The New Physical Education for Elementary School Children

**Houghton
Mifflin
Company**

Boston
Atlanta
Dallas
Geneva, Ill.
Hopewell, N.J.
Palo Alto
London

The New Physical Education for Elementary School Children

Elsie Carter Burton

Florida State University

Printed in the U.S.A.

Library of Congress Catalog Card Number: 76-11981

ISBN: 0-395-20658-8

Contents

Preface

The New Physical Education for Elementary School Children is written for prospective physical educators and classroom teachers who will assume the responsibility of providing meaningful learning experiences for children. It is not a handbook of traditional activities organized into structured teaching units. This book is child-centered rather than activity-centered. It contains a systematic presentation of learning experiences designed to enable children to move experientially, expressively, and efficiently.

In order to be educationally relevant, movement activities must contribute to the child's optimal development in the cognitive, affective, and psychomotor domains. Thus the content of this book has been selected and organized in such a way as to be readily translatable into educational objectives for each domain.

Part One presents a rationale for a new system of physically educating children. It provides background information necessary for developing a child-centered program and explores the educational potential of movement experiences.

Part Two introduces a six-step model designed to provide a sound theoretical basis for curriculum development. It begins with an assessment of each child's educational needs and ends with an evaluation of the learning outcomes.

In Parts Three, Four, and Five, the subject matter of physical education is presented clearly and sequentially. Part Three focuses on learning activities designed to develop children's bodily, spatial, and kinesthetic awareness. Part Four outlines a systematic sequence of learning experiences designed to enhance children's basic skill development. Individual chapters examine the development of the basic movement skills, the manipulative skills, the basic sports skills, and the fundamental physical skills. Part Five relates the skills and concepts developed by participation in the learning activities described in Parts Three and Four to the three principal movement forms: educational dance, games, and gymnastics.

Appendix A contains an observation form developed to help students appraise a physical education program. Appendix B is an annotated bibliography, and Appendix C lists sources for rhythmic accompaniment.

The content of this book reflects my own learning experiences, and therefore the influences of all those who have taught, challenged, and stimulated me. I wish to express my sincere gratitude to the colleagues, students, and friends who have encouraged and assisted me, and especially to three of my master teachers whose guidance and expectations of excellence prepared me to write this book. My deep appreciation is extended to Katherine Ley, who taught me how to move skillfully; to Marion Broer, who taught me how to analyze movement; and to Margaret H'Doubler, who helped me develop an understanding of movement. I also wish to thank Andrew H. Breiner, Ruth Davis, Patricia K. Fehl, Bonnie L. Johnson, Leo O'Donnel, Theresa Smith, Patricia Tanner, and Joan Tillotson for so thoroughly reviewing the manuscript. Their valuable suggestions led to revisions that clarified and enhanced the message of the book. Finally, for their generosity in allowing me the use of their facilities for photography sessions, I am grateful to the Developmental Research School, Florida State University; the Creative Dance Center, Tallahassee, Florida; the Creative Pre-School, Tallahassee, Florida; the Tallahassee YMCA; and the Boston Public Schools.

Elsie Carter Burton

The New
Physical
Education
for
Elementary
School
Children

Part One

The New Physical Education

Part One introduces the world of the moving child and the environmental structure of modern educational processes.

Chapter 1 examines factors that have contributed to the need for a new system of physically educating today's children. Humanistic education provides the theoretical framework on which this system is based. Chapter 2 is devoted to familiarizing you with the *new physical education,* a child-centered program that utilizes movement as an educational medium. Chapter 3 considers how movement relates to children's development and how, in turn, their developmental needs relate to their movement experiences. In Chapter 4 the numerous factors that affect the nature of the child's movement experiences are discussed. An understanding of the content of these four chapters is a necessary prerequisite to the development and conduct of a meaningful and educationally sound learning environment.

1   A Humanistic Education

To learn is to change; education is a process that changes the learner. This definition of education sounds relatively simple until you recognize that as a contemporary educator you must meet the needs and stimulate the interests of children who have been and are rapidly being changed by the world in which they live. Before discussing the educational potential of particular learning media, therefore, let us review some of the factors that are influencing the development of children today, as well as some of the educational innovations that appear to enhance their learning.

TECHNOLOGICAL ADVANCEMENT AND EDUCATIONAL CHANGE

Until recently children gained most of their information from direct experience. The only other informational source available to them was the printed page, and the vicarious experiences they gained through reading provided the only extension of their horizons beyond direct personal experience. Since children usually did not begin to read until they entered school, they ordinarily assimilated a vast amount of direct experience before they became accustomed to vicarious experience. Learning to read was at best a slow process; during the early school years most of the children's experiences continued to be *real*. As they became better readers the children's vicarious experiences increased in number, but usually did not exceed their direct experiences.

The emergence of electronic technology has changed all this. Artificially induced experience is no longer a delayed, slowly developed supplement to real experience. Rather, it is an early and major component of children's total experience. The modern child's world of electronic media is *information-rich* but *action-poor* (Coleman, 1972).

The media explosion has given all of us a new view of our internal and external worlds (Toffler, 1970). It has forced educators to recognize that traditional programs and teaching methodology are inadequate, that new approaches to teaching are essential. One new approach is humanistic education.

HUMANISTIC EDUCATION DEFINED

Humanistic educators do not view the intellect as the single most important attribute of humanity. Rather, they attempt to resolve the traditional dualism between cognitive learning and affective experience by looking on the learner as both a thinking and a feeling human being. Known also as confluent education, humanistic education is in practice a synthesis of the affective domain—consisting of feelings, emotions, attitudes, and values—and the cognitive domain, which includes the intellect and the activity of the mind associated with knowing (Brown, 1971). Children's emotions and cognitive functions are seen as inseparable, because feelings influence intellectual powers and, conversely, intellectual performances help to determine emotional states.

Humanistic education thus consists of learning processes designed for emotionally responsive human beings. It is a search for ways to bring students' humanness to fuller realization, to awaken and develop all their sensibility, creativity, and awareness. It implies not only that the learning process is more enjoyable when it is humanized, but also that retention of the human element in the classroom makes learning more relevant to life. In this school of thought the qualities of pleasure, spontaneity, and feeling are considered to be as vital, if not more so, then intellectual achievement (Lyons, 1971).

THE IMPORTANCE OF FEELING

It has been said that children who enter school today face a twelve- to twenty-year apprenticeship in alienation. They learn to manipulate words and numbers fluently, but they do not learn to experience the real world. At the end of their schooling they have been conditioned to live in modern society, but are out of touch with the reality of their own feelings (Petersen, 1972). The importance of feeling to learning is evident when one recognizes that learning involves an interaction between the learner and his or her environment. The nature and extent of the learning that occurs depends on the frequency, variety, and intensity of that interaction.

EXPERIENTIAL LEARNING

The goal of humanistic education is to open up the world to children and enable them to experience it, enjoy it, and cope with it. In order to attain this goal, the learning environment must be child-centered rather than subject-centered. In a curriculum that is subject-centered, meaning is thought to reside within the curricular materials. In a child-centered curriculum it is thought that meaning exists *within* the learner, and that therefore the subject matter's only relevance is that assigned to it by the individual. Anything unrelated to a child's experience is meaningless for that child; it has no reality. Recognition of this fact focuses attention on learning experiences or, to reverse the emphasis, on experiential learning. The essential elements of experiential learning are described by Rogers as follows:

> *It has a quality of personal involvement*—the whole person in both his feeling and cognitive aspects being *in* the learning event. *It is self-initiated.* Even when the impetus or stimulus comes from the outside, the sense of discovery, of reaching out, of grasping and comprehending, comes from within. It is pervasive. It makes a difference in the behavior, the attitudes, perhaps even the personality of the learner. *It is evaluated by the learner.* He knows whether it is meeting his need, whether it leads toward *what* he wants to know, whether it illuminates the dark area of ignorance he is experiencing. The focus of evaluation, we might say, resides definitely in the learner. *Its essence is meaning.* When such learning takes place, the element of meaning to the learner is built into the whole experience (Rogers, 1969).

Experiential learning is thus interplay between the child's self and the immediate universe. It is intense involvement designed to heighten awareness.

In an experientially oriented learning environment, the student's responses are of primary concern. Therefore, the teacher's attention must not be so narrowly focused on subject matter as to preclude acute awareness of the learner's actions. Lessons are developed partially in light of students' responses, rather than wholly in conformity to a predetermined logical structure. In other words, part of the curriculum originates with the students themselves.

A class atmosphere that encourages open and honest student response has three interrelated qualities: (1) there is a sense of freedom; (2) the student feels secure, respected, trusted, and loved; (3) it encourages discovery.

Experiential learning is a discovery process that employs multiple modes of exploration. The acquisition of experiential knowledge is stressed as the basis for development of concrete concepts, and personal subjective experience is regarded as the foundation for relational thought. In other words, children learn by playing with, exploring, enjoying, and contemplating their inner and outer worlds, which are considered inherently interesting. Experiential learning is an *open system* that recognizes degrees of rightness, rather than a system in which all the knowables are fixed and an answer is either right or wrong.

As a teacher you will be responsible for enhancing all aspects of the child's development. The content of this introductory chapter will help you comprehend the nature of this responsibility.

TOPICS FOR REVIEW AND FURTHER STUDY

1. Compare and contrast your own childhood experiences with those of the children you will be teaching, considering such matters as:
   a. the things you did for fun
   b. where and with whom you played during the various seasons of the year
   c. your responsibilities and domestic chores within the family
   d. the kinds of toys you played with
   e. the things your family did together
   f. your school environment, the nature of the subject matter, and learning experiences

2. What evidence do you see that the world has become information-rich and action-poor? What are the educational implications of this phenomenon? How does it affect children's need for physical activity and their need to learn through direct experience?

3. Technological advances have made children no longer useful in the home. In most instances it is no longer necessary for them to help care for the family or contribute to the family's income. Do you believe this phenomenon affects children's feelings of worth and/or development of the skills of everyday living? Does it alter the role of the school and necessitate different kinds of learning experiences?

4. Do you agree that humanistic education is more relevant to life than other types of education? What elements of humanistic education are also important factors in everyday human relationships?

5. How is feeling related to learning? Is it necessary to feel in order to learn? Is learning to feel an important aspect of the child's education?

6. What is meant by the statement "the subject matter's only relevance is that assigned to it by the learner"? Are there subjects that have very little meaning for you? Can you determine why?

7. Have you read any of the references listed at the end of this chapter or any other books or articles that criticize traditional educational practices? Do you consider their criticism just? How do you think education should change in order to meet the needs of the children who will live in tomorrow's world?

SUGGESTIONS FOR FURTHER READING

ASSOCIATION FOR SUPERVISION AND CURRICULUM DEVELOPMENT. *Perceiving, Behaving and Becoming.* New York: ASCD, 1962.

BROWN, GEORGE ISAAC. "Human Is as Confluent Does." *Theory Into Practice* 10 (1971): 191–195.

COLEMAN, JAMES S. "The Children Have Outgrown the Schools." *Psychology Today* 5 (Feb. 1972): 72ff.

GOODMAN, PAUL. *Compulsory Mis-Education.* New York: Random House, 1964.

GROSS, RONALD, and GROSS, BEATRICE, eds. *Radical School Reform.* New York: Simon & Schuster, 1969.

ILLICH, IVAN. *Deschooling Society.* New York: Harper & Row, 1970.

LEONARD, GEORGE B. *Education and Ecstasy.* New York: Dell, 1968.

LOWEN, ALEXANDER. *Pleasure.* New York: Lancer Books, 1970.

LYONS, HAROLD C. *Learning to Feel—Feeling to Learn,* Columbus, Ohio: Charles E. Merrill, 1971.

MCLUHAN, MARSHALL. *The Medium is the Massage.* New York: Bantam Books, 1967.

PETERSEN, JAMES R. "Eyes Have They, But They See Not: A Conversation with Rudolf Arnheim." *Psychology Today* 6 (June 1972): 55–58, 92–96.

POSTMAN, NEIL, and WEINGARTNER, CHARLES. *Teaching as a Subversive Activity.* Dell, 1969.

POWELL, JOHN. *Why Am I Afraid to Tell You Who I Am?* Chicago: Argus, Communications Company, 1969.

ROGERS, CARL R. *Freedom to Learn.* Columbus: Charles E. Merrill, 1969.

TOFFLER, ALVIN. *Future Shock.* New York: Bantam Books, 1970.

VAN TIL, WILLIAM, ed. *Curriculum: Quest for Relevance.* Boston: Houghton Mifflin, 1971.

2 The Educational Value of Movement Experience

Modern educational concerns are reflected in the emergence of a new physical education. Traditional elementary-school physical education has primarily emphasized teaching skills and developing fitness by means of a series of such activities as games, dance, gymnastics, and exercises. These programs have tended to be activity-centered; that is, teachers have selected activities designated as appropriate for certain grade levels and organized these activities into structured teaching units. The sequence of such units has typically been determined by the traditional association of given activities with certain seasons of the year. In the upper grades, for instance, a soccer unit is usually taught in the fall; volleyball, basketball, and dance in the winter; and softball or track and field in the spring. Each unit is usually presented as a separate entity, and some class time at the beginning of each unit is devoted to teaching the skills and rules specific to it. Furthermore, physical education has traditionally been considered a separate subject in the school curriculum. The physical education class has been viewed as the exclusive domain of the physical education specialist, and classes have been conducted in a multi-purpose room or on the playground.

The new physical education curriculum, by contrast, is designed to help children develop an awareness of their moving beings and to encourage total involvement in their learning experiences. Emphasis is placed on skills that will enable children to utilize their physical beings as functional and expressive movement instruments.

MOVEMENT AND LEARNING

Educators are beginning to recognize that sequences of apparently unrelated activities cannot adequately educate the modern child. There is growing awareness of the need to integrate the child's learning experiences. For over fifty years educators have been talking about the need to educate the "whole child," but most have failed to realize that one cannot teach the whole child effectively unless *the child as a whole* is involved in the learning process. When education is viewed in this way, physical education assumes a new importance.

Among the child's most urgent needs is the need to move. Vigorous physical activity is one of the dominant characteristics of normal elementary-school children. During the preschool years much of children's learning results from exploratory movement activities. When children go to school, however, they enter a sedentary environment that requires them to become increasingly sedate. In order to meet these expectations, it is necessary for children to suppress their natural urge for physical activity. This process in turn necessitates shutting out sensory stimulation that demands movement as a response. Thus, bit by bit, children are desensitized. They adjust to the demands of the schoolroom by becoming alienated from their natural beings. By adulthood most have adjusted so well that they have lost the ability to experience pleasurable movement, and have become habitual "watchers" rather than "doers." It seems evident that, in order for the educational process to meet the real long-term needs of today's children, the learning potential of movement experiences must be developed and utilized.

In the modern educational setting, movement experiences have a dual role: children learn *to* move and they learn *through* movement. The responsibility for seeing to it that children learn to move effectively, expressively, and experientially rests primarily with the physical educator. But all teachers share responsibility for utilizing movement to promote learning of other curricular subjects.

When human movement is seen as the substance of physical education, that field of study is broadened in perspective. Treating movement as the central concern places "the moving child" at the center of his or her own education and enables one more readily to view physical education as an ongoing process. The relevance of this approach

The Educational Value of Movement Experience

becomes apparent when one asks, "When does the individual's physical education actually begin and how long does it continue?" The prevailing opinion among contemporary theorists is that human beings' physical education begins the moment they become capable of movement and continues as long as they live. It is believed that the movement of the fetus *in utero* provides sensory stimulation necessary to normal development. It is known that the infant's early exploratory movements play a vital role in learning and that, normally, all of a child's basic movement patterns are developed before he or she enters school at age six. (The sequential development of these patterns is discussed in detail in Chapter 3.) A person's movement patterns gradually become well defined and largely habitual. Throughout one's lifetime, however, there persists a need to adapt physically to changing life styles and physical environments.

Movement Education   *Movement education,* a recent development in the field of physical education, emerged concurrently in England and the United States. In England this approach was stimulated by the theory of Rudolph Laban, while in the United States physical educators were becoming aware of the potential in Margaret H'Doubler's educational dance. Both believed that people can and should develop a strong kinesthetic awareness of their movements, and that the spontaneous and exploratory aspects of movement have essential expressive and educational value. Exchange visits following World War Two enabled American physical educators to become acquainted with the English system of movement education. Since that time this system has been adapted and enhanced to meet the objectives of American education. Movement education is defined by Tillotson (1970) as "that phase of the total education program which has as its contribution the development of effective, efficient, and expressive movement responses in a thinking, feeling, and sharing human being." Movement education can thus serve as the basis for a new kind of elementary-school physical education program that assists children to discover and develop their inherent natures. Emphasis is placed on *self-* and *body awareness, basic skill development, creative satisfaction,* and a *sense of total involvement* in the learning experience. Such a physical education program provides for creative learning through the medium of movement. Exploration is the principal teaching method employed in movement education. "Exploration is a 'child-centered' approach or method of teaching which allows for individuality, creativity, spontaneity, and self-discovery" (Tillotson, 1970). The purpose of movement education is to develop simultaneously the child's basic skills and understanding of why the body moves as it does. This necessitates teaching the child to recognize and analyze the various components of movement (listed on pages 80−81).

Creating Child-Centered Movement Experiences

There are three prerequisites to the development of child-centered learning experiences:

1. You must know the learner.

2. You must try to envision the world in which the child lives now and that in which he or she will live in the future.

3. You must know what makes an activity an "educational" experience.

In order to provide meaningful child-centered learning experiences, you as a teacher must possess a functional knowledge of children's developmental characteristics; and if you intend to personalize their learning experiences, you must become acquainted with your students as individuals. It is assumed that you have studied the growth and development of children. However, because an understanding of developmental change is vitally important and because teachers need to see clearly the relationship between developmental characteristics and the child's educational needs, Chapter 3 reviews these subjects.

In addition to developmental factors, you must also recognize the role of phenomena unique to the electronic age, some of which were reviewed in Chapter 1. It has been pointed out that the world of modern children is information-rich and action-poor, and that much of their learning results from vicarious rather than direct experiences. The child's world is changing so rapidly that researchers have not had time to conduct the longitudinal research necessary to identify accurately all the effects of these changes. However, the available evidence strongly suggests a need for innovative educational practices that will provide action-centered learning environments, learning media that will enable the child to become actively involved in the learning process. Providing this kind of learning environment necessitates viewing the child as a thinking, feeling, acting person who is growing and changing. You must see children's bodies as their equipment for living, intricate mechanisms through which they receive impressions from the world about them and with which they express their thoughts and feelings and manipulate the people and things in the world around them.

Education has been defined as a process that changes the learner, for the purpose of preparing him or her to become a fully functioning human being by maximizing the development of inherent capacities.

There are three interrelated domains in which this development occurs: the cognitive, the affective, and the psychomotor. Cognitive functions include remembering and relating information, as well as creating and synthesizing new ideas. The affective domain encompasses all aspects of feeling, such as emotions, interests, attitudes, appreciations, and values. It also includes feelings about one's acceptance or rejection by others. The psychomotor domain is composed of physical or motor skills that allow for gross motor movement of the body and the manipulation of objects. As we have said, classroom subjects have traditionally been taught as if only cognitive functions were involved; physical education has focused primarily on the psychomotor domain, and the affective domain has been largely neglected. Now, however, we are moving toward the development of educational experiences that integrate the three domains.

Movement is children's natural learning medium; their everyday movement experiences contribute to their physical, cognitive, and affective development. However, such incidental learning does not result in the full development of the child's movement potential or movement awareness. Nor does this development occur automatically when the child is required to participate in certain kinds of physical education activities. In order for children to learn to move effectively, expressively, and experientially, they must be purposefully and carefully taught. In this kind of teaching both the content and the methodology of teaching are vitally important.

The view of physical education as pertinent only to the psychomotor domain has resulted in programs consisting primarily of activities that provide for the release of excess energy and develop skill and physical fitness. The cognitive learning associated with these programs consists principally of learning the rules and strategies of various sports and games. The affective content is limited to the development of attitudes of fair play and good sportsmanship. These are undeniably vital aspects of the physical education experience, but modern educational goals seek to provide for the child's optimal development in all three educational domains.

Figure 2.1 shows the relationship between movement experiences and the child's development in each of the educational domains. Though in this figure and the following discussion the domains have been separated for purposes of clarity, development occurs concurrently in all three domains; in fact, one of the unique characteristics of movement is the way in which it unites the cognitive, affective, and psychomotor domains.

Movement and Learning

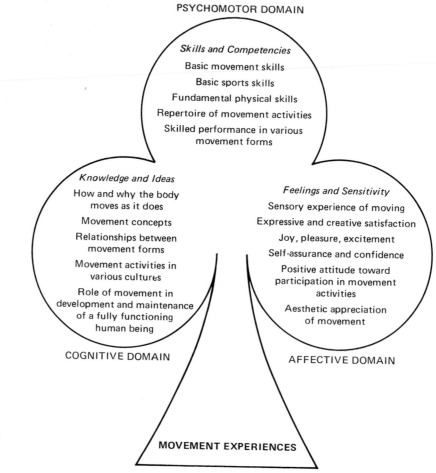

PSYCHOMOTOR DOMAIN

Skills and Competencies
Basic movement skills
Basic sports skills
Fundamental physical skills
Repertoire of movement activities
Skilled performance in various
movement forms

Knowledge and Ideas
How and why the body
moves as it does
Movement concepts
Relationships between
movement forms
Movement activities in
various cultures
Role of movement in
development and maintenance
of a fully functioning
human being

COGNITIVE DOMAIN

Feelings and Sensitivity
Sensory experience of moving
Expressive and creative satisfaction
Joy, pleasure, excitement
Self-assurance and confidence
Positive attitude toward
participation in movement
activities
Aesthetic appreciation
of movement

AFFECTIVE DOMAIN

MOVEMENT EXPERIENCES

Figure 2.1 The Relationship Between Movement Experiences and Educational Outcomes

MOVEMENT COGNITION

The cognitive components of movement involve conceptualization, analysis, synthesis, and utilization of various aspects of movement. The subject matter of this domain is the structural, mechanical, spatial, temporal, and rhythmic dimensions of movement. Development of basic concepts germane to these matters enables children to understand how and why their bodies move as they do and to envision relationships among different forms of movement (dance, games, gymnastics, and the like). Elementary-school children should also develop an understanding of similarities and differences among the movement activities of people in various cultures. They should learn how forms of movement have developed historically and been influenced by such factors as geography, climate, occupations, and religion. (The study of

The Educational Value of Movement Experience

these factors should, of course, be integrated with the social studies curriculum.)

Physical education consists all too often of the teacher telling the children what to do, rarely with a valid explanation of the reason for doing it. The goal of skill development is often to win a game or championship, and the desired outcome of conditioning activities is usually the President's Award for Physical Fitness. Rarely do children receive meaningful instruction on the real and long-term value of participation in physical activity. The new physical education, however, emphasizes "why" as well as "how." Learning is maximized by carefully coordinating the content of the physical education program with those aspects of the science curriculum that deal with the functioning of the human body. Furthermore, those who teach in the physical education program should draw children's attention to the relationships between what and when one eats and one's energy level; between active play or exercise and development of different parts of the body; between rest and exercise; and to the need for participation in both indoor and outdoor activities throughout the year. Teaching physical education in this way helps develop children's awareness of their physical needs and the importance of caring properly for the complex mechanisms in which they live, their bodies.

AFFECTIVE PHYSICAL EDUCATION

The affective components of physical education include all the feeling states associated with movement experiences. Movement is highly affective, due to the potential for feeling inherent in the sensory experience of moving one's body. However, development of this domain does not occur automatically when children move. Rather, they must be taught to become *sensorily aware* of their moving beings. They must learn to feel and think with reference to their moving bodies. They must become consciously aware of their feeling selves and of what is happening in their sensory environments. These goals require that children develop multi-sensory awareness, and learn both how feeling states evoke movement and how movement evokes feeling states. (See Figure 2.2.) This kind of learning is dependent on the provision of movement experiences that *actualize* the child's feeling potential.

Though physical education is now often defined as "the art and science of human movement," the artistic aspects of movement continue to be the most frequently neglected aspect of the curriculum. One reason for this circumstance is the narrowness with which art has been defined. People have traditionally tended to think of art as a product, and to regard artistic ability as the unique endowment of the gifted. In

Figure 2.2 Experiencing Movement
Bonnie Unsworth

modern usage, however, the terms *artistic* and *aesthetic* have acquired much broader meanings that acknowledge the capacity for aesthetic experience of anyone who is aware of artistic qualities. Artistic qualities include the harmonious effects of line, color, form, proportion, and rhythmic motion. Human movement has unlimited potential to develop awareness of these qualities and the ability to utilize them expressively.

THE PSYCHOMOTOR DOMAIN OF PHYSICAL EDUCATION

The psychomotor domain includes all learning experiences designed to improve the quality of movement responses. In the elementary-school physical education program, such experiences are addressed to the development and utilization of basic skills. There are four classes of such skills: *basic movement skills, manipulative skills, basic sports skills,* and *fundamental physical skills.* (A detailed description of these skills is provided in Chapter 7.) The new physical education emphasizes the universal application of these skills, and encourages children to develop a variety of movement skills that can be applied in all forms of movement and in the activities of everyday life.

THE PHYSICALLY EDUCATED CHILD

The development of effectual physical education has been hindered by failure to specify adequately what it means to be physically educated. It has often been assumed that a person is physically educated if he or she can perform a sport well or attain a certain performance level on a physical fitness test. This chapter has introduced a much broader view of what it means to be physically educated. This outlook has been summarized by H'Doubler (1967), who states that education has two aspects, the capacity to "take in" or be impressed and the capacity to "give out" or express. This statement implies the need for heightened sensory awareness that will enable the child to take in much more of the world. It also suggests how cognitive learning and skill development are essential to utilization of the body as an expressive instrument. Thus, in terms of modern educational goals, the physically educated child is one who:

1. is sensorily aware of his or her moving being and of the feelings and emotions associated with and expressed by movements

2. has a functional knowledge of how and why his or her body moves as it does and of the relationships between basic and complex movement forms

3. moves skillfully, rhythmically, and confidently in various activities and situations

TOPICS FOR REVIEW AND FURTHER STUDY

1. How can the whole child be actively involved in the learning process? How does this goal relate to the dual role of movement experiences in the modern educational setting?

2. When does an individual's physical education begin and how long does it continue? How does conceiving of physical education in this way relate to viewing it as an ongoing process? What does this approach tell educators about the need for physical education in early childhood?

3. Why is it necessary to consider the child's present and future world in order to provide relevant educational experiences? Do you think the existing educational system reflects this kind of vision?

4. What are the three interrelated domains of education? How do movement experiences relate to the child's development in each of these domains?

5. What is involved in teaching children the "why" of physical activity? How does such learning relate to the long-term value of physical education?

6. If a teacher, asked what he or she is teaching, answers, "I'm teaching folk dance," or "We're in the volleyball unit," what does this suggest about the teacher's focus? Is a different attitude conveyed by

the response, "I'm teaching the children to folk dance," or "I'm teaching the children how to play volleyball"?

7. How does the definition of a physically educated child presented in this chapter differ from the traditional view? Is the new physical education more educationally relevant than the programs you experienced? Do you believe that the approach to physical education presented here will have an effect on the content and methodology of future programs?

SUGGESTIONS FOR FURTHER READING

BLOOM, BENJAMIN S., et al. *Taxonomy of Educational Objectives, Handbook I: Cognitive Domain.* New York: David McKay, 1956.

HARROW, ANITA J. *A Taxonomy of the Psychomotor Domain.* New York: David McKay, 1972.

H'DOUBLER, MARGARET. *Dance, A Creative Art Experience.* Madison: University of Wisconsin Press, 1967.

KRATHWOHL, DAVID R.; BLOOM, BENJAMIN S.; and MASIA, BERTRAM B. *Taxonomy of Educational Objectives, Handbook II: Affective Domain.* New York: David McKay, 1964.

LANESE, MARTY M. "Movement Education Confuses Me." *Ohio High School Athlete* 33 (Feb. 1974): 159.

TILLOTSON, JOAN. "A Brief Theory of Movement Education." In *Selected Readings in Movement Education,* edited by Robert T. Sweeney. Reading, Mass.: Addison-Wesley, 1970.

3   Movement and Child Development

Providing meaningful movement experiences depends on understanding what children are like. The term *understanding* here implies more than basic knowledge of developmental characteristics: it also involves ability to comprehend the needs, interests, and behavioral patterns of each child. Thus, if you are to help children develop and utilize their full movement potential, you must possess an understanding of (1) growth, maturity, and learning in successive developmental stages; (2) the factors that have determined individual differences; and (3) the role of movement in the developmental and learning processes.

Although the psychomotor (physical) cognitive (intellectual), and affective (emotional) spheres are functionally interrelated, their complexity necessitates discussing them individually. Let us first examine the sequential pattern of physical and motor skill development.

MOTOR DEVELOPMENT

Infancy and early childhood are characterized by rapid physical growth and maturation of the body's systems and organs. Most children triple their birth weight by their first birthday and double their birth length by age four. Equally significant changes are occurring simultaneously in the structural development of the internal systems that govern movement.

Movement of the body and body parts is brought about by action of the muscles and controlled by the nervous system. Thus motor skill development is determined by the growth and maturational level of the child's neurological and muscular fibers. Stimuli that generate movement responses are received by the senses (particularly the visual, auditory, tactile, and kinesthetic senses) and transported through neural fibers to the central nervous system (the brain and spinal cord), where an association with memory occurs and a movement response is initiated. The messages that direct this response then travel through the nerves to the appropriate muscle fibers. In early infancy this action is reflexive and uncoordinated. However, as the nerves and muscles develop, the child's movements become more controlled and coordinated; and as the association area of the brain matures, movements become more purposeful.

General Trends in Motor Development

Newborn infants' movements are global and generalized. In other words, infants tend to respond with movement of their entire bodies and uncoordinated movements of their body parts. As development progresses, more controlled and specific patterns of movement emerge. Development proceeds in a progressive and orderly manner and is characterized by three simultaneous trends (Thompson, 1962):

1. The cephalocaudal and proximo-distal trends. The cephalocaudal trend implies that muscular development proceeds longitudinally from head to foot. That is, the muscles of the head and neck mature first, followed by maturation of the muscles of the trunk and then of the legs and feet. The proximo-distal trend is a tendency for the muscles of the trunk to develop first, followed by those in the more distal (further from the center) portions of the body.

2. The bilateral to unilateral trend. During the early stages of development, the child's movements tend to be symmetrical and bilateral. The infant uses either hand to pick up objects and the young child uses both hands to hold or manipulate things. Preference for a given hand develops gradually, in conjunction with an increase in motor control of the preferred hand.

3. The mass to specific trend. Because children gain coordinated control first over the large muscles located in the neck, trunk, legs, and arms, their early movements involve use of the whole body. As development progresses, they become able to differentiate between body parts and therefore to move various parts independently. Finally they gain control over the smaller muscles of the wrists, fingers, and feet.

These three principles are evident in the sequential progression of motor development. Though orderly, development is individualized, and there is wide variation in when and how different children perform particular developmental movement patterns.

The Development of Basic Movement Skills

The infant gains control first over movements of the head and neck. A rudimentary form of such control begins to appear by the end of the first month. Between four and six months, most infants become able to lift the upper part of their bodies and, using their arms for support, to maintain this position for a short time. During this period the infant also gains sufficient control over the trunk muscles to roll over and assume a supported sitting position. By nine months most children can sit unassisted. (See Figure 3.1, top.)

Crawling

Between seven months and one year, most infants become capable of executing their first locomotor movements, which are characterized by wide variations in individual style. Some children begin to move across the floor by lying prone and pulling or pushing with their hands; some maintain a sitting posture and scoot across the floor by means of a hitching motion; still others raise their bodies from the floor and creep on their hands and knees or hands and feet. (See Figure 3.1, middle.) A few children pass through this stage of development without performing any kind of crawling.

Standing

Children begin standing erect around the age of eight months. Most must be supported under the armpits at this age. Arm and leg strength gradually increases until the child can pull his or her body to a standing position and maintain balance by holding onto a piece of furniture. Maintaining a standing posture is a significant motor achievement: in order to do so, the child must have gained sufficient strength and control to withstand the force of gravity. He or she then enters the phase of development devoted to mastering basic locomotor movements.

Walking

Children usually begin walking between the ages of ten and fifteen months. The first steps are executed while holding onto someone or something, and the child gradually progresses to walking independently. At first children walk hesitantly, on their entire soles. They must compensate for lack of strength and coordination by walking with their feet wide apart to broaden the base of support, flexing their knees slightly to lower the center of gravity, and raising their arms to facilitate balance. (See Figure 3.1, bottom.) Gradually the width and variability of the steps decrease, the length of the stride increases, and a heel-toe progression ensues. By age four most children have developed an easy, rhythmic stride that enables them to walk in a straight line and to turn sharp corners.

Running

Running employs the same basic movement pattern as walking. However, the increased tempo and the momentary period of nonsupport

Figure 3.1 One Pattern of Locomotor Development
Top: sitting; Middle: crawling; Bottom: walking
Mickey Adair

Movement and Child Development

while the body is suspended in space require additional strength and balance. Most children develop the ability to run between ages two and three, and a skillful running pattern emerges by ages five to six.

Jumping

Jumping is characterized by a takeoff from one or both feet, a two-foot landing, and a momentary suspension in mid-air. Therefore, before a child can jump he or she must develop the sense of balance necessary to orient oneself in the air and when landing. The child's first approximation of jumping is frequently stepping down from a stair-step or stool, which is usually accomplished between one-and-a-half and two years of age. Again, the development of children's jumping patterns varies greatly. Some children acquire the necessary leg strength to initiate the upward thrust of the jump by age three, but most cannot execute a skilled jump until approximately age five.

Hopping

A hop differs from a jump in that it is characterized by a one-foot takeoff and a one-foot landing on the same foot. The hop is a more difficult movement because greater strength is required to propel the body upward and forward with one foot and leg. It is also more difficult for the child to maintain balance while hopping, because the base of support is much smaller and the body's center of gravity must be shifted laterally over this small base. Although some children are able to hop by age four, this skill is ordinarily not fully mastered until approximately age six.

Leaping

A leap is actually an elongated running step in which the body is lifted higher into space. Leaping requires the same kind of skill as running, and is therefore accomplished at approximately the same time.

Skipping, Galloping, and Sliding

Because they represent combinations of locomotor movements, these skills are the most complex basic movements. A skip consists of a step and a hop on alternate feet. Galloping is a combination of walking and running, with the same foot leading continuously. A slide is the same as a gallop except that the movement is executed sideways. Some children develop rudimentary forms of these skills by age four, but most cannot perform them skillfully until approximately age six.

Nonlocomotor Skills

The ability to execute basic nonlocomotor skills parallels mastery of locomotor skills. Young children readily perform some nonlocomotor movements: infants 10 months to 15 months push objects away and roll round objects across the floor by executing a pushing motion; children 10 months to 2 years pull their bodies to a standing position and reach out to grasp a toy. The various push-and-pull toys now available stimulate children to execute such movements. (See Figure 3.2.)

As young children explore the world about them they bend their trunks, arms, and legs, and stretch to reach and stand. They twist their bodies to see and reach objects that are not directly in front of them. Turning is a more complex skill than twisting, because one must maintain a balanced upright posture while changing the position of the base of support.

Falling and rising are inevitably familiar movements in the life of the young child. (See Figure 3.2, bottom.) The toddler who becomes fatigued or loses balance usually drops from a standing position to a sitting or prone position. Executing the locomotor skills, the child must cope with body positions that are momentarily unstable, and inability to maintain the necessary bodily control in these situations causes the child to lose balance and fall.

Swinging and swaying are rhythmic movements that require a balanced body position, and a child cannot execute them fluently until he or she is capable of well-coordinated bodily movements. Some children display this ability at an early age, while others acquire it more slowly.

Essential Activities

As we have seen, children usually develop all the basic movement skills during the preschool years. Because these skills appear to develop naturally, their significance is frequently overlooked. Most people fail to recognize that, during these formative years, children are acquiring the skills they will use all their lives in movement activities. This is why it is so vitally important for the young child to practice these skills frequently *and correctly* in a wide variety of situations.

Movement is the dominant characteristic of young children's lives. During their waking hours they are constantly active, and active play is by no means an inconsequential aspect of childhood. Rather, it is an essential learning medium. As children become structurally and functionally ready to learn, it is imperative that they be provided opportunities to explore, experience, and practice in a stimulating and challenging physical and social environment. They should be encouraged, but not forced, to explore their full movement potential.

By the time children are five years old, they can usually execute all the basic movement skills. From this point on, their skill development consists of refining and coordinating these skills. Children who have difficulty executing the hop, skip, slide, and/or gallop, which are relatively complex movement patterns, should receive immediate individual help: the troublesome skill should be subdivided into its component parts, and each part should be practiced separately. While children are in the early elementary grades, their large muscles are better

Movement and Child Development

Figure 3.2 Early Nonlocomotor Movements
Top left: pushing; Top right: reaching and grasping; Bottom: rising
Mickey Adair

developed than are the smaller muscles in the hands, fingers, and feet. These children are still far-sighted and lack fluent visual control, which results in poor hand-eye and foot-eye coordination. For this and other reasons, children in this age group should be provided ample opportunities to participate in gross motor activity. They should also receive instruction and supervised practice in the manipulative skills, particularly the ballhandling skills of rolling, catching, bouncing, and tossing. Children of this age should work with yarn balls, beanbags, and playground balls, which are relatively easy for them to handle and control.

Children in grades 3–6 have greater control over the use of their small muscles, and demonstrate marked improvement in coordination and agility. Because strength and endurance are also rapidly increasing, these children are ready for activities requiring more highly refined skills such as striking, accurate throwing, controlled response to a rhythmic beat, and games involving quick and agile movements.

In grades 4–6 children usually grow slowly and steadily, though at the end of this period some (especially girls) may be undergoing the rapid changes characteristic of prepubescence. Girls tend to be taller, heavier, and more mature than boys. The increased muscular and neurological development of children of this age is apparent in their improved reaction time, strength, and endurance. These characteristics suggest that children of this age need activities that are physically challenging, such as skills practice, conditioning activities, team games, rhythms, and individual activities like gymnastics and track and field. It is essential for children of this age to find *pleasurable* ways of satisfying their need for vigorous physical activity.

COGNITIVE DEVELOPMENT

Among a number of well-defined theories of cognitive development, the one that is having the greatest impact on current educational practice is Jean Piaget's developmental system. Piaget's work makes repeated reference to infantile and childhood behaviors that involve movement, and the relevance of his theoretical formulations to the content of this book is unmistakable.

Piaget has identified four stages of intellectual development: (1) the sensorimotor period (0–2 years), (2) the preoperational stage (2–7 years), (3) the stage of concrete operations (7–11 years), and (4) the period of formal operational thought (11–15 years).

In the sensorimotor period the infant progresses from movements that are purely reflexive through a stage during which movements result in chance discoveries. By the end of this period, the child's movement behavior is clearly intentional and goal-directed.

Piaget has subdivided the preoperational phase into the preconceptual stage (ages 2–4 years) and the stage of intuitive thinking (ages 4–7 years). During the preconceptual stage the child's cognitive development centers on extracting *preconcepts* from real and direct sensory experiences. The informational source is the child's moving body. During the stage of intuitive thinking these data are translated into basic concepts that are in effect static images of reality. For example, the child becomes capable of distinguishing such movement-related factors as number, distance, length, area, speed, and time. Though he or she may be able to count, estimate distance, and tell time, however, the child does not actually conceive of the quantity involved. Quantity is an abstract concept children of this age are not yet capable of conceptualizing, and they thus perform functions and employ language they do not fully understand.

During the stage of concrete operations the child's thinking becomes increasingly logical and systematic, but is still focused exclusively on objects and events experienced first-hand. Faced with a situation he or she cannot explain on the basis of direct experience, the child of this age relates it to a comparable familiar situation. The child is still unable to think abstractly, and learns logical operations by thinking in terms of the actual or concrete aspects of the situation. Solutions are no longer intuitive or impulsive, but are the result of rational thinking; the child's learning is now characterized by an understanding of cause-and-effect relationships.

The beginning of the period of formal operational thought corresponds to the onset of adolescence. The distinctive difference between the phase of concrete operations and the phase of formal operations is that the child in the former deals only with the actual, while the adolescent in the latter can deal with conjecture and understand the relationship between the possible and the actual. Thus the adolescent moving into the objective world of ideas and realities is capable of logically deducing possibilities and consequences and of thinking about his or her own thoughts in a reflective way.

Piaget's Explanation of Play

An aspect of Piaget's theory particularly relevant to physical education is his explanation of the role of play in cognitive development. Piaget distinguishes between play and imitation, designating as *play* all forms of make-believe and dreamlike activity, as well as other kinds of spontaneous creative behavior, and as *imitation* all overt or covert imitative behavior (Flavell, 1963). This distinction is less clearcut in practice than in theory, since children frequently play by imitating the behavior of others. (See Figure 3.3.) In fact, this aspect of Piaget's theory is so complex and extensively articulated that he devoted an entire volume *(Play, Dreams and Imitation in Childhood)* to exploration of these phenomena.

Figure 3.3 Role-Playing
Mickey Adair

Rudimentary forms of both play and imitation first appear in the early phases of the sensorimotor stage. By the end of this stage, children intentionally imitate the actions of others and repeatedly perform actions that give them pleasure and satisfaction. Children's play activities (which are largely physical in nature) are the medium in which they begin to discover and relate the essential aspects of their environments (Boyle, 1969). Children of this age frequently indulge in role-playing, pretending to be cowboys, astronauts, doctors, actors, athletes, television figures, and the like. (See Figure 3.3.) They enjoy enhancing the realism of their role-play by wearing costumes or using equipment that resembles that used by adults. Children of this age also enjoy imitating the actions of animals and mechanical devices. Through role-play, they thus begin to identify the characteristic attributes of animate and inanimate objects. During this stage children's play becomes more socially oriented. They develop the ability to play cooperatively with others and become capable of comprehending such essential social conventions as respecting the rights of others, taking turns, and abiding by rules.

During the stage of concrete operations children's play becomes increasingly formalized and socialized. They become more peer-oriented and their play reflects awareness of the expectations of others. As they become capable of relating to more complex situations, they enjoy the challenge inherent in organized play activities. And because they can now anticipate the possible outcomes of a situation, they enjoy the element of chance.

In the period of formal operational thought the individual's interests resemble those of adults. Adolescents are developmentally ready to participate in highly complex recreational activities. At the same time, the adolescent is undergoing the self-testing and self-discovery that are essential to establish one's own identity and prove one's capability of functioning in an adult world.

The Implications of Piaget's Theory

Piaget characterizes learning as a process whereby *unknown externals* become *known internals* (Flavell, 1963). During the sensorimotor period infants learn by repeating behaviors they discover by chance. In subsequent stages of development children's behavior is intentional and goal-directed—that is, they strive purposefully for satisfying outcomes.

According to Piaget, an individual's basic knowledge of the world is derived from direct experience. He theorizes that the first step in the development of representational thought is the acquisition of nonverbal mental images, and that these images are formed through direct contact with objects and events. Thus, in order to know an object, the child must *act on it* and mentally assimilate its properties. However, the ability to "take in" such information is a function of the pre-existence of the essential intellectual structures. In other words, children cannot learn until they are developmentally ready to assimilate the kind of information being presented. For example, children cannot receive verbal information until they comprehend language. Thus learning is facilitated and enhanced by teaching materials and methods that permit children to explore sensorily mental images (symbols) that can be translated into linguistic signs. Later, direct experience provides the input necessary for acquisition of the symbols that must be manipulated in complex cognitive operations.

Piaget's theory of the function of imitation is also directly applicable to the learning process. By imitating the observable actions of others, he proposes, children acquire internal representations of those actions. In this way they develop the symbols that enable them to recall and reproduce given actions. These symbols also allow for the development of signifiers (words and gestures) that make it possible for the child to communicate with others. It is therefore important for children to be continuously exposed to a variety of action patterns they can imitate. (See Figure 3.4.)

Piaget also emphasizes the importance of peer interaction, arguing that seeing a situation from another person's point of view causes the

Figure 3.4 Imitation
Mickey Adair

child to compare that viewpoint with his or her own frame of reference and thus to gain a broader perspective. Through repetition of this process, the child becomes less egocentric and more rational and objective (Flavell, 1963). Thus group activities and a free interchange between children are essential aspects of the elementary-school learning environment.

Piaget's theoretical position strongly supports the educational principle of "learning by doing." Flavell summarizes Piaget's prescription for action-centered learning as follows:

The child should first work with the principle in the most concrete and action-oriented context possible; he should be allowed to manipulate objects himself and "see" the principle operate in his own actions. Then, it should become progressively more internalized and schematic by reducing perceptual and motor support, e.g., moving from objects to symbols of objects, from motor action to speech, etc . . . (Flavell, 1963, p. 84).

The educational implications of Piaget's theories may be summarized as follows: (1) the child must be developmentally ready to assimilate the kind of information being presented; (2) certain kinds of experiences are essential to optimal development of the child during each developmental period; and (3) the child's ability to learn in each successive stage is partially determined by the adequacy of his or her

Movement and Child Development

experiences in the earlier stages of development. Thus it is imperative for children to be provided the right kinds of learning experiences during each stage of development and not to be expected to achieve beyond their level of readiness.

AFFECTIVE DEVELOPMENT

Development in the affective domain involves a combination of social and emotional interactions. The two cannot be separated, since children's feelings about themselves are markedly affected by the actions and reactions of others.

The emotions of the newborn are nonspecific. Infants tend either to be content in their surroundings or to express their discomfort through crying and gross bodily movements. Even at this very early age, however, infants are developing feelings about those who fill their needs. Because the infant lives in a world of physical sensations, social contact is limited to the person who removes unpleasant sensations and provides for comfort. Over time the infant develops a feeling of closeness with this person, usually the mother. Gradually the infant's social world enlarges to encompass other people who contribute to the fulfillment of his or her needs. The infant initially lives in a sensorimotor world, responding physically to bodily sensations, and gradually becomes capable of cognitively preceiving the relationship between his or her sensations and actions. This transition marks the beginning of self-awareness. Thus, as we have said, the infant progresses during the sensorimotor period from simple body awareness to a cognitive awareness of other entities and objects in the environment. Because the young child is completely self-centered, however, every perception is translated into a form of self-awareness.

Preschool children's principal activities involve fulfillment of biological needs and active play, and in both spheres they are dependent on and influenced by other people. In order to fulfill their biological needs children must eat, eliminate, rest, and exercise. These functions are not separate from the child's social and emotional interaction; they are an integral part of it.

Eating is a social occasion, and is in some instances heavily weighted with emotional overtones. Some children have consistently or periodically poor appetites, or do not develop a liking for the foods that are essential to a well-balanced diet. Parental insistence that the child eat everything and "clean the plate" may create emotional turmoil or result in the child's use of the situation to gain attention. Children with hearty appetites and those in whose families mealtime is usually a happy occasion tend to look forward to eating, anticipating that it will be sensorily and socially satisfying. A child's appetite is also affected by participation in physical activity and the condition of his or her health. The body of a child who is physically inactive does not develop a need for normal food intake; an overly active child may be too busy or tired to eat.

The need to move is inherent in the child's biological makeup, and frequent participation in a well-rounded program of physical activities is essential to full development and optimal functioning. Furthermore, movement is sensorily satisfying to children. As they move they develop feelings about their bodies and an essential awareness of their physical beings. Modern life places many restrictions on the child's freedom and opportunities to participate in vigorous movement activities. Such inventions as the playpen, television, and the automobile, as well as the nature of urban living, deprive children of movement experiences that were once commonplace.

The lack of environmental demands to move necessitates development of activity programs that can serve as adequate substitutes. Children should spend several hours a day in large-muscle activity like running, climbing, jumping, and other vigorous locomotor and nonlocomotor movements. These activities not only fulfill a physiological need, but also serve as an essential social medium by offering the child a proving ground on which to test and display physical achievements. It is essential that the child's efforts be recognized and encouraged by significant others. Movement skills older children and adults execute automatically are major learning tasks for young children. As they experiment with their developing ability to perform these skills, they frequently meet with failure. If they are ridiculed or chastised when they fail, children tend to "play it safe" by avoiding attempts to meet physical challenges in the world around them. However, if their efforts are positively reinforced, they will come to see their unsuccessful attempts as a natural outcome of trying.

Children should also be encouraged to use their bodies as expressive outlets for both positive and negative feelings. Children naturally jump for joy and run to meet people they are happy to see. (See Figure 3.5.) They also tend to express feelings of frustration, anger, or fear physically. Though it is common practice for parents to say, "Don't act that way," such statements are in essence requests that children mask and deny their feelings. As children grow older and learn the implicit lesson, the parent's admonition often becomes, "You shouldn't feel that way." Both remarks represent a failure to realize that feelings are caused and are real. It is relatively easy to constrain overt manifestation of emotional reactions, but inhibiting their expression does not eliminate their source. For example, fear of the dark is common in children.

**Figure 3.5 Moving to
Express Happiness**
Mickey Adair

A child who is ridiculed and forced to enter dark places may obey, but obedience does not mean that the fear has been overcome. In fact, such experiences may increase the child's anxiety.

There are two psychologically sound ways of dealing with children's emotional reactions: to help them find socially acceptable emotional outlets and to help them recognize and gradually come to terms with the source of their feelings. Movement activities can play a role in both processes. The acquisition of physical skill and prowess helps children develop feelings of mastery. As they begin to feel more competent, they gain the confidence necessary to cope with further challenges. Each successful experience reinforces the child's positive self-image, thus reducing negative feelings toward the self and others. Physical activity can also serve as a constructive emotional outlet: children are naturally active, and when physically confined for long periods of time tend to overreact emotionally. The same thing occurs when they become overly fatigued. Emotional control is therefore enhanced by a proper balance between activity and rest.

Through play, children discover themselves and learn to relate to their worlds physically, socially, and emotionally. Children's play develops sequentially, and during the development process takes on several forms and dimensions. Babies' play is comprised of activities that give them sensual pleasure and exercise their developing motor abilities. At the same time, their play has a social-affective dimension: they begin to discover the pleasure and satisfaction of human contacts. During this period the social environment is family-centered, and play consists primarily of interaction with adults. As awareness and autonomy develop, children become capable of entertaining themselves for increasing periods of time. Gradually the social world enlarges, and the child progresses from solitary play to playing with other children.

At first children tend to play side-by-side, rather than sharing an activity; this form of limited interaction has been termed *parallel play* (Stone and Church, 1973). As children become more aware of other people, and as their linguistic abilities develop sufficiently to permit an exchange of information, *cooperative play* emerges. Finally, most children learn to cooperate well enough to participate in *group play*.

Most children entering kindergarten have not matured enough to participate successfully in play activities requiring group interaction. With children of this age, therefore, it is advantageous to use a form of class organization that allows them to participate as individuals or as partners. As their social skills increase and they begin to comprehend the meaning of being organized, the size of a group can be increased to three. Following simple rules, sharing equipment, and taking turns are major developmental tasks for children of this age. In fact, some first-graders may have difficulty doing so: they are typically very individualistic and want to be "first" in everything. However, interest in group activities is increasing, and by the time they reach the second grade most are usually quite group-oriented.

In the second grade children begin to evaluate their own achievements and to compare them with the accomplishments of others. The performance of motor skills is a major subject of such comparisons. Children begin to place value on the ability to move effectively, which causes motor skills to become a factor in social recognition and acceptance. Children of this age are becoming more confident, sensitive, and outgoing, and are also learning to be more responsible, orderly, and cooperative.

In grades 4–6 motor skill and bodily development are important factors in social acceptance, and this in turn stimulates children's interest in how their bodies develop and how fitness and skill can be increased. Social activities are peer-centered, and children are more concerned with peer-group acceptance than adult approval. Characteristically, children of this age are adventurous, like being outside, and love to play. Such activities can serve as ideal opportunities for them to develop socially and emotionally. However, it is essential that the nature and conduct of these activities promote self-reliance, self-respect, and self-direction. In other words, activities should not be adult-dominated. Instead, adults should serve as facilitators, companions, and resource persons.

One of the principal goals of affective education is to increase children's self-awareness and enhance their self-concepts. Development of the child's self-awareness involves two interrelated processes, one of which grows out of the feelings associated with doing things. When a child meets the challenge presented by a situation, he or she has a sense of mastery and achievement. Another aspect of self-awareness develops in response to the reactions of other people. An atmosphere of acceptance and affection reinforces the child's sense of being important and deserving of love. Conversely, an atmosphere of disapproval, reproach, or hostility inhibits the child's natural inclination to experiment and explore by arousing feelings of being unclean, inept, and unworthy of love. Thus the child's self-respect depends on others' respect (Stone and Church, 1973). Through action and interaction, the child unconsciously discovers who he or she is and what others are like. From these processes emerge the child's concepts of self and others. The term *identity* is used to refer to the developing self-image, which results from ongoing identification of the self with others, role-playing, and evaluation of one's own behavior and accomplishments. A positive self-image emerges if one is genuinely loved, accepted, and positively reinforced. Children need the attention and approval of significant others. As a teacher, you will be such a person for the children and will markedly influence this aspect of their development. It is therefore essential to become acutely aware of the role you play in the lives of developing children, and to interact with them in a manner that enhances their self-concepts.

TOPICS FOR REVIEW AND FURTHER STUDY

1. What is the difference between a knowledge of developmental characteristics and an understanding of children?

2. Describe the three principal trends that characterize motor development.

3. Trace the sequential development of the locomotor movements.

4. How can you help a child who is having difficulty executing the hop, skip, slide, or gallop?

5. Why should younger children practice ballhandling skills with playground balls?

6. Note four examples of the relationship between children's development in the psychomotor domain and the types of physical activities they should pursue.

7. How does the child's body serve as an informational source during the early stages of cognitive development?

8. How do the child's movement activities relate to the development of such concepts as distance, length, area, and speed?

9. Why is role-playing an essential developmental activity?

10. Explain the statement "Learning is a process whereby unknown externals become known internals." Relate this proposition to the discussion in Chapter 1 of the child's discovery of personal meaning.

11. How does Piaget's theoretical position support educational practices that involve "learning by doing"?

12. How does Piaget's position support the concept of readiness?

13. What is the relationship between bodily sensations and self-awareness?

14. How does modern life inhibit the child's movement potential? How can this circumstance be compensated for by a program of activities provided by an agency outside the home?

15. What do remarks like "Don't act that way" and "You shouldn't feel that way" suggest about the speaker's understanding of the relationship between a child's feeling states and his or her behavior?

16. What kinds of movement activities offer children a way of expressing their feelings in a socially acceptable manner?

17. What is the potential contribution of movement experiences to the development of a positive self-concept? How can adults' verbal and nonverbal behavior promote such development?

18. What are the three kinds of play activities? Give illustrations of each from your own experience.

19. Why should a workable group of kindergarteners contain no more than three children?

20. What is the relationship between the development of a child's self-awareness and the actions and reactions of other people?

21. Observe children of a specific elementary-school grade in the classroom, in physical education, and on the playground. Which of the developmental characteristics discussed in this chapter can you see in the behavior of these children? Are the children's needs for age-appropriate movement activities, social interaction, and positive self-concepts being met in the learning environments you observed?

SUGGESTIONS FOR FURTHER READING

BIEHLER, ROBERT F. *Psychology Applied to Teaching.* Boston: Houghton Mifflin, 1971.

BOYLE, D. G. *A Student's Guide to Piaget.* New York: Pergamon Press, 1969.

CORBIN, CHARLES B. *A Textbook of Motor Development,* Dubuque, Iowa: Wm. C. Brown, 1973.

ESPENSCHADE, ANNA S., and ECKERT, HELEN M. *Motor Development,* Columbus, Ohio: Charles E. Merrill, 1967.

FLAVELL, JOHN H. *The Developmental Psychology of Jean Piaget.* New York: Van Nostrand Reinhold, 1963.

FLINCHUM, BETTY M. *Motor Development in Early Childhood,* Saint Louis: C. V. Mosby, 1975.

FLINCHUM, BETTY, and HANSON, MARGIE. "Who Says the Young Child Can't?" *Journal of Health, Physical Education and Recreation* 42 (June 1972): 16–19.

GALLAHUE, DAVID L.; WERNER, PETER H.; and LUEDKE, GEORGE C. *A Conceptual Approach to Moving and Learning.* New York: John Wiley and Sons, 1975.

GERHARDT, LYDIA. *Moving and Knowing: The Young Child Orients Himself in Space.* Englewood Cliffs, N.J.: Prentice-Hall, 1973.

HAMACHEK, DON E., ed. *The Self in Growth, Teaching and Learning.* Englewood Cliffs, N.J.: Prentice-Hall, 1965.

HORROCKS, JOHN E., and JACKSON, DOROTHY W. *Self and Role: A Theory of Self-Process and Role Behavior.* Boston: Houghton Mifflin, 1972.

ILG, FRANCES L., and AMES, LOUIS B. *Child Behavior,* New York: Harper and Row, 1955.

MUSS, ROLF E. *Theories of Adolescence,* 2nd ed. New York: Random House, 1962.

PIAGET, JEAN. *Play, Dreams and Imitation in Childhood.* Translated by C. Gatteguo and F. M. Hodgson. New York: W. W. Norton, 1962.

STONE, L. JOSEPH, and CHURCH, JOSEPH. *Childhood and Adolescence,* 3rd ed. New York: Random House, 1973.

THOMPSON, GEORGE. *Child Psychology,* 2nd ed. Boston: Houghton Mifflin, 1962.

4   The Movement Experience

Every act of movement consists of two kinds of experience, *individual* and *general*. Individual experiences are those that are uniquely personal and therefore cannot be fully shared. General experiences are those that are common to a group of individuals sharing the same physical environment. Thus all the children in a class may be sharing the experience of a certain activity, but each child in the group is having a uniquely individual movement experience. For example, children who are playing Beat the Ball are sharing the general experience of throwing the ball; but those children who can throw skillfully will have a different individual experience from those who cannot.

Different types of activities provide differing kinds of general experiences. For instance, practicing skills in a drill formation differs from using the same skills in a game. And playing the same game in a more highly competitive situation is yet another kind of movement experience.

Although the variables that affect the nature of the movement experience are complexly interrelated, they can be specified and classified for purposes of discussion. There are two major classifications of these variables: environmental variables—the physical and sociocultural factors that influence the learner—and personal and perceptual variables—the characteristic physical and psychological attributes that determine one's movement potential and affect the way one perceives the learning environment.

ENVIRONMENTAL VARIABLES

Environmental variables include the features of the physical setting in which a given movement activity takes place, as well as pertinent social and cultural factors. The principal environmental variables that commonly affect movement experiences are:

Physical

1. space
2. time
3. sounds
4. weather
5. accessories
   a. dress
   b. equipment
6. spectators
   a. number
   b. type
7. movement media

Sociocultural

1. customs and roles
   a. male–female
   b. parent–child
   c. teacher–student
   d. coach–player
2. expectations
   a. achievement level
   b. success vs failure
   c. rewards
3. type of competition
4. group interaction

The Physical Environment

Space

The space in which the child moves affects the nature of his or her movement experiences. Three classes of space may be utilized by the moving person: *available space, prescribed space,* and *conceptual space.*

There are two types of available physical space: *open space* and *closed* space. (See Figure 4.1.) Open space consists of a large area within which the individual can move in any direction, such as a gymnasium or a playfield. This type of space allows for large, expansive, rapid movements, and therefore tends to stimulate feelings of

Figure 4.1 Playing in Closed Space and Open Space
Bonnie Unsworth

freedom and abandon. Closed space consists of an area that is physically small or crowded. It may contain objects to which the child must relate physically while moving about, such as the desks in a classroom. Closed space tends to restrict freedom of movement and to limit the variety of possible activities.

Children differ in the ways they are affected by physical space. Some seem to feel more comfortable in closed spaces, which give them a sense of intimacy or obscurity, while others prefer open spaces that permit large unrestrained movements.

Prescribed spaces are areas limited by specified boundaries, rules, or formations. An example is the playing area for Nine-Court Basketball, a regulation-size basketball court subdivided into nine rectangles, each of

Figure 4.2 Prescribed Space: Nine-Court Basketball

which is the designated playing area for two players. (See Figure 4.2.) The rules of the game specify that the two players may utilize as much or as little of the rectangle as they desire, but must remain within its boundaries; stepping outside it is a violation of the rules. This spatial limitation is one of the factors that makes Nine-Court Basketball experientially different than the official sport of basketball.

Another kind of prescribed spatial limitation is imposed by a specified formation. For example, a single circle is the prescribed formation for the Danish folk dance Seven Jumps, and this formation must be maintained if the dance is to be correctly executed. (See Figure 4.3.) The children's movements are also spatially limited by the type and prescribed number of movements utilized in the dance: the children may move forward around the circle only as far as they can progress while executing seven skipping steps, and then retrace their original steps. Thus throughout the dance they are spatially limited to moving back and forth over a short distance. The spatial limitations imposed by this dance make it differ experientially from unstructured rhythmic

Figure 4.3 Prescribed Formation: The Folk Dance *Seven Jumps*

activities. In an unstructured situation the children would be free to move in any direction and to execute a variable number of skipping steps. In Seven Jumps, they must execute a certain number of steps and a specified series of movements in a curved pathway.

Movement educators utilize movement exploration to develop childrens' spatial awareness and to enable them to conceptualize spatial dimensions. By means of this exploratory approach, children develop concepts of two kinds of space; these two kinds of *conceptual space* are *personal space* and *general space.*

Personal space is the area occupied by the child's body and the unoccupied space immediately surrounding him or her. This space, also referred to as *self space,* is limited to the distance a child can reach in any direction while executing nonlocomotor movements. Thus the upper limit of a child's personal space is the uppermost point the fingertips can reach when the child stands on tiptoe with the arms extended straight overhead. The lateral limitation of personal space is the distance a child can reach with arms outstretched horizontally. The supporting surface on which the child is standing constitutes the lower limit of his or her personal space. (See Figure 4.4.) The moving child is constantly creating a new personal space.

General space is all the unoccupied space beyond one's personal space. Its outer limits are formed by boundary lines, walls, fences, or buildings. Like personal space, general space is constantly being altered as children move about. Figure 4.5 illustrates how both personal and general space are altered when two children turn away from each other and change the positions of their bodies.

Movement experiences are influenced by the child's level of awareness of his or her body's position in space, and by the ability to conceptualize and relate to the demands created by alterations in the spatial dimensions of the physical environment. Some children may feel fear or frustration because they lack the confidence or bodily control necessary to avoid running into objects or other children, while more highly skilled children enjoy the challenge presented by a situation that demands spatial adjustments.

The elementary-school physical education program should utilize a wide variety of spatial environments. Varied experiences in these environments should promote in children familiarity with the different types of space and awareness of the different feelings they evoke.

Time

The time available helps determine the kind of activity in which children may participate, the extent of their participation, and the feelings evoked. A short time period is best suited to young children, because their attention spans are short and they tire easily. Overlong

Figure 4.4 Exploring Personal Space
Mickey Adair

Figure 4.5 Change in Personal and General Space
Mickey Adair

activity periods may give rise to boredom and undue fatigue at this age. Longer time periods are appropriate for the more extensive, varied, and complex activities of older children.

A temporal limitation may inhibit learning if the children feel unduly hurried. If forced to complete a learning task hastily, they may execute it incorrectly or fail to assimilate all the significant factors associated with it. In physical education classes, children are frequently introduced to new skills or activities and then put in a competitive situation in which winning depends on completing the task in the shortest possible time. This teaching methodology does not allow for adequate practice periods, and winning rather than learning becomes the desired outcome.

In creative activities, in particular, a sense of timelessness is essential: children need sufficient time to explore possibilities fully, recognize relationships, and make discoveries. And other types of activities benefit from ample time for leisurely exploration of their "feeling" aspects. For example, children should be encouraged to internalize the feelings of moving slowly and moving rapidly in different kinds of activities. They should also become aware that changing the speed of a movement alters its quality and that moving to an even rhythm differs experientially from moving to an uneven beat.

Sometimes it is impossible or inadvisable to conduct classes free of temporal limitation. Because young children's experiences tend to be instantaneous, prompt fulfillment of expectations and immediate observable outcomes are desirable in some learning situations. Also, prolonged performance of a single activity promotes distraction and preoccupation. Furthermore, temporal limitations are essential elements in some physical education activities. In a tag game like Hill Dill, for instance, the object is to see who can escape being caught; the winner is the child who remains uncaught for the longest time. The opposite objective is characteristic of some relays. In the over-and-under relay, for instance, the winning team is the one that takes the shortest time to complete the required number of movements. And some activities are regulated by prescribed time limits. The teacher may specify that a game will continue for a certain length of time, and that the team with the most points at the end of that time will be the winner. In races a child's score may be determined by the length of time taken to complete the required task, making the contest a race against time. The effect of the time element is also dependent on the level of the child's temporal awareness and the value attached to a temporal criterion.

Sound

Children react in different ways to the sounds that characterize the physical education environment. The sounds most commonly associated with movement activities are the human voice, music, a drumbeat, and the sound of a whistle; these sounds are frequently used as teaching aids or to stimulate or control movement. For example, a teacher may use a drumbeat to acquaint students with the metric structure of a movement sequence and/or the concept of an accented beat. The teacher may then ask the students to respond to the sound of the drumbeat by clapping their hands or walking, and perhaps to stop moving when the drumbeat ceases. Music may be utilized in the same and many other ways.

In addition to serving a directive function, sounds may be used to enrich and enhance children's sensory awareness. Children should be encouraged to attend to the sounds that accompany their movements. They should, for example, become aware of how it sounds to run or jump correctly and incorrectly. If a child runs or jumps flatfooted, the impact of the entire bottom surface of the feet on the floor will produce a sound distinctly different from that of the ball of the foot hitting the floor. Walking sounds different than running, and hopping or jumping produce sounds that differ from either. Skipping, sliding, and galloping each produce a characteristic sound. Variations in the tempo of these movements result in alteration of the sound pattern. Children should also be encouraged to note environmental sounds and to relate them to the movement of people, animals, machines, and objects.

Weather

Weather affects the way children feel, and thus influences the selection of activities during different seasons of the year and under differing climatic conditions. On a hot day children may feel lethargic and need activities that will stimulate them without requiring a great deal of rapid or exhaustive movement. On cold days they may feel energetic and need activities that require more vigorous movements. Gray days may depress children, making lively music and colorful movement stimulators appropriate. Bright and sunny days tend to arouse peppy feelings and a need for free and active movement. A gentle breeze may stimulate rhythmic swinging movements, whereas a strong wind may evoke feelings associated with pushing. A gentle rain may encourage a child to respond openly to the natural environment, while a hard rain arouses a desire to escape the forces of nature. Many children are afraid of thunder and lightning; when these conditions exist, teachers should be alert to the need for activities that will divert the children's attention.

Modern life tends to insulate children from their natural environment. Movement experiences offer unlimited opportunities to enrich children's awareness of the real world, and the physical education program should include a number of activities designed to familiarize students with the outdoor world and the feelings evoked by the natural elements.

It is common practice in many schools to keep children indoors during cold or inclement weather. This practice usually reflects the wishes of teachers or maintenance personnel, rather than fulfillment of the children's needs. A child's need for active play does not diminish just because the temperature drops or the ground is wet. Every child is entitled to regular physical activity, regardless of the restrictions imposed by weather conditions, and it is the teacher's responsibility to provide for such activity. Even if this means altering schedules and utilizing new teaching methods, the dedicated and competent teacher will make an effort to provide learning experiences that meet the children's real needs.

Accessories

Clothing and equipment affect the experiential nature of movement activities. For several reasons, elementary-school physical educators are becoming less and less prone to require children to wear specified uniforms. First, the crowded schedule of the school day often does not allow sufficient time for children to change clothes. Most regularly scheduled physical education periods are from twenty to thirty-five minutes long, and all of this time is needed for instruction and practice. Also, many elementary schools do not have adequate dressing room facilities. However, the principal reason for having children wear ordinary clothing for physical education activities is an outgrowth of the prevailing view of movement's educational potential. It is widely recognized that children are constantly participating in movement activities, and that the learning that occurs in the gymnasium must be applied in everyday life. In order to facilitate this transition, characteristics of the learning situation must resemble as closely as possible those of the child's usual environment. One factor is the child's attire. The clothing worn in class should be similar to that worn elsewhere, so long as it permits the child to move freely and safely. Thus all children should wear shorts or pants and appropriate footwear. Examples of inappropriate and appropriate dress are shown in Figure 4.6.

Clothing can markedly affect a child's feelings about participation in different movement activities. Casual clothing promotes feelings of freedom to move, while dressy clothes inhibit certain kinds of movement. And uniformity encourages conformity, while individualized dress emphasizes individuality.

On the other hand, certain kinds of costumes or uniforms may enhance children's self-esteem and encourage them to emulate the people they associate with such attire. When children are playing basketball lead-up games, for example, they will feel more like basketball players if they are wearing approximations of basketball uniforms. When learning the folk dances of a certain country, they will more readily experience the feelings associated with the dances if they wear the traditional dress of the country.

Clothing is an extension of the individual, and therefore both reflects and affects how one feels. Thus if children wear clothing that permits an unlimited range of motion and allows for considerable tactile stimulation, movement experience is enhanced.

Children's movement experiences are also affected by the size, weight, color, texture, and variety of equipment utilized. It is vitally important that the size and weight of equipment be appropriate to the body size, strength, and skill level of the children. Equipment that is too large or heavy inhibits correct movement patterns and arouses feelings of frustration and failure.

Bright colors attract children's attention and stimulate their interest. Manufacturers are now producing a wide variety of colorful equipment including balls, bats, mats and parachutes, for movement activities.

The composition and texture of equipment are also consequential. Most children like to touch, hold, and throw yarn balls, which are light, soft, and fuzzy. They also enjoy squeezing and throwing nerf balls. It is relatively easy to throw and catch a beanbag, and when dropped it stays where it lands rather than rolling away. Most children delight in pushing, kicking, and throwing themselves on a cage ball. Using a variety of objects adds interest to ballhandling lessons, as well as

Figure 4.6 Inappropriate Dress and Appropriate Dress
Bonnie Unsworth

providing differing sensory experiences associated with touching and handling these objects. (See Figure 4.7.)

The amount of equipment available is also a significant variable. Children lose interest—and discipline problems ensue—when they must wait to participate. If all the children are to be actively involved most of the time, it may be necessary to use teaching stations which allow the size of each group of children to be adjusted to the amount of equipment available.

Spectators

The number and type of observers affect a child's feelings *about* performing and the feelings evoked *during* the performance. These feelings are also influenced by the child's personality and degree of confidence in his or her ability to execute the required skills. Some children are more highly motivated when they are being observed, while others tend to be inhibited by observers. Both types of children need to be reinforced by the recognition and approval of others, and teachers should provide for children to perform satisfactorily before adults and other children, as shown in Figure 4.8. This process should be gradual; that is, the child should not be required to perform before the whole student body or a group of adults until he or she feels at ease performing for the teacher and the other children in the class.

The Movement Experience

Figure 4.7 Playing with a Variety of Objects Top: playing with yarn balls; Bottom: playing with a cage ball
Mickey Adair

Figure 4.8 Performing for Different Kinds of Spectators
Top: Bonnie Unsworth; Bottom: Mickey Adair

The Movement Experience

| The Movement Environment | The environment in which children move affects the nature of their activities and determines the types of sensory stimulation that are available. There are four types of movement environments: (1) land or solid surfaces, (2) water, (3) suspension, and (4) air. (See Figure 4.9.) |

Supporting surfaces for movement activities include natural outdoor surfaces, such as grass, sand, packed earth, snow, and ice; artificial outdoor surfaces, usually concrete or asphalt paving; and indoor floors, usually wood, tiled, or carpeted. Tumbling mats and thick foam-rubber mats are also used. Each of these surfaces evokes a particular feeling state.

Water is a novel and stimulating movement medium for children. They should become sensorily aware of the feelings associated with wading in water of different depths, being supported by the buoyancy of water, and moving through water.

A special thrill is evoked by being suspended in space. In the physical education setting, suspension activities usually involve gymnastics and the use of such equipment as rings, ropes, and bars.

Aerial activities such as jumping, diving, and flipping may be performed on mats, but an experiential dimension is added when they are performed from a springboard or on a trampoline.

Different movement media are subject to different physical laws. Gravitational pull, buoyancy, friction, and the counterpressure of the supporting surface are factors that differentially affect the execution of the movement, as well as varying the nature of the movement experience. The child's physical education should provide for movement in a variety of media, and thus for development of an awareness of the ways in which such experiences differ.

The Sociocultural Environment

A child becomes a member of society at birth, and from then on his or her movement activities and experiences are markedly influenced by cultural heritage and social expectations.

Customs and Roles

Social customs determine the type and breadth of movement situations available to children, and influence their attitudes toward certain activities. Some such customs are specific to particular social *roles*, or traditionally prescribed patterns of social behavior. The roles whose dimensions most decisively affect participation in movement activities are listed on page 39.

Parents play the principal role in determining the nature and extent of a child's movement activities in infancy and childhood. Some parents allow or encourage their children to participate freely in active play, while others restrict and inhibit children's natural tendency toward a wide variety of exploratory movements. For example, some

**Figure 4.9 Experiencing
Movement in Different
Environments**
Mickey Adair

The Movement Experience

children are permitted to roam freely about the house or yard, while others are confined to playpens or other designated areas. Some children are permitted to climb fences and trees; others are not. Some parents play active games and go on outings with their children, and some enroll their children in clubs or groups that offer instruction and participation in certain physical activities. Thus parental attitudes and practices influence children's movement behavior.

Another highly significant factor is sex role identity. Certain kinds of active play are traditionally ascribed to the male or the female role in American culture. Boys are expected to take part in activities that elicit aggression, fearlessness, hardiness, roughness, and self-assertion, while girls are expected to display sensitivity, affection, compassion, kindness, fastidiousness, and demureness. It is socially acceptable for boys' play to be rambunctious, unrestrained, and daring, while girls are traditionally expected to be more quiet, meticulous, and dainty.

Unfortunately, children are usually given play equipment, and encouraged to participate in play activities, that reinforce sex-appropriate behavior: boys traditionally receive balls, bats, wagons, and guns; girls are more frequently given playthings associated with household tasks. Girls take dancing lessons while boys play ball. Boys often display negative attitudes toward activities they consider "for girls." By the same token, some girls resist taking part in activities they associate with boys.

However, when children's play is observed objectively, individual differences appear to belie stereotypes. Some girls like to participate in team sports and track-and-field events, and some boys enjoy jumping rope and dancing. Fortunately, social change is undermining sex role stereotypes. As more and more women enter businesses and professions that were once exclusively male domains, and as men assume more responsibility for the maintenance and nurture of the family, rigid sex roles are giving way to recognition of individual needs, feelings, and preferences. These changes are in turn reflected in the modification of attitudes toward certain movement activities. It is becoming more socially acceptable for girls to undertake vigorous physical activities and boys to participate in rhythmic activities. We are entering an era in which it is widely recognized that movement is appealing, interesting, and necessary for every individual.

Expectations

Children are constantly subject to the direct or indirect supervision and influence of adults, and to the needs and wishes of other children. A child's experiences are therefore continuously affected by others' values and expectations. The child's self-evaluation is in turn a function of the degree to which he or she obeys the rules of conduct and achieves the goals prescribed by significant others. Educational environments are by nature achievement-oriented, and children soon learn that, in one way or another, they are rewarded for success and penalized for failure. They also learn that there are degrees of success and failure. Inevitably, each child begins to measure his or her achievements against those of other children. If the teacher compares the achievements of different children or judges them with reference to a fixed standard, the element of competition is introduced.

Type of Competition

Competition may be defined as a striving for supremacy. Loy (1968) has identified five types of competitive relationship, four of which occur at the elementary-school level:

1. competition between one individual and another; examples are four-square, hopscotch, Ping-Pong, and Indian wrestling

2. competition between two or more teams; examples are relays, team tag games, line soccer, gym hockey, kickball, and volleyball

3. competition between an individual and an ideal standard or established norm; examples are throwing a ball a specified distance, running the thirty-yard dash in a certain time, and executing a designated number of curl-ups

4. competition in which one individual achieves supremacy over all others; for example, any contest in which there is only one winner, such as the last person caught in tag, the first to reach the finish line in a race, or the one who throws a ball farthest

In the past it has been common practice to include competitive activities in physical education programs, on the assumption that competition would stimulate interest, motivate children to learn, and prepare them to cope with a highly competitive society. It is now recognized that competition is a highly complex phenomenon that challenges some children and discourages others. Combs (1957) argues that competition motivates only those who believe they have a chance of winning; those who do not believe they can succeed tend instead to be threatened by it. Competition is risky for children who are unsure of themselves. A child who succeeds will gain confidence in his or her ability, but failure may cause humiliation and unwillingness to try again. Some such children may gain self-esteem from being members of teams, to which they can contribute while remaining relatively inconspicious.

Competition can be used advantageously, to provide variety and create interest and excitement, when children have achieved a satisfactory level of skill. At a plateau of development, children may benefit from an incentive to match their skill against others' or against an established standard. However, teachers should recognize that premature competition can cause children to sacrifice form in an effort to increase speed. That is, the end may become more important than the means. And some children who have developed satisfactory skill may be socially or emotionally unready to compete against others.

The eventual outcome of a competitive situation is largely determined by the nature of the objective and the value ascribed to the reward. If the contest is casual and winning is not crucial, simple enjoyment of the activity can be an end in itself. But if winning is made all-important, children may be forced to use any means they can to achieve victory.

Teachers should also recognize that in modern society people are highly dependent on each other, and that the ability to work cooperatively is thus far more crucial than the ability to compete successfully. In the class situation, therefore, it is probably far more important for children to learn to help each other and share in common endeavors.

Group
Interaction

How children relate to each other in the movement environment affects the nature of each child's movement experiences. If the other children are friendly, cooperative, and helpful, the child will tend to respond freely and to be positively reinforced; if the children behave antagonistically and selfishly, the child will not be so inclined.

PERSONAL AND
PERCEPTUAL
VARIABLES

When children enter a learning environment they bring with them the effects of their past experiences, which have resulted in characteristic ways of viewing themselves and the various factors in the learning situation. Called the learner's *set*, this uniquely personal way of perceiving the environment determines the nature of his or her anticipation of an activity and expectations of its outcome. In any given situation the child's set will be located somewhere on a continuum between highly positive and completely negative. For example, a highly skilled sixth-grader who has had many pleasurable and satisfying experiences playing baseball will probably have a positive set toward the game. By contrast, an unskilled child who is always the last one chosen for a team and who almost always strikes out will probably have a negative set toward playing baseball. Still another child, who has developed neither a liking nor a dislike for the game and has no particular feelings about participating in it, may have a neutral set.

A child's set is not static; it fluctuates in response to new experiences. The principal factors affecting set are:

1. Previous experience
   a. success vs. failure
   b. satisfaction vs. frustration
   c. pleasure vs. pain

2. Ability
   a. skill
   b. knowledge
   c. developmental level

3. Characteristics
   a. attitudes
   b. needs
   c. interests
   d. desires
   e. fears
   f. habits
   g. goals

4. Perception
   a. of self
   b. of others
   c. of the nature of the activity
   d. of the complexity of the task
   e. of the consequences of the performance
   f. of gratification
      (1) potential
      (2) immediate vs. delayed

The interaction of these factors to alter a child's set toward a particular activity is illustrated by the situations portrayed in Figure 4.10. At the left, the child's performance is being positively reinforced by the teacher. His need to succeed has been satisfied, and he is being warmly acknowledged by a significant other. The teacher's recognition of his success creates a feeling of pleasure and satisfaction that enhances his self-confidence and motivation. Thus the child's needs for success, recognition, and affection have been met, and he will perceive himself, the teacher, and the game positively. A contrasting situation is illustrated on the right. This child has been unsuccessful in his attempts to complete the task satisfactorily, and his failure is being negatively reinforced by the teacher. As a result, he is experiencing psychological pain and negatively perceiving himself, the teacher, and the game of baseball.

**Figure 4.10 Positive
and Negative Feedback**
Mickey Adair

As these two examples illustrate, a child's set is continuously being altered by perceptions of his or her own behavior, the behavior of others, and the outcomes of events. This process is further complicated by the fact that the child is constantly changing—growing, maturing, learning, and developing. These changes in turn give rise to new interests, needs, and goals. As ability increases, enabling the child to cope with more complex tasks, he or she becomes capable of comprehending the necessity of delaying gratification of some needs.

To envision how these factors alter an individual's set, it is necessary to understand the perceptual process. *Perception* may be defined as "the process whereby an individual organizes current sensory input and relates it to his or her past experience."[1]

With children most activity originates in sensory stimulation. The three principal modalities that provide sensory input during movement

[1]Some psychologists use the terms *perception* and *cognition* interchangeably; others differentiate between the two, treating the latter as a more inclusive term.

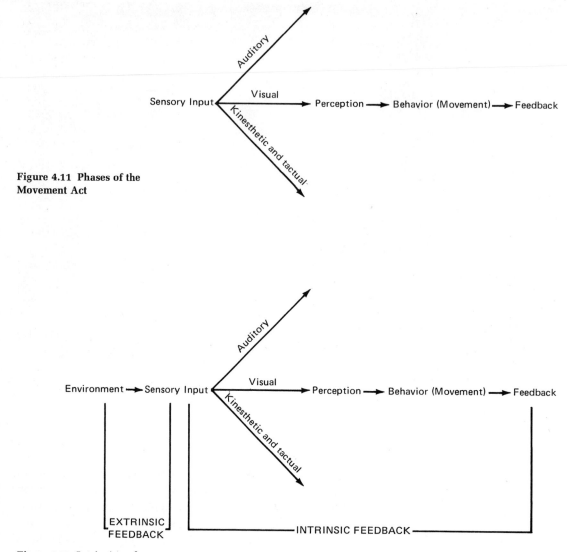

Figure 4.11 Phases of the Movement Act

Figure 4.12 Intrinsic and Extrinsic Feedback

activities are the auditory, the visual, and the kinesthetic. The receptors for the kinesthetic sense are located in the muscles, tendons, and joints. This sense modality provides information on the position in space of the body and its parts. Because movement usually involves touching someone or something, the kinesthetic sense is closely related to the tactile sense. Human sense modalities function interrelatedly, and an individual's movements are thus stimulated by the totality of what he or she hears, sees, and feels at any given moment. The relationship of sensory input to perception and behavior is illustrated in Figure 4.11. Data from the senses are received in the brain and related to information stored in the memory, and on the basis of this combination a decision is made. This decision can result in either overt or covert behavior. *Overt* behavior always involves movement and is thus observable. *Covert* responses are thoughts and feelings, which cannot usually be detected by another person.

Behavior in turn produces *feedback*, which can be either intrinsic or extrinsic. (See Figure 4.12.) *Intrinsic feedback* is sensations arising from within the learner; it is internal recognition of the results of one's behavior. *Extrinsic feedback* has external sources; it is information obtained from someone or something outside the learner. For example, the learner may see the ball rolling foul, the teacher may explain why the ball went foul, or another student may react positively or negatively to the student's performance: all are examples of extrinsic feedback. Feedback is an important variable in the learning experience because it acts as a reinforcing agent, influencing both the student's set toward participation in the activity in question and his or her subsequent movements.

A movement experience is comprised of a series of acts, whose contiguity in time necessitates that each affects those that follow. Because movements necessarily take place in a physical and sociocultural environment, these variables also affect the learner's set. When one considers that a child's experience of a particular situation is determined by the combined effects of significant elements in the present environment, past experience, and the outcome of the immediate event, it is apparent that each child's learning experiences are of necessity unique and individualized.

EXPERIENCE AND PERFORMANCE

There is a subtle but distinctive difference between a movement experience and a movement performance. A movement *performance* is an overt act executed for the purpose of achieving a definable end. It is purposely planned, and its outcome can be observed and evaluated. A movement *experience*, on the other hand, is intrinsic; it is a function of awareness of the sensations, feeling tones, and meaning associated with one's moving being. It is spontaneous, subjective, and uniquely personal. A movement experience is enjoyed as an end in itself, while a movement performance results in recognition of an achievement. The difference between these two aspects of movement becomes more apparent when their specific characteristics are compared as follows:

Performance	Experience
Objective	Subjective
Can be evaluated, critically analyzed, labelled, classified	Must be viewed as a totality and thought about imaginatively
Judged according to a value criterion	Cannot be judged
A means to an observable, definable end	An end in itself
An attempt to satisfy the expectations of others	Self-satisfying
Planned and purposeful	Spontaneous
Extrinsically rewarding	Intrinsically rewarding
Motivated by extrinsic factors	Motivated by intrinsic factors
An achievement	A feeling state

It is not always possible or necessary to distinguish between a performance and an experience, since the two are intimately interrelated. Children's experiences are markedly influenced by their performance levels, and performances in turn gain meaning and purpose from their experiences. But as a teacher you should be aware of the difference between these two aspects of the educational environment, since they have differing effects on the outcome of learning.

Educational systems have traditionally been performance-oriented. The value structure that has characterized education emphasizes tangible achievements that can be measured and qualified. However, modern educational goals increasingly reflect both recognition that some significant behavioral changes are not immediately evident and growing awareness of the importance of affective education. What a child learns in the physical education setting is determined by the nature of his or her movement experiences. As you plan and conduct learning activities, therefore, it is essential to be aware not only of the factors that influence skill development, but also of those that affect children's feelings, attitudes, and values.

TOPICS FOR REVIEW AND FURTHER STUDY

1. a. What is the difference between individual and general experiences?

b. Which is emphasized most by current educational practices?

2. Imagine yourself in the following sets of situations, and think about how they differ experientially.

a. walking to class alone versus walking to class with a close friend

b. walking to class versus walking in the woods on a beautiful spring day

c. responding freely to stimulating, expansive music in an open space versus responding identically in a closed space

d. having five minutes to get to a class across campus versus having thirty minutes to do so

e. being hailed by a friend as you cross a street versus being honked at by a stranger

f. walking to class on a bright sunny day versus walking to class in the rain

g. walking across a lawn barefoot versus walking on the sidewalk, a sandy beach, or a soft carpet

h. walking on a hardwood floor versus walking on ice

i. walking in ankle-deep water versus wading in waist-high water

j. performing a folk dance with the rest of the class versus performing a movement sequence while the class watches you

3. a. Thinking back to your own childhood, can you recall some ways in which your participation in movement activities was determined by sociocultural and parental expectations?

b. Watch children of different ages playing, and try to detect some of the social expectations that are influencing their choices of activities.

c. Why are girls cheerleaders while boys play team sports? Why don't girls' teams have boy cheerleaders? In what other ways is participation in physical education activities affected by sex role identification? How is this situation changing?

4. a. How does competition affect the nature of the movement experience?

b. How does the nature of the reward affect the child's attitude toward winning and losing?

c. How is the child who always loses likely to feel about competing?

5. a. What is your own set toward the following activities? Do you have different sets toward different activities? What accounts for the differences?

(1) playing a game of tennis with a friend who is much more skilled than you

(2) running a thirty-yard dash

(3) taking a physical fitness test

(4) learning a folk dance in which you must do a polka step

(5) doing a forward roll

b. Discuss with three or four other people how each of you feels about these activities. Does your set toward certain activities differ from theirs?

c. How would your set be affected if the situations were altered as follows:

(1) You could play tennis as well as your opponent.

(2) Your grade in a physical education class would be partially determined by your performance in the thirty-yard dash.

(3) Your scores on the physical fitness test were going to be posted for public scrutiny.

(4) You received instruction in the polka step and felt confident about executing it before you were expected to learn a folk dance that included it.

(5) You had to demonstrate a forward roll to the children in your third-grade class.

6. How would your movement experience be differentially affected by the extrinsic feedback received in the following two situations? You are participating in a relay race and your team is ahead. You are the last to run, and you slip and fall flat on your face. *Situation A:* Your teammates and the other members of the class laugh at you. *Situation B:* Two of your teammates run out to pick you up, and the teacher and other members of the class ask if you are hurt.

7. a. What is the difference between an experience and a performance?

b. Do you agree that the prevailing American educational systems are performance-oriented?

c. How important do you think it is for children to have experiences that cannot be objectively measured?

d. Have you observed teachers emphasizing the experiential aspect of learning?

SUGGESTIONS FOR FURTHER READING

COMBS, ARTHUR W. "The Myth of Competition." *Childhood Education* 33 (Feb. 1957): 264–269.

GENTILE, A. M. "A Working Model of Skill Acquisition with Application to Teaching." *Quest* 17 (1972): 3–23.

GOULD, LOIS. "A Fabulous Child's Story." *MS* 1 (Dec. 1972): 74–76, 105–106.

INBAR, MICHAEL. "The Socialization Effect of Games Playing on Pre-Adolescents." *Journal of Health, Physical Education and Recreation* 43 (June 1972): 49–50.

LOY, JOHN W., JR. "The Nature of Sport, a Definitional Effort." *Quest* 10 (May 1968): 1–15.

SINGER, ROBERT N. *Motor Learning and Human Performance: An Application in Physical Education Skills,* 2nd ed. New York: Macmillan, 1975.

ULRICH, CELESTE. *The Social Matrix of Physical Education.* Englewood Cliffs, N.J.: Prentice-Hall, 1968.

Part Two

Developing the Movement Curriculum

Learning experiences are the result of an interaction between the learner and the learning environment. Thus the purpose of the physical education curriculum is to provide a learning environment that will stimulate interaction that extends and enhances the personal development of every child.

It is relatively easy to create a curriculum by adopting a list of physical education activities recommended for a given grade level. This approach is not educationally sound, however, because its central focus is the activity rather than the child and the educational potential inherent in the movement medium. It also tends to isolate the content of the physical education program, rather than integrating it with the child's other learning experiences within and outside of school.

The content of a child-centered physical education curriculum is determined by examining the role it is to play in the context of the child's total educational experience. It is designed to implement answers to the question, "What must this child be able to do in order to live a full and satisfying life?" Chapters 5–10

outline the steps to be taken in developing this type of curriculum. The process begins with an analysis of the learner and proceeds through a series of steps designed to guide exploration of the factors that are determinants of content. Chapters 9 and 10 discuss planning and conducting effective learning experiences. The final step in the initial cycle is to evaluate the learning outcomes and effective-

ness of your teaching procedures. On the basis of this information, a new starting-point is determined and the whole process begins again. In this way curricular content never acquires rigid finality. Instead, revisions necessitated by discovery and development on the part of both teacher and learner are constantly being implemented. Thus the procedure for designing a child-centered curriculum is circular rather than linear.

5 Determining the Children's Educational Needs

The development of a child-centered curriculum begins with analysis of the child's characteristics. The teacher must determine the child's developmental and skill levels, strengths and weaknesses, interests, and individual needs. Decisions about curricular content are based on the outcome of this analysis.

APPRAISING THE CHILDREN'S ABILITIES AND INTERESTS

If the child is to be the center of his or her own education, the teacher must become thoroughly familiar with the factors that affect the child's *ability* to learn and *interest* in the learning medium. This is accomplished by collecting and analyzing all available objective and subjective data on each learner.

School Records

The physical educator should first become familiar with the information contained in the child's permanent school records, which should include:

1. the results of periodic health examinations and the physician's recommendation for the type of physical education in which the child should participate

2. data on the child's growth and developmental patterns

3. reports of accidents, illnesses, and absences

4. results of tests conducted in the school

5. a record of the child's academic achievements

6. notations from educational specialists and former teachers

Sources of Subjective Data

Subjective data should be obtained from all those who share responsibility for the child's education. The physical educator should be receptive to the comments and suggestions of classroom teachers, who often discern individual needs and capabilities that are not apparent in the physical education setting. If the school employs such specialists as a nurse, counselor, psychologist, or special education teacher, they should be asked to recommend types of movement experiences that will be most beneficial to the child. And conversations with parents are essential if one is to become acquainted with the child's needs and interests. Such contacts elicit valuable information, acquaint others with the purposes of the modern elementary-school physical education program, and promote harmonious working relationships.

The most important source of information is the child. Subjective data can be gathered by observing and studying students' reactions in different learning environments. The teacher should note how and on what level individual children respond, and these data should be recorded in such a way that they can be used to assess the progress of individual students and to evaluate the effectiveness of instructional procedures.

When working with older students, who have probably already developed strong interests and preferences, the teacher may undertake formal and informal surveys. The formal survey may consist of a checklist on which the children indicate the activities they prefer. Additional insights may be obtained by asking them to describe what they like and dislike about particular activities. The informal survey consists of students' comments. In an open system children feel free to express their feelings, knowing the teacher is receptive and nonjudgmental. You may stimulate informal student comments by asking questions such as these:

"What kinds of activities do you like the best, those in which you work alone or those in which you work in a squad or a small group? Or do you like team activities the best?"

"Do you prefer being outdoors for classwork, or would you rather be indoors?"

"Do you like games in which you play with just a ball, or do you prefer games in which you use an implement like a bat, paddle, or racket?"

"Do you like activities involving music?"

"Do you like to compete against another person or team, or would you rather participate in activities in which everyone is a winner?"

"Do you like activities in which you receive an individual score, such as how fast you can run, how far you can jump, or how accurately you can throw?"

"Do you like other people to watch you perform, or do you prefer activities in which the attention of others is not focused on you?"

These questions can be used either to elicit comments from individual students or to stimulate group discussion.

Sources of Objective Data

Because it is difficult to analyze subjective data accurately, the physical educator must also obtain objective information on the child's educational needs. Three types of diagnostic tests are used for this purpose: tests of motor skill development, motor ability tests, and physical fitness tests. All three types involve performance of certain kinds of movement skills.

Motor Skills Tests

The three kinds of motor skills tests assess performance of (1) the basic movement skills (locomotor and nonlocomotor), (2) the basic sports skills, and (3) specific sports, dance, and self-testing skills.

Assessment of the child's ability to perform the basic movement skills correctly and efficiently usually occurs at the kindergarten or first-grade level. The instruments utilized are highly subjective, consisting primarily of checklists on which the teacher rates the child's performance on the basis of observation. The same type of subjective measure is also frequently used to evaluate children's performance of the other two types of motor skills. There are, however, a few objective motor skills tests. The Hanson Motor Performance Tests of Elementary Grade Children (1965) and the Johnson Fundamental Skills Test (1962) were constructed to assess the skills of children in grades 1–6. Percentile norms are reported for each of these test batteries. The Latchaw Motor Achievement Test (1954) was developed to assess general and specific motor skills in grades 4–6. The American Alliance for Health, Physical Education and Recreation has published a series of sports skills tests, accompanied by national norms for ages ten through eighteen. This series includes test manuals for archery, basketball, football, softball, and volleyball.

Motor Ability Tests

Motor ability tests were originally designed to assess factors thought to be general predictors of an individual's ability to perform various motor skills. Because it is now recognized that motor learning is a highly complex phenomenon whose contributory factors cannot all be accurately measured, these tests have not been widely used in recent years. There remains, however, a need for objective measures that can be used to identify children who need remedial motor activities. At present, such assessment is usually undertaken in conjunction with perceptual-motor training programs. A number of test batteries are being used in these programs, but there is no general agreement on the adequacy of any of these tests. There does, however, seem to be a consensus on the factors that are essential prerequisites to satisfactory performance in motor learning activities: body awareness, gross motor coordination, hand-eye coordination, static balance, dynamic balance, strength, and agility. Arnheim and Pestolesi have developed a Basic Motor Ability Scale (1973) that can be utilized as a preliminary screening device for five- and six-year-old children. Although this instrument has not yet been widely tested, it contains test items that have been used in other testing programs.

Physical Fitness Tests

The need to enhance the physical fitness of American schoolchildren has been recognized since World War Two, and organized efforts to do so gained impetus and leadership in 1956 when President Eisenhower established the President's Council on Youth Fitness. Five years later President Kennedy's support led to specific recommendations for school programs designed to assess and improve children's physical fitness. Among these recommendations were the following:

1. All schools should conduct screening tests designed to identify underdeveloped children and those with remedial defects.

2. Schools should provide a minimum of fifteen minutes of vigorous physical activity for every child every day.

3. Valid tests should be employed periodically to measure the children's progress.

These recommendations continue to be endorsed by what is now called the President's Council on Physical Fitness and Sports.

The capacities most commonly measured by physical fitness tests are endurance, speed, strength, agility, flexibility, and balance. Numerous tests have been developed for use with children in the intermediate grades. Physical fitness tests are not widely used in the primary grades, however, because most children in this age group are not developmentally ready to be tested in a manner that would yield reliable results; their attention spans are too short, they are easily distracted, and they are not naturally motivated to exert maximum effort. Thus other types of screening devices, including the objective and subjective tests described above, are more appropriate for use with children in this age group.

The most widely used physical fitness test is the Youth Fitness Test developed under the auspices of the American Alliance for Health,

Physical Education and Recreation (AAHPER) and adopted by the President's Council on Physical Fitness and Sports. It is a seven-item test battery designed to assess strength, speed, agility, coordination, and endurance. Testing procedures and national norms for youths from ten to eighteen and for the mentally retarded from eight to eighteen are provided in the AAHPER test manuals listed at the end of this chapter. Standards for elementary-school children from five to fourteen are provided by Arnheim and Pestolesi (1973, pp. 278–285).

USING THE DATA YOU HAVE GATHERED

Information obtained from the sources noted above can be utilized in curriculum design in several ways. (1) It can be used to assign children to homogeneous groups. (2) It indicates the initial level of skill of each child. (3) It provides for the development of individualized instruction. (4) It serves as a basis for comparison when evaluating the child's progress and the effectiveness of the instructional content.

Groups

Children are usually assigned to regular physical education classes on the basis of grade level, all the children in a particular classroom attending the same physical education class. This practice is administratively convenient, but it does not provide the best distribution of students for instructional purposes. The developmental levels of the children in any chronological age group vary a great deal and, although commonalities outweigh differences, individualized instruction is facilitated by grouping children more homogeneously.

The feasibility of classifying students on the basis of needs, interests, and abilities is largely determined by the administrative structure of the school. At present, most schools do not employ the type of flexible scheduling that permits teachers to assign students to classes on the basis of these factors or to adequately prepare and conduct small-group learning situations. However, interest in flexible scheduling is growing. In the meantime, the teacher can assign children to subgroups within each class.

Special Classes

Many schools provide separate physical education classes for children with special needs. The types of specialized classes offered include:

1. a perceptual-motor program for children with body management problems

2. classes for children with neurological or orthopedic impairments

3. classes for mentally retarded children

Children are usually selected for these classes on the recommendation of several specialists, including the child's physician, the school nurse, the special education teacher, the counselor, classroom teachers, and the physical education specialist. The purpose of specialized classes is to provide individualized developmental motor activities for children whose limitations prevent full participation in the regular physical education program. In some instances, the children in specialized programs also participate in regular physical education classes. If such a child can participate in the regular program in a manner that is experientially satisfying, he or she should be enrolled in both types of classes, for two reasons. First, the specialized class isolates such children from their normal social environment; the regular class represents an opportunity to share in the activities of their peers. Second, these children need to be encouraged to participate in a variety of motor activities, in order to acquire maximum practice and to develop confident and positive attitudes toward their movement potential. Sometimes the parents of these children are asked to serve as volunteer assistants in the specialized programs. This is an excellent practice, because it both permits more individualized supervision and familiarizes the parent with the physical activities in which the child should participate on a regular basis.

TOPICS FOR REVIEW AND FURTHER STUDY

1. What can you expect to learn about a child by reviewing his or her permanent school record?

2. Where can you obtain subjective data on a child's needs and interests?

3. Describe the three kinds of motor skills tests used to evaluate the performance of elementary-school children.

4. What do the recommendations of the President's Council on Physical Fitness and Sports imply about the school's responsibility to provide an adequate physical education program for every child?

5. Explain why physical fitness tests are not widely used with children in the primary grades.

6. List the components of fitness most commonly assessed by physical fitness tests.

7. Describe the advantages and disadvantages of the various methods of grouping children in physical education classes.

8. What is the purpose of specialized classes for children with special needs? How are children usually selected for membership in these classes?

9. Visit an elementary school and obtain the following information.
a. What kind of information is contained in the children's permanent records?

b. What motor skills tests does the physical education teacher utilize?

c. Does the school regularly administer a physical fitness test? What are the items in the test battery? How are the results utilized by the physical education teacher?

d. Is any attempt made to group the children homogeneously in physical education classes?

e. Does the school provide specialized physical education classes for children with special needs? If so, how are children selected for membership in these classes and what learning activities are engaged in?

SUGGESTIONS FOR FURTHER READING

AMERICAN ALLIANCE FOR HEALTH, PHYSICAL EDUCATION AND RECREATION. *AAHPER Youth Fitness Test Manual*, rev. ed. Washington, D.C.: AAHPER, 1975.

AMERICAN ALLIANCE FOR HEALTH, PHYSICAL EDUCATION AND RECREATION. *Special Fitness Test Manual for the Mentally Retarded*. Washington, D.C.: AAHPER, 1968.

ARNHEIM, DANIEL D., and PESTOLESI, ROBERT A. *Developing Motor Behavior in Children*. St. Louis: C. V. Mosby, 1973.

FLINCHUM, BETTY M. *Motor Development in Early Childhood*. St. Louis: C. V. Mosby, 1975.

HANSON, MARGIE. "Motor Performance Testing of Elementary School Age Children." Ph.D. dissertation, University of Washington, 1965.

JOHNSON, ROBERT D. "Measurement of Achievement in Fundamental Skills of Elementary School Children." *Research Quarterly* 33 (March 1962): 94–103.

LATCHAW, MARJORIE. "Measuring Selected Motor Skills in Fourth, Fifth and Sixth Grades." *Research Quarterly* 25 (Dec. 1954): 439–449.

MATHEWS, DONALD K. *Measurement in Physical Education*, 3rd ed. Philadelphia: W. B. Saunders, 1968. Chapters 5 and 6.

SCHURR, EVELYN L. *Movement Experiences for Children*, 2nd ed. Englewood Cliffs, N.J.: Prentice-Hall, 1975. Chapters 6 and 8.

6   Formulating General Goals

The first step in curriculum development is to analyze the learner's educational needs. The second step is to make decisions about what the child can, will, and should learn. In order to do so, you must be familiar with the broad general goals of elementary-school physical education, including concepts, skills, and attitudes.

The overall goal of the modern elementary-school physical education program is to enable each child to move efficiently, expressively, and experientially. In order to move efficiently, the child must have achieved satisfactory skill and physical fitness (psychomotor domain). He or she must also be able to solve the movement problems that occur in everyday life and to execute these movements in a manner that will be personally satisfying and promote physical well-being. In order to do so, the child must understand how and why his or her body moves as it does and the effects of the principles that regulate and control movements (cognitive domain). And, finally, the child must become aware of his or her moving being, and thus develop an appreciation of physical activity, the aesthetic qualities of human movement, and the intrinsically satisfying feeling states that result from using the body as an expressive and effective movement instrument (affective domain).

Becoming physically educated is an individualized process, and educational goals must ultimately be personalized. However, children of the same age tend to be somewhat alike, because they are biologically similar and because they have been exposed to similar physical, social, and educational environments. It is therefore both possible and justifiable to specify broad educational goals for given learning levels. Table 6.1 is designed to serve as a guide to the learning sequence that is generally recommended for elementary-school children.

Table 6.1. General Goals of Elementary School Physical Education

Psychomotor Domain	Cognitive Domain	Affective Domain
Beginner		
Correctly execute all the locomotor and nonlocomotor movements.	Identify all the body parts.	Follow simple rules, take turns, share equipment, and be responsible for putting equipment away.
Demonstrate a basic awareness of laterality and directionality.	Understand the concepts of moving in personal and general space.	Demonstrate emotional control and basic social awareness by satisfactorily participating in individual, dual, and small-group movement activities.
Control a playground ball while rolling, bouncing, tossing, and catching it.	Recognize the directions right and left and the body surfaces front, back, and side. Demonstrate ability to relate these concepts to own body and to objects and surfaces in the environment.	Demonstrate awareness of the sensory stimulation associated with touching and moving different body parts.
Freely and appropriately respond to movement stimuli provided by stories, music, sounds, objects, and tactile stimulation.	Recognize basic environmental directions (over, under, into, out of, and the like).	Demonstrate the ability to follow directions while participating in simple games and rhythmic activities.
Demonstrate bodily control while starting and stopping on signal, changing direction, and moving through space without touching anyone.		
Advanced Beginner		
Correctly execute all the locomotor and nonlocomotor movements while responding to various movement stimulators and exploring the dimensions of time, space, and force.	Recognize differences in body positions and shapes and sizes of movements.	Participate in individual, dual, and group activities without fearing failure, fighting, or arguing.
Demonstrate the following ballhandling skills:	Identify the locomotor and nonlocomotor movements.	Use imagination freely in expressive movement and pantomime.
a. accuracy in rolling	Demonstrate knowledge of the basic formations used in physical education classes (circles, lines, squads).	Respond in movement to stimulation of the kinesthetic, tactile, gustatory, olfactory, visual, and auditory senses.
b. controlled bouncing and tossing	Demonstrate knowledge of the rules of class routines and simple games.	Share, take turns, and be responsible for the use of equipment.
c. correct catching form (without fear)	Demonstrate knowledge of the basic elements of rhythmic activities.	Assume some responsibility for making and obeying rules, and giving and following directions.
d. use of correct form while executing an underhand throw of a yarn ball, beanbag, and playground ball.		Manifest a positive attitude toward the moving self.
e. control of a playground ball while kicking and dribbling.		
Respond to a rhythmic beat while executing simple movement patterns.		
Demonstrate bodily control while balancing, climbing, hanging, and rolling.		

Intermediate

Execute all the locomotor movements in response to rhythmic accompaniment.

Utilize the basic movements in response to various rhythms and tempos.

Use different body parts to lead movements, support and transfer body weight, and demonstrate various spatial relationships.

Increase physical fitness by participating vigorously in activities requiring increasing strength, endurance, speed, and agility.

Satisfactorily execute all the basic sports skills.

Execute the basic dance patterns utilized in folk and square dance and in gymnastics routines.

Identify similarities and differences among movements varying as to time, space, and force.

Identify the structures of various games and dances and the basic movements they utilize.

Recognize the effects of time, space, and force factors on the qualities of movement.

Demonstrate improved memory for movement by participating in increasingly complex movement sequences, games, and dances.

Recognize similarities between movements utilized in physical education activities and those used in other types of activities.

Demonstrate knowledge of the basic components of games by inventing games and contests.

Demonstrate self-direction, self-control, and initiative in planning and carrying out individual and group activities.

Participate cooperatively in student-led activities and activities characterized by mutual assistance.

Utilize imagination and creative ability in responding to movement stimulators and creating movement sequences.

Participate in activities for purposes of enjoyment and self-fulfillment rather than to receive extrinsic rewards or avoid punishment.

Assume some responsibility for improving physical fitness and skill by means of self-directed movement activities.

Advanced

Correctly apply and utilize all the basic skills while participating in lead-up games, gymnastics routines, track-and-field events, and structured and creative dance.

Correctly execute the fundamental physical skills.

Improve physical fitness by participation in movement forms and self-testing activities.

Develop movement sequences exemplifying:

a. functional combinations of the basic movements

b. smooth transitions

c. the dimensions of the movement elements

Demonstrate the acquisition of a functional repertoire of movement activities representative of the various movement forms and media.

Participate in a variety of outdoor activities, such as orienteering, biking, and camping.

Identify the rhythmic structure of locomotor movements.

Describe the basic structural elements and design of the human body and relate them to the possibilities of and limitations on human movement.

Identify and apply the basic mechanical principles that affect and control human movement.

Mechanically analyze the basic movement skills, sports skills, and fundamental physical skills.

Demonstrate knowledge of the rules and procedures governing the conduct of games and other movement activities.

Recognize the basic steps, sequence of movements, and rhythmic structure of selected dances.

Demonstrate knowledge of the cultural origin and significance of games and dances.

Demonstrate friendliness, mutual respect, and concern for others during and after participation, whether winning or losing.

Help plan and conduct some in-class, extra-class, and self-directed individual activities.

Assume some responsibility for setting own goals and evaluating own performance

Demonstrate sensory awareness of own physical being and of the feelings and emotions associated with and expressed by bodily movements.

Respond freely, confidently, and expressively while creating movement sequences.

Demonstrate an aesthetic appreciation of movement.

Demonstrate a positive attitude toward participation in a variety of movement activities.

The purpose of the foregoing list is to help you select goals that are appropriate for a given group of children. By reviewing a child's developmental characteristics and the data obtained from the sources noted in Chapter 5, you will be able to determine his or her levels of development and prior achievement. Comparing the child's competencies with those in the foregoing list will enable you to determine the child's learning level in each of the educational domains. You can then review the general goals of that learning level and select the immediate and long-range goals toward which you and the children should work.

A child's learning level may not be the same in all three domains. He or she may, for example, be an advanced beginner in the cognitive domain but lack some of the competencies that characterize the beginning level in the psychomotor domain. This is one reason why goals are specified by learning level rather than grade level. Another is to avoid the restrictive and confining expectations that often ensue when children are classified according to age or grade level.

When you have determined the children's educational needs and selected the appropriate educational goals, you are ready to undertake the third step in curriculum development, selecting the subject matter that will serve as a learning medium in order to achieve these goals.

TOPICS FOR REVIEW AND FURTHER STUDY

1. What are some of the ways you are required to move in your everyday life? How can you modify the extent or execution of these movements to enhance personal satisfaction and/or promote physical fitness?

2. How can you help children develop an appreciation of the value of physical activity?

3. Explain the implications of the statement, "Becoming physically educated is an individualized process."

4. What factors tend to make children of the same age somewhat alike? What are some factors that cause them to differ?

5. Why should general goals be specified for *each* of the educational domains?

6. Why should general goals be specified according to learning level, rather then age group or grade level?

7. a. Observe a group of children in a physical education setting. Determine as much as you can about their educational needs. What specific charateristics and needs can you detect?

b. On the basis of your observation, select the general goals in each of the educational domains that you believe these children should work toward.

Formulating General Goals

SUGGESTIONS FOR FURTHER READING

DAUER, VICTOR P. and PANGRAZI, ROBERT P. *Dynamic Physical Education for Elementary School Children,* 5th ed. Minneapolis: Burgess, 1975. Chapter 2.

METZGER, PAUL A., JR. *Elementary School Physical Education Readings.* Dubuque, Iowa: Wm. C. Brown, 1972.

SWEENEY, ROBERT T., ed. *Selected Readings in Movement Education.* Reading, Mass.: Addison-Wesley, 1970.

VAN HOLST, AUKE. *Physical Education Curriculum for Elementary Grades.* London, Canada: London Free Press, 1974.

7 Outlining the Curriculum

Physical education is usually thought of as limited to activities conducted in the gymnasium or on the playground. This text, however, has introduced a much more comprehensive definition of physical education as encompassing all the learning experiences that contribute to knowledge of, skills in, and positive attitudes toward participation in gross motor activities. Viewed from this perspective, it is obvious that much of the child's physical education has already occurred by the time he or she enters school. It also becomes apparent that much of what the child learns during the school years will be acquired outside of school, when he or she is much more physically active. Thus the content of the physical education curriculum must be determined in light of three time frames, the past, present, and future.

The child's past experiences must be studied in an attempt to determine their effect on his or her present attitudes, interests, and developmental level. The following exercise will illustrate why this process is essential. Can you determine the probable effects of each of the following five situations on the development of the child's skills and attitudes and describe how his or her participation in physical activities might be affected?

1. A six-year-old boy's mother forbids him to run, climb, or play in the dirt because he might ruin his clothes or get hurt.

2. A third-grade girl's parents think it is unladylike to climb, ride a boy's bike, or play ball.

3. A fourth-grade boy's father and older brother have told him it is "sissy" to jump rope or dance.

4. A sixth-grade girl's three older brothers have made her a regular member of their baseball team.

5. A sixth-grade boy's father wants him to become captain of his high-school football team and to win an athletic scholarship to a major university.

These situations might, of course, have various effects, depending on the other factors involved. They serve, in any case, to illustrate some of the environmental variables that can affect children's physical education and bring about characteristic ways of responding in certain movement media.

The concept of time is abstract, but children think concretely. They live in the here and now. They are means- rather than end-oriented, and are therefore motivated by the stimuli in their immediate environments. They love to play, and participate spontaneously in activities that are enjoyable and satisfying. Thus the mode of learning that naturally motivates them is learning that is pleasurable and immediately gratifying. Your task as a teacher is to discover the activities that stimulate the most interest on the part of the children with whom you work.

And you must also look to the child's future, asking yourself, "What must this child be able to do in order to live a full and satisfying life?" In other words, you must think in terms of immediate goals with long-range effects.

Keeping in mind the first two steps in the curriculum development model while discussing content will help minimize the tendency for the curriculum to become content-oriented rather than child-centered.

The three subject-matter components that should characterize the elementary-school physical-education curriculum are shown in Figure 7.1 in relation to the learning medium (physical education) and the general learning outcomes. The components are arranged hierarchically to indicate the sequence in which they should be taught. *Movement awareness* is at the top of the hierarchy because the child needs a certain level of perceptual development if he or she is to execute the movement skills. *Basic skills* are listed next because they are a necessary prerequisite to successful performance in movement forms. *Movement forms* are listed last because they are complex activities requiring acute movement awareness and a high level of skill development. The three components are, of course, interrelated. The child must be aware in order to move, and must move in order to increase his or her awareness and skill levels. The difference between the content of the awareness component and that of the other components is largely a matter of

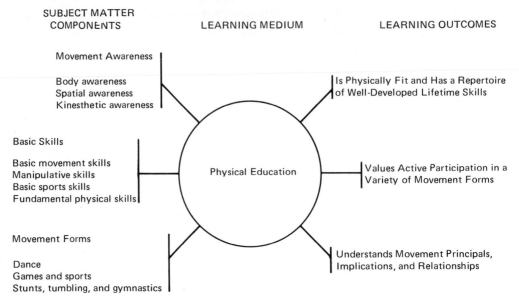

SUBJECT MATTER COMPONENTS   LEARNING MEDIUM   LEARNING OUTCOMES

Movement Awareness

Body awareness
Spatial awareness
Kinesthetic awareness

Basic Skills

Basic movement skills
Manipulative skills
Basic sports skills
Fundamental physical skills

Movement Forms

Dance
Games and sports
Stunts, tumbling, and gymnastics

Physical Education

Is Physically Fit and Has a Repertoire of Well-Developed Lifetime Skills

Values Active Participation in a Variety of Movement Forms

Understands Movement Principals, Implications, and Relationships

Figure 7.1 The Relationship Between Subject Matter Components, the Learning Medium, and Learning Outcomes

emphasis. The awareness component emphasizes activities that enable the child to perceive his or her movement potential, while the skill components emphasize performance levels.

MOVEMENT AWARENESS

The purpose of movement awareness activities is to help the children become sensorily aware of their moving beings and discover their bodies' movement possibilities. This is a sequential process in which children first become consciously aware of their own bodies (body awareness) and then develop awareness of where and how their bodies can move (spatial awareness, kinesthetic awareness). The principal steps are:

Body Awareness

1. perception and identification of body parts
2. development of laterality and directionality
3. recognition of body positions and relationships of body parts
4. awareness of sensations associated with moving and touching

Spatial Awareness

1. awareness of spatial dimensions
a. range and size of movements (small to large)
   (1) in personal space
   (2) in general space

b. direction (forward, backward, sideways)

c. level (high to low)

d. shape (narrow, wide, curved, angular, twisted)

e. pathway (straight, angular, curved)

2. awareness of spatial relationships

a. between body parts

b. between the self and other people or objects

c. between the self and the physical environment

Kinesthetic Awareness

awareness of

1. the body in stillness and in motion

2. how the body parts are used to support the body and control movement

3. the effects of varying time and force

4. the relationship between the body's structure and how it functions

Body Awareness

In becoming aware of his or her body, the child develops a *body image*. This process involves learning to identify all the body parts, knowing their locations, recognizing different body positions, and knowing how the body parts relate to one another. It also involves the development of increased sensory awareness.

Body awareness is also characterized by *laterality* and *directionality*. Laterality is the ability to differentiate functionally between the two sides of the body and to identify the body parts on each side. Directionality is the ability to use awareness of laterality and the dimensions right, left, up, down, front, and back to relate to objects in external space.

Body awareness is a prerequisite to successful participation in movement activities, because children's own bodies are their central reference-points. They perceive the dimensions and locations of objects in external space in relation to their own body positions.

Spatial Awareness

While the purpose of body awareness experiences is to familiarize the child with their bodies as instruments of movement, the purpose of spatial awareness experiences is to familiarize them with space as a medium of movement. The spatial awareness unit consists of activities designed to help children recognize spatial dimensions. As we have seen, the body moves in two types of space, personal and general. It also moves in some *direction* and on some *level*. Any given movement is characterized by a size, ranging from small to large, and changes in the position of the body alter its *shape*. If the body parts are close together, the body will have a narrow or a curved shape; if they are far apart, it will have a wide shape. Bending gives the body an angular shape, and rotating gives it a twisted shape. And as the body moves across the floor, its pathway creates a pattern.

The human body is a physical object that exists among other objects in a physical environment, and thus has relationship to the things that surround it. The body parts also have physical relationships to each other. In movement education, these factors are referred to as *spatial relationships* (see pages 186–189).

Human beings use their own bodies as central reference-points in spatial relationships. Thus spatial awareness experiences should be designed so that children first experience spatial factors in relation to their own bodies and subsequently relate to other people and objects in space.

Kinesthetic Awareness

Kinesthesia, one of the five senses, is sensation of the movement, position, and tension of body parts. *Kinesthetic awareness* is the goal of curricular components that promote recognition of the ways different body parts are used to perform various movements. This phase of the curriculum is designed to enhance children's awareness of their movement potential by emphasizing sensory input and cause-and-effect relationships. Attention is given to the ways in which the body's structure determines its function, how different body parts are used to support body weight and to initiate and control movement, and how variations in time and force affect the resultant movement.

The structure of the human body determines what it can and cannot do. On the primary level children learn about the relationship between structure and function by *experiencing* their own movements and *comparing* them to the structures and functions of other animate and inanimate objects. On the intermediate level children also learn about the mechanics of effective and efficient movement patterns.

The human body is always either in motion or motionless. (See Figure 7.2.) In both states (except during those brief moments when it is suspended in mid-air) it must have a base of support. The position of the body determines the type of base that is necessary and, conversely, the base of support determines the body positions that can be assumed. The most common body positions are standing, sitting, and lying. Thus the body parts most frequently used as bases of support are the feet; the buttocks; and the back, front, and sides of the prone body. By using these body parts in different ways or by using other body parts and combinations of body parts, numerous other body positions can be created. Children need to experience the sensations aroused by different body positions and to learn to make smooth transitions between one position and the next.

All changes in the body's motion and position must be initiated by

MOTIONLESS (STILLNESS)

IN MOTION (MOVEMENT)

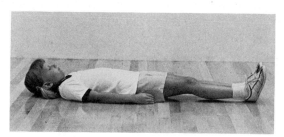

To get from here

to here

Back

Feet

Some body part and/or combination of body parts must initiate and control the movement . . .

Figure 7.2 The Two Body States
Mickey Adair

And in either state the body must have a base of support.

contraction of the muscles that control the pertinent body parts. If the trunk of the body is involved in a movement to the point that a major shift in the body's center of gravity occurs, weight must be transferred from one body part to another.

Execution of movement patterns that are smooth, efficient, and rhythmic depends on control of the time and force factors. The effects of these two factors interrelate to produce different tempos, rhythms, and other qualities. Children should experience and learn to recognize similarities and differences in time and force factors, and should learn to control them consciously in the reproduction of structured movement skills and the invention of their own activities. By controlling force and experiencing how it affects the quality of the resultant movement, children experience the *flow* of a movement and learn to recognize the two types of flow, *bound* and *free*. Bound movements are characterized by the sudden exertion of force to stop and hold a certain body position, while free movements are characterized by fluency and smooth, continuous transitions from one movement to the next.

The factors that control movement and determine bodily positions, referred to as *movement elements*, are *space*, *time*, and *force*. Each of these elements has several dimensions, which may vary in certain ways:

Space

1. range and size (small to large)
2. direction (forward, backward, sideways)
3. level (high to low)
4. shape (narrow, wide, curved, angular, twisted)
5. path (straight, angular, curved)

Time

1. tempo (slow, medium, fast)
2. duration (short, long)
3. rhythm (even, uneven)

Force

1. exertion (strong, heavy, hard; weak, light, soft)
2. acceleration (sudden, gradual)
3. flow (bound, free)

Through physical education every child should become cognitively and sensorily aware of these factors, which are the basis for experiencing and understanding movement. These concepts should thus be directly and purposefully taught, and learning should be reinforced by frequent review and application in increasingly complex activities. Children do not develop lasting movement awareness simply by participating in physical activities. Consciousness of movement must permeate all of a child's movement experiences.

THE BASIC SKILLS

As we have said, the goal of modern elementary-school physical education is to improve the quality of the child's movement responses. The basic skills component contributes to this goal by developing the skills that enable children to utilize their physical beings as functional and expressive movement instruments.

The Basic Movement Skills

The child's physical education should begin with the development of a basic vocabulary of movement. This vocabulary is comprised of eighteen basic movement skills. These are of two types, locomotor and nonlocomotor. Locomotor skills are those that move the individual through space from one place to another; nonlocomotor movements may be executed without moving one's base of support. There are eight locomotor and ten nonlocomotor movements. Five of the locomotor movements have even rhythms and three have uneven rhythms.

Locomotor Skills

Even Rhythm

1. walk
2. run
3. jump
4. hop
5. leap

Uneven Rhythm

6. skip
7. slide
8. gallop

Nonlocomotor Skills

1–2. bend and stretch

3–4. twist and turn

5–6. push and pull

7–8. swing and sway

9–10. fall and rise

All movements of the human body are variations on these eighteen basic movements. For instance, crawling is a combination of bending and walking; throwing represents a swinging movement of the bent arm combined with one or more walking or running steps.

Teaching the basic movement skills that comprise motor learning[1] is analogous to teaching the alphabet in verbal learning or the numbers in mathematical learning. In verbal learning two kinds of letters (vowels and consonants) are joined to form words, and words are combined to form sentences. Sentences may in turn be combined to form paragraphs, and paragraphs may be joined to convey complex messages. The eighteen basic movement skills are used in motor learning just as are the twenty-six letters in verbal learning. That is, the two types of basic skills (locomotor and nonlocomotor) are combined to form movement sequences that may vary in length and level of difficulty from the very simple to the highly complex. For instance, running across the room is a simple sequence characterized by repetition of the same movement. When the running steps are combined with a leap, the sequence becomes more difficult. And, finally, when a football player running down the field leaps to avoid being tackled, his movements are part of a highly complex sequence with twenty-two participants. Yet all these undertakings use basic movement skills. In terms of basic skills, a football game may be described as follows:

All the linemen *bend* over to assume the starting position for the play. The center snaps the ball and the players *run* at or away from their opponents. If it is a pass play, the quarterback will *stretch* to pass the ball while the receiver *runs* into position and *swings* his arms up to catch the pass. If it is a running play, some of the defensive players will be *pushing* and *pulling* to tackle while the runner is *twisting* and *turning* to avoid being tackled. Others are *running, jumping, leaping,* or *sliding* to gain better positions for assisting in the play. Finally most of the players have *fallen* on the ground. They must *rise* and *walk* back to the position they are to assume for the next play.

The success of these highly skilled athletes in this highly complex movement sequence is dependent on their ability to execute the basic movement skills they began to acquire in early childhood. In order to play football, one must also be able to handle, project, and control a football effectively. The development of this highly specialized skill begins when the child learns how to manipulate various kinds of objects.

---

[1]*Motor learning* may be defined as learning to execute motor skills effectively and efficiently.

| **The Manipulative Skills** | When children have developed basic control of their own bodies, they are developmentally ready to learn to relate to and control external objects. The second class of basic skills are those that are essential for handling, controlling, and projecting movable objects of various sizes, shapes, and composition. Those commonly used in the physical education program include beanbags, hoops, wands, paddles, ropes, and balls. |

Children are frequently forced to participate in competitive games and sports before they are developmentally ready to execute the complex skills required. Teaching the manipulative skills provides for a necessary transition between the relatively simple basic movement skills and the more highly specialized sports skills.

The Basic Sports Skills

Sports skills are basic movement and manipulative skills that have been modified to serve a specialized function in sports and games. They are: (1) running, (2) hopping, (3) jumping, (4) leaping, (5) throwing, (6) catching, (7) striking, (8) kicking, and (9) swimming. The first four skills are locomotor movements. They are also classified as basic sports skills to emphasize the fact that skilled execution of these movements is necessary to successful participation in lead-up games[2] and sports. Skills 5–8 are manipulative skills, which are used for specialized purposes in sports. For example, the baseball pitch and the football pass are specialized kinds of overarm throwing patterns. Tennis and golf swings are specialized striking skills. A high level of motor skill development is necessary to execute these movements correctly. If children are to do so, they must be developmentally ready. Thus the manipulative skills are appropriate subject matter for younger children, and the sports skills should not be introduced until children demonstrate mastery of these more basic skills.

Swimming is considered a basic sports skill because it requires adaptation of the basic movement skills. Swimming requires children to adjust physically and psychologically to a different movement environment. They should be introduced to swimming as early as possible so they can become familiar with movement in water before fear and self-consciousness develop.

The Fundamental Physical Skills

A component of the recommended elementary-school physical education curriculum that has been almost completely neglected is correct execution of the physical skills required in everyday living. Let us consider the physical skills you require in daily life.

---

[2]For a definition of lead-up games, see page 90.

During your physically active hours, you are usually either standing or sitting. You move from place to place by walking. While shopping, travelling, doing household chores or yardwork, you repeatedly stoop, lift, hold, carry, push, or pull various objects.

Let us examine a typical trip to the grocery store to identify the fundamental physical skills you perform.

You *stand* up, *walk* to the car, *pull* open the car door, and *sit* inside. You *hold* the steering wheel and *push* down alternately on the accelerator and the brake. Arriving at the store, you *push* open the car door, *stand,* and *walk.* You *lift* objects from the shelves and place them in the shopping cart. You *stoop* to retrieve articles from the bottom shelves. You *push* and *pull* the cart around the store. Then you *lift* the objects out of the cart and place them on the checkout stand. After they are bagged, you *lift* and *hold* the parcel while *carrying* it to the car. You repeat the movements involved in driving and then perform those involved in transporting the sacks of groceries.

In discharging this ordinary task, you have repeatedly performed the following skills: (1) standing, (2) walking, (3) sitting, (4) stooping, (5) lifting, (6) holding, (7) carrying, (8) pushing, and (9) pulling. These are the nine principal skills utilized in work and play. Although standing is a static activity rather than a movement skill, it is classed with the latter because it is necessary to move in order to assume a standing position and because correct standing posture is essential to some of the other basic skills. Walking, a locomotor skill, is also listed as a fundamental physical skill because it is the most common movement utilized in everyday living. Walking patterns must be modified in various ways in order to engage in ordinary work and play. Pushing and pulling are nonlocomotor movements that become fundamental physical skills when they are performed to move external objects. Sitting, holding, stooping, lifting, and carrying are combinations of locomotor and non-locomotor movements.

How did you learn to execute these fundamental movements? Like most people, you probably learned through imitation and trial-and-error. And you perform adequately, as long as your tasks are not too strenuous or demanding. But do you know how to stand, sit, or walk for long periods of time without becoming unduly fatigued? Can you lift objects from an overhead position without risking injury to your back? How would you lift a thirty-pound box of books? If you are going on a long trip, should you take one large suitcase or two smaller ones? What is the advantage of a bag with a shoulder strap? Why is a backpack an efficient means of carrying external weight?

The rationale for teaching correct execution of these skills is probably self-evident, but why should we teach them on the elementary level?

For several reasons it is essential to teach these skills as early as possible. One involves the development of attitudes and habits. For example, the maintenance of correct posture is largely a matter of attitude. Children's posture is unlikely to be affected by adults who chastise them for failing to sit up straight or stand without slumping: people stand and sit in the positions that feel most comfortable. On the elementary level, then, the most important learning occurs in the affective domain. Children will stand and sit correctly if they feel good and if the position feels good.

Habits result from repeated practice; once a habit is established, it feels right. In order to break a habit, therefore, the feeling states associated with it must be altered, the habitual responses extinguished, and new response patterns established through practice. The elaborateness of this process indicates why early learning is so important. Children learn to walk when they are about one year old. This, then, is when habitual walking patterns are formed, and when correct practice should occur. As we have said, children are required to submit to hours of sitting once they enter school. Since it requires maintenance of this posture, the school has a responsibility to provide furniture that encourages correct sitting and to help children develop efficient sitting postures.

Children in the intermediate grades are curious about their bodies and capable of comprehending relatively complex cognitive relationships. These developmental characteristics enable children of this age to learn to analyze movement principles and see factual relationships. The science curriculum of the upper elementary grades ordinarily includes the mechanical principles that control human movement. Teaching children to execute the fundamental physical skills efficiently and to analyze the mechanical principles at work allows such learning to be applied and reinforced.

THE MOVEMENT FORMS

A *movement form* is a group of activities that are similar in nature.[3] The principal forms of movement are dance; games and sports; and stunts, tumbling, and gymnastics. Each of these groups of activities is characterized by a given combination of basic movements executed in a particular manner. The movement forms are educational media in which the basic skills are applied, and each form plays a unique role in the physical education of the child.

Dance

Dance is a rhythmically and spatially structured form of human movement. Of the numerous kinds of dance, those that have the most

[3]For an in-depth discussion of movement forms, see Felshin (1972, Ch. 3).

educational value for elementary-school children are *creative, folk,* and *square* dance.

Creative dance is a medium in which developing children can expressively explore their movement potential. As soon as they have acquired basic movement vocabularies, children can begin to create dances by varying the spatial, temporal, and rhythmic dimensions of the basic movements. While children are discovering *how* they can move in creative dance, they should also become aware of the *expressive potential* of their movements. They should be encouraged to express their thoughts and feelings in pantomime and improvisation and to observe and interpret the nonverbal expressions of others.

While children are learning to invent their own dance patterns, they should learn patterns devised by others. Folk and square dance are media in which children can apply their knowledge of the basic movements and the movement variables. However, teaching should not be limited to the performance and analysis of dances; folk and square dance should be taught as folk art, and attention should be given to the origin and significance of the dance and the beliefs, customs, legends, occupations, costumes, and festivals of the people. Taught in this way, dance serves to enhance understanding and appreciation of people in other countries and other times, which is imperative for children today. Another such avenue of learning is the study of various cultures' games.

Games and Sports

Games are classified according to the level of skill required and the complexity of the rules. There are three kinds of games: games of low organization, lead-up games, and sports.

Games of low organization are simple, have very little structure, and do not require a great deal of skill. Examples are Squirrels in Trees, Tunnel Ball, and Steal the Bacon. The elements of play in such games are (1) fun, (2) an element of suspense, (3) immediate outcomes, and (4) no serious consequences. Because they are brief, a wide variety of games can be played within a relatively short time. Games of low organization allow children to practice the basic movement skills and manipulative skills.

Lead-up games, so called because they lead up to participation in official sports, have more complex rules, require higher levels of skill development, are played for a longer period of time, and are more keenly competitive than games of low organization. Lead-up games contain the same elements of play as do games of low organization, but successful participation requires a more serious attitude. Lead-up games provide practice in the basic sports skills, acquaint children with

Outlining the Curriculum

some of the rules of certain sports, and provide practice in the particular skills they utilize. For instance, newcomb leads up to volleyball, kickball leads up to softball, line soccer leads up to official soccer, and endball provides practice in some basketball skills. Lead-up games are an important aspect of upper elementary physical education programs because they provide for both practice in essential skills and the challenge and excitement inherent in competitive activity.

Sports are highly organized games. Successful participation in sports requires a high level of skill and a fluent knowledge of their rules. Furthermore, sports are usually more highly competitive than games, and there is a marked difference in the selection of team members and the roles they play. In games, team members are usually selected rather spontaneously; the team typically disbands following the contest. In sports, team members are usually carefully selected; once the team is organized, it remains intact for an entire season (Loy, 1968).

Games are characterized by very little role differentiation: players may change roles frequently without altering the outcome of the game. In a simple tag game, for example, the runner becomes It when tagged, and the tagger simultaneously becomes a runner. In a lead-up game like line soccer there is no role differentiation: any player may kick the ball toward the opposing team's goal line and then be required to play goalie by attempting to prevent the ball from crossing his or her team's goal line. In official sports, however, each participant plays a specific and specialized position. The roles of these positions are clearly defined, and successful strategy requires that each player perform his or her role correctly and skillfully. In football, for example, only the center is allowed to snap the ball, and only the backfield players can receive it. The linemen are not allowed to touch the ball during offensive play, except in the case of a fumble. Because sports are highly specialized movement forms and because considerable value is attached to winning in American culture, the outcome of the sporting event is usually quite serious. Most of the elements of play are absent in sports.

As is shown in Table 7.1, play is characterized by broad, diffuse activity; games of low organization are circumscribed by a few rules; lead-up games are more highly restricted; and sports are highly specialized. Viewed in terms of children's developmental needs and interests, play and games of low organization are suitable learning media for young children, lead-up games provide the kinds of learning experiences necessary for older children, and sports competition is an appropriate learning medium for more highly skilled and emotionally mature individuals. As long as there is more to be learned through participation in less specialized movement forms, adults should refrain from

Table 7.1. Play, Games, and Sports Compared

	Play	Games of Low Organization	Lead-Up Games	Official Sports
Equipment	Unspecified	Modified or improvised	Specified, but may be modified	Type, size, and weight specified
Area	No limitations	Arbitrary limitations	Boundaries and divisions specified, but may be modified	Exact size, shape, and dimensions specified
Time	No limitations	Arbitrary limitations	Flexible limitations	Specified limitations
Rules	None predetermined	A few, which may be changed or modified	Comprehensive, but may be modified	Specific and all-inclusive
Roles	None specified	Some general, but may change	Specified, but participants may alternate	Established and highly specialized
Skills	Unspecified	Specified basic movement and manipulative skills	Specified basic sports skills and locomotor movements	Highly specialized
Competitiveness	Outcome uncertain and inconsequential	Slight—playing is more important than winning	Usually competitive—winning may be important	Highly competitive
Rewards	No extrinsic reward	Praise or criticism	Evaluation or grading	Status and material rewards

forcing children into competitive sports. When a child is physically and psychologically ready, however, he or she should be offered opportunities to develop the higher levels of skill required for successful sports participation. A few children are ready to participate in sports on a limited scale by the fourth grade; others are not. An adequate physical education program provides appropriate learning activities for children at both ends of the continuum and all those in between.

Stunts, Tumbling, and Gymnastics

Most children naturally love to climb, hang, roll, balance, and imitate. Thus stunts, tumbling, and gymnastics are ideal educational media. Children aged five to eight are in an exploratory stage; they have vivid imaginations and boundless energy, and tend to respond spontaneously. For these reasons an exploratory approach to such activities is recommended at the primary level. This approach is called *educational gymnastics* to emphasize the primacy of the child's learning experience over the execution of a specific skill. In traditional gymnastics (now called *olympic gymnastics*), the goal is body mastery. The skills are precisely prescribed and their execution is performance-oriented. Older children who are interested and have developed the necessary bodily control should receive instruction in olympic gymnastics. However, children should not be forced into this type of structured activity before they have fully explored their creative movement potential.

TOPICS FOR REVIEW AND FURTHER STUDY

1. What environmental factors have influenced your physical education and interest (or lack of interest) in different kinds of movement activities?

2. What does the statement "Children are means- rather than end-oriented" suggest to you as a teacher?

3. Why should a child's physical education program be designed in light of his or her past, present, and future?

4. Why should the question "What must this child be able to do in order to live a full and satisfying life?" be kept in mind while designing physical education curricula? Select a child in a specific age group and attempt to answer this question by considering his or her present and future needs. Compare your answer to the answers of your classmates who selected the same age group. What are some of the similarities and differences between your answers?

5. Define the terms *laterality* and *directionality*.

6. Why is body awareness a prerequisite to successful participation in movement activities?

7. List the spatial dimensions taught in the spatial awareness component of the curriculum.

8. Define *kinesthesia*.

9. Describe the content of the kinesthetic awareness component of the curriculum.

10. Why should children learn about the concepts of time, space, and force?

11. How is teaching a movement vocabulary analogous to teaching a verbal vocabulary?

12. What is the purpose of teaching children to execute the manipulative skills?

13. What is the difference between manipulative skills and basic sports skills?

14. Why is it essential for elementary-school children to learn to execute the fundamental physical skills correctly?

15. Select a period during the day when you are usually physically active, and identify the fundamental physical skills you use to perform various tasks.

16. What is a movement form?

17. Describe the educational value of teaching children to dance.

18. What are the three kinds of games? What are the differences between them?

19. Why is participation in sports an inappropriate activity for most elementary-school children?

20. Read some of the references listed in the Suggestions for Further Reading. In light of your reading, explain the educational value of one or more of the following: (a) play, (b) games of low organization, and (c) one of the movement forms.

SUGGESTIONS FOR FURTHER READING

BRUNER, JEROME S. "Play is Serious Business." *Psychology Today* 8 (Jan. 1975): 81–83.

COTTLE, THOMAS J. "Play is the Magic Word." *Learning: The Magazine for Creative Teaching* 1 (Jan. 1973): 15–18.

DIGENNARO, JOSEPH. "The Purposes of Physical Education In the 70's." *The Physical Educator* 28 (Oct. 1971): 125–126.

ELLIS, MICHAEL. *Why People Play.* Englewood Cliffs, N.J.: Prentice-Hall, 1973.

FELSHIN, JAN. *More Than Movement: An Introduction to Physical Education.* Philadelphia: Lea and Febiger, 1972.

FRALEIGH, SONDRA H. "Dance Creates Man." *Quest* 14 (June 1970): 65–70.

GRAY, LARRY. "Games Can Wait." *Journal of Health, Physical Education and Recreation* 36 (May 1965): 34–35.

LOY, JOHN W., JR. "The Nature of Sport: A Definitional Effort." *Quest* 10 (May 1968): 1–15.

MOFFITT, MARY W. "Play as a Medium for Learning." *Journal of Health, Physical Education and Recreation* 43 (June 1972): 45–47.

RIZZITIELLO, THERESA. "Movement Education Challenges an Inner-City School." *Journal of Health, Physical Education and Recreation* 43 (Jan. 1972): 35–37.

STONE, GREGORY P. "The Play of Little Children." *Quest* 4 (April 1965): 23–31.

TODD, KIRBY. "Love Can Be Taught in Dance." *Journal of Health, Physical Education and Recreation* 41 (Jan. 1970): 89–90.

WHITEHURST, KATURAH E. "What Movement Means to the Young Child." *Journal of Health, Physical Education and Recreation* 42 (May 1971): 34–35.

8　Influences on Curriculum Development

The third step in curriculum development is appraisal of factors that determine the kinds of learning experiences that can be provided: the psychological climate, temporal and spatial factors, the physical plant and equipment, and available personnel.

ATTITUDES TOWARD PHYSICAL EDUCATION

The possibilities of the physical education program are largely determined by the attitudes of the school administrators, other teachers, and the parents. If physical education is viewed as an essential aspect of the elementary-school curriculum, attempts to establish meaningful programs usually receive the necessary support. But if prevailing opinion has it that physical education is primarily a "play" period or that sports should be the central focus, the teacher's efforts to develop an educationally sound program may be undermined. The modern elementary-school physical education curriculum is a relatively recent development, and most people are not yet aware of its educational potential. Thus the physical educator must assess the current status of the school's program and work toward establishing the human relationships that will permit program innovation.

The school should provide the teacher with a statement of philosophy that clearly specifies the role of physical education in the children's total educational experience. If such a statement is not available, the physical education teacher should confer with the school's administrators to determine whether physical education is considered an essential component of the curriculum and is treated like any other subject. Such a conference makes apparent the framework in which the teacher is expected to operate and clarifies his or her rights and responsibilities. In some schools, for example, classroom teachers are permitted to prevent children from attending physical education classes if they fail to complete academic assignments or for disciplinary reasons. This practice is unfair to both the child and the physical education teacher. It is very difficult to provide meaningful instruction when it is held in such low esteem that others have the privilege of interrupting its continuity. This practice is also educationally unsound. Preventing children from participating in an aspect of the school program they enjoy *will not* contribute to the development of positive, self-motivating attitudes toward learning. In order to prevent or abolish this or any other such intrusion, the physical educator must attempt to impress on the school's personnel the child's need for regular physical activity and the educational benefits of participation.

STRUCTURAL AND ORGANIZATIONAL FACTORS

The structural and organizational composition of the school markedly influences the type and extent of its offerings. Structural factors include the size, number, and design of the teaching stations and the type and amount of available equipment. Organizational aspects of the school include the scheduling of classes, recess periods, specialized classes, and extra-class activities.

Structural Factors

Indoor Facilities

The physical education facility most common in elementary schools, a multi-purpose room, is inadequate for several reasons. It is usually shared with all other school programs that must accommodate large numbers of people, including the hot lunch program, school assemblies, and such special events as PTA meetings and special holiday programs. When these programs are being prepared and presented, physical education classes must be conducted elsewhere, a situation that interrupts the normal flow of the curriculum and imposes severe temporal limitations on the program. If, for example, five-and-a-half hours of actual instructional time are available during the school day and the multi-purpose room is being used by the hot lunch program for two of those hours, only enough time remains to schedule seven thirty-minute physical education classes. If each class contains 30 students, physical education classes can accommodate only 210 children a day.

Many new schools have regulation-size gymnasiums. In addition to permitting a longer schedule of classes, such a facility provides for more adequate instruction and practice. In multi-purpose rooms the furniture must usually be stored along the walls, which makes the wall space unavailable for practice and the display of posters, charts, or pictures.

In schools whose enrollments are decreasing, empty classrooms are sometimes used as physical education teaching stations. Such rooms are quite satisfactory for less active learning experiences and for some specialized classes.

The physical structure of traditional school buildings thwarts and inhibits freedom of movement, and thus discourages active play. Some of the newer buildings designed to accommodate open classrooms and/or modular scheduling do contain areas that permit freedom of movement. Some of these schools have physical activity "learning centers" similar to those for other subject matter areas. Ezersky (1972) advocates turning the entire school into a physical education learning center, whose halls and classrooms are equipped to serve as "mini-gyms" and "fitness corners." He suggests installing chinning bars, pegboards, and balance beams in the hallways, padding some corridor floors, using other corridors as indoor tracks, and installing stationary bicycles and rowing machines in classrooms. Ezersky's ideas are probably impractical in view of the noise level that would occur and the school's liability in case of accident. However, it is often possible for the imaginative teacher to turn an ordinary classroom into a movement medium. The desks can be moved and the available space used as an obstacle course, volleyball court (substituting a balloon for a ball), bowling alley, orienteering course, or dance floor. It may also be possible to create an activity center in a corner of the classroom or in an empty room. Such a center might contain equipment to stimulate individual activity: hoops, wands, beanbags, yarn balls, scoops, targets, a balance board or balance beam, and a mat. Children could participate individually in the activities in this center when they have free time or when they feel the need for a change of pace. The center could also be used for small-group instruction.

Outdoor Facilities

The school's outdoor playground should be arranged and equipped in a manner that invites and enables every child to participate freely and safely in a variety of physical activities. It should have natural and manmade structures that present a variety of physical challenges. The playground should be an exciting place that allows children to use their imaginations to invent activities, as well as stimulating them to practice the skills taught in physical education classes. In other words, the terrain and the equipment should say to the children, "Come on! Let's run, jump, climb, swing, hang, roll, and balance!"

The school's outdoor environment should have areas that can be used for physical education classes, outdoor education, and recreation. There are five types of areas that should be available: multi-purpose hard-surfaced areas, playing fields, apparatus areas, open grassy areas, and natural settings. Each area should be designed in a manner that will enable children at each grade level to participate in age-appropriate physical activities.

The hard-surface area should be marked with boundaries for various games and readily accessible so it can be used on wet days. The playing field and open grassy area should be designed to permit diversified use for games and track-and-field events. The apparatus should be varied in size, color, and design. Traditional swings, slides, and jungle gyms are things of the past. In their place, modern playgrounds have structures such as tunnels, climbable walls, nets, arches, and cages. Manufacturers of playground equipment are now producing simulated forts, treehouses, ships, space stations and lunar jungles designed to provide children a variety of movement possibilities. Because many children have little contact with the natural environment, playgrounds with natural features are desirable. Such features may include a wooded area, hills, a stream, a pond, boulders, and logs.[1] If natural settings cannot be retained or restored, they may be simulated by using improvised materials or by purchasing commercially manufactured equipment.

Community Facilities

If the school's facilities cannot be improved due to spatial or budgetary limitations, an attempt should be made to utilize such available community facilities as parks and recreation centers. For example, every elementary-school child should have access to a swimming pool. However, the cost of construction and maintenance usually makes it impossible for the school to provide one. Most schools use the lack of a pool as an excuse for failing to provide swimming and water safety instruction. A few, however, provide such instruction by working out agreements to use pools that belong to the recreation department, YWCA, YMCA, or a swim club. These pools are seldom used by the regular clientele during the school day, and the sponsors are usually willing to cooperate with the school to provide swimming instructors. The same kind of arrangement is made by some schools to provide instruction in bowling, golf, archery, skating, skiing, and camping.

There is a trend in modern school construction to build facilities that can be used as community centers.[2] This is much more practical than

[1]For examples of such playgrounds, see Hanson (1969) and Miller (1972).
[2]An example of this type of facility is described by Bailey and Rowley (1969).

leaving the school's physical plant unused during evening hours, weekends, and school vacations. The expense of constructing and equipping a school site is not a sound dollar investment if the structure is utilized on such a limited scale. And it makes no sense for a community to build school facilities that are used only during the day *and* recreational facilities that are used primarily when school is not in session. In sum, there are two advantages to constructing multi-use areas: more adequate facilities can be provided, and these facilities will be readily available for children's free-time use.

Equipment

A list of recommended equipment and supplies is included in the observation form in Appendix A. The amount of equipment that should be available is not specified, since it varies with variations in scheduling, available teaching stations, the number of students in classes, and teaching methods. The principal criterion is that enough of any given type of equipment be available to prevent children from having to waste valuable class time waiting their turns.

If equipment is in short supply, the teacher must improvise by varying the organization of the classes and/or producing additional equipment. Types of class organization that permit small-group instruction are squads, stations, and circuits. The development of equipment should be undertaken by the students as well as the teacher. Useful references for producing equipment are *Inexpensive Physical Education Equipment for Children* (Werner and Simmons, 1976); *Inexpensive Equipment for Games, Play and Physical Activity* (Corbin, 1972); and *The Beanbag Curriculum* (Christian, 1973).

Equipment should be selected according to the following criteria:

1. Does it provide novel and age-appropriate movement stimuli?

2. Will it evoke a variety of movement patterns or does it tend to prescribe limited possibilities for movement?

3. Is it structurally appropriate to children of the size and age range for whom it is intended?

4. Is it appropriate for children of different interests and varied skill and ability levels?

5. Is it durable, attractive, colorful, and easily maintained in a safe condition?

6. Will it enable children to play safely with minimal supervision?

7. Can the surface areas under and around the equipment be easily maintained?

8. What is the initial cost and maintenance cost in light of the expected life of the equipment?

9. How well does it meet childrens' need to:

a. explore

b. play imaginatively

c. move energetically over, under, around, and through objects

d. be uninhibited

e. manipulate and rearrange objects

f. develop movement skills

g. improve fitness levels

h. play alone and with others

i. participate in a variety of self-directed movement activities?

A review of this list will reveal that it addresses four major considerations: movement possibilities, safety, cost, and maintenance. Before selecting equipment, you should consult the people responsible for these matters: the children, parents, teachers, administrators, and custodians.

Technological advances have brought about a staggering variety of new equipment, which necessitates your being a careful shopper. You should review catalogues from various companies, which may be obtained at professional conventions or by writing to the manufacturers. The addresses of a number of major companies are printed in the November-December 1968 issue of the *Journal of Health, Physical Education and Recreation.*

Organizational Factors

Scheduling of Classes

Physical education requires the same amount of time and attention as any other aspect of the school curriculum. Therefore, if children are to be provided adequate instruction and sufficient opportunities for supervised practice, the numbers both of scheduled class periods and of students in each class should be the same as in any other subject. It is generally recommended that children receive *at least 150 minutes per week of actual physical education instruction.* In schools where scheduling is traditional, daily physical education should be provided. Some schools allocate 30 minutes for all grade levels, while others provide shorter and more frequent periods for younger children. Due to the fatigue factor and the short attention spans of primary children, it is desirable to organize their school day so as to permit frequent changes of pace. However, these children need as much physical education instruction as do older children; thus if class periods are shorter, they should be scheduled at more frequent intervals.

Class Size	The number of children enrolled in a given physical education class for grades 1–6 should not exceed thirty, and twenty-five is more desirable. Kindergarten classes should be no larger than twenty, to provide for the necessary individual attention. Occasionally all the children in two regular classes are scheduled for physical education simultaneously, making it necessary for the physical educator to try to teach as many as sixty children at once. This practice is educationally unsound. It prevents the teacher from providing appropriate learning experiences and robs the children of adequate instruction, practice, and individual attention.
Excusing Children from Class	Though there are many reasons why it may be necessary to excuse a child from active participation in physical education classes, it can generally be assumed that a child who is in school is able to learn and that physical education is an essential aspect of learning. Therefore, the physical educator is responsible for providing meaningful activity for the child. How this is done depends on the nature and extent of the child's limitations and the time and facilities available. If a child's activities are only temporarily restricted, you may allow him or her to assist you and the other children in the conduct of activities. If the limitation on activity is long-term, it may be necessary to assign the child to a specialized class. Rarely should a child be totally excluded from class participation. If an adequate physical education program is being provided, and if the physician and parents are informed about the content and relevance of the program, it is usually possible to work out a mutually satisfactory plan for limited participation. When a child's activities must be modified, the examining physician should be asked to specify the nature and extent of the limitation. When parents ask to have their child excused, they too should be expected to explain why and for how long. If parental excuses become a chronic problem, the need for a parent-teacher conference is indicated.
Recess Periods	Children need periodically to be freed from the temporal and spatial restrictions of the ordinary school day. Therefore, recess periods should be provided *in addition* to regularly scheduled physical education classes. Children need to be on the move; their bodies naturally urge them toward activity. One of the purposes of modern education is to provide learning experiences that enhance children's sensory awareness and enable them to respond to this desire to move in a way that is both self-fulfilling and socially responsible. The recess period is a laboratory in which this kind of learning can occur. A learning situation is created when children are allowed to respond to their natural urge to play by participating in worthwhile activities: they learn that it

Influences on Curriculum Development

is OK to respond to such feelings *but* that the response must be controlled. It is not OK to respond any old way any time you feel like it; there are conditions. If you wait until the time is right, you can be free to do what you want to do, as long as your choice of activity is reasonable and constructive.

As a teacher you should recognize behavior that signals a need for a period of relaxation or outdoor activity. When children become sleepy, inattentive, hyperactive, or noisy, they are telling you something; if the message suggests the need for physical activity you should attempt to provide it. You should also be aware that children's need for physical activity does not evaporate because the weather is inclement. In fact, such weather may increase the childrens' need for active play. Children should be encouraged to dress appropriately and to play outside as much as possible. The outdoor environment provides physical and psychological stimulation that can help to rekindle the childrens' interest and enthusiasm.

In some schools children are prohibited from playing outside in wet weather because the teachers are reluctant to go outside or to dress the children properly. Sometimes children are not allowed to go outside because they would "track up" the school floors. Such schools exist for the convenience of the teachers and the custodial staff, rather than to meet the needs of children. There are, of course, times when it is not desirable for children to be outside; then appropriate indoor play activities should be provided. Many games and rhythmic activities can be satisfactorily conducted within the confines of the classroom, and you should be prepared to do so.

It is the responsibility of the teachers who supervise the children during recess periods to lead them in worthwhile activities. Some teachers see as the sole role of a playground supervisor to keep children from fighting and to prevent bodily injury. These tasks are necessary, but it is much more productive to deal with the causes of such problems than with their effects. The best prevention is to enable the children to participate in activities that hold their interest and to provide for adequate supervision. Teachers who stand inside the school building and peer out the windows or who hover next to the building with their hands in their pockets are not supervising effectually. You should be actively involved with the children on the playground, just as you are in the classroom.

THE TEACHER

The key factor in any class situation is the teacher, because he or she establishes the learning environment and controls the learner within it. Therefore, the teacher's characteristics and competencies are the primary determinants of the learning that will occur. Our individual characteristics largely determine the kinds of competencies we can and will develop and the manner in which we will utilize them. They also determine how we will interact with others.

In order to specify the characteristics that facilitate the teacher's effectiveness, it is necessary to ask, "What is the function of the teacher?" How one answers this question will be influenced by one's value structure and definition of the purposes and processes of education. The answer most consistent with the premises of this text is that the function of the teacher is to serve as an intermediary who helps the child *feel, experience,* and *come to know.* It follows then that the most desirable characteristics in a physical educator are those that will enable one effectively to help children come to know themselves and others through movement. These characteristics are difficult to specify and define because they are subjective and qualitative. However, it is possible to specify some general traits that appear to be significant factors in teaching effectiveness. These factors are listed in Table 8.1, in conjunction with lists of related competencies and effects on the actual teaching situation.

Teachers who possess the competencies listed in Table 8.1 are secure, understanding, empathetic individuals who view themselves as humanistic "facilitators" of learning. These teachers recognize that children are *self-learners* and that their role as teachers is to provide a learning environment for each child that will stimulate interest, encourage participation, and extend learning.

The Physical Education Specialist

Ideally, every elementary school would have the services of a highly qualified elementary physical education specialist, whose primary responsibility would be to develop and implement a daily physical education instructional period for every child, the content of which would be based on the child's individual needs and interests. This view suggests that the physical education specialist and the classroom teacher consider themselves partners in the provision of adequate and educationally sound movement experiences. They will be mutually responsible for the planning and conduct of the physical education program. Shared responsibilities enable the physical education specialist to plan with other specialists in the school, such as the art and music teachers, and allow the physical educator to conduct movement activities with children who have special needs and to supervise extra-class activities.

It has been common to certify elementary physical education teachers on completion of one or two elementary physical education methods courses in addition to those courses required for secondary physical education certification (Hanson, 1972). It is now recognized,

Table 8.1. Characteristics of Effective Physical Education Teachers

Characteristics	Competencies	Effect on Teaching Practices
Curious, enthusiastic, eager to learn, dedicated, and responsible	Perceives learning as a constant and continuous process without temporal limitations. Is aware of the need to expend time and energy to continue own development and is willing to do so	Utilizes own learning to create new lesson content and to develop more effective ways of stimulating children to learn in the present and future
Enjoys physical activity, is healthy and energetic	Enjoys playing with the children and is able to perform a wide variety of movement activities confidently	Participates with the children. Accurately demonstrates execution of certain skills when necessary
Is basically secure and self-confident. Believes in own capabilities and the attributes of others. Sees the world as a friendly place and is willing to take the necessary risks in establishing meaningful interpersonal relationships	Is able to utilize strengths and compensate for weaknesses, and to encourage children to believe in themselves and be self-directing and mutually supportive	Establishes an atmosphere of freedom with responsibility. Encourages children to explore, analyze, discover, and evaluate
Sensitive, warm, open, responsive, patient, kind, respectful, tactful, flexible yet firm and consistent	Knows how to create an open and unthreatening learning environment in which each child is appreciated, secure, free to respond, and self-controlled	Makes each child feel comfortable, useful, wanted, and needed. Provides for the needs of atypical children
Insightful and empathetic	Is a keen observer. Sees into situations and behaviors. Is aware of and understands nonverbal communications. Can perceive the "real" messages in what children say	Utilizes children's responses in planning, conducting, and revising lesson content. Plans learning content on the basis of children's immediate and long-term needs
Creative, resourceful, and knowledgeable	Knows how to create and evaluate situations in which learning results from active, dynamic behavior. Understands children's growth and development, motor learning theories, curriculum content, and various teaching methods and evaluation procedures. Is aware of the relationship, order, and relative value of all aspects of the elementary curriculum	Encourages children to explore and discover by utilizing their movement potential. Adapts and improves content and equipment in a manner that interests, stimulates, and meets the needs of every elementary-school child. Utilizes a holistic rather than a fragmented approach in teaching. Works with other teachers in the development of integrated learning experiences

however, that elementary physical education is a specialty requiring much more extensive preparation. Though state certification laws and professional preparation programs vary a great deal, there is a general trend toward upgrading both the quality and the quantity of required courses (Hoffman, 1972; Johnson, 1972).

One factor that inhibits innovation in elementary-school physical education is the number of teachers who received training and certification under prior regulations and who have not been motivated to update their training. There is a real need for teachers to be given incentive and opportunities to gain competency in the new physical education, curricula for children with special needs, and movement activities for preschool children.

The Classroom Teacher

As we have said, elementary classroom teachers should be prepared to share responsibility for the conduct of educational movement activities. There are four ways in which classroom teachers' competencies can serve to provide children essential learning experiences:

1. The classroom teacher and the physical educator can jointly plan the child's learning activities so that classroom learning experiences are reinforced in the movement environment, and the reverse.

2. The classroom teacher can use movement activities to enhance learning in such curricular areas as science, math, social studies, and language arts.

3. The classroom teacher can provide more adequate playground supervision and conduct more meaningful recess activities.

4. When the physical education specialist cannot teach certain classes, or when the schedule only permits him or her to teach certain classes two or three times a week, the classroom teacher can provide physical education instruction.

Ancillary Personnel

One of the most critical problems in individualized instruction is to obtain sufficient personnel. The use of parents and other volunteers has been previously mentioned. But because it is difficult to provide continuity of leadership relying entirely on volunteer assistance, it is frequently necessary to secure other kinds of help, such as that of students.

There are many students who can effectively assist in the conduct of physical education classes. They include students within the class, older students in the school, high-school students, and college students.

Because children need to learn how to be responsible for the conduct of their own activities and how to help each other reach learning goals, development of leadership potential should be a high-priority objective. More is involved in this process than simply that a child helps you conduct the class. It is necessary to develop in the child the skills and understandings that will enable him or her to effectively guide the other children. Managing things is easier than managing people, and self-control is a prerequisite to controlling others successfully. Thus children should demonstrate self-mastery and the ability to use and care for equipment properly before being made responsible for the conduct of other children. It is common practice to select children who appear to be natural leaders to be in charge of squads or teams. This practice may be necessary when initiating student leadership, but as soon as possible other children should be prepared and encouraged to assume leadership roles. Some children are natural leaders; others are not. But all children need to learn to be responsible and functional members of a group and to feel that their roles are important ones. Therefore you must attempt to assess each child's potential and to stimulate its development.

Children in the intermediate grades can work very effectively with younger children in the conduct of learning activities. Older children may act as tutors, spotters, small-group leaders, and officials. They can assist with demonstrations, preparation of learning materials, and arrangement of equipment. Giving older children opportunities to work with younger children can improve the quality of the educational experiences for both age groups in several ways. (1) Younger children naturally like and admire older children, and the self-esteem of the older children is enhanced by such attention. (2) Motivation is increased. (3) Small-group instruction permits more varied activities and increases practice time, since children need not wait their turns. (4) In order to lead, the older children must understand the content and conduct of activities much more thoroughly than when they merely participate. (5) The older children tend to develop more efficient work patterns when the reward for completing their assignments is extra time in the gym.

Some high schools offer elective physical education classes designed to prepare students for leadership roles in instructional programs and recreational activities. Field experiences are required as part of the course work, and some students elect to work with elementary physical education teachers. Many colleges now require students preparing for careers in teaching to have field experience. As teacher aides these students can perform all the functions described above, and they are usually expected to assume more responsibility for the actual conduct of instructional classes and extra-class activities. Thus college students facilitate instruction by performing many of the tasks of teaching, and in turn become more familiar with the characteristics of children, the role of the physical education teacher, and the content of the program. Such experience equips them much more adequately to decide on a career.

Occasionally college students conduct physical education classes in schools that cannot hire regular physical education teachers. Students assuming such responsibility should be properly trained and supervised and should be assisted by the classroom teachers. They should not be expected to fill the role of a regularly employed teacher.

Whenever student leadership is utilized, the principal concern should be the learning experiences of the student leaders. Students should not be required to perform menial tasks unless they wish to. Students are in school to learn, and their time should be devoted to activities that are educationally sound.

TOPICS FOR REVIEW AND FURTHER STUDY

1. How do the attitudes of the school administrators, classroom teachers, and parents affect the physical education program? How can the physical educator influence these attitudes?

2. Why is it important for the school to issue a statement of philosophy specifying the role of physical education in the children's total education?

3. Discuss the different types of indoor facilities commonly used as physical education learning environments. Why is a regulation-size gymnasium desirable in an elementary school?

4. Describe the five types of outdoor teaching area that should be available on the grounds of an elementary school.

5. Design an educational playground for a school in your community. Include structures and surfaces that stimulate a wide variety of vigorous exploratory movements. Provide areas for individual and small- and large-group activities. Specify the movement possibilities provided by each structure.

6. What are the advantages of building a school facility that can be used as a community center?

7. Survey and evaluate the physical education facilities and equipment of a given elementary school. If you detect inadequacies, recommend improvements.

8. Outline the factors that should be taken into consideration when purchasing equipment.

9. Why is it essential for children to have a daily physical education period at least thirty minutes long?

10. What is the recommended class size for physical education?

11. Under what conditions should a child be excused from active participation in physical education classes? What kinds of learning activities should be provided for these children?

12. Why do children need recess periods? What is the responsibility of the teachers who supervise recess activities?

13. Explain how a teacher's characteristics relate to his or her teaching competencies, and how these in turn affect teaching practices.

14. Describe some of the characteristics of an effective teacher.

15. Describe the respective roles of the physical education specialist and the classroom teacher in a physical education program.

16. How can elementary, high-school, and college students assist in the conduct of physical education classes? How can these experiences enhance the education of the students who work as assistants?

SUGGESTIONS FOR FURTHER READING

Facilities and Equipment

AITKEN, MARGARET H. *Play Environments for Children: Play Space, Improvised Equipment and Facilities.* Bellingham, Wash.: Educational Designs and Consultants, 1972.

BAILEY, SHERM, and ROWLEY, LLOYD. "A School for Today and Tomorrow." *Journal of Health, Physical Education and Recreation* 40 (Sept. 1969): 31−35.

BELKA, DAVID. "Improving a Primary Playground." *Journal of Health, Physical Education and Recreation* 44 (Jan. 1973): 72.

BENGTSSON, ARVID, ed. *Adventure Playgrounds.* New York: Praeger, 1972.

BUDD, BERTEL. "Lacking Facilities? Improvise!" *The Instructor* 82 (Jan. 1973): 52−53.

CHRISTIAN, QUENTIN A. *The Beanbag Curriculum.* Wolfe City, Texas: The University Press, 1973.

CORBIN, CHARLES B. *Inexpensive Equipment for Games, Play and Physical Activity.* Dubuque, Iowa: Wm. C. Brown, 1972.

EZERSKY, EUGENE. "Mini-Gyms and Fitness Corners." *Journal of Health, Physical Education and Recreation* 43 (Jan. 1972): 38−39.

GALLAHUE, DAVID L. *Developmental Play Equipment for Home and School.* New York: John Wiley, 1975.

GREY, ALEXANDER. "Creative Learning in Children's Playgrounds." *Childhood Education* 45 (May 1969): 491−499.

HANSON, ROBERT. "Playgrounds Designed for Adventure." *Journal of Health, Physical Education and Recreation* 40 (May 1969): 34−36.

HEWES, JEREMY J. *Build Your Own Playground.* Boston: Houghton Mifflin, 1974.

HOLTER, PATRA, and SCHAETER, ANNE. "Playground Design Club." *The Instructor* 81 (March 1972): 76.

HURTWOOD, LADY ALLEN OF. *Planning for Play.* Cambridge, Mass.: MIT Press, 1968.

LEDERMANN, ALFRED, and TRACHSEL, ALFRED, *Creative Playgrounds and Recreation.* New York: Praeger, 1968.

MILLER, PEGGY L. *Creative Outdoor Play Areas.* Englewood Cliffs, N.J.: Prentice-Hall, 1972.

MITTELSTAEDT, ARTHUR. "Planning School Grounds." *Journal of Health, Physical Education and Recreation* 40 (May 1969): 37–40.

PENNINGTON, GARY. "Slide Down the Cellar Door—The New Approach to Playgrounds." *The Instructor* 81 (March 1972): 74–76.

PUCKETT, JOHN. "Two Promising Innovations in Physical Education Facilities." *Journal of Health, Physical Education and Recreation* 43 (Jan. 1972): 40–41.

SIXTH ANNUAL DIRECTORY: Sources of Equipment and Supplies for Athletics, Physical Education, Recreation, School Health." *Journal of Health, Physical Education and Recreation* 39 (Nov.-Dec. 1968): 53–62.

SLEZAK, E. "50 Checks for a Safe Playground." *Journal of Health, Physical Education and Recreation* 36 (May 1965): 47.

VANNIER, MARYHELEN; FOSTER, MILDRED; and GALLAHUE, DAVID. *Teaching Physical Education in Elementary Schools,* 5th ed. Philadelphia: W. B. Saunders, 1973. Chapter 5.

WERNER, PETER H., and RINI, LISA. *Perceptual-Motor Development Equipment: Inexpensive Equipment Ideas and Activities.* New York: John Wiley, 1976.

WERNER, PETER H., and SIMMONS, RICHARD A. *Inexpensive Physical Education Equipment for Children.* Minneapolis, Minn.: Burgess, 1976.

State Requirements

GRIEVE, ANDREW. "State Legal Requirements for Physical Education." *Journal of Health, Physical Education and Recreation* 42 (April 1971): 19–23.

Physical Education Personnel

AMERICAN ALLIANCE FOR HEALTH, PHYSICAL EDUCATION AND RECREATION. *Professional Preparation of the Elementary School Physical Education Teacher.* Washington, D.C.: the Association, 1969.

———. *Preparing the Elementary Specialist.* Washington, D.C.: the Association, 1973.

———. *Professional Preparation in Dance, Physical Education, Recreation Education, Safety Education and School Health Education.* Washington, D.C.: the Association, 1974.

BOWERS, LOUIS; CRICHENBERGER, MARGARET; HOFFMAN, HUBERT; KLESIUS, STEPHEN; SMITH, CHARLES; STOVALL, JACK; and TANNER, PATRICIA. "Personal Professional Preparation in Physical Education." *Journal of Health, Physical Education and Recreation* 41 (Nov.-Dec. 1970): 23–25.

CALHOUN, NEZ. "Sophomores Launch Elementary School Physical Education Program." *Journal of Health, Physical Education and Recreation* 42 (Feb. 1971): 44−45.

HANSON, MARGIE R. "Professional Preparation of the Elementary School Physical Education Teacher." *Quest* 18 (June 1972): 98−106.

HOFFMAN, HUBERT A. "National Survey of Professional Preparation for the Elementary School Physical Education Specialist." *Journal of Health, Physical Education and Recreation* 43 (Feb. 1972): 25−28.

JOHNSON, LOIS. "Optimistic Prospects in Elementary School Physical Education Professional Preparation." *Journal of Health, Physical Education and Recreation* 43 (Feb. 1972): 29−31.

9   Developing Effective Teaching Methods

"We learn by doing." This statement is true but incomplete. Because all learning above the level of reflex involves cognition, it should read, "We learn by *thinking* about *what* we are doing" (Cronbach, 1966). But something is still missing. When we talk about learning in an educational context, it is assumed that the goal is to maximize learning. In order to do so, we must enhance the student's interaction with the subject matter *and* insure retention of the outcome of that interaction. Whether or not this goal is attained depends on the nature of the individual's learning experience. Learning is intrinsic and the learning experience is personal. It seems, therefore, that we should be saying, "Learning is enhanced when the individual discovers the personal meaning in what he or she is doing." This formulation assumes that the subject matter is relevant to the learner. (In actuality, however, this is not always the case.) Therefore, the purpose of any teaching method is to help the child sense, discover, and apply the content. (It would be useful at this point to review the discussion of experiential learning in Chapter 1.) Let us return to our starting-point, the child, and ask, "How can I create learning situations that will enable each child to discover the personal meaning in what he or she is doing?" In other words, we shall view teaching methods as tools to facilitate the child's comprehension of the content and mastery of the necessary skills. Thus the purpose of any teaching method is *to activate the learning process and guide the child's interaction with the content.*

Teaching methods are usually described in terms of the level of the teacher's control over the content and conduct of the lesson. The teaching methods that are most appropriate to elementary-school physical education can be classified in three broad groups: command, guided exploration, and problem solving.

TEACHING BY COMMAND

Teaching by command is also called *the direct method,* because the teacher is in complete control. He or she selects the activity, specifies how and when it is to be performed, regulates its conduct, and evaluates its outcome. Because the content and performance level are predetermined, the learning outcome can be evaluated by means of objective measures.

Modern education endorses the open system of teaching, and the command method is often discredited as a result. We should not, however, hastily conclude that it is entirely bad. There are some distinct advantages to this method.[1] It is not necessary for the teacher to be overly authoritarian in order to teach successfully by command. Your human relationship with your students will not be adversely affected by use of this method if you remain in touch with the children and if they sense that your being in complete command expedites the conduct of the learning activity. (Remember that we are assuming your students are aware of the purpose of the activity and of the goals they as individuals are seeking to attain.) For example, let us assume that your class is ready to receive instruction in the underhand throw, a highly complex motor skill requiring exact timing of the sequential movements of a number of body parts. The skill is specific, and there is very little leeway for individual variations in execution. Use of the command method to teach the underhand throw is described on page 336. This skill can be taught by means of an exploratory approach, but doing so requires more individual attention and more time for trial-and-error. It is therefore usually more expedient to use the command method to instruct the class as a whole in each phase of the movement pattern.

Let us look at another example of the command method as an appropriate teaching procedure. Your second-grade class has explored the locomotor and nonlocomotor movements and practiced them in response to appropriate rhythmic accompaniment. You conclude that the children's learning would be best reinforced by participating in a lively structured folk dance. Selecting Seven Jumps, you say, "Let's all take hold of hands and form one large circle," and tell the children you want them to do a folk dance with you. You then explain that they are to take seven skipping steps counterclockwise (indicating their right) followed by one jumping step in place. Practice this phase of the dance.

[1]Chapter 3 of Bilbrough and Jones (1968) contains a comprehensive discussion of the advantages of the direct method and information on the use of the indirect and limitation methods.

(It is assumed that the children have practiced the transition from a skip to a jump and that they are all capable of executing the movements satisfactorily.) Then explain that the next part of the dance is exactly like the first part except that they will move clockwise (indicating their left). Practice this part. Explain that in the next part of the dance they are to do exactly what you do and that the dance then starts over again, so they will have to be ready to skip. You then start the music and begin.

In this situation you have used two common command techniques, verbal directions and demonstration. The children must execute a prescribed sequence of movements, and thus the content of the lesson is entirely predetermined. Yet this lesson comes alive. Why? How does this lesson differ from ordinary lessons utilizing the command method? Analyze this lesson in terms of its place in the learning progression, the teacher's role, the type and amount of verbal instruction, the conduct of demonstrations, and behavioral outcomes. Analyzing these factors will give you real insight into the meaning of the statement, "It's not just *what* you do that affects learning outcomes. It's also how you do it." Keep this point in mind as we discuss the inquiry methods of teaching.

GUIDED EXPLORATION

Guided exploration is also called the "limitation method" (Bilbrough and Jones, 1968) or "guided discovery" (Mosston, 1966). It is here being designated *guided exploration* because exploration is a *process*, while discovery is a *learning outcome*. Using this method, you will be guiding the child's exploratory processes.

This method is most effectively utilized with primary-school children. At the primary level learning tasks are designed to help children develop intellectual awareness of the components of movement (cognitive domain), sensory awareness of their moving beings (affective domain), and bodily control (psychomotor domain). Children explore their movement potential by moving their bodies and body parts in various ways and by manipulating external objects. This exploration is guided by the teacher, who provides different types of verbal cues.

Phrasing of Verbal Cues

A verbal cue is a message designed to evoke a certain movement response. These cues may be classified in the following ways:

1. specific instruction
"Let your elbow lead the movement."
"Slide around the room in a curved pathway."
"Move forward on a high level and backward on a low level."

2. question
"Can you run among your classmates without touching them?"

"Can you move quickly about the room and stop when you hear the drumbeat?"

"Can you make a different shape with your body each time you stop?"

"Can you hold that position very still?"

3. challenge

"How can you move from here to there without using your feet?"

"How many times can you clap while the tossed ball is up in the air?"

"Try to run very quietly."

"Try to keep your body in a twisted shape while you move in a curved pathway."

All the types of cues just listed can be used to elicit *mental images* that serve as movement stimulators. Throughout this book you will find suggestions for evoking such images.

1. specific instruction

"Make a machine with two parts moving in different directions."

"With a partner, make a building with two windows."

"You are a balloon being blown up, floating through space, bursting!"

"Be a big paintbrush, painting the inside of your personal space."

2. question

"How does a bear move when it's waking from hibernation? when it's trying to get honey from a tree? when it's frightened?"

"How would you move if you were walking into a strong wind? on ice? on the moon?"

"How do you move when you're happy? when you're angry? when you're afraid?"

3. challenge

"Can you show me how a cat moves when it's being chased by a dog?"

"Can you show me how a flower moves when it's growing? when it's blooming? when it loses its petals?"

"Can you show me the difference between the way a ball moves when it's bouncing and the way it moves when it's rolling?"

The verbal cue must convey all the information the child will need in order to complete the movement task in question. It must be clear, concise, and definite, not broad and general. It must specify *what* is to be moved (the body as a whole or certain body parts), *where* it is to be moved, *how* it is to be moved, and *when* the movement is to occur. Answers to some of these questions may be implicit. For example, you may establish the precedent that the children are to begin moving when you finish speaking. The location may be implied as general space. The challenge, "Try to run very quietly," contains two words that specify *how* the child is to move: he or she is to *run quietly*. The answers to all the other questions are implied. Analyze some of the other cues listed above, identifying the key words that specify or imply what, where, when, and how. Can you discern how statements must be worded in order to convey the necessary implied messages?

Verbal cues should also be used throughout the lesson to *encourage* student responses and to *redirect* the learning task. Such cues may be directed toward the entire class, the members of a certain group, or an individual.

The teacher may encourage the children's efforts by saying, "That's good," "That's an unusual idea," or "You did that very well." To reinforce correct responses, the teacher may say such things as, "You were very large (tall, fast, strong) animals!" "That was very good, because none of you touched anyone else even when you were moving very fast," or "That was a good roll, Bill. Will you show it to the rest of the class?"

Students' responses should be utilized to extend and redirect the lesson content, and challenging the class is an effective means of doing so. If the teacher wants the children to experience *contrasting* movements, he or she might say, "Can you make it (the movement) bigger (smaller, higher, lower, faster, slower, stronger, weaker, closed, more open, straighter, more twisted)?" In place of "Can you?" the teacher might vary cues by substituting "Try to . . ." "See if you can . . ." or "What would happen if . . .?" To *extend* the range of movement possibilities, the teacher might say, "Can you change the direction you're moving?" "Can you change the level on which you're moving?" "Can you change the size (speed, shape) of your movements?" "Can you gradually (suddenly) change the amount of force?" Another way to extend movement possibilities is to alter the base of support; to elicit this response the teacher might ask, "Can you do the same movement while you're supporting your weight on a different body part?"[2]

Levels of Difficulty

The determinants of difficulty level are the *number* and *type* of specifications contained in the verbal statement and the *nature* of the implied messages. Let us analyze two such statements.

Specific instruction: "Walk around the room."
Analysis: "Walk (*how*) around the room (*where*)." [Implied: now

---

[2]Numerous examples of verbal cues that may be used in guided exploration are provided by Gilliom (1970).

(when), using the feet as the base of support and source of locomotion (what).]

Specific instruction: "Run around the room among your classmates without touching anyone."

Analysis: "Run (how) around the room among your classmates (where) without touching anyone (second how)." [Same implied message as in the preceding statement.]

The level of difficulty is raised by specifying more difficult movement skills and by increasing the number of movement elements in the task. The second instruction requires the child to move faster (run), relate spatially to the movements of the other children, and rapidly readjust his or her body position by dodging and turning.

Question: "Can you run among your classmates without touching anyone, stop when you hear the drumbeat, and hold that position very still?"

The movement elements in the first part of this question are the same as those in the preceding instruction, except that the where is now implied because the children already know where they are to move. The second part of the question requires the children to respond to an instantaneous when, and therefore to attend closely to the signal for this response. They are also being required to exercise higher levels of coordination and bodily control:

"Hold (how) that position (what) very still (second how)."

These examples illustrate why it is essential for the teacher to be thoroughly familiar with the movement elements, and to understand how they can be organized into learning tasks that become progressively more difficult.

Types of Movement Response

The purpose of verbal cues is to evoke a movement response. The differences among cues have been pointed out to emphasize that phrasing affects the type of movement response elicited. There are two types of movement responses, *imitative* and *interpretive*. Imitative responses are elicited by instructing the child to move *like* someone or something else—either to replicate a demonstration or to "gallop *like* a pony" or "sway *like* a flower." The focus is external, since the model of what the child is to do is extrinsic.

All the above examples of verbal cues are designed to elicit interpretive movements. To perform the movement task, the child must interpret the cues in personal terms. Even when the instructions are specific, such as, "Slide about the room in a curved pathway," the child is permitted to make choices that reflect the meaning of the experience. He or she may elect to complete the task by moving in either direction, facing forward or backward, performing movements of various sizes, moving fast or slow, or using any part of the body as a base of support. In fact, the purpose of guided exploration is to enable the child to discover all these possibilities.

Imagery cues used to evoke interpretive movement responses must be phrased in a manner that emphasizes "being" and "feeling." For example, the challenge "Can you show me the difference between the way a ball moves when it is bouncing and the way it moves when it is rolling?" requires the child to "be" the ball and "feel" the difference. The child can, of course, go through the motions without genuinely attending to the feeling states; this is why you must present the lesson content in such a way as to insure development of the affective domain. The learning outcome will be affected by the child's experiences in each phase of the movement response.

Phases of the Movement Response

You were introduced to the phases of the movement act in Chapter 4. It would be beneficial now to review Figure 4.11 in order to relate its content to the present discussion.

Since we are concerned here with the effects of verbal cues, the primary source of sensory input is auditory. The child will hear your words, your tone of voice, and the emphasis you put on certain words. In the perceptual process, the child attempts to match incoming information with data stored up from previous experiences. On the basis of this association the child selects a response pattern. You will evoke the movement response you anticipate if you verbally convey the message you intend, if your words mean to the child what you think they mean, and if your words stimulate the child to move as you intend. But look at how many "ifs" are involved. You may not have said clearly what you intended to say. For example, suppose you intend the children to experience what it feels like to execute a series of hops and you say, "Can you hop like a rabbit?" The answer to your question is "no": a rabbit doesn't hop; it jumps, by alternately transferring weight from its back feet to its front feet. Also, you have instructed the children to perform an imitative rather than an interpretive movement. If you intend the child to experience the movement of his or her own body, you should say something like, "How would it feel if you had to move about the world using only one foot?"

The second "if" has to do with the child's repertoire of stored concepts and his or her ability to recall and relate these concepts to incoming messages. For example, if you tell the children to gallop around the room, some may run rather than gallop because they have not developed a clear concept of a gallop step. Or they may be able to execute a gallop step but not know its name. Thus you must determine the children's learning levels before you select learning tasks. Children in the upper elementary grades often do not possess a complete vocabulary of the basic movement components. Though able to execute the skills in question, their cognitive comprehension of the verbal cues may be quite elementary.

The third "if" in our analysis of verbal cues has to do with motivation. The purpose of the cue is to motivate the child to move in a certain way in order to discover a new dimension of his or her movement potential. The value of the cue as an incentive depends on its relevance to the child. Cues that are relevant to older, more experienced children differ from those that stimulate younger children. Children in the stage of intuitive thinking (ages four to seven) respond more readily to static images and instructions requiring singular movement responses. Children of this age react to their environments, rather than initiating responses on the basis of relational thought. Thus instructions to these children must evoke a single specific mental image, such as a certain body part, position, or shape; an animal; or a certain inanimate object. Children in the stage of concrete operations (ages seven to eleven) are cognitively capable of relational thought, and movement cues should promote the development of this ability. This is why the problem-solving method is most appropriate for children in this age group. They are very quickly bored by imitative movements, and need to be challenged to analyze, compare, and interpret. Bored when told to jump like a kangaroo, they will be challenged by the movement task of analyzing how to jump higher and farther. Young children move just because it feels good to be moving, but older children are entering the age of reason, and their activity must be more purposeful.

The final phase of the movement response involves feedback, which is vitally important because it reinforces learning. As we have seen in Chapter 4, there are two types of feedback, intrinsic (originating at a sensory source inside the learner) and extrinsic (originating externally). Any movement act provides both types of feedback, since the movement itself stimulates the internal sensory mechanisms and alters the external environment in some way. The alteration may be simply a change in the space occupied by a body part (such as when you raise your hand), a change in the position of an object (such as when you pick up a pencil), or something more extreme. In any case, feedback always occurs, but the learner may not be aware of it.

Since one of the primary goals of the new physical education is to enhance the child's awareness of his or her moving being, we must ask,

"How can verbal cues be used to increase awareness?" To answer adequately, we must consider when the two types of feedback occur. Intrinsic feedback is present *while* the person is moving, whereas most extrinsic feedback resides in the messages that *follow* the movement act. This is significant in that *when* you provide verbal feedback can be as important as *how* you do it. This point is best illustrated by comparing the approaches of two teachers to the movement task of balancing on one foot and comparing the sensation of doing so with that of standing on both feet. The two components of the task are maintaining balance and focusing on a relative feeling state. (The children are instructed to close their eyes, in order to minimize extraneous sensory input.)

While the children perform the task, Teacher A stands in one spot and quietly observes the class, noting the students who appear to be having difficulty maintaining their balance. When she senses the children tiring or becoming bored, she signals them to stop and tells them to sit down and rest while they discuss their experience. After a short discussion of points relevant to the two aspects of the movement task, she instructs the children to return to their personal spaces and try the experiment again, this time balancing on the other foot.

Now let us look at Teacher B. Observing that a few children are having trouble maintaining their balance, she says, "Some of you are pretty wobbly. Try to hold the position standing on one foot." Then she walks over to Sally, who has been having more trouble than the others, and tells Sally to shift her weight over the foot on which she is attempting to stand. How do you think Teacher B's actions will alter the outcome of the movement task? What happens to the children's attention as she speaks? On what will their attention be focused while she is speaking? What effect do her actions have on Sally, and how does her contact with Sally affect the learning experiences of the other children? How do the learning experiences of these children differ from those of the children in Teacher A's class?

Do you see how extrinsic feedback during the movement may inhibit learning? In the perceptual process a person sorts out the incoming stimuli to which he or she will attend. In this instance the children automatically attend to what the teacher is saying, rather than to their own feeling states, because they have been very thoroughly conditioned to respond immediately to an authority figure. Thus, if you want children to experience a feeling state, you must explain clearly what you want them to attend to, design a learning task that will provide appropriate sensory input, and create and maintain an atmosphere in which extraneous stimuli are minimized.

One of the most important (but frequently neglected) sources of extrinsic feedback is the follow-up discussion, which can enhance learning in three ways. (1) It can provide an opportunity for the child to review the learning experience, thereby reinforcing it. (2) It can serve as a source of new information, such as suggestions for correcting errors or for altering or extending some phase of the movement act. (3) It can help the child to generalize the experience—that is, to recognize how its movement components are used in other situations.

During the class discussion, if possible, some or all of the children should respond in movement as well as in words. This practice helps to create and maintain interest, and provides opportunities for learning to be reinforced by concrete images and additional sensory input.

The four types of verbal cues described earlier can also be used to guide class discussion, as the following examples illustrate.

1. specific instructions (review of the task components)
"Let's look at the differences between balancing on one foot and on two feet. When you stand on two feet you have a larger base of support, so it's easy to keep your center of gravity within this base. It's harder to stand on one foot because your base of support is very small. You must shift your body weight to one side in order to keep your center of gravity over this small base."

In this example, the teacher is acting as the informational source. This approach has some advantages: it saves time; the content is always appropriate and correct; and the facts are presented in an orderly, sequential manner. But it has one big disadvantage: the children are probably not attending to what is being said. They are not cognitively activated.

2. question (directed toward the group as a whole, a subgroup, or an individual)
"What is the difference between the base of support when standing on two feet and when standing on one foot?"
"When you change from standing on two feet to standing on one foot, what change must you make in the position of your upper body? Why?"
"In which position do you get tired the quickest—when you stand on one foot or when you stand on both feet? Why?"

Questions motivate children to pay attention, because they need and want the recognition they will receive by answering. Their disadvantages are that it is time-consuming to develop good questions and arrange them in an appropriate progression; some children will not try to answer, and only a few may respond; and some answers will not be correct.

    3. challenge (similar to a question, but with the connotation of "are you able to?" or "will you try to?")

"Who can tell me where your center of gravity is located?"

"Who can tell me why it is harder to maintain your balance when you are standing on one foot than on two feet?"

"Can you describe how it feels to stand on one foot as compared to how it feels to stand on both feet?"

"Can you show me an object in this room that has a large base? a small base?"

    4. imagery (used to stimulate recall and to help the children see relationships)

"Who can name an animal that has a large base of support?"

"Which is more stable, a bicycle or a tricycle? a tricycle or a wagon? Why?"

Imagery can be very effective in follow-up discussions, because it enables children to focus on the image of a concrete object while reviewing the elements of the lesson. You should remember, however, that the children must be familiar with both the object and the concept if they are to see a relationship between the two.

    We have been discussing feedback as a reinforcing agent in guided exploration, but the extrinsic feedback techniques discussed above can, of course, also be used in conjunction with other teaching methods. This discussion has emphasized types of feedback that encourage the children to explore the *content* of the learning experience mentally. Teachers sometimes tend to assume that children learn entirely by doing, and that the activity itself acts as the necessary reinforcing agent. This is partially true; the activity reinforces learning in the psychomotor domain because it causes the child to practice certain skills. (The child may, however, be practicing wrong. If so, the teacher must evaluate the child's performance and provide supervised practice in which correct execution of the skill is reinforced.) The child will probably also learn cognitively and affectively simply by participating in the activity. (He or she may learn some rules and it may be fun.) Nevertheless, the learning potential of the movement activity is not fully utilized unless the child is motivated to attend to, think about, and reflect on its content. The child must be challenged to think about the meaning and application of what he or she is doing, and must be cognizant of both the factual and the sensory content.

Using the guided exploration method, we are trying to develop the children's ability to execute a wide variety of movement skills, to expand their awareness levels, and to enable them to apply their learning. By causing them to interact with the subject matter, we are attempting to help them discover their own answers and become responsible for their own learning. The following list of statements illustrates the kinds of personal discoveries we are attempting to facilitate.

"I discovered how to:

1. roll a ball along a straight line."

2. use my feet to move and control the ball."

3. keep my balance while hopping backwards on the balance beam."

4. play a game by throwing a ball through a hoop."

"I discovered I can:

1. form different shapes with my body."

2. support my body weight on different body parts."

3. jump higher when I bend my knees and use my arms to help lift me."

4. use my hands to help me walk from one end of the horizontal ladder to the other without having to let go."

"I discovered I need to:

1. practice running so I can run faster and keep from getting tired so quickly."

2. be stronger so I can climb the rope and throw the ball farther."

3. practice throwing and catching so I can have more fun and help my team more when we play games."

4. pay attention when the teacher is telling us what to do, so I won't mess it up or get left out."

"I discovered how it feels:

1. when I let the music tell me how to move."

2. different when I move fast or slow, move high or low, bend or stretch."

3. when I make a strong movement and when I make a weak one."

4. when my body is making a wide shape and when it is making a narrow one."

"I discovered that I feel:

1. like running when the music is fast."
2. happy when I skip."
3. sad when I walk slowly with my head down."
4. warm inside when I rub the yarn ball on my face."

Whether or not children's exploration culminates in such discoveries is largely determined by their expectations, awareness of what they are doing and why, and recognition of what they have done.

Children need to have a wide variety of exploratory experiences before being expected to complete the learning tasks of the problem-solving method, which is an extension of guided exploration.

PROBLEM-SOLVING

In the cognitive domain the problem-solving approach is the combination of two or more basic principles in order to arrive at a higher-order principle. In the psychomotor domain it is the process of combining basic movement skills and applying basic principles in order to create and reproduce more complex movement sequences. In physical education this process occurs when the teacher structures a series of goal-directed movement experiments. The children must then solve problems by progressing sequentially through the following steps:

1. sensing and comprehending the problem

2. defining and analyzing the elements or component parts of the problem

3. using various strategies to approach the problem and to search out and collect the relevant facts

4. formulating possible solutions

5. selecting and testing alternative solutions

6. selecting the most appropriate solutions

If children are to progress functionally through these steps, certain conditions must exist. (1) The subject matter must stimulate the child's curiosity so he or she will attend to the description of the problem. (2) Both the content and the complexity of the problem must be in keeping with the child's level of readiness, so he or she can comprehend the subject matter and effectively manipulate the variables in the problem. (3) The child must be given or have previously acquired the information essential to solve the problem. (4) The child must be developmentally ready to focus attention on the relevant facts and capable of ignoring irrelevant information. (5) The incentive value of the process and the resultant discovery must be high enough to motivate the child to complete the task. (6) The child must be sufficiently self-controlled to keep his or her attention and activity focused within the confines of the problem. (7) Sufficient time must be available to permit adequate searching, formulating, and testing. (8) The child must be capable of recognizing the correct solution.

These criteria make it evident that problem solving is a complex process requiring a long attention span, basic understanding of the problem, and the ability to think logically and systematically. These characteristics are sometimes displayed by third-graders, and usually by children in the upper elementary grades.

The following are problem-solving tasks of progressive difficulty:

1. With a partner, make
a. a statue that has four angular shapes
b. a statue that has two small and two large angular shapes
c. a statue that has two large angular shapes on a low level and two small angular shapes on a high level
d. an object with two or more moving parts that have an angular relationship

2. Develop a movement sequence
a. expressing how you think three different objects feel in the spring
b. including the following dimensions: moving on a low level and on a high level; moving fast and slow
c. using contrasting movements to show how you think three objects feel in spring and autumn

3. Make up a game with the following elements
a. competition with a partner using a playground ball and a hoop
b. four players, two on each team, and four paddles and a tennis ball

Several factors can increase the difficulty level of a problem. Task 3b is more difficult than 3a because more people are involved. Tasks 1a and 2a are relatively easy to solve because they contain only two elements; the succeeding steps of both are more difficult because of additional elements. Task 3 is more difficult than the first two because it is more open-ended and involves skills that require manipulation of external objects. Keep in mind that increasing the difficulty level of the problem also increases the amount of time the children need to arrive at a satisfactory solution.

Successful use of the problem-solving process is largely dependent on two factors: (1) the children's readiness to participate in such learning experiences, and (2) the teacher's ability to present meaningful problems and guide the problem-solving process. When the children are solving a problem, you must be both available to them and sensitive to when and how to give assistance. What constitutes too much or not enough help varies with different children, kinds of problems, and learning levels. The problem-solving method is very time-consuming, both prior to and during the actual teaching, but in terms of the quality and extent of learning outcomes is well worth the effort.[3] Children will not learn to discover and solve genuine problems if they are always being told what to do and how to do it. Movement problems are common and universal. During their every waking moment, individuals make conscious and unconscious decisions involving gross motor movement. They decide whether or not to move at a given moment. When they decide to move they must choose what, where, when, how, and how much to move. How and what people learn during their elementary-school years influences the movement choices they will make the rest of their lives.

[3]Examples of types of movement problems and a more extensive discussion of the problem-solving process may be found in Mosston (1966, ch. 8).

Table 9.1. Breadth of Learning Experiences in Three Teaching Methods

Instructions	Interaction with Subject Matter	Response
Command		
Instructions *prescribe*	Specified and restricted	Predetermined acceptable response
Guided Exploration		
Instructions *permit*	Several possibilities	Alternative responses acceptable
Problem-Solving		
Instructions *require*	Multiple interactions involving choice of strategy, collection of data, formulation of solutions, selection of responses, testing of responses, and selection of best responses	Optional acceptable responses, determined by choices made during interaction

A COMPARISON OF TEACHING METHODS

The learning experiences associated with each of the three teaching methods are compared for breadth in Table 9.1. In the command method the type and extent of the child's interaction with the subject matter are limited, since a response is either correct or incorrect. In guided exploration the child is encouraged to interact with the subject matter in order to discover alternative responses. Problem solving necessitates extensive interaction with the subject matter in order to discover and test alternative responses.

For a composite description and comparison of the three teaching methods, see Table 9.2.

Table 9.2. Summary and Comparison of Three Teaching Methods

Command	Guided Exploration	Problem Solving
Teacher-directed	Somewhat self-directed	Almost completely self-directed
Subject matter entirely predetermined	Some of content provided by children	Most of content provided by children
Lesson content and conduct structured and inflexible	Lesson content and conduct modified by students' response	Children develop much of the lesson content and conduct their own learning experiences
Rote learning— children absorb predetermined answers and perform prescribed actions	Children discover some of their own answers and select some of their own actions	Emphasis on sensing, comprehending, and relational thought as processes whereby answers are discovered
Single possible correct response	Several acceptable responses	Many possible correct responses
Emphasis on product and performance level	Emphasis on process and learning experience	
Outcome can usually be assessed by objective criteria	Evaluation criteria highly subjective	
Outcome evaluated by teacher	Students must share in evaluating outcomes	
Limited student-teacher interaction	A great deal of student-teacher interaction	

INDEPENDENT STUDY

Independent study, or self-directed learning, is a teaching procedure that is being increasingly widely adopted in elementary schools. The advantages of this type of instruction are that it:

1. allows the child to learn at his or her own rate

2. offers the child opportunities to pursue in depth the curricular areas in which he or she need additional practice or has particular interest

3. encourages the child to participate in physical activities outside the regular instructional program

4. provides opportunities for the child to receive instruction in skills that cannot be offered by the regular instructional program, such as swimming, hiking, skating, bowling, and riding

This instructional procedure also has the following limitations and disadvantages:

1. The preparation of materials and conduct of activities is time-consuming.

2. It is difficult to provide adequate supervision for each child.

3. The children must initiate and pursue the learning task on their own, and thus must be responsible and self-directing.

4. Accurate evaluation and achievement records must be maintained.

5. Ancillary personnel may have to be recruited and trained.

Self-directed learning tasks vary in the amount of autonomy they grant the child. When initiating such instruction, it may be necessary for you to supervise the children's activities closely. As they become more independent and self-reliant, they can assume more responsibility for their own learning.

The children may be introduced to self-directed learning by means of task cards or contracts. A task card specifies the task to be completed. It may also supply the performance criterion or challenge the child to perform to his or her maximum. (See Figure 9.1.) If a performance criterion is supplied, it should be individualized so as to be an appropriate goal for the child in question. When you challenge a child to perform to his or her maximum, you are introducing self-testing. (See Figure 9.2.) Responsibility for assessing one's own achievement honestly and accurately is an essential aspect of self-directed learning. Task cards are appropriate for any curricular area involving the practice of

Figure 9.1 Task Card Specifying Performance Criteria

Stunts

Name_____

Grade_____

Room No._____

1. Bouncing Ball   10 times
2. Crab Walk   around the circle 3 times
3. Turk Stand   10 times
4. Jack-in-the-Box   15 times
5. Walrus Walk   around the circle 2 times

Name_____

Grade_____

Room No._____

Stunts

How many times can you: Score

1. do a Turk Stand?   _____
2. Duck Walk around the circle?   _____
3. do a Coffee Grinder in a complete circle
   a. using your right arm as a support?   _____
   b. using your left arm as a support?   _____
4. do a Jack-in-the-Box?   _____
5. Walrus Walk around the circle?   _____

Figure 9.2 Task Card for Self-Testing

individual skills. Cards used in the upper grades may include lists of the basic concepts germane to correct execution of the skill.[4]

A contract is simply a written statement of what the child is to do in order to fulfill a particular assignment. There are two types of contracts. One is similar to task cards in that it is designed to help the child learn a group of related skills, such as stunts, tumbling, or ballhandling. (See Figure 9.3.) A contract specifies a series of skills, and is therefore longer and more inclusive than a task card. A series of such contracts has been published.[5] Or you may create your own by extracting items from the lists of learning activities in Parts Four and Five of this text.

The second type of contract specifies all the learning experiences and performance criteria for a given achievement level in a particular activity, such as beginning swimming, bicycling, hiking, or team games. (See Figure 9.4.) Because use of this type of contract on the

[4]Additional examples of task cards may be found in Mosston (1966, pp. 84–90).

[5]The series of seventeen contracts, developed primarily for use by classroom teachers responsible for teaching physical education, is suitable for use in grades 1–6 and includes ballhandling, hula hoops, balance beam, stunts, and rhythm sticks. Contracts may be ordered from ELPE, 8749 E. Coronado Road, Scottsdale, AZ 85257 for $1.00 each or $15.00 for the set of seventeen.

```
                    Ballhandling        Name_____
                                        Grade____Room No.____
                                        Date_____

1. Bounce the ball with your right hand.
2. Bounce it with your left hand.
3. Bounce it while turning your body around in a circle.
4. Bounce it while walking forward.
5. Bounce it while walking backward.
6. Bounce it while running.
7. Bounce it while keeping it away from an imaginary person.
8. Using both hands, bounce the ball as hard as you can and catch it before it bounces
   again.
9. Bounce the ball, turn all the way around, and catch it before it bounces again.
10. Toss the ball into the air and catch it before it bounces.
11. Toss the ball up and clap as many times as you can before catching it.
12. Toss the ball up, turn all the way around, and catch it before it hits the floor.
13. Throw the ball against the wall and catch it after it bounces once.
14. Throw the ball against the wall and catch it before it bounces.
15. Single out a spot on the wall above your head. Throw the ball against the wall and
    try to hit that spot.  Catch the ball before it bounces.
```

Figure 9.3 Ballhandling Skills Contract

```
                    Bicycling          Name_____
                                       Grade____Room No.____
                                       Date_____

1. Do one of the following:
   a. Collect four newspaper or magazine articles on bicycles or bicycling.
   b. Make a collage showing people riding bicycles in different ways. Critique the
      manner in which each is riding.
2. Plan an organized bicycle ride for two or more people. Include in your plan points of
   interest and an appropriate location to eat a picnic lunch.
3. Draw a diagram of the major parts of a bicycle and identify the safety factors affecting
   each part.
4. Be prepared to demonstrate to the teacher:
   a. how to select a bicycle of the appropriate size
   b. the different body positions one can use when riding
   c. proper mounting, dismounting, and maneuvering
   d. pedaling to attain various speeds
   e. braking at various speeds
   f. hand signals and correct roadside driving
5. Pass a written or oral test on the following subjects:
   a. bicycle safety regulations
   b. the bicycle safety code
   c. proper care of a bicycle
   d. the mechanical principles of a bicycle
6. Play five bicycle games with at least two other people.
7. Observe all bicycle safety regulations and obey the bicycle safety code while riding the
   following distances:
   a. three miles, at one-half-mile intervals
   b. five miles, at one-mile intervals
   c. ten miles, at intervals of two or more miles
```

Figure 9.4 Bicycling Contract

elementary-school level is still experimental, it will be necessary to design a contract to meet your particular needs if you wish to use one.

Some contracts designed for use on the secondary level include far too much written work. The primary goal of self-directed learning—to encourage active participation in the movement medium—should be paramount in the learning experiences you prescribe. The knowledge aspect of the contract is vital—the child should know and be able to explain how to execute the activity correctly and safely—but in the physical education setting such learning is significant only in conjunction with active participation.

Careful preparation and communication with the learner are essential in self-directed learning. To administer this type of learning situation, the following steps should be taken:

1. Introduce the children to the different kinds of learning experiences available.

2. Have each child select the subject he or she wishes to pursue.

3. Discuss the process and performance objectives with the child.

4. Provide instructions on:
a. how the task is to be completed
b. where equipment and supplies may be obtained
c. the time limit
d. when and how the child's achievement will be evaluated

5. Provide reference and enrichment materials, such as pictures, posters, charts, records, films, and books.

The school ought to have a physical education learning center; the provision of reference materials and resources enables children to work toward their own goals individually, with a partner, or in a small group. Making such learning opportunities available also promotes the concept that one is responsible for one's own physical education and that it is a continuous process.

For purposes of clarity each teaching method has here been presented separately, but it is usually not necessary or desirable to maintain this separation in practice. Methods can in some instances be effectively combined. For example, some of the subject matter the children employ in problem-solving is highly specific. It may therefore be advisable to use the command method for initial presentation of this material and the problem-solving approach to reinforce and extend learning.

1. What is the purpose of any teaching method?

2. Describe the command method of teaching and give examples of its effective utilization.

3. Why is guided exploration an effective way of teaching children in the primary grades?

4. Develop a lesson plan for first-grade children, using several types of verbal cues.

5. Work with a small group of children, using different types of verbal cues to stimulate and redirect their movement responses.

6. Practice using verbal cues to stimulate contrasting movements.

7. Practice phrasing verbal cues that will extend the number of movement possibilities the child explores.

8. Practice phrasing verbal cues that elicit movement responses of different levels of difficulty.

9. Discuss the difference between imitative and interpretive movements.

10. Discuss the three principal reasons why a child may not respond to your verbal cues as you anticipate.

11. How can verbal cues be used to raise awareness levels?

12. Explain the implications of the statement, "*When* you provide verbal feedback can be as important as *how* you do it."

13. Describe three ways follow-up discussion can serve to enhance learning.

14. List the advantages and disadvantages of using each of the four types of verbal cues to guide class discussions.

15. Why must children be cognizant of both the factual and sensory content of the subject matter if the learning potential in the movement activity is to be fully realized?

16. How does the guided exploration method help children take responsibility for their own learning?

17. Solve some of the movement problems on page 125, using the steps listed on page 124. Does this experience help you understand why problem solving is a teaching method appropriate to the upper elementary grades?

18. What factors determine the difficulty level of a movement problem?

19. What variations in learning outcomes result from use of the three types of teaching methods?

20. What are the advantages and disadvantages of independent study?

21. Develop a set of task cards the children can use for a series of self-testing activities.

22. Describe the two types of contracts.

23. Develop a contract that can be used to teach an area of the elementary-school physical education curriculum.

24. Why should the school provide a physical education learning center? What kinds of materials should be available there?

SUGGESTIONS FOR FURTHER READING

BARRETT, KATE R. *Exploration—A Method for Teaching Movement.* Madison, Wis.: College Printing & Typing, 1965.

———— "I Wish I Could Fly—A Philosophy of Motion." In *Contemporary Philosophies of Physical Education and Athletics,* edited by Robert A. Cobb and Paul M. Lepley. Columbus, Ohio: Charles E. Merrill, 1973.

BILBROUGH, A., and JONES, P. *Physical Education in the Primary School,* 3rd ed. London: University of London Press, 1968.

CHRISTINE, CHARLES T., and CHRISTINE, DOROTHY W. *Practical Guide to Curriculum and Instruction.* West Nyack, N.Y.: Parker, 1971.

CRONBACH, LEE J. "The Logic of Experiments on Discovery." *Learning by Discovery: A Critical Appraisal,* edited by Lee S. Schulman and Evan R. Keislar. Chicago: Rand McNally, 1966.

GILLIOM, BONNIE C. *Basic Movement Education for Children: Rationale and Teaching Units.* Reading, Mass.: Addison-Wesley, 1970.

MOSSTON, MUSKA. *Teaching Physical Education: From Command to Discovery.* Columbus, Ohio: Charles E. Merrill, 1966.

MURRAY, RUTH L. *Dance in Elementary Education,* 3rd ed. New York: Harper and Row, 1975.

10 Planning and Evaluating the Learning Outcomes

This chapter examines the final stage of curriculum development, planning learning experiences and evaluating learning outcomes. Effective planning involves coordination and application of all you have learned about the children, the situation, the subject matter, and teaching in order to create learning opportunities that will stimulate each child to raise his or her learning level in each of the educational domains. The first step in designing this kind of learning environment—to define clearly what you and the children want to achieve—necessitates translating the general goals of a particular learning level into specific objectives for each child.

DEVELOPING SPECIFIC OBJECTIVES

The purpose of stating objectives is to guide instruction and facilitate learning. Clearly defined objectives serve as a systematic framework within which you and the children can function more effectively. When objectives are effectively stated, they fulfill this purpose in the following way.

1. They serve as a guide in the selection of:
   a. the content to be included in the curriculum
   b. the content to be emphasized in a given learning situation
   c. the learning experiences that will be emphasized
   d. the behavioral outcomes that will be evaluated

2. They communicate to the children essential information about:

a. the purpose of the activity

b. the anticipated outcome

c. the results of the outcome

3. They provide for accurate evaluation by specifying verifiable learning outcomes.

Objectives must be clearly and definitively stated if they are to communicate to the child *exactly* what is to be accomplished in a *specific* learning situation. Though objectives can be stated in a number of ways, the current trend in education is toward objectives that explicitly describe measurable learning outcomes. Such statements are called *behavioral* or *performance objectives*[1] because they specify the *behavioral outcome* or *performance level* expected to result from participation in the learning activity. The development of this type of objective is a product of growing awareness of the need for *accountability* in education. Accountability means that the school and the teacher will be held responsible for defining the behavioral changes that occur as a result of participation in the learning activity, and for proving that these changes do in fact occur. Thus it will be your task to select appropriate goals for each child and to identify subsequent behaviors that indicate achievement of these goals. In other words, you must write performance objectives for each child in each subject matter area of the curriculum.

Writing Performance Objectives

A performance objective clearly specifies three things:

1. *who* will perform the activity

2. *what* activity is to be performed (and possibly also the conditions under which the learner is to perform)

3. the *criterion* of acceptable performance (how well the child must perform)

The following example illustrates how a performance objective is constructed:

[The learner] will [run a distance of thirty yards] in [five seconds.]
    who   *what*   *criterion*

[1]There is no general agreement in the literature on terminology. Some authors use the term "behavioral objectives"; others speak of "operationally defined objectives," "instructional objectives," or "performance objectives." In this text the term *performance objectives* will be used to denote learning outcomes that can be measured immediately and objectively. The term *process objectives* will be used to designate subjective outcomes and those that cannot be immediately assessed.

The following examples of jumping objectives for different age groups illustrate why a high degree of specificity is essential.

1. a two-year-old:

[The child] will [jump from an object] [nine inches high] and
   who   what   criterion 1

[land in a balanced standing position.]
          criterion 2

2. a five-year-old:

[From a standing position.] [the child] will [jump over a balance
      what 1   who   what 2

beam] [nine inches high] and [absorb the force of landing by flexing
      criterion 1   criterion 2

his or her hip, knee, and ankle joints.]

3. an eight-year-old:

[From a standing position,] [the child] will [jump a distance] of [four
     what 1   who   what 2

feet] and [land in a balanced standing position.]
criterion 1   criterion 2

In these examples the basic skill is the same but the conditions and performance criteria differ because the children are on different learning levels.

It is sometimes necessary to state part or all of *what* is to be done prior to stating *who* will do it; examples 2 and 3 above are both phrased in this manner. Sometimes there is more than one criterion for an acceptable performance level; examples 1, 2, and 3 above each specify two criteria, a distance and a landing form. It may sometimes be necessary to itemize criteria, as in the following example.

[The learner] will [demonstrate the ability to execute a backward
   who   what

roll] in [the following manner:
      a. knees tucked and body rounded
      b. hips moving directly over face
      c. the hands exerting equal amounts of force while pushing
      off from the mat
      d. landing in a balanced standing position]
               criteria

All preceding examples of performance objectives involve the psychomotor domain. Performance objectives should also be specified for the cognitive domain, and the following examples illustrate how they should be written.

[The learner] will [respond to a verbal command by touching] the
   who   *what 1*

[correct] [body part as it is named.]
criterion   *what 2*

[The child] will [describe the execution of a one-hand underhand
   who   *what*

throw.] The description will identify the [correct position and action of the following body parts:
   a. feet
   b. throwing arm
   c. hips and trunk]
       criteria

The Limitations of Performance Objectives

It is relatively easy to write performance objectives for the cognitive and psychomotor domains, because many learning outcomes can be readily observed and objectively evaluated. Children can describe and reproduce cognitive learning verbally, and psychomotor abilities can be displayed in physical performances. But it is much more difficult to specify and evaluate learning in the affective domain, which involves changes in attitudes, values, and feeling states. Assessment of these changes is possible only if the child openly displays his or her feelings. If a child has learned to mask his or her feelings or to role-play, affective learning may not be apparent.

Thus performance objectives are limited in suitability to aspects of behavior we can observe and manipulate. Another limitation is that performance objectives can measure only what the child *can* do; there is no objective way of assessing what the child *will* ultimately and freely do. In other words, *measurement is restricted to those aspects of learning the child can be motivated to display during a specified time period.*

Another consideration is that performance objectives focus on the *products* of learning; the learning *process* is evaluated only in terms of immediate results. However, what children *will do* is determined by how they learn, as well as by what they learn. Children are process-oriented; to them, the means is more important than the end. They do not value impersonal rewards or fully comprehend the meaning of delayed gratification. Therefore, *children's learning must be evaluated in terms of the process as well as the product, and of long-term as well as immediate outcomes.*

Writing Process Objectives

As we have seen, teachers need objectives that focus on subjective outcomes and on the learning process which this text will call *process objectives.* Such objectives have to do with how the child feels while learning and will feel about what he or she has learned. In other words, process objectives specify essential educational outcomes in the affective domain. The following examples illustrate different kinds of learning outcomes that may be specified by process objectives:

The child will discover and contrast how it feels to move fast and to move slowly.

The child will discover how he or she moves when feeling happy, sad, or tired.

The child will display a willingness to follow simple rules, take turns, and share in the use of equipment.

The learner will manifest increased emotional control and basic social awareness by working satisfactorily with a partner.

The child will show that he or she enjoys playing as well as achieving.

As is apparent in these examples, a process objective states exactly what the child is to do, but does not include a performance criterion.

Objectives will be purposeful only if the children accept the challenge they present. In order to do so, each child must clearly understand what is expected. Furthermore, the expectation must be realistic and the learner must sense its relevance. Thus the process of writing these kinds of objectives must allow for student input. You must confer with each child about what he or she wants to achieve and how to go about it. This procedure also serves to motivate children; letting them share responsibility for determining their own goals gives them more incentive to learn.

STRUCTURING THE LEARNING ENVIRONMENT

When you have defined what is to be learned, the next step is to identify the learning experiences that will enable the children in question to attain these goals. This task involves selecting appropriate learning activities and teaching methods that will intensify the children's interaction with the subject matter. You should then organize the subject matter sequentially. How this is done depends on the nature of the subject matter. The learning sequence should *follow a progression, have continuity, and demonstrate relationships.* The learning

Planning and Evaluating the Learning Outcomes

activities described in the following chapters on particular areas of the curriculum have been arranged in this manner. Careful study of these chapters should enable you to plan a meaningful learning progression for a group of children by determining their learning level and selecting learning activities that will provide for a systematic coverage of the subject matter.

When determining the activities you will utilize as learning media, you should explore all the possibilities and then select those that best meet the following criteria:

1. to enable the children to interact effectively with the subject matter

2. to hold the attention and stimulate the interest of the children

3. to provide a novel way for the children to practice skills and develop concepts

4. to provide for most children to be actively involved most of the time

5. to bring about maximum learning by each child in each of the educational domains

6. to resemble closely the physical activities in which the children participate outside of school

Your plan should also include a list of all the equipment, supplies, teaching aids, and extra-class activities that will be required in the conduct of the learning experiences. Such a list will enable you to obtain or make the necessary equipment and teaching aids and to arrange extra-class activities well before they are needed. When all this initial planning has been completed, you are ready to plan the content of the daily instructional program.

An effective plan of action requires a great deal of thought and advance preparation. As you plan, you must think about the children and try to anticipate how they will respond. You must also specify exactly what is to be achieved and how, and how you will evaluate the learning outcomes. As a beginning teacher, you will need to put your plan in writing in order to be sure you are adequately prepared.

In the new physical education, a lesson usually consists of the following components.[2]

1. Theme. The lesson theme specifies the aspect of the curriculum of which the lesson is a part. For example, if the children are studying

[2]An example of a lesson plan with this format is provided on pages 413–416.

body awareness, several lessons will be devoted to body awareness concepts. Thus the themes of individual lessons might be "Identifying Body Parts," "Recognizing Different Body Positions," or "Relating to Objects in Space."

2. Objectives. Your plan must include the specific objectives that are to be attained as a result of the children's interaction with this lesson's learning content. Because it should include objectives for each of the educational domains, you should specify both performance and process objectives.

3. Equipment and supplies. You should specify the kind and amount of equipment necessary if all the children are to participate actively in the lesson.

4. Teaching aids. The plan should include a list or description of the materials you will use to arouse interest or to enrich and extend the children's learning experiences. Music, stories, poems, objects, pictures, posters, diagrams, bulletin boards, and costumes are all potential teaching aids.

5. Pre-preparation. This part of the plan outlines what you must do in advance to prepare to teach the lesson. It may specify, for example, how to arrange the equipment, how to instruct the students who will give demonstrations, or how to prepare student leaders for their roles. It may specify a method of advance selection of squads or teams in order to provide for balance and conserve class time.

6. Learning activities. A lesson has three distinct phases: the activities that initiate the lesson (the beginning), the learning tasks that comprise the main body of the lesson (the middle), and the concluding activity (the end).

a. Introductory activity. The initial activities should prepare the children physically and psychologically for what is to follow. They should be stimulating and invigorating. Some elementary-school teachers routinely begin every class period with warm-up exercises, but this practice is highly questionable since most children are already "warmed up." If the lesson includes activities that use muscles and joints infrequently exercised by the children's ordinary activities, they should of course be exercised before being used in the performance of specific skills. The point is that the initial activity should introduce and have a direct bearing on the remainder of the lesson. Sometimes the introductory activity can consist of a few brief statements by the teacher to review the previous lesson, introduce the new activity, or relate the lesson to previous lessons or to some other area of the child's educational experiences.

b. Main activity. The part of your plan that describes the principal learning activities should specify: (1) how the class will be organized; (2) your verbal instructions to the children; and (3) the verbal cues you will use to reinforce the children and to extend or redirect their learning. If you employ the exploratory method, you should list the various responses you expect from the children and the modifications in content or procedure that may be desirable in view of these responses. If you are teaching highly specialized skills by the command method, you should list both anticipated errors in execution and ways to correct the children's movement patterns.

c. Concluding activity. The purpose of the concluding activity is to bring about closure of the learning experience. It may consist of review, discussion, or a slow-down activity. If the children have been extremely active during the lesson, it is advisable to provide a short period at the end of class during which they can readjust to the necessity of sitting quietly in their seats when they return to the classroom.

7. Self-evaluation. As a student you have become accustomed to being evaluated by other people; as a teacher you will be responsible for evaluating yourself. You will have to determine the adequacy of the learning activities you selected and the effectiveness of your interaction with the children. Asking yourself the following questions will help you assess possible strengths and weaknesses.

a. Did all the children seem interested and actively involved?

b. If some children were uninterested or uninvolved, can you determine why?

c. Which teaching procedures worked best; which, if any, failed to evoke the desired responses?

d. Was your presentation orderly and sequential, and was there a smooth transition between activities?

e. Were you able to maintain order in the conduct of the class without becoming restrictive or authoritarian?

f. Did you positively reinforce the efforts of as many children as possible?

g. Could the children readily comprehend your verbal cues? Did the level of your verbal descriptions match the developmental level of the children?

h. Was the pitch and volume of your voice and the tempo of your speech appropriate?

i. Do you feel you were adequately prepared to guide the children's learning in this situation? If not, what should you do to be more adequately prepared in the future?

EVALUATING THE LEARNING OUTCOMES

Evaluation is a continuous process; it should be undertaken before, during, and after the child's participation in the learning situation. Its purpose is twofold: (1) to assess the effectiveness of the learning process and (2) to appraise the child's achievements. Evaluation may therefore be defined as *a systematic means of obtaining information about learning.* Because this information should be employed to improve the instructional process and to motivate the learner, emphasis should be given to individualized evaluation and self-evaluation. Determining the relative standings of students on a competitive basis is justifiable only if and when it serves to augment learning. (The discussion of the effects of competition on page 54 is applicable here.) In most instances, each child should be evaluated in terms of his or her own progress toward the specified goals. Self-evaluation is stressed because it fosters self-direction, self-reliance, and self-knowledge. It also helps the child take ultimate responsibility for his or her own learning. The degree of such responsibility children can assume is dependent on their level of maturity and prior experience. As is true of all aspects of learning, they must begin where they are and become progressively more self-sufficient.

It has been pointed out that one of the purposes of writing specific objectives is to provide for more accurate evaluation. Well-defined performance objectives are the means by which you can measure learning outcomes objectively, and clearly specified process objectives enable you to evaluate behavioral changes subjectively.

Several sources of evaluative data were listed in Chapter 5, and additional sources are noted in conjunction with descriptions of specific learning activities in the latter parts of this text. In most instances these assessment instruments can be used to obtain both pretest and posttest data.

In most school systems evaluation of the child's achievement culminates in a report to the parents, which necessitates translating the results of the assessment into a progress report. Fortunately, letter grades are seldom used for this purpose; they do not adequately indicate whether or not the child is developing satisfactorily in each of the educational domains. It is common practice to report simply that the child's efforts are satisfactory or unsatisfactory, but this approach too fails to convey an adequate message; it says that the child's progress does or does not meet the teacher's expectations, but does not define these expectations or describe the nature of such progress. The report to the parents can be a vital aspect of the school's public relations program if it is viewed as an opportunity to communicate with the parents. If this is its intent, the report should contain information on what the

```
             PHYSICAL EDUCATION PROGRESS REPORT

For _____  Date_____
            (Child's name)

                              Participation and
Unit: Basic Sports Skills     Performance Level          Comments
Specific Skills

      Throwing

      Catching

      Kicking

      Striking

Understanding of Content

Self-Management


Key
  +  Very good
  √  Good
  △  Needs improvement
```

Figure 10.1 Sample Progress Report

child is learning and how adequately he or she is achieving. Because the usual report card is not designed for this purpose, the teacher must usually develop an appropriate form. Figure 10.1 shows one possible format.

Because the time devoted to physical education instruction is extremely limited in most schools, it is unrealistic to expect a child to demonstrate marked improvement solely as a result of what he or she does in class. Therefore, it is recommended that the progress report indicate what the child should practice outside of class. Reporting the skills that are being practiced in school says to the parent, "These skills are included in the curriculum because they must be correctly learned and practiced." The skills the child should practice at home may be noted under "Comments," or a statement like the following could be included:

_____ would progress much more rapidly if you could help him/her practice the following skills as frequently as possible:

Obviously an attempt to personalize such reports is a time-consuming project. Each teacher must find a way of meeting this responsibility. Ideally, all reports would be accompanied by periodic parent-teacher conferences, because dialogue is much more effective than monologue.

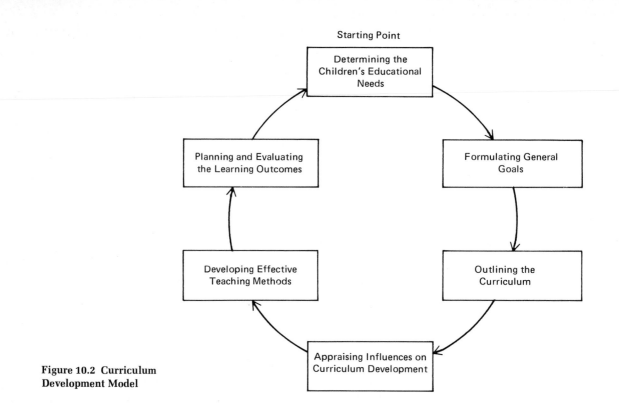

Figure 10.2 Curriculum Development Model

But this approach, too, presents problems, notably that the parents you most need to see are usually unable or unwilling to come to school.

Whatever grading and reporting procedure you adopt, two points should be kept in mind. First, the child should understand that a grade *does not* mean that learning has been terminated. Rather, the child should see the grade as a mutual evaluation of his or her achievement, and should recognize that its primary purpose is to establish the basis for new learning goals. Second, when you grade a child, you are simultaneously grading yourself. When a child fails to learn, you have failed him or her as a teacher. Teachers tend to assume that the responsibility for failure resides with the child. But this outlook is highly questionable in physical education, since children naturally enjoy movement. Rather than looking first to the child as the source of the problem, it is advisable to examine the subject matter and teaching methods, and then attempt to determine why these three factors are not interacting effectively.

Finally, it should not be forgotten that curriculum development is a circular process. Development does not end with planning and evaluation, but begins anew. (See Figure 10.2.) The teacher who has completed an evaluation has only begun to develop an even better curriculum.

TOPICS FOR REVIEW AND FURTHER STUDY

1. How do effectively stated objectives help to facilitate instruction and evaluation?

2. Read some of the current literature on accountability in education. Write a report on your reading, explaining what this concept implies for you as an educator and what effect you think it will have on teaching.

3. Practice writing performance objectives for the psychomotor and cognitive domains. Check to be sure you have included all the necessary information in each objective.

4. What are some of the limitations of performance objectives?

5. Practice writing process objectives that specify learning outcomes in the affective domain.

6. Why should children participate in the process of determining their own learning goals?

7. How should you go about selecting and organizing learning activities in a particular subject?

8. Observe a group of children and determine their learning level. Plan appropriate learning experiences for these children. If possible, apply your plan with the children; evaluate its adequacy and your ability to translate it into action in the learning situation.

9. Why is self-evaluation a vital educational experience?

10. What is the twofold purpose of evaluation?

11. Describe how you plan to evaluate the objectives of the lesson you developed in Topic 8 above.

12. Why is it unsatisfactory to grade a child's performance in terms of a letter grade or "satisfactory"/"unsatisfactory"?

13. Design a progress report that will convey to the parents the nature and extent of their child's learning in a specific subject.

14. What two points should you keep in mind when you grade a child?

SUGGESTIONS FOR FURTHER READING

BAKER, EVA L., and POPHAM, JAMES W. *Expanding Dimensions of Instructional Objectives.* Englewood Cliffs, N.J.: Prentice-Hall, 1973.

BLOOM, BENJAMIN S., ed. *Taxonomy of Educational Objectives I: Cognitive Domain.* New York: David McKay, 1956.

CLARK, D. CECIL. *Using Instructional Objectives in Teaching.* Glenview, Ill.: Scott, Foresman, 1972.

CORBIN, CHARLES B. *Becoming Physically Educated in the Elementary School.* Philadelphia: Lea and Febiger, 1969. Chapter 20.

DAVIS, ROBERT. "Writing Behavioral Objectives." *Journal of Health, Physical Education and Recreation* 44 (April 1973): 47–49.

FIELD, DAVID. "Accountability for the Physical Educator." *Journal of Health, Physical Education and Recreation* 44 (Feb. 1973): 37–38.

HARROW, ANITA J. *A Taxonomy of the Psychomotor Domain.* New York: David McKay, 1972.

KAPPER, MIRIAM. *Behavioral Objectives in Curriculum Development.* Englewood Cliffs, N.J.: Educational Technology Publications, 1971.

KEMP, JERROLD E. *Instructional Design.* Belmont, Cal.: Fearon, 1971.

KRATHWOHL, DAVID; BLOOM, BENJAMIN; and MASIA, BERTRAM. *Taxonomy of Educational Objectives Handbook II: Affective Domain.* New York: David McKay, 1964.

MAGER, ROBERT F. *Preparing Instructional Objectives.* Palo Alto, Cal.: Fearon, 1962.

POPHAM, W. JAMES; EISNER, ELLIOT W.; SULLIVAN, HOWARD J.; and TYLER, LOUISE L. *Instructional Objectives.* Chicago: Rand McNally, 1969.

SHOCKLEY, JOE JR. "Needed: Behavioral Objectives in Physical Education." *Journal of Health, Physical Education and Recreation* 44 (April 1973): 44–45.

SHURR, EVELYN L. *Movement Experiences for Children*, 2nd ed. Englewood Cliffs, N.J.: Prentice-Hall, 1975. Chapters 5 and 6.

SIMPSON, ELIZABETH. "The Classification of Educational Objectives, Psychomotor Domain." *Illinois Teacher of Home Economics* 10 (Winter 1966–1967): 110–144.

SINGER, ROBERT N., and DICK, WALTER. *Teaching Physical Education: A Systems Approach.* Boston: Houghton Mifflin, 1974. Chapter 3.

WEBB, I. M. "The Theoretical Content of Physical Education," *Conference Report of the Association of Principles of Women's Colleges of Physical Education*, 3–6 January 1972, at Dartford College of Education, Dartford, Kent, England.

Part Three

Developing Movement Awareness

It has traditionally been assumed that, because children move, they comprehend movement, and have no need to study it. But as teachers have begun to investigate this subject systematically, they have discovered that some children are not sensorily aware of certain parts of their bodies; some cannot identify their body parts; and most cannot identify the factors that affect, regulate, and control their bodily movements. Apparently, children have learned to execute movement patterns without developing the ability to experience their moving bodies and to understand their movement potential. These aspects of the human being are, however, a central concern of the new physical education. As this text has repeatedly emphasized, if what a child does is to be an educational experience, it must culminate in the discovery of personal meaning. Or, to reverse it, if what a child is doing is meaningless to him or her, it is not an educational experience. In fact, it is less an experience than a performance.

The movement awareness component of the curriculum, therefore, ought to be a learning medium in which children are totally involved, and through which they come to know their own bodies in stillness and in motion. The proposed subject matter is designed to achieve these goals, but their attainment depends on your skill in directing the learning experiences. To assist you in this endeavor, the curricular content of Part Three is outlined in terms of concepts that are to be developed, and the learning content in the form of teaching suggestions.

No attempt has been made to formulate specific lessons. Instead, the material is presented sequentially so that you may select certain portions for use as self-contained lessons or in combination with thematically related areas of the curriculum. Because the content of this part of the curriculum is conceptual, it tends occasionally to be less active than other parts. These learning experiences should therefore be combined with more active aspects of the curriculum when developing specific lesson plans. Because each part of the curriculum is arranged in terms of the movement concepts to be developed or reviewed, you will have no trouble recognizing relationships among the various areas once you have become familiar with the entire curriculum.

11   Body Awareness

Children cannot be expected to use their bodies as effective movement instruments until they are familiar with what they are to move. They must develop a sensory awareness and a mental image of each body part as it exists and functions in stillness and in motion. Once they have become aware of the physical reality of their own bodies, they can cognitively and physically relate to the existence of other people's bodies. At the same time each one is also developing the ability to relate the aspects of his or her own physical being to other kinds of objects in external space.

THE BODY PARTS

A child is naturally interested in his or her own body and fascinated by the discovery of its functions and feeling states. These discoveries are essential elements in the development of the self-concept, and are therefore an integral aspect of the child's education.

Key Concepts
□ *My body has different parts, each with a name.*
□ *I can move each of my body parts.*
□ *I use my body parts to move through space.*
□ *I must listen for the signals that tell me what to do.*

Activities for Children

I can touch each of my body parts.

1. Have the children sit on the floor in their own personal spaces. Tell them what they are going to do: "Today we will be working with different body parts, so first of all I need to see if you know all the parts of your body. Hold up your foot. Your leg. Your arm. Your knee."

"You did that very well, so let's go on."

"Hold up your hand again. I want you to use that hand to touch the body part I name. Ready?"

"Touch your other hand. Your foot. Your other foot. One leg. The other leg. Your knee." (Continue until all the body parts numbers 1–14 on the Evaluation Scale in Figure 11.1 have been touched.)

To help the children become sensorily aware of their body parts and the feelings associated with touching those parts, you may have them close their eyes. Instruct them to *think* about how it feels when they touch each part. Review some of the body parts named in the preceding activity and add some of those listed as numbers 15–27 on the Evaluation Scale. Having the children close their eyes also prevents them from merely copying other children and will help you identify those who are having difficulty.

I can touch and name my body parts.

2. "This time I want you to say the name of the body part while you are touching it. If I say 'leg,' you touch your leg and say 'leg.' You may keep your eyes open. Ready. Leg." (Review some of the body parts already identified and add some new ones.) Depending on the needs of the children, you may wish them to repeat this activity with their eyes closed.

I can move each body part.

3. "This time when I call out a body part I want you to move that part. Continue moving that part until I call out the next part. Move your hand (leg, arm, head, both elbows, shoulders, knees, all your fingers, all your toes)."

I can move and name each body part.

4. With their eyes closed, have the children move and name various body parts.

I can shake my body parts.
Shaking makes me feel loose.

5. The children have been sitting while doing these activities, and they probably need more vigorous action. "You did that very well while you were sitting down. Now let's stand up and loosen up those body parts by shaking them. Shake your hands (arms, head, shoulders, one foot, one leg, the other foot, that leg)."

Child's Name _____ Date _____

Body Parts	Responds to teacher's touch by moving	Responds to verbal command by:		Responds by naming body part*
		Moving body part	Touching body part	
1. Hand				
2. Foot				
3. Leg				
4. Arm				
5. Knee				
6. Tummy				
7. Chest				
8. Head				
9. Back				
10. Buttocks				
11. Elbow				
12. Shoulder				
13. Fingers				
14. Toes				
15. Face				
16. Nose				
17. Mouth				
18. Chin				
19. Neck				
20. Eyes				
21. Ears				
22. Forehead				
23. Cheek				
24. Wrist				
25. Thumb				
26. Ankle				
27. Heel				
Overall rating				

Scoring: + Child responds readily
0 Child responds with only slight hesitation
— Child experiences difficulty in responding

Figure 11.1 Evaluation Scale for Body Part Identification

*The teacher may point to one of his or her own body parts or to the body part of a cardboard manikin, or may touch one of the child's body parts.

"Now that you've loosened up your body, let's move all around the room, staying very loose. Be careful not to run into anyone. Ready, go!"

"Stop! You have to move kind of slow when you're staying loose, don't you? So now let's tighten up a bit and move faster, but be careful not to run into anyone. Go!"

The drumbeat is a signal that tells me to stop moving.

6. "Stop! You did very well moving fast and not running into anyone, so let's try something new. This time I'll use a new signal for you to stop. Whenever you hear a drumbeat like this (*beat drum once*), that's your signal to stop. Let's try that and see if you can stop whenever you hear the signal."

"That's good, so let's go on. Now you'll have to listen very carefully. I'm going to call out the name of a body part. When you hear the name, begin moving around the room. And when you hear the drum beat, stop with that part of your body pointing toward me. If I say 'foot,' you'll stop so that one foot is pointing toward me. Does everyone understand? All right, let's try it. Foot (hand, knee, tummy, head, back, elbow, shoulder, both hands, both feet, both elbows, both knees)."

"This time, instead of pointing the body part toward me, I want you to hide it when you hear the drum beat. Really hide it so no one can see it. Hand (one elbow, both hands, tummy, both knees, head)."

Different body parts can lead my movements.

7. This activity makes use of imagery. "Very good! This time I want you to pretend there's a string tied to the body part and that string is pulling you around the room. I'll name a body part, and as soon as you hear the name let the string start pulling you. When you hear the drumbeat, stop and listen for the next body part where we will tie the string. Hand (foot, knee, elbow, back, shoulder, nose, ear)."

Key Concept
□ *It feels different when I use my body parts in different ways.*

I can press (push) different body parts against a surface and against each other.
The floor is hard; mats are soft.
Some of my body parts are hard and some are soft.
It feels different when you touch hard and soft body parts.

It feels different when you press hard and soft body parts against the floor.

8. Have the children lie on their backs on the floor with their eyes closed. Ask them to press their body parts against the floor, beginning with the head and moving down (for example, neck, shoulders, arm, hands, back, buttocks, legs, heels). Then have them press their whole bodies as hard as they can, hold the position, and relax. Discuss how it felt (that is, the floor was hard). Ask them to press with their whole bodies again and to try to discover which body parts feel padded and which ones feel hard because there is no padding between them and the floor. (They may name head and back.) Ask if they know what makes their other body parts feel softer. Briefly discuss how their muscles pad certain body parts, and have them feel the padded parts (upper and lower legs and arms, neck, cheek, buttocks) and unpadded parts (spine, skull, ribcage, knees, elbows, wrists, hips).

If mats or carpeted surfaces are available, have the children experience the difference between pressing their body parts against these surfaces and against the bare floor.

Review names and location of body parts.
Contrast feelings associated with muscular tension and relaxation.

9. Have the children lie on their backs on mats or a carpeted floor. You can help them to sense their body parts by instructing them to lift very slowly the body part you name, and when you say "drop" to let that body part fall suddenly back to the floor. For example, "Slowly raise your hand up into the air (*talking slowly*). Drop! Now the other hand (each leg, each shoulder, both arms, both legs, both arms and legs at the same time)."

"Now I want you again to lift each body part I name, but this time hold it up in the air until it becomes so tired you can't hold it any longer—then let it drop. Think about how it feels when you are lifting, holding, and dropping the body parts. Think how it feels when the body part hits the mat and how it feels while it is lying there." Repeat the sequence of body parts indicated. Then discuss how it felt. The children may not be able to describe the feeling states verbally, because this experience is nonverbal. This is an excellent discussion point: that it feels, but you can't really describe exactly how it feels. (Note: This activity may be used with older children to study the effects of the force of gravity. With these children you would emphasize how it feels to "give in" to the force of gravity. You would also have them experiment with the difference between the amount of muscular force needed to resist the force of gravity when the body parts are held at a 45-degree and at a 90-degree angle.)

10. Coming Alive! You can help the children experience the feeling of "coming alive" with this activity. Have them get down on their hands and knees and make themselves as small as possible. Tell them, "Make believe you are nothing—nothing at all. You can't feel, you can't move. You are just a blob in space. Bit by bit, you are going to feel your body come alive. First there is a little pulse deep inside you. It stirs the middle of your body just a little bit, then it slowly moves up through your neck and into your head. You find you can slowly and ever so slightly move your head."

"The stirring moves through your shoulders and down through your arms and into your fingers. Your fingertips begin to come alive and to move. Now your hands, arms, and upper body begin to move ever so slowly."

"The stirring goes down through your legs and feet into your toes. Your toes begin to wiggle. Now your feet come alive."

"Your whole body begins to rise as all your body parts come alive."

"They bend and stretch."

"They begin to move a little faster."

"You discover you can walk."

"You move through space, looking and feeling."

"It feels so good to be alive; you run and leap; you see the trees, the sky, the grass. Would you like to roll in the grass? Everyone roll in the grass. It feels good just to roll over and over."

"Finally, you realize you're getting tired. You stop rolling, stop moving, and fall back to the earth where you can rest. All the stirring goes away and your body is very quiet. But you *are alive,* so you can still feel. You feel your body against the floor and you feel the quiet of just lying there. And it feels good to be alive."

(Note: This sequence introduces the concepts of increasing and decreasing the tempo of movements. If the children are cognitively ready, these concepts should be pointed out and discussed.)

11. The following images can be used to evoke movement responses involving the feelings associated with different body parts: a statue (let the statue's body parts come alive sequentially); rag doll; puppet with strings attached to different body parts; snowman being built piece by piece; melting snowman.

12. Ask the children to imagine that one body part (a hand or foot) is glued to the floor. "You must catch a bug with another body part."

13. Ask the children to wave goodbye with various body parts.

Some of my body parts are always moving.

14. Have the children lie on their backs, arms at their sides.
"Let your body feel very loose and relaxed."
"Think about your breathing."
"Feel yourself breathing in and out."
"Place your hands on your chest with your fingertips touching."
"Feel your chest move up and down as you breathe."
"Your chest is like a balloon. It gets bigger when the air goes in and smaller when the air goes out."
"Take a very deep breath and feel how big your chest gets."
"Let the breath all the way out and feel how small your chest becomes."
"Take a deep breath and hold it. Let it out."
"Put your hands on the side of your chest and breathe in and out."
"Can you feel the sides of your chest moving?"

15. Have the children run or gallop around the room until they are breathing heavily. Then have them lie down and feel their chests. Emphasize awareness of the tempo of their breathing as well as the movement of their chests. On the intermediate level you may also have them measure their pulse rates by palpitating the carotid artery on *one* side of the neck. Discuss the relationship between respiratory rate and heart rate, emphasizing that the heart is always moving.

Objects and materials have different textures.
Different textures feel different.

16. Have the children touch and then rub different body parts with a variety of articles that have different textures. Try feathers, cotton balls, and pieces of fabric (flannel, silk, burlap, plastic, fur).

Have the children wrap themselves up in such large articles as towels, blankets, rugs, and pieces of cloth with different textures. Have them wiggle and roll around while wrapped. (Note: Some children will be afraid if their heads are covered, and others will want to wrap themselves up completely.) Because as much of the body as possible should be exposed to contact with the material, short-sleeved shirts and shorts are the best attire for this activity.

Different feelings result from:
touching, rubbing, and pressing
pressing slow and fast
pressing easy and hard
pressing against resistance

17. Have the children touch, rub, and then press the palms of their hands together. Have them touch, rub, and then press on different body parts. Contrast these feelings with clapping and slapping.

18. Have the children sit on the floor, put one hand on the floor, and gradually increase the pressure by raising the body until that hand and the feet are supporting all of the body weight.

19. "With your right hand, grasp your left wrist. Let the right hand lead the left hand around in space. Then have the left arm resist the movement—push away from the body with the left hand and attempt to pull it back with the right. Do the same while raising and lowering the left hand. Change hands." Then explore the same kinds of resistance movements with other body parts (head, elbows, knee, ankle). Emphasize the difference in feeling states between the body part that is resisting movement and the one attempting to move the resisting part.

Thus far the children have been required to relate only to their own body parts. Once they have grasped these basic concepts, they are ready to move on to more complex concepts. The next step in the sequence is to have the children identify the body parts of another person.

Key Concept
□ *Other people have body parts that are like mine.*

Name and locate another person's body parts.

20. Arrange the children in pairs. With a felt-tip pen, apply a red dot to the back of one child's right hand and a blue dot to the back of the other child's right hand. Arrange the pairs so the child with the red dot is facing you and the child with the blue dot has his or her back toward you. Tell them what you are going to do:

"I will call out the name of a body part. I want the people who have red dots on their hands to reach out and touch that part of their partner's body. Everyone with a red dot hold up the hand that has the dot on it. Touch your partner's hand (arm, chest, head, leg, knee, foot, and so on)." You may either have them touch all the frontal body parts or select those you think need to be reviewed.

Then have the children with blue dots touch their partners' body parts. (Be sure to move to the other side of the room so as to face the children who will be responding to your commands.)

Instruct one child in each pair to turn around, and have his or her partner touch the parts of the bodies on the back surface. Then have the children trade roles.

21. Statues. Have one child stand inside a circle (for example, a hoop) and his or her partner stand outside the circle. Have the child on the outside arrange the body parts of the child on the inside so as to make interesting shapes and designs. Play music while the children work, and ask the statues to hold whatever position they are in when the music stops. While the children hold their positions, move around the room pointing out such factors as the size, shape, and level of various body parts. Have the children change places and repeat the exercise.

Some body parts match.
Body parts can be used to greet another person.

22. "Sometimes when people meet each other, they shake hands. Have you seen people shaking hands? Let's do that. Shake hands with your partner."

"Shaking hands is a form of greeting, isn't it? You are actually saying 'hello' or 'how are you?' That's a nice thing to do when you meet someone, but wouldn't it be more fun if people used other body parts to greet each other? Now that you know lots of body parts, let's see if you can use these to greet each other."

"I'll call out a body part and you and your partner touch that part together. If I say foot, put your foot beside your partner's foot. Let's try it. Foot."

Check to see that all the children understand and then proceed, naming various body parts. As soon as all the children are responding readily, have them move around the room, greeting different people.

"Remember when you walked around the room and when you heard the drumbeat you stopped and pointed a body part toward me?"

"Now we'll do the same thing, only you'll greet a person near you by touching the body part I've named. I'll call out a body part and then you'll move around the room. When you hear the drumbeat, find someone near you and put that body part next to theirs."

When the children appear confident, have them select the body parts they will put together.

When the music stops, it's a signal for me to stop walking.

23. "You've done so well we'll have music with our greeting. I'll play music while you walk around the room. When the music stops, find a person near you and the two of you put one of your body parts together." (With young children a demonstration may be necessary; you are requiring them to respond to a new signal and to recall and select the body part they will use.)

"Let's try it." (If all the children seem to know what to do, instruct them to start walking again as soon as the music starts.)

I can use different body parts to play a game.

24. Busy Bee. Arrange the children in pairs. One partner has a red dot and the other a blue dot. One child is without a partner; this child has a blue dot on one hand. The child without a partner is the Busy Bee. The children with red dots are stationary players.

The Busy Bee calls out a body part and says "Busy Bee." This is the signal for all the children with blue dots to run to new partners (children with red dots) and touch the designated body part. The Busy Bee tries to get a partner, and the child left without a partner becomes the new Busy Bee. This child calls out a different body part and gives the signal "Busy Bee." After a few turns, have the children with red dots run. (The new It will have to change the color of his or her dot from blue to red.)

This activity has at least two variations.

The children are not assigned to teams; when It says "Busy Bee," everyone runs.

The Busy Bee calls out two or more body parts.

My reflection in the mirror moves the same way I move.
I can move my body parts in the same way my partner moves.

25. Mirroring. Arrange the children in pairs. One partner has a red dot and one a blue dot, and they stand facing each other.

"Everyone with a red dot raise your hand. You will pretend you are looking into a mirror and your partner is your reflection in the mirror."

"Everyone with a blue dot raise your hand. You are your partner's mirror reflection, so you must move in exactly the same way your partner moves."

"Let's try it. Everyone with a red dot move one hand around very slowly. Everyone with a blue dot follow the movement of your partner. Try to stay right with him or her."

"Don't try to hurry. Think about what your partner is doing and stay right with him or her."

When all the children seem to have grasped the idea, instruct them to add other body parts and/or positions.

As soon as children are familiar with the concepts that apply to identifying and using isolated body parts, they may be introduced to activities that involve associations between numerical concepts and body part concepts. A good way to begin is to have the children use one or more body parts to perform various actions.

Key Concept
□ *When I move, I use one or more body parts.*

I can begin moving with one body part and keep adding more parts.

26. Have the children sit on the floor in their own personal spaces. Have them begin moving one body part, then another and another until the whole body is moving. You may select one or more children who added parts in interesting sequences or moved in unusual ways to demonstrate their movements to the class.

27. Have the children stand and begin shaking one body part, then another and another until the whole body is shaking. Music may be used to stimulate shaking movements. ("Going Out of My Head" from the Kimbo album *And the Beat Goes On* is excellent.)

28. Bicycle tires, hoops, or jump ropes may be used to form circles on the floor. Have the children put one body part inside the circle, then another and another until their entire bodies are inside the circle. Children usually place a hand or foot inside the circle first, followed by knees, elbows, and head. Some make the mistake of sitting in the circle, which limits them to five body parts (seat, two feet, and two hands). If they face the floor they will be able to put a total of nine body parts in the circle (two hands, two feet, both knees and both elbows, and the head).

I can tuck my body parts together and make myself very small.

29. Have the children sit on the floor in their own personal spaces. Challenge them to see how many body parts they can touch together at

one time. This task will cause them to squeeze their bodies into very small shapes, providing an opportunity to introduce the concept of size.

I can touch different parts of my body to those of other people.

30. Arrange the children in pairs.

"Touch one body part against the same body part on your partner. Good. Now touch a different body part to your partner. Now a different one."

"This time I want you to touch two body parts to the same parts on your partner. Now two different parts. Now touch three parts to your partner. Can you touch four parts to your partner? Five?" Have the children continue adding parts until as many as possible are touching.

Play music and have the partners touch a part together. When the phonograph needle is lifted, have them change to a different body part. Then have them touch two or three parts at each change.

Combine two sets of partners. Have the four people touch the same body part together and, at a signal, touch a different part. Then have them touch two or more parts together.

Combine two groups of four and do the same thing. Continue combining groups until the entire class is a single group.

LATERALITY

Key Concept
□ *My body has two sides, a right side and a left side.*

The children learn to identify the right and left sides of the body.

Activities for Children

1. Have the children sit in their own personal spaces and raise their right hands. List some functions they usually perform with their right hands (eat, draw, salute the flag, open the door). Identify the left-handed children and note that they usually perform these tasks with their left hands.

"Using your *right* hand, I want you to touch some of the body parts on the right side of your body. Touch your right foot (knee, ankle, hip, ear, cheek, eye)."

"What side of your body are you touching?"

If the children need the practice, have them touch left body parts with the left hand.

Have the children touch the body parts on the *left* side with the *right* hand, and then the body parts on the *right* side with the *left* hand.

The children are now ready to progress to the activities listed in

Child's Name _____ Date _____

Identifying Left and Right	Responds by moving		Responds by touching	
	Eyes open	Eyes closed	Eyes open	Eyes closed
1. Left hand				
2. Left elbow				
3. Left leg				
4. Right arm				
5. Right knee				
6. Left ankle				
7. Right shoulder				
8. Left foot				

Moving Separate Body Parts in Unison and in Opposition

Lying on back	Score	Comments
1. Slide both arms along the floor and touch hands together overhead.		
2. Slide both legs apart as far as possible.		
3. Slide both arms and both legs.		
4. Move *right* arm along floor to overhead position.		
5. Move *left* arm overhead.		
6. Move *right* leg to the side.		
7. Move *left* leg to the side.		
8. Move *right* arm overhead and *right* leg to the side.		
9. Move *left* arm overhead and *left* leg to the side.		
10. Move *right* arm overhead and *left* leg to the side.		
11. Move *left* arm overhead and *right* leg to the side.		

In a standing position,
 1. Turn head to right while raising left arm (and vice versa).

 2. With arms straight out to the side, hold arms still while (a) turning head from side to side; (b) bobbing head forward and backward.

 3. With arms straight out to the side, hold head still while rotating arms in a circular motion.

Scoring: + Child responds readily
         0 Child responds with only slight hesitation
         — Child experiences difficulty in responding

**Figure 11.2 Evaluation
Scale for Laterality**

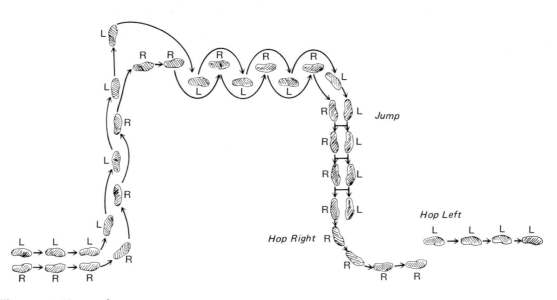

Figure 11.3 Diagram for the Activity *Stepping Stones*

Figure 11.2, the Evaluation Scale for Laterality. This scale has been designed for various uses. When used as a screening test, it ought to be reproduced in such a way as to provide space to note the children who experience difficulty. These children can then be tested on a one-to-one basis, and individual difficulties noted. The items on the scale may also be used as class activities.

2. Have the children run around the room and stop with a right or left body part pointing toward you. Then have them place the body part inside a circle. Have them clap their hands on the right side of their bodies, and then on the left side.

3. Stepping Stones. Arrange pieces of construction paper or cardboard on the floor in a pattern that indicates the steps to be taken with the right and left feet. (If desired, permanent marks may be painted on the floor or the hard-surface outdoor play area.) For young children, the papers may be in the shapes of right and left feet, the right feet cut out of red paper and the left out of blue. It may also be necessary to tie a piece of red yarn around the child's right foot to help him or her distinguish between right and left. For young children a pattern that simulates ordinary walking steps should be used first. This activity can then be made more challenging by arranging the steps so the children must put one foot directly in front of the other, cross the feet over each other, and jump or hop. A suggested pattern is shown in Figure 11.3.

Laterality   163

DIRECTIONALITY

Key Concept

☐ *My body has physical relationships to other objects, persons, and surfaces.*

Objects are located on my right or left.
Objects are in front, beside, or in back of me.
I can move up and down.
I can move over, under, around, and through other objects.

Activities for Children

All the items in Figure 11.4, the Evaluation Scale for Directionality, can be used to teach and reinforce these concepts. As soon as the children are familiar with the terms and capable of relating to them while moving, the following activities will provide additional reinforcement.

1. Beanbags. Have the children stand about the room in their own personal spaces.
"Hold the beanbag in your right (left) hand."
"Put it on your right (left) shoulder."
"Put it on the bottom of your body."
"Put it on the floor in front of (in back of, beside) you."
"Move around the beanbag."
"Move over it."
"Move it forward (backward, to the side) using a body part other than your hands."
"Hold the beanbag in your right hand. Pass it to your left hand, around your body, and back to your right hand."
"At the signal, pass the beanbag in the opposite direction."
"Pass the beanbag around your knees in a figure eight pattern, first passing it behind your right knee and in front of your left." Reverse the direction.

2. Have the children stand in pairs. One child remains stationary while the other moves in response to the command. Then they exchange roles.
"Move around your partner."
"Move over your partner."
"Can you move under your partner?"
"Can you move through some of your partner's body parts?"

3. Obstacle Course. The obstacle course illustrated in Figure 11.5 requires the children to apply the various concepts of directionality. These concepts should be reinforced by reviewing with the class those associated with each movement task.

Child's Name _____   Date _____

	Score	Comments

Individually,

1. Point to the *front* of the room.

2. Point to the *back* of the room.

3. Walk to the *front* of the room.

4. Walk to the *back* of the room.

5. Slide *sideways* across the room to your *left*.

6. Point the *left* side of your body toward the *front* of the room.

7. Point your *right* side toward the doorway.

8. Stand *inside* the circle.

9. Stand *outside* the circle.

10. Stand on your *right* foot *inside* the circle.

11. Stand on your *left* foot *outside* the circle.

12. Go *over* the pole on top of the wood cones.

13. Move *under* the pole.

14. Move from one end of the ladder to the other while stepping *into* each space between the rungs.

15. Move down the ladder, stepping *inside* the ladder with your *right* foot and *outside* the ladder with your *left* foot.

16. Walk *between* two poles waist high. (Poles should be angled so the child begins moving through a wide space and adjusts to a narrower space as he or she progresses. The space should become so narrow that the child must turn sideways to get through.)

17. Crawl *through* the cylinder.

With a partner,

1. Touch the *top* of your partner.

2. Touch the *bottom* of your partner.

3. Stand *behind* your partner.

4. Stand *beside* your partner.

5. Stand in *front* of your partner.

6. Touch each of your partner's body parts as I name them:

Left hand

Left wrist

Right arm

Right knee

Left shoulder

Right ear

Left elbow

Right ankle

Right hip

Figure 11.4 Evaluation Scale for Directionality

Scoring: + Child responds readily

0 Child responds with only slight hesitation

− Child experiences difficulty in responding

Directionality

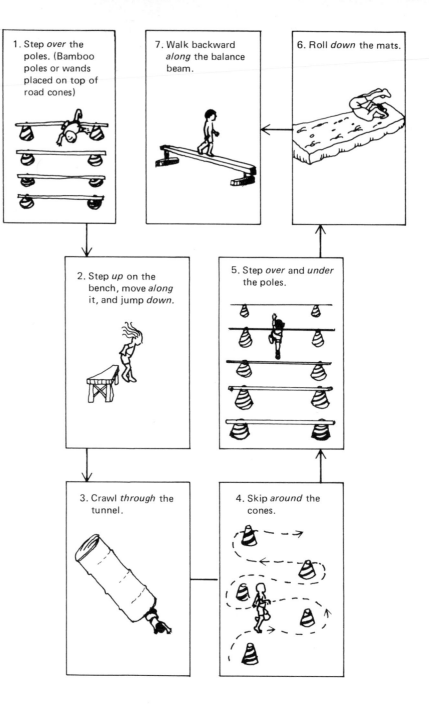

1. Step *over* the poles. (Bamboo poles or wands placed on top of road cones)

7. Walk backward *along* the balance beam.

6. Roll *down* the mats.

2. Step *up* on the bench, move *along* it, and jump *down*.

5. Step *over* and *under* the poles.

3. Crawl *through* the tunnel.

4. Skip *around* the cones.

Figure 11.5 Obstacle Course for Development of Directionality

**Figure 11.6 Beanbag
Circuit for Development
of Directionality**

The stations contain the following text:

STATION 1
Toss a beanbag *under* the pole 5 times. Toss a beanbag *over* the pole 5 times.

STATION 2
Pass a beanbag *around* your body to the *left* 5 times. Then pass it back to the *right*.

STATION 3
Toss 5 beanbags *through* the hoop. (Adjust the height of the hoop and the throwing distance according to the skill level.)

STATION 4
Balance a beanbag on your left elbow while moving *forward* on the balance beam. (Have the more highly skilled children walk backward.)

STATION 5
Pass the beanbag *around* your knees in a figure 8, to the *left* 4 times and then to the *right*.

Key Concept

☐ *When I hear a signal, I can move to the next station in our circuit.*

When the children have become familiar with movement from one place to another in order to perform a task, they are ready to be introduced to a circuit. (See Figures 11.6 and 11.7.) A circuit is a novel method of practicing skills and reinforcing concepts.

I must perform the tasks at each station and then wait until I hear the signal before moving on to the next station.
I must perform the task at each station according to the directions given.

4. Because participation in a circuit requires the children to be self-directing, they must be adequately prepared.

STATION 5   Camel Walk (Moving the whole body *forward* and *backward* while moving some body part *upward* and *downward*)
The child bends forward from the waist and places the hands behind the back, making a fist with one hand and holding the fist with the other hand so it looks like the hump on a camel's back. The child walks slowly forward and backward, bobbing the head and chest upward and downward on each step.

STATION 3   Bear Walk (Moving *right* and *left* sides of the body separately)
With hands and feet touching the floor, the child moves forward and backward using unilateral movements. (The right arm and right leg move forward or backward at the same time, or the left arm and left leg move at the same time.)

STATION 4   Rooster Hop (Moving *forward* and *backward* in different pathways)
The child stands on one foot with hands under the armpits and hops forward and backward in straight, curved, and angular pathways marked on the floor. (Variation: have the child stand on the right foot with left foot behind the body. The child grasps the left foot with the right hand and hops while using the left arm to assist in maintaining balance.)

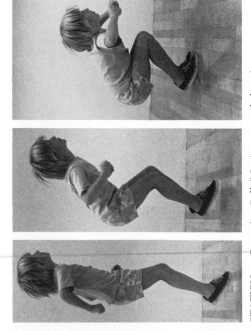

STATION 1   Bouncing Ball (Moving *up* and *down*)
The child executes a series of jumps, gradually lowering the height of each jump and the level of the body until the hands touch the floor. The action of the body simulates a ball that is tossed into the air and continues to bounce until it comes to rest on the floor.

STATION 2   Measuring Worm (Moving body parts *toward* and *away from each other*)
The child assumes a front-leaning position and walks with feet forward, keeping legs straight and hands stationary. The child brings the feet as close as possible to the hands and then walks with hands forward while the feet remain stationary.

Figure 11.7 Stunt Circuit for Development of Directionality
Mickey Adair

Circuits for first-graders should be limited to five stations, since the children have short attention spans and tend to become confused if the situation is too complex. (Seven or more stations can be used with older children.)

The children should be thoroughly familiar with each task on the circuit, so that it serves to provide additional practice and reinforce learning. You should demonstrate each task before the class is divided into groups, and it may also be advisable for each group to review by practicing some of the skills. If possible, a leader should be assigned to each station to help young children and to note those who have difficulty.

A sign should be posted at each station designating the station number and the activity to be performed. Pictures or diagrams can be used to convey the message to nonreaders and to stimulate the interest of older children.

The class is divided into groups of equal size, and each group is assigned to a station. The children are instructed to begin at a signal and to progress to the next station as directed. The preferred method is to play music and to lift the needle to signal a move to the next station. However, a bell, whistle, or verbal signal is satisfactory.

Key Concept
□ *I can dance with the movements I have been practicing.*

5. Folk Dance. Once children have been introduced to the basic movements and to rhythmic response to music, laterality and directionality concepts may be effectively reinforced through participation in elementary folk dance. Some of the dances that can be utilized are Hansel and Gretel, Seven Jumps, Chimes of Dunkirk, Dance of Greeting, Kinderpolka, and Looby Loo.

6. Creative Movement. The Dance-A-Story *The Toy Tree*[1] contains a number of movement stimuli that suggest various ways of moving one's body parts while relating to surfaces and objects. The concepts emphasized are up and down; high and low; forward, backward, and side to side; stop and go; and increasing and decreasing the speed of the movements.

EXTRA PRACTICE IN THE BASICS

Ability to identify one's body parts and to relate laterally and directionally to one's environment is a prerequisite to successful participation in any movement activity. The relationship of these factors to movement skills and other movement variables will be pointed out later. Because

[1]The Dance-A-Story series is available from RCA Records (see page 474).

these skills are vitally important and because some children have difficulty learning them, the following activities are provided for use as supplementary learning experiences. They may be used in the following ways:

1. as introductory activities

2. to stimulate discussion during review periods

3. to provide instruction on a one-to-one basis and in small groups for children who need additional help

4. as classroom learning experiences

5. as learning center materials available for use by individual children

Activities for Children

1. Using a cardboard mannikin with movable joints, the teacher or another person points to various body parts and asks the child to name each.

Remove various body parts from the mannikin, and ask the child to identify the missing part or parts.

Ask the child to move his or her own corresponding body part while naming the one indicated on the mannikin.

Have the child touch his or her own body part or that of a partner while naming it.

2. To help reinforce recognition of how the body parts are arranged, use cardboard replicas of the major body parts—head, torso, upper arms, lower arms, hands, upper legs, lower legs, feet.

Instruct the child to put the body together by placing the body parts in the correct positions (like a puzzle).

Remove one or more parts and ask the child to identify the missing part or parts verbally or by touching his or her own or the partner's body.

Draw in the facial features, hair, and ears.

Have the child put together only the parts on the right or left side of the body.

3. To help children understand how animals and people use their body parts to move in different ways and how people use machines to move their bodies greater distances, you will find the book *Going Places* by Aileen Fisher (1973) useful.

Read selected parts of the book to the children and show them the illustrations. Challenge them to move as the birds, fish, insects, and animals are moving.

Body Awareness

Ask them to identify the body parts these animals use to move their bodies.

Have the children compare the ways these animals move with the ways they move when they are "going places."

Challenge the children to move the way machines move when they are taking people places.

Have the children make up stories about "going places" and tell these stories verbally and nonverbally. Identify the ways they move and the body parts they use.

Have different children imitate various animals and machines. Identify the speed of their movements and the level on which they move.

4. To promote recognition of similarities and differences between animal and human body parts, have a supply of pictures of animals, birds, and reptiles—dog, cat, horse, giraffe, kangaroo, elephant, snake, lizard, bird standing and bird flying.

Ask the child to name the animal's body part as you point to it.

Have the child move as he or she thinks the animal would move.

Ask the child to describe how the animal's body parts differ from his or her own in number and/or size.

Ask the child to describe (verbally and nonverbally) how these differences affect the way the animal moves—for example, it may walk on four legs, jump, slide, or fly.

5. To demonstrate how various body parts are used in work and play, you can use pictures of children participating in different kinds of movement activities. Ask the child to tell you what the people in the pictures are doing. Then ask him or her to name the body parts the people are using.

Let the child make up a story about the way the people in the picture are moving and tell the story verbally and nonverbally.

6. Supply each child with a piece of clay. Ask the child to mold the clay into a figure resembling his or her body, and to arrange the body parts first in one position and then in another.

Have the child copy each of the figure's positions with his or her own body.

Organize the children in pairs, and have one partner make the clay model and the other imitate its positions with his or her body.

Have the partners mold their figures so certain body parts are touching.

7. To promote recognition of the verbal symbols that designate body parts, you can use cards on which the names of the body parts are printed in lower-case letters and pictures of body parts mounted on cardboard.

Ask the child to match the name of a body part with a picture of it.

Remove some of the pictures of body parts so that the child has a surplus of name cards and cannot arrive at answers by the process of elimination.

TOPICS FOR REVIEW AND FURTHER STUDY

1. Why must the child be aware of the physical reality of his or her own body?

2. Use the scale on page 152 to evaluate a child's ability to identify his or her body parts.

3. Select one of the subjects below and construct a lesson plan that will help children develop and utilize its basic concepts.
   a. body part identification
   b. laterality
   c. directionality

4. Conduct your lesson with a group of children and critique its effectiveness.

5. Design an obstacle course or circuit that will provide an interesting and novel way for children to review the concepts of directionality.

6. Describe how supplementary activities can be used to enhance learning.

7. Develop a supplementary activity and use it with one or more children.

SUGGESTIONS FOR FURTHER READING

CAPON, JACK. "Group Activities to Reinforce Body Image Development." *Journal of Health, Physical Education and Recreation* 45 (Nov.-Dec. 1974): 82.

———. "Perceptual-Motor Balance Puzzles." *Journal of Health, Physical Education and Recreation* 45 (Nov.-Dec. 1974): 82–83.

CHANEY, CLARA M., and KEPHART, NEWELL C. *Motoric Aids to Perceptual Training.* Columbus, Ohio: Charles E. Merrill, 1968.

CHERRY, CLARE. *Creative Movement for the Developing Child.* Belmont, Cal.: Fearon, 1971.

CLURE, BETH, and RUMSEY, HELEN. *How Does It Feel?* Glendale, Cal.: Bowmar, 1968.

———. *Little, Big, Bigger.* Glendale, Cal.: Bowmar, 1968.

———. *Me!,* revised ed. Glendale, Cal.: Bowmar, 1971.

FISHER, AILEEN. *Going Places.* Glendale, Cal.: Bowmar, 1973.

FISHER, SEYMOUR. "Experiencing Your Body: You Are What You Feel." *Saturday Review of Science* 55 (July 1972): 27–32.

HATCHER, CAROL, and MULLINS, HILDA. *More Than Words: Movement Activities for Children.* Pasadena, Cal.: Parents-For-Movement Publication, 1967.

LOGSDON, BETTE J., and BARRETT, KATE R. Teachers's manual for *Ready? Set . . . Go! Level One.* Bloomington, Indiana: National Instructional Television, 1969.

LOWNDES, BETTY. *Movement and Drama in the Primary School.* London, England: B. T. Batsford, 1970.

VAN HOLST, AUKE. *Kindergarten: Physical Education Curriculum for Elementary Grades.* London, Canada: London Free Press, 1974.

WERNER, PETER H. and RINI, LISA. *Perceptual-Motor Development Equipment. Inexpensive Equipment Ideas and Activities.* New York: John Wiley, 1976.

SUGGESTED TEACHING AIDS

BARLIN, ANNE, and BARLIN, PAUL. "The Toy Tree." Dance-A-Story Series. New York: RCA Records Educational Department.

BRAZELTON, AMBROSE. "And the Beat Goes on for Physical Education." L.P. Record Album No. KEA 5010-B. Deal, N.J.: Kimbo Educational.

CARR, DOROTHY B., and CRATTY, BRYANT J. "Listening and Moving." L.P. Record Album No. 605 and 606–607. Freeport, N.Y.: Educational Activities.

LICCIONE, GEORGIANA. "Developmental Motor Skills for Self-Awareness." L.P. Record Album No. 9075. Deal, N.J.: Kimbo Educational.

PALMER, HAP. "Getting to Know Myself." L.P. Record Album No. AR 543. Freeport, N.Y.: Educational Activities.

12 Spatial Awareness

Once children have become familiar with their own physical beings, they are prepared to use their bodies to explore the physical environment. Within this environment spaces are either occupied or unoccupied. Thus the first spatial concept children must develop is that their own bodies are objects that occupy space. As soon as they comprehend this fact, they are ready to explore other concepts concerning their physical relationships to the world around them.

PERSONAL SPACE AND GENERAL SPACE

Key Concept

□ *My body is a physical object that occupies space.*

I have a personal space that moves with me wherever I go.

Activities for Children

1. Have the children sit on the floor in their own personal spaces. Tell them what they are to do:

"Move one hand around your body."

"Move it as many different places as possible."

"Can you move it all around in the space above your head?"

"Can you move it all around your body at shoulder level?"

"Can you move it low around your hips? around your legs and feet?"

"Now move both hands all around your body."

"Stretch and reach as far as you can in front of you, to the sides, in back of you, above your head."

"Let's use another body part."

"Move one foot all around to as many places as you can reach."

"Now move both feet all around."

"You reached as high as you could while sitting on the floor. What must you do in order to reach higher? That's right—you must stand up. Everyone stand up!"

"Reach as high as you can."

"What must you do with your feet in order to reach really high? That's right—stand on tiptoe. Everyone reach as high as you can and s-t-r-e-t-c-h."

"You reached very high. Now can you reach low?"

"How low can you reach? That's right, you can reach clear to the floor."

"You've reached high and low. Now can you reach into all the space in between high and low?"

"Can you reach all around in front of you and behind you? Good. Now sit down right where you are."

"You've just reached into all the spaces clear around your body. You reached as far as you could from very high to very low and all around in between. This space has a name. It's called your *personal space*. Your personal space is all the space around you as far as you can reach."

2. You can use imagery to illustrate the concept of personal space.

"Let's pretend you have a big paint brush. Can you paint the inside of your personal space? Did you remember to paint the top, the bottom, and all the way around?"

"What happens to your personal space when you move? That's right—it goes with you, doesn't it?"

As I move from place to place, I move through general space.

3. "There is another kind of space. It is called *general space*. General space is all the empty spaces in the room—all the spaces that are not being used by other people."

"Look around you. Can you see some spaces that are empty? Point to some of them."

"Let's explore general space. When I say 'go,' I want you to get up and move about into all parts of the room, but remember to stay out of everyone else's personal space. Ready, go!"

"Have you been in the corners of the room? in the middle?" Have the children sit down and review the concepts of personal and general space.

<table>
<tr><td>THE RANGE
AND SIZE
OF MOVEMENT</td><td>Key Concepts
□ My movements may be large or small.
□ I may cover a lot of space as I move or only a small amount of space.
□ It feels different when I move in small and large spaces and when I make big and small movements.</td></tr>
</table>

I can make small and large movements with each body part.

Activities for Children

1. Have the children sit on the floor in their own personal spaces.

"Using just your fingers, make a very small movement. Let your hands join the movement, but keep it small. Let your arms join in . . . and your shoulders . . . and finally your head and chest. Now the whole upper part of your body is making small movements. Let those movements get slower and s-l-o-w-e-r u-n-t-i-l y-o-u s-t-o-p."

"This time let's use the same body parts, but we'll make very big movements." Repeat the sequence. You may continue by having the children start moving at the toes and proceed to the feet, ankles, and legs.

"What kind of space were you using as you moved your body parts? That's right, you were moving in your personal space.

"Now let's explore small and large movements while you move through general space. First I want you to walk through general space taking very small steps. Ready, go!"

"Now add another body part. Make very small movements with another body part while you're walking." Continue adding body parts until the entire body is involved.

"Now I want you to take big walking steps." Gradually add body parts.

When I have lots of space, I can make big movements.
When the space is small, I must make small movements.

2. Have the children stand in a straight line, one behind the other and close together. Have them walk around the room. Ask them what size steps they must take.

Then have them space themselves in the line so that each is two arms' lengths in front of the next child. (Have the children extend their right arms in front of them and their left arms behind. Their fingertips should barely touch those of the children ahead of and behind them.)

Now have them walk around the room using lots of space. Ask them what size steps they used this time.

3. Have the children hold hands and form a big circle. (It will be necessary to teach young children how to form a circle. Have them form a line, along a wall or sideline, and hold hands. Then take the hand of the first child and lead the line around in a circle until you meet the child who is last in line. Take that child's hand and have the group move back to round out the circle.)

"Walk forward toward the center of the circle." Have the children continue walking until they are squeezed together. Have them stop and think about the feeling of being so close to other people and about the size of the movements they can make.

Have them walk backward until the circle is stretched out, drop hands, and make large movements all around their personal spaces.

Have the children hold hands, form a circle, and slowly walk toward the center. When they are again squeezed together, have them sit down and move inward until they are as close together as possible. Ask how this feels. Have the children compare this feeling with that of making big movements in their personal spaces. Ask how big their personal spaces are now.

"Because your personal space is small, how must you move? What would happen if you tried to make a big movement now?" (Caution the children not to move so as to hurt themselves or someone else when their personal spaces are small.)

4. Have the children close their eyes and walk through general space until they touch another person. Tell them to stand by that person until you call out the name of a body part (arm, foot, nose, ear). They must then find that part of the other person's body while keeping their eyes closed.

5. An activity called Trees in the Forest (Dimondstein, 1971) reinforces these concepts by means of imagery.

Have half the children stand around the room as though they were trees in the forest, and have the other half move around the trees. Vary the spacing between the trees so the children experience moving in large and small spaces. Have the trees assume different body positions so as to vary in size and shape. Then have the two groups switch roles.

6. Show the children the pictures in the book *Little, Big and Bigger* (Clure and Rumsey, 1968), and have them form the shapes of little, big, and bigger houses and bowls of candy. Then have them move like little, big, and bigger dogs, elephants, and cars.

Ask the children to think of other animate and inanimate objects and to replicate them in various sizes.

DIRECTION AND LEVEL

A number of concepts involving direction and level were introduced in the section on directionality; others will be presented in the lessons on spatial relationships. Therefore only the Key Concepts up, down, forward, backward, and sideways and will be treated in this section.

Key Concept
☐ *I can move up, down, forward, backward, and sideways.*

Up is above me.
Down is below me.
Forward is in front of me.
Backward is behind me.
Sideward is on my right or left side.

Activities for Children

1. Have the children sit on the floor.
"Point to something above you." (ceiling, light, windows)
"Point to something below you." (the floor)
"Point up. Point down."
"Stand up. Sit down."

2. Imagery is useful at this point. "Who can name something that moves up and down?" (Examples are a ball, a seesaw, an elevator, birds, an airplane.) Let the children imitate the things they name.

3. "Everyone walk toward the front of the room. Stop. What direction were you moving?" (forward) "Now, without turning around, walk to the back of the room. Stop. What direction were you moving that time?" (backward)

"Keep your body facing me, but look at that end of the room." (Point to the end of the room that is to their right.) "Move toward that end of the room. Stop. What direction did you move?" (sideways) "Move sideways toward the other end of the room."

Next have the children move forward four steps, backward four, to the right four, and to the left four. Repeat. Then perform to a count (forward, two, three, four; backward, two, three, four; and so on). Execute to a drumbeat in 4/4 meter, instructing the children to change direction on the accented beat.

Have the children walk in general space, changing direction whenever they approach a wall or meet another person.

Have them move forward through general space on a low level. At the signal of a single drumbeat, have them move backward on a high level. Continue alternating the movements.

Challenge the children to see how many ways they can move forward, backward, and sideways on different body parts. Add the challenge of changing both direction and level.

Have the children move in different directions and on different levels while performing various locomotor movements, such as a hop forward, jump backward, and slide sideways.

4. Shadow Figures. Take the children outside on a sunny day and let them experiment with making shadow figures (see Figure 12.1).

"Can you stand with your shadow in front of you? behind you? beside you? Can you touch your shadow? Can you make your shadow very big? very small? tall? short? Can you make your shadow finger touch someone else's shadow? Can you stand on someone else's shadow head? Can you touch someone's shadow hand with your shadow hand? Can you touch an object with your shadow hand?"

Have the children form pairs and experiment with making different kinds of shadows. Then have them make shadows of contrasting dimensions—one shadow big, one small; one tall, the other short; and so on.

Ask the children to describe the dimensions of the shadows cast by such visible objects as trees, poles, playground equipment, and buildings.

5. Direction Game. Have four sets of six to eight cards, each set a different color. On the cards are printed instructions specifying how the child is to move: forward four steps, backward two steps, sideways three steps, and the like. The instructions are the same on each set of cards.

Divide the children into four teams, each of which is assigned a color corresponding to the color of one set of cards. Each team lines up in relay formation at one end of the gym. Mark a goal line determined by the total number of steps indicated by a set of cards.

Shuffle all the cards together. Then take a card from the top of the pile, name the color of the team that is to move, and read the instructions from the card. Each succeeding player begins beside the teammate who last moved. The team that reaches the goal line first wins. Have the children who did not get turns move to the front of the line so they will be able to participate in the next game.

A variation is to add locomotor movements to the instructions: hop forward four steps, jump backward two steps, skip forward three steps, slide sideward four steps, and the like.

If the children can read, a set of cards can be placed on the floor in front of each team. Each child in turn picks up a card, runs up beside the teammate who last moved, reads the instructions on the card, and executes the movement. The team whose players first finish moving wins. Each set of cards should be stacked in the same order so the teams can be compared for accuracy of performance.

**Figure 12.1
Experimenting with
Shadow Figures**
Mickey Adair

Spatial Awareness

6. Either "Little Duck" or "Balloons" from the Dance-A-Story series (RCA) may be used to review concepts relating to body parts, size, direction, and level.

SHAPE

Key Concept

□ *My body and body parts have shapes, and as I move the shape of my body changes.*

I can make shapes with my body and body parts that are narrow, wide, curved, angular, or twisted.

Different body shapes feel different.

Activities for Children

1. Have the children find a personal space and lie on their backs. "Place your arms on the floor above your head."

"Stretch your body, making it just as thin and long as you can. Ready: S-t-r-e-t-c-h."

"Stretch your arms, legs, fingers, and toes."

"Let go and let your body become saggy." Repeat this sequence several times, emphasizing the contrast between the feelings of stretched and relaxed body positions.

"Stretch your arms and legs out to the side, making your body as *wide* as possible. Notice how it feels to be open."

"Now close your body shape. Hold your arms tight against the sides of your body."

"Pull your legs as close together as you can. Relax."

"Starting with your legs together and your arms at your sides, open your body way out. Now close it." Repeat this sequence.

"This time move only your arms. Open your upper body shape by extending your arms clear out to the sides. Now bring them on up until your hands touch. Stretch. Relax. Slowly move your arms back down to your sides." Repeat.

Have the children turn over and repeat the preceding sequences while lying face down on the floor.

"Lie down on your side with your arms extended overhead and your head resting on your bottom arm. Make your body as thin as you can. Is your body wider or narrower than when you were lying on your back? Now, while lying on your side, make your body shape wider. Make it as wide as you can. What body parts did you move? Where did you place those body parts? Make your body shape as small as you can. What must you do to make yourself very small? What kind of a shape does your body have now?" (rounded or curved)

Have the children sit up. "Can you make a rounded shape with just your arms? With your fingers? Can you make a round shape with your arms while they are over your head? Can you make a curved shape with your back? with both your arms and your back? Can you make a curved shape with your legs and feet? Now add your arms and back. Make as many body parts as you can into curved shapes."

"Now let's make another kind of shape. Extend your right arm straight out in front of you. Keep your upper arm still, but bring your right hand in toward your body and touch your chest. Look at the shape of your right arm. How would you describe that shape?" (The children may say "bent" or "sharp.") Tell them they are correct, but that we have a special name for that shape, *angular*. Angular shapes have corners.

"Can you make an angular shape with your other arm? Can you make angular shapes with your legs? your legs and feet? See how many angular shapes you can make with your body parts."

"Let's all stand up. How can you make an angular shape with your body? That's right, you bend over. Can you make more than one angular shape while standing? That's right, you can if you bend your knees and ankles as well as your hips. Now can you add the arms and hands to make more angular shapes?"

"Now lie down and see how many angular shapes you can make while lying on your back (front, side)."

"You've made narrow shapes, wide shapes, curved shapes, and angular shapes. There's one more kind of shape we can make. Stand up. Without moving your feet, look at the wall behind you. What is the shape of your body? (twisted) What other body parts can you twist?" (arms and hands, legs and feet, neck)

Review the five kinds of shapes by having the children make each one with their bodies. While they are holding each shape, reinforce the concept with the following descriptions, which may be phrased as questions:

"When we're making *narrow* shapes, we try to keep our body parts close together so we are thin."

"When we want to make *wide* shapes, our body parts must be far apart."

"When you're making a *rounded* shape, your body parts must be curved."

"*Angular* shapes have corners, so we can make an angular shape with any body part that bends."

"We make *twisted* shapes by having one body part face one way and another body part move so it faces another way."

2. Have the children identify the shapes created by the boundary lines on the gym floor and challenge them to match the shapes of their bodies to those lines. You may create additional shapes by cutting out large pieces of colored cardboard and taping them to the floor.

This activity can be made into a game by playing music. Each time the music stops, each child must find a shape, stand beside it, and replicate it with his or her body. It is an additional challenge to require the children to maintain the shapes while moving through general space.

3. Blindfold half the class members. Have a child who is not blindfolded lead a blindfolded child along the outline of a shape. The blindfolded child must guess the shape.

4. Give each child a jump rope. Instruct the children to make the ropes into different shapes. Have them make their bodies the same shapes as their ropes. Then have each child make a shape with the rope and an opposite shape with his or her body: the rope straight, the body angular; the rope curved, the body straight; the rope narrow, the body wide; and so on.

5. Movement Mural. Have each child lie down on a large sheet of colored paper and make a shape with his or her body. Trace the outlines of the bodies. Then have each child cut out the shape and write his or her name on the front. Mount the shapes on the gymnasium walls. (See Figure 12.2.)

6. Shadow Shapes. Have the children make narrow, wide, curved, and angular shadow shapes, using a variety of body parts. Ask that some of the shapes be solid and others have empty spaces (Anderson, Elliot, and LaBerge, 1972). Then have the children work with partners. Shadow shapes may also be used to reinforce the concepts introduced below.

Key Concept
□ *Everything has a shape.*

    shapes of specific animate and inanimate objects
    shapes of numbers
    shapes of letters

7. Show the children a variety of inanimate objects (for example, a ball; pencil; book; yardstick; roll of tape; pair of scissors, open and closed; umbrella, open and closed). Have them name each shape and make a similar shape with their bodies or body parts.

Show the children pictures of various animals and have them identify the shapes of each animals' body parts. (See Figure 12.3.)

Have the children form numbers and letters with their body parts and describe the shapes they create.

8. For intermediate and advanced students, you can invent movement problems that must be solved by creating various shapes. Examples of such problems are:

Figure 12.2 A Movement Mural

Curved

Angular

Figure 12.3 Animals with Body Parts of Different Shapes

Straight

a. to keep one or more body parts on the floor while making a specified shape

b. to keep one or more specific body parts on a certain level while making certain shapes. For example, "Keep your arms high while you make an angular (curved, twisted) shape." "Keep your hips higher than your head while you make a curved (angular, twisted) shape."

c. to maintain a specific relationship between two or more body parts while making a shape. (For example, "Keep your knees and elbows close together while creating three different shapes.")

Make the problems more complex by combining people. Have the children work with partners, and then in groups of three and four. (With older children as many as seven may be in one group.) Have the groups create a single composite shape by creating individual shapes that fit harmoniously together. Have them initially form static shapes and then progress to moving shapes.

The following images are effective in eliciting shapes from groups of children: a room with windows and doors, a house, telephone poles and lines, a cage containing an animal, a fireplace and fire, a phonograph, other machines.

Introduce geometric shapes and have the children form triangles, squares, rectangles, pentagons, hexagons, and the like.

PATHWAY

When the children have mastered spatial concepts, they are capable of visualizing pathways. Because pathways are abstract concepts, the children will have to be introduced to them by means of concrete images. The concept of pathways on the floor (floor patterns) should be introduced first.

Key Concept
□ *As I move across the floor, I create a pattern.*

The pattern I create on the floor may be straight, curved, or angular.

Activities for Children

1. Have the children walk along the lines marked on the gymnasium floor. Point out the straight, angular, and circular pathways they follow while walking.

Describe how joining angular pathways in a series can result in a zigzag pathway.

Instruct the children to move through space creating pathways on the floor.

Play music, challenging the children to change pathways each time the music stops.

Challenge the children to create pathways while moving on different body parts and various numbers of body parts.

Blindfold half the children. Have each child who is not blindfolded lead a blindfolded child along a pathway. The blindfolded child must guess the type of pathway. Then have the partners reverse roles.

2. Have the children name all the things they can think of that follow pathways. Examples are rainwater running down a street, a car on a road, a train on a track, a boat on a river, a ball rolling across a floor. This activity can be made a game if you divide the class into teams and challenge each team to create the longest list.

Ask the children to describe the pathways they follow when they walk from place to place in the school building and when they go home from school.

Key Concept
□ *As I move through space, my body and body parts create a pathway.*

I can create straight, curved, and angular pathways in space.

3. Have the children sit on the floor in their own personal spaces. Instruct them to create each kind of pathway by using a hand, and then by using other body parts.

Have them move through general space creating pathways by varying the level, direction, and size of their movements.

Play follow-the-leader, emphasizing pathways.

Give each child a balloon, and challenge the children to make their balloons follow different pathways.

SPATIAL RELATIONSHIPS   The activities involving identification of body parts and practice in directional concepts have already introduced the child to most of the spatial relationships. Thus the purpose of the activities that follow is to enable the child to extend and apply these concepts to more complex situations.

Key Concept
□ *When I am still and when I am moving, my body and body parts have relationships to all other people and objects.*

My partner and I can stand and move, face-to-face, back-to-back, side by side, close together, or far apart.

1. Stand at the front of the room and have the children stand in pairs along one side, one partner next to the wall and one nearer the center of the room. "Stand so you are facing your partner. Now stand so your backs are together. Stand facing each other again and hold your partner's hands. Take four sliding steps toward the side of the room where I'm standing. Slide back to where you were."

"Now stand back-to-back and hook elbows. Slide four steps toward me. Now slide back."

"Stand beside your partner and face the front of the room." (The couples should be lined up one behind another along the side of the room.) "Are you standing close to or far away from your partner?" (close)

"Now I want each person on the inside to slide across the room and stand next to the opposite wall. Ready, go!"

"Now are you standing close together or far apart?"

"Now all of you who stood still slide across the room, stand beside your partner, and take hold of his or her hand. Now you're close together again!"

"Staying side by side and close together, slide back across the room."

"This time the people on the inside will slide across to the opposite wall, and as soon as they arrive their partners will slide across the room, grab their hands, and start back. Ready, go!"

I can lead or follow my partner.

2. Arrange the children in pairs. "The two of you are going to play follow-the-leader. I'm going to play some music and I want one of you to lead the other all around the room. When the music stops, you stop."

"Now let the other person lead."

"Each time the music stops, reverse roles."

Follow-the-leader may also be played by a group of children. The leader goes to the end of the line each time the music stops.

I can move toward and away from my partner.

3. Have the children move certain body parts toward and away from those of their partners.

Add a drumbeat. Have the body parts approach each other to a count of four and retreat to a count of four.

Have the children walk (or perform other locomotor or nonlocomotor movements) toward and away from each other. Specify other dimensions, such as to move away from each other on a high level and toward each other on a low level; away slow, toward fast; and the like.

I can move in unison with or in opposition to my partner.

4. Arrange the children in pairs. Have everyone bend and stretch to a drumbeat in 2/4 meter. Tell the children they are moving in unison, because everyone is doing the same thing.

Then tell them to move in opposition, one stretching while the other bends.

Variations are for one to move high while the other moves low; small/large; fast/slow; weak/strong; straight/angular.

I can move along (beside), across, or around lines, objects, and surfaces.

5. Have the children form a line along a side of the room. Instruct them to move along the lines on the gym floor, then back and forth across the lines and around the center circle. (Jump ropes may be used to form lines.)

Have them move along the walls, back and forth across the room, and around the room.

Challenge them to show you how many objects, lines, or surfaces they can move along (across, around).

Have the children form pairs. Let one partner lie on the floor while the other moves along (beside), back and forth across, and around him or her.

Have the children explore these relationships using gym scooters.

I can move into, out of, and through spaces and objects.

6. Introduce these concepts by explaining to the children that they are moving into, out of, and through spaces whenever they move.

Have the children form one large circle. Call out a color and have everyone wearing that color move through the circle and find a new space. Call out other colors. Explain that in order to go through the circle, they had to go into and then out of it.

These concepts should be reinforced and applied by means of realistic experiences in the child's everyday physical environment. An ideal way to do so is to take the children on a field trip. (See Figure 12.4.) If it is not possible to take them outside, the outdoor environment can be simulated in the gym. This is an excellent final activity for the unit, because it provides for review of the basic concepts and enables the children to generalize their learning experiences.

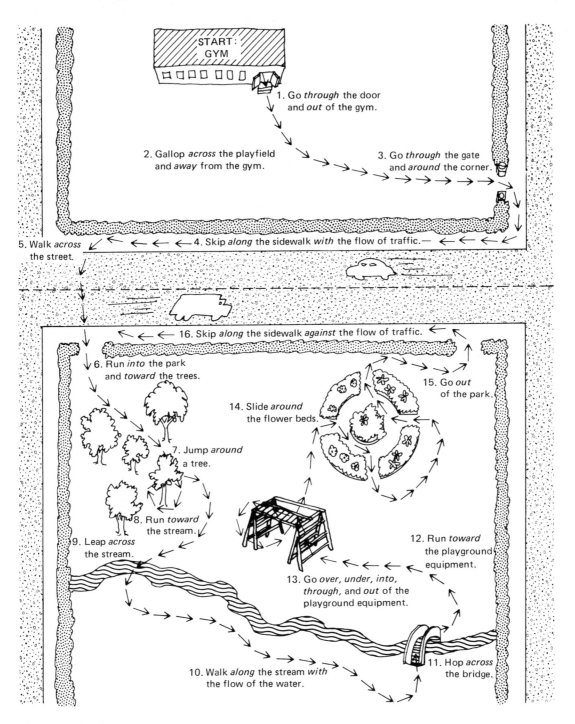

Figure 12.4 Plan for a Field Trip Emphasizing Spatial Relationships

The labeled steps within the figure:

1. Go *through* the door and *out* of the gym.
2. Gallop *across* the playfield and *away* from the gym.
3. Go *through* the gate and *around* the corner.
4. Skip *along* the sidewalk *with* the flow of traffic.
5. Walk *across* the street.
6. Run *into* the park and *toward* the trees.
7. Jump *around* a tree.
8. Run *toward* the stream.
9. Leap *across* the stream.
10. Walk *along* the stream *with* the flow of the water.
11. Hop *across* the bridge.
12. Run *toward* the playground equipment.
13. Go *over, under, into, through,* and *out* of the playground equipment.
14. Slide *around* the flower beds.
15. Go *out* of the park.
16. Skip *along* the sidewalk *against* the flow of traffic.

**TOPICS FOR
REVIEW AND
FURTHER STUDY**

1. Develop a series of learning experiences in which the children explore one or more of the following concepts:

a. personal and general space

b. the size of movements

c. the relationship between the size of a movement and the amount of space it occupies

d. moving in different directions

e. moving on different levels

f. forming shapes with the body as a whole and with different body parts

g. creating different kinds of pathways

h. creating different spatial relationships with a partner

i. relating spatially to objects, lines, and surfaces

2. Develop an obstacle course or circuit that will provide opportunities for the children to review and utilize spatial concepts.

3. Plan a field trip that will stimulate children to relate spatially to the outdoor environment.

**SUGGESTIONS
FOR FURTHER
READING**

ANDERSON, MARIAN; ELLIOT, MARGARET; and LABERGE, JEANNE. *Play with a Purpose,* 2nd ed. New York: Harper and Row, 1972.

DIMONDSTEIN, GERALDINE. *Children Dance in the Classroom.* New York: Macmillan, 1971.

GILLIOM, BONNIE. *Basic Movement Education for Children: Rationale and Teaching Units.* Reading, Mass.: Addison-Wesley, 1970.

MURRAY, RUTH. *Dance in Elementary Education,* 3rd ed. New York: Harper & Row, 1975.

STANLEY, SHEILA. *Physical Education: A Movement Orientation.* Toronto: McGraw-Hill of Canada, 1969.

13   Kinesthetic Awareness

The bodily and spatial concepts the child has already mastered will be utilized in this chapter to enhance awareness of his or her movement potential. Stimulation of the kinesthetic sense will be the child's primary informational source. Learning will be extended and reinforced through heightened cognitive awareness of kinesthetic sensations and increased understanding of the body functioning as a movement instrument.

THE BODY IN STILLNESS AND IN MOTION

All movement concepts are related to the basic concepts of two contrasting states, *stillness* and *motion*. It is therefore essential for children to develop an awareness of these two conditions of being.

Key Concepts
☐ *My body is always either still or in motion.*
☐ *Being still feels different than moving.*

   I can create stillness by being tense.
   I can create stillness by being relaxed.
   I can be still while my body is in various positions.
   When I move I must change the position of my body.

1. Have the children stand in their own personal spaces. "I want you to stand very still. Close your eyes and think about how it feels to be still. Can you feel your different body parts? Keep your eyes closed and slowly wiggle your fingers. Can you feel them more? Hold them still again. Which way can you feel more keenly, when your fingers are still or when they are moving?"

"Make your hands into fists and squeeze them tight. How do they feel?"

"Put your hands together in front of you. Can you feel them being together? Press your hands together hard. Does that feel different?"

"Lie down on your back. Can you feel the floor? How does it feel?" (hard, cold, slick) "Press your head (shoulders, arms and hands, back, seat, legs, heels) against the floor. Press your whole body hard against the floor and hold it still."

"Now let go. Don't move, just lie still and think about how you feel. Do you feel different than you did when you were pressing against the floor?"

2. At the intermediate level, you can proceed to the following exercises.

"This time we won't press, we'll just tighten the muscles in different body parts. Let's start with your face. Can you tighten all the muscles in your face? Make a smile with your cheeks and forehead. Now make a hard frown with your forehead, cheeks, mouth, and even your neck. Does a smile feel different from a frown?"

"Tighten the muscles in your neck, so your head is pulled down toward your shoulders. Hunch your shoulders up toward your head. Relax."

"Tighten your arms and make your hands into a fist."

"Tighten your back and abdominal muscles so that your lower back and hips press against the floor."

"Tighten your legs. Keep your legs tight and press your heels against the floor."

"Now tighten your whole body and become very tense."

"Let go and relax." Discuss the contrasting feelings of tension and relaxation, and point out that one can be still and tense or still and relaxed.

3. At the beginning level, the following exercises are suitable.

"Stand up and find yourself a big personal space. I want you to think about how it feels when you are moving through space and how it feels when you are standing still."

"When I say 'go,' step slowly forward with your right foot and bring your left foot up beside your right like this (demonstrate). Then hold that position. Ready, go."

"Now I want you to close your eyes and do the same thing. Go. This time I want you to think about how it feels when you are taking a step and how it feels when you stop and hold that position."

Have the children repeat the same movement with the left foot. Then instruct them to step right, left, close. (With older children you can proceed to right, left, hold in an open position, and take several steps.) Have them keep their eyes closed. Emphasize moving slowly and thinking about the contrasting feeling states associated with movement and stillness. Provide for a more extreme contrast by having the children walk fast and stop, and then run and stop.

At both the intermediate and advanced levels, discuss the relative amount of muscular force that must be exerted to stop when one is moving fast, and relate this phenomenon to the amount of tension created in the body.

SUPPORTING THE BODY WEIGHT

Study of the base of support pertains initially to the body parts that are touching the floor, and then to the fact that these body parts support the rest of the body. This material prepares the children to learn the concepts involving the body's base of support.

Key Concept
□ *When I move across the floor, part of my body is always touching the floor.*

I can name the parts of my body that touch the floor.
Different parts of my body touch the floor when I am in different positions.

Activities for Children

1. Have the children sit on the floor in their own personal spaces. "Who can name something that keeps its whole body on the ground when it moves?" The children will probably name a snake, so you can say, "Let's see how it feels to be a snake moving along the floor."

"Now who can name an animal that has four legs?" The children will give various answers, which you can reinforce by saying, "Let's see how it feels to be an animal that has four legs. Let's be a cat" (or whatever the children have mentioned). "Now let's be a dog. Now be an elephant."

Next you can ask, "Who can name something that moves about on two legs?" The children may name a bird, a monkey, or a kangaroo. Have them imitate these creatures.

You should then review and compare the three ways they have moved. "Let's look at the different ways you moved. Who can show me the first way you moved?" Call on one of the children to demonstrate.

"Who can tell me what part of Sally's body is on the floor? That's right, the whole front of her body. Good, Sally. Now who can show me the second way you moved?" Pick another child. "What parts of Jack are touching the floor? That's right, his hands and feet. Thank you, Jack. Now who can show me the last way you moved? What parts of Tom are touching the floor? Only his feet, that's right."

"Tom, will you just stand still right where you are? Sally and Jack, will you go over by Tom and get into the positions you were just in, without moving this time?"

"Class, let's think about the body parts supporting Sally, Jack, and Tom."

"How much of Sally is touching the floor?" (lots of her)

"How much of Tom is touching the floor?" (just his feet)

"What parts of Jack are touching the floor?" (hands and feet)

"Who has the biggest part of their body on the floor?" (Sally)

"Who has the smallest part of their body on the floor?" (Tom)

"Good. Let's remember about big body parts and small body parts touching the floor, because we're going to talk about this again."

When reviewing these concepts you can have the children put small body parts—such as hands and feet—on the floor inside a circle and large body parts—such as the back, front, seat, and legs—on the floor outside the circle.

Key Concept

□ *Whether I am still or moving, my weight must be supported by some body part(s).*

I can use different body parts to support my body while I am moving on the floor.

I must change body positions when I use different body parts to support my body.

2. Have the children scatter and stand. "What part of your body is touching the floor? That's right, your feet."

"Now sit down. What body part is touching the floor?" (seat)

"Stand up again. Close your eyes. Can you feel the weight of your body pressing your feet down against the floor?"

"Sit back down and put your legs straight out in front of you. Can you feel your body weight pressing your seat against the floor? Can you feel the weight of your legs and feet pressing the backs of your legs and your heels against the floor? We say that the parts of you that are touching the floor are *supporting* your body weight. What body parts are supporting you now? What body parts were supporting you when you were standing up? Can you use other body parts to support your weight?"

Guide the children in exploring the use of a wide variety of body parts to support their weight. (See Figure 13.1.) Ask children to demonstrate the different positions they discover. You may play music, instructing the children to change their base of support each time the music stops. Challenge them to support their weight (1) with a certain number of body parts, (2) on different levels, and (3) while making different kinds and sizes of shapes.

Challenge the children to move through space without using certain body parts to support their weight. For example, if you challenge them to move without using their feet as a base of support, some possible solutions are:

sliding on the abdomen
sliding on the seat
crawling
walking on the knees
rolling sideways

The parts of my body that are not supporting my weight can move about in space.

3. Guide the children in exploring how different body parts can be moved while the body weight is being supported on other body parts. For example, you can ask, "How can you move your head (arms, legs) while supporting your body weight on your back?"

"Show me how many different ways you can move your head (arms, shoulders, upper body) while supporting your body weight on your knees and feet."

"Make an angular shape with your arms while supporting your weight on your seat and legs."

Challenge the children to change the level, direction, size, and shape of movements in various ways.

I can use my body parts to support my partner's weight.

4. Have intermediate and advanced children experiment with various ways of supporting the body weight of their partners. (See Figure 13.2.) Emphasize the feeling states associated with relying on a partner to support one's body weight.

I can use my body parts to support my weight while I am moving in the air.
I can move in the air by climbing, hanging, and swinging.

BODY SURFACES

Back straight   Back rounded

Front straight   Front rounded

FEET

**Figure 13.1 Using
Different Body Parts as a
Base of Support**
*Body Surfaces: back,
Mickey Adair; front,
Bonnie Unsworth; Feet:
Mickey Adair; Body Parts
in Bent Positions: hands
and feet, Mickey Adair;
hands and knees, knees
and elbows, Bonnie
Unsworth; knees and feet,
knees, feet, Mickey Adair;
Hands and Feet in
Triangular Positions:
Mickey Adair; Seat:
Mickey Adair; Inverted
Positions: Mickey Adair*

Together   Forward stride   Sideward stride   One foot

Figure 13.1 (cont.)BODY PARTS IN BENT POSITIONS

Hands and feet

Hands and knees   Knees and elbows

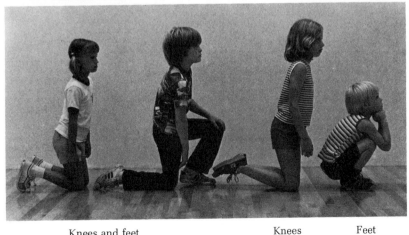

Knees and feet   Knees   Feet

Supporting the Body Weight   197

Figure 13.1 (cont.)

HANDS AND FEET IN TRIANGULAR POSITIONS

| Back to floor | Facing floor | Facing sideward |

SEAT

| Hands, seat, and feet | Seat and feet | Seat and legs | Seat |

INVERTED POSITIONS

| Shoulders and toes | Shoulders and head |

| Hands and head | Hands |

FEET AS A BASE OF SUPPORT

Leaning forward, hands together   Leaning backward, feet together   Backs pressing together

HANDS AS A BASE OF SUPPORT

Figure 13.2 Supporting a Partner's Body Weight
The Feet: leaning forward, Mickey Adair; leaning backward, Bonnie Unsworth; backs pressing together, Mickey Adair; Other Body Parts: Mickey Adair

5. The type and extent of climbing, hanging, and swinging activities that can be provided for are largely determined by the equipment available. Examples of appropriate equipment are shown in Figures 20.1 and 20.3. Among the ways children can be challenged to explore such activities are the following.

"Show me how many ways you can climb while using your hands and feet." (use a vertical wooden or metal ladder, rope ladder, cargo net, log structure, arch climber, climbing rope, or pegboard)

"Show me how many different body parts you can use to support your body weight while you are hanging." (use hands to hang on horizontal bar, parallel ladder, peg board, peg pole, arch climber, climbing rope, or cargo net; hang by knees, hips, or elbows on horizontal bar)

"Show me how many ways you can swing while supporting your body weight in the air." (swing while arms, hands, knees, or hips are supporting body weight on the horizontal bar; while hands and/or feet support body weight on the climbing rope; while hands hang onto the horizontal ladder)

Some of the activities listed above require considerable strength and coordination; others are a bit frightening at first. You must therefore know the capabilities of your group and guide their exploration at an appropriate level. Children cannot be expected to explore movement concepts if they are totally absorbed in mastering a skill. It is sometimes best to have certain children demonstrate certain movements while the rest of the class watches. The following points should be reviewed and discussed:

1. how the body is supported in the most common body positions—lying, standing, sitting in a chair, and sitting on the floor (Analyze the different feeling states associated with these positions.)

2. how different shapes and feelings are created by the use of different body parts to support one's weight

3. the different feeling states created by being supported on the floor and in the air

TRANSFERRING THE BODY WEIGHT

Key Concept

☐ *I move my body by transferring weight from one part of my body to another.*

While using my back or my front as a base of support, I can transfer my body weight by rocking or sliding.

In order to rock, my body must have a rounded shape.
Rocking feels different than sliding.
It feels different to rock or slide in different directions.

Activities for Children

1. Have the children lie on their backs. "What part of your body is supporting your weight? Who can show me how you can move with your weight on your back?" Select the children who discover they can rock or slide and have them demonstrate for the class.

Have everyone rock back and forth. "Now close your eyes and think about how it feels to rock." Ask the children to describe the shape of their bodies while they rock, and explain that the back must be rounded. Explain that, when they rock, weight is transferred from their hips to their shoulders and back again. (With older children, say, "from one end of the spine to the other.")

"Close your eyes and think about how it feels when weight is transferred upward from your hips, along your back to your shoulders, and back down again."

Have the children make rocking motions big enough to transfer weight to the seat and feet at one end and to the shoulders and head at the other. Point out that this exaggerated rock transfers weight to more body parts.

Ask the children if they can rock on any other body part. Have a child who rocks on his or her front demonstrate. Ask the entire class to rock that way.

"Can you rock farther on your back or your front?" Explain that they can rock farther on the back because it can be made more rounded.

Have the children rock on their fronts, turn over, and rock on their backs. Have them compare the feeling states aroused by these two positions.

"Can you rock in any other direction?" Have everyone rock from side to side. Ask the children to compare the feelings aroused by rocking forward and backward with that of rocking from side to side.

Have the children stand in a forward stride position. Ask them to rock forward and backward, transferring weight from the forward foot to the back foot and back again.

Have them stand in a sideward stride position and rock from side to side, shifting body weight from one foot to the other.

2. "Some of you discovered you could slide while using your back as a base of support. Let's all do that. What body parts must you use to help you slide?" (feet and hands)

"Everyone point your toes toward me. Now slide toward me. Slide away from me."

"Do that again, and this time think about how you use your hands and feet differently moving toward me and away from me."

Point out that they use their hands and feet to *pull* their bodies when sliding forward and to *push* when moving backward.

Have the children turn over and slide on their fronts.

Challenge them to slide in a direction other than backward or forward. When they discover they can slide sideways and circularly, discuss the differences.

Have them close their eyes and think about the different feeling states associated with sliding on their backs, on their fronts, and in different directions.

Have the children rock and then slide. Ask them to think about the feeling states aroused by these two movements.

Discuss how weight is transferred in rocking and in sliding.

If I rock from side to side hard enough, I will be rolling.

In rocking and rolling, my weight is transferred on rounded surfaces.

3. Have the children lie on their backs with their bodies fully extended, arms overhead.

"I want you to begin rocking from side to side. Make your rocking movements bigger and bigger. Finally let the movement tip you over on your front."

"Rock from side to side on your front, making your movements bigger and bigger until you tip over on your back."

"This time close your eyes. Think about how it feels to make your rocking motion bigger and bigger. Think about how it feels when you tip over. Now keep rolling over from back to front to back in the same direction."

Have the children do a series of sideward rolls in both directions. Challenge them to think of another direction in which they can roll. If the children can execute forward and backward rolls satisfactorily, you can encourage them to develop simple sequences involving rocking and rolling. If certain children cannot make the transition between rocking and rolling, it will be necessary for you to work with them individually, spotting them and encouraging them to execute the movements correctly.

Discuss the fact that in rocking and rolling weight is transferred on rounded body surfaces. Have the children execute rocking-to-rolling sequences, and identify the adjacent body parts utilized. In rocking forward into a roll, for example, the weight is transferred from the feet to the hands, then to the back of the head, neck, and shoulders, along the back of the body to the hips, and back to the feet. Point out that in a sequence of continuous rolls, the rock is part of the roll. Challenge the children to identify the part of this rolling sequence in which weight is transferred between body parts that are not structurally adjacent. (the transfer of the weight from the feet to the hands)

I can transfer my body weight by taking different kinds of steps on different body parts.

When I transfer my body weight with steplike movement, I must use nonadjacent body parts.

4. Have the children stand in their own personal spaces.

"Show me how many different ways you can move through general space using only your feet as a base of support." If the children have already learned to identify the locomotor movements, this challenge should evoke the full range of these movement possibilities. If they have not yet identified these movements by name, you can initiate them with appropriate verbal cues. Then list them on the board and explain that these movements are called locomotor movements because we use them to move through space.

"Show me how many different ways you can move using your hands and feet as a base of support." (See Figure 13.1.) Modify the challenge by instructing the children to use three body parts consisting of hands and feet. (See Figure 13.1.)

"Show me how many ways you can move by using your seat and feet as a base. Add your hands if you like." (See Figure 13.1.)

"Move through space transferring your weight from one body part to another. See how many different body parts you can use as a base of support."

Add movement elements to the assignment by challenging the children to move forward using one set of body parts and backward using another. Challenge them to move on a high level using two body parts (for example, both feet) as a base of support, and on a low level using one (or more) body parts (such as the back or the back and feet). Point out that when they transfer body weight using steplike movements, they must use nonadjacent body parts.

Challenge the children who are sufficiently skilled to create inverted body positions, such as moving from a headstand into a forward roll or from running into a cartwheel.

Identify the various body parts they use to move in the ways described above. ("What body parts did you use when you moved on a high level? on a low level? forward? backward?" and so on.)

Gradually add further movement elements by challenging the children to transfer their weight from one body part to another while they create different pathways, make large and small movements, make various shapes, and move fast and slow.

Challenge the children to use different body parts to support their weight in stillness and in motion. For example, "I'm going to play music. I want you to move through space using one set of body parts and, when the music stops, to transfer your weight to another set of body parts and hold that position very still as long as there is no music (demonstrate). When the music begins again, transfer your weight to another set of body parts (continue demonstrating) and again move through space."

These concepts may be reviewed and reinforced by having the children move through an obstacle course or circuit that requires them to transfer the body weight by using different body parts.

5. Have intermediate-level children develop a movement sequence with three distinct phases: a beginning, a middle, and an end. Prescribe that the sequence use different body parts as bases of support and that there be smooth transitions between phases.

Have some of the children demonstrate their sequences. Then ask each what body parts he or she used as bases of support, whether the weight transfers involved adjacent or nonadjacent body parts, and whether or not the sequence fulfilled the assignment. (That is, did it have three distinct phases and were the transitions smooth?) Point out the strengths and weaknesses of each sequence, and make suggestions for improving it.

Challenge the children to develop another sequence, and to polish and refine its structure and execution.

6. For advanced students, design movement problems involving the use of various body parts as bases of support and various movement elements in a sequence of three phases. Some examples of such problems follow.

a. "Begin your sequence with a slow movement on a high level, use your back as a base of support in the second phase, and conclude your sequence with your body in an inverted position." (Sample solution: step forward slowly, execute a forward roll, and end in a tripod or headstand.)

b. "Move on a low level throughout your sequence. Use your feet, hands, shoulders, and back to support your weight." (Sample solution: move from rocking on the back into a backward roll and then a back-lying position.)

c. "In the first and last phases of your sequence, transfer your weight onto adjacent body parts; in the middle phase, transfer it to nonadjacent parts. Move in two different directions and create an angular pathway on the floor."

MOVING ON AND OFF BALANCE

Key Concept

□ *When I move I am either balanced or off balance.*

My body has a center of gravity, which is an imaginary point in the center of my body.

When I am balanced, my center of gravity is above and within my base of support.

I am off balance when my center of gravity is outside my base of support.

When I am off balance, I must regain my balance or I will fall.

Activities for Children

1. Introduce advanced beginners to the concept of the center of gravity by pointing out its location. Explain that the body's center of gravity is located a little lower than the navel and in the center of the body.

Have the children place the middle finger of one hand on the front of the body and a finger of the other hand on the back at the height of their centers of gravity. Ask them to close their eyes and press gently toward the center of the body. Have them concentrate on that point at the center of the body.

Have the children walk, jump, and slide. Then discuss the locations of their centers of gravity in relation to their bases.

Have them roll sideward, backward, and forward. Explain that rolling causes the center of gravity to fall outside the base of support, making the body tip over.

"Sit down on a mat, your legs extended on the floor in front of you. Extend your arms parallel to your legs. Now slowly tilt your upper body backward until your center of gravity falls outside your base and you must lie down to regain your balance." (See Figure 13.3.)

"Repeat the same movement, but this time stop right at the point where your center of gravity begins to fall outside your base and hold your body in that position."

"Let go and fall backward."

**Figure 13.3 Moving from
On to Off Balance: Tilting
Backward**
Mickey Adair

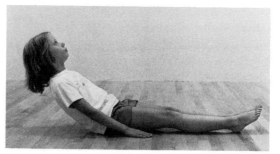

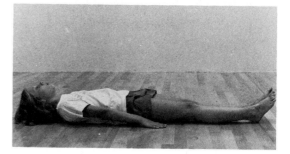

Kinesthetic Awareness

"Repeat the movement again, and this time think about how it feels to hold your position and resist the force of gravity."

Key Concept
□ *When I fall I must land.*

When I land some body parts must support my weight.
The force of the landing must be absorbed.
Force may be absorbed by bending my body parts.
A soft surface absorbs some force.
I will not land as hard if force is absorbed gradually.

2. "Assume a position in which your weight is supported on your knees and feet, your body is upright, and your hands hang down at your sides." Have the children lean forward until their centers of gravity fall outside their bases. (See Figure 13.4.) Caution them to use their hands to catch themselves. "Why do you fall over so soon when you start moving forward? Why do you have to use your hands when you fall forward?" (to keep from falling so hard; to catch themselves)

Explain that they were off balance and falling forward, and so they had to land on some body part and absorb the force of the landing. Their hands became new bases of support, and the force was absorbed gradually by flexing the wrists, elbows, and shoulder joints.

Repeat the experiment, instructing the children to catch themselves with their hands, but to keep their arms straight. Discuss why this position makes them stop suddenly, rather than gradually, and how it jars their bodies. Have them repeat the movement flexing the joints of the arm. Discuss the difference between the two movements.

Have one child perform a forward roll without rounding his or her back. Then have the child repeat the movement with a very rounded back. Point out that when the back is flat the whole back hits the mat at once. When the back is rounded, the parts of the back touch the mat one after the other, thereby absorbing force gradually.

Arrange the tumbling mats in a pile and have the children jump off the pile onto a mat. Then have the children repeat the jump, instructing them not to bend their legs when landing. Explain that landing in this manner jars the body because the entire body must absorb the force. Have them jump again, flexing their ankle, knee, and hip joints. Discuss how flexing the joints absorbs the force of the landing. (see Figure 13.5).

Figure 13.4 Moving from On to Off Balance: Tilting Forward
Mickey Adair

**Figure 13.5 Flexing
Ankle, Knee, and Hip
Joints to Absorb the Force
of a Landing**
Mickey Adair

Moving on and off Balance

Figure 13.6 Correct Body Position for a Downward Fall

Top across: Land with feet close together, on the balls of the feet. Flex hip, knee, and ankle joints to absorb more force. Bottom across: Use hands as an additional base of support and flex arms to absorb the force. Round the body and go into a forward roll.
Mickey Adair

Explain to the children that cushioned surfaces absorb some of the force of landing, and that they should always be sure mats are placed where they may fall, purposely or accidentally.

Explain that the soles of tennis shoes provide some cushioning for the feet and therefore absorb some of the force of landing.

3. With intermediate-level students, compare the "hardness" of such supporting surfaces as concrete, asphalt, wood, carpeting, tumbling mats, and builder's mats. Explain that the body must absorb any force that is not absorbed by the landing surface, and discuss the bearing of this fact on the possibility of injury.

Have the children fall from a standing position and gradually absorb the landing force by executing forward, backward, and sideways rolls.

4. Advanced Level. Have one child suddenly push his or her partner over. Instruct the child who is pushed to land by flexing his or her joints and going into a roll.

Have the children practice falling from various heights and landing in a variety of positions. Cover the following points.

a. When falling straight down:

(1) Land with the feet hip width apart. This position provides a wider base than if the feet are together. Spreading the feet more than hip-width creates a wide, angular position of the legs, predisposing the person to ankle and knee injury. (See Figure 13.6.)

(2) Land on the balls of the feet so that some of the landing force can be absorbed by extending the joints of the foot. This position also allows for greater range of motion in the ankle joints.

(3) A fall from a considerable height will create more landing force. Safely absorbing this force may necessitate the use of additional body parts. You can use your hands as an additional base of support, and flex your arm joints to absorb some of the force. If still more force remains to be absorbed, you may go into a forward roll.

b. When falling forward:

(1) Avoid landing on your knees, elbows, or head.

(2) Attempt to land as described in (a) above.

(3) You may twist your body, so as to land on your rounded shoulder, and go into a roll.

(4) You may twist your body so as to land on your seat (the body's best-padded surface).

c. When falling backward:

(1) Flex your joints and, if possible, go into a roll.

(2) If you cannot roll, take your body weight on your hands, flex your arms, and land on your seat.

STABLE VERSUS UNSTABLE BODY POSITIONS

Key Concepts

☐ *The force of gravity is always acting on every object on the earth.*

☐ *The stability of my body is affected by the size and shape of its base of support and by the relationship of my center of gravity to that base.*

☐ *Maintaining a balanced position without moving is called static balance. Moving in a balanced position is called dynamic balance.*

The force of gravity is exerted vertically downward toward the center of the earth.

My center of gravity is an imaginary point in the center of my body, around which all my body parts exactly balance.

The movements of my body and all other objects are affected by the line of gravity, an imaginary line extending vertically downward through the center of gravity toward the center of the earth. (See Figure 13.7.)

In order to maintain my balance, the line of gravity must fall within my base of support.

Activities for Children

1. Intermediate and Advanced. Explain the concept of the line of gravity, by using a chart or by holding a plumb line beside one of the children.

Have the children stand up. "Tilt your body forward as far as you can. When you have to move another way, do so." (They will be forced to take a step forward to avoid falling over.)

"Now repeat the movement and concentrate on how far you can tilt before you have to take a step."

Explain that one can tilt forward until the line of gravity falls outside the base of support; then one must establish a new base of support in order to regain balance. Point out that such balance is *dynamic* because the body is moving and there is a changing relationship between the location of the center of gravity and the base of support.

"Now tilt backwards and notice how far you can tilt before having to adjust your base of support. Why can you tilt farther forward than backward?" (because the line of gravity soon falls beyond the heel, whereas the front of the foot serves as a larger base of support)

**Figure 13.7 The Line of
Gravity**
Left: The line of gravity
extends vertically
downward through the
center of the base of
support; Middle and right:
If the line of gravity falls
outside the base of support,
the body loses stability.
Mickey Adair

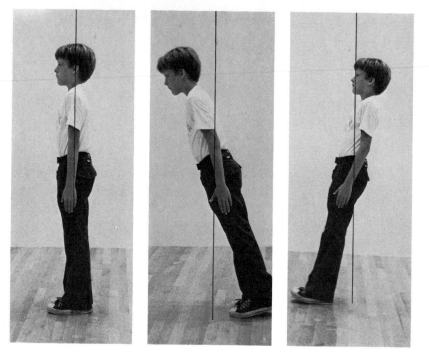

Challenge the children to lean sideways and answer the same
question.

Discuss the size of one's base of support when standing on two feet.

Ask the children to lie down on their backs, and to compare the size
of this base of support and that of a standing position.

Have the children crawl. Explain that this body position is very stable
due to the number of body parts supporting the body weight, the size of
the base, and the fact that the line of gravity is constantly within the
center of their base of support.

Have the children walk on their knees. Discuss the relative sizes of
the knees and feet as bases of support, and relate this factor to the
instability of this body position.

Have the children stand on two feet, and then on one foot. Ask them
which position is more stable and why.

Ask the children to rock and then to roll. Point out that the line of
gravity always remains within one's base of support while rocking, but
falls outside the base during a roll, requiring a new base of support to be
established.

Have the children use different body parts as bases of support in positions of static balance. (See Figure 13.1.) Ask them to locate their centers of gravity and to relate the line of gravity to their bases of support in each position.

WHY THE BODY MOVES THE WAY IT DOES

Key Concept

□ *My body has a structure and, as is true of any object, its structure determines the ways in which it can function.*

My skeleton is my body's framework.
My skeleton is made up of bones.
The bones in different body parts are formed differently.
The form of the bones in each of my body parts determines how I can move it.

Activities for Children

1. Show the children a model of the human skeleton. (Those sold for decorative purposes at Halloween can be used.)

Explain that the skeleton is the framework of the body and that many objects have frameworks. Ask the children if they have seen a house being built; if they have, ask how it looked before the walls and roof were put on. Show them pictures of the frameworks of a bicycle and an umbrella. (See Figure 13.8). Point out that the framework of each object gives it a shape and determines how it can be used. In a house, for example, the doors, windows, and walls are made for different purposes, and are thus shaped differently and placed in certain locations. The front of a bicycle is made so as to provide a place to attach the handlebars, and the framework allows the front wheel to turn from side to side. An umbrella is made so it can open and close (change from big to little), and when it is open the top is curved. Ask why an umbrella is shaped this way and why it is made to open and close. Demonstrating with an umbrella will stimulate the children's interest and help them recognize that it has moving parts. You may also have the children move like the umbrella and simulate its curved shape.

Have the children look at the skeleton again, and discuss the relationship between the shapes and functions of given bones. The following examples will illustrate exploration of these points.

a. Skull. Have the children feel the bony structure of their skulls. "Which part of your skull can move?" (the lower jaw) "Now move your jaw. What do you do that involves moving your jaw?" (eat or chew, talk, laugh) Have them explore ways to move their whole heads. (tilt backward, forward, and sideways; rotate it from side to side)

**Figure 13.8 Frameworks
of Different Objects**

Kinesthetic Awareness

b. Shoulders. Have the children touch their clavicles and scapulas. "How many ways can you move your shoulders?" (up, down, forward, backward) Have them touch their clavicles and feel how the end nearest the arm moves up and down when they move their shoulders.

c. Rib Cage and Spine. Ask the children to touch the front, back, and sides of their rib cages and to run their fingers down their spinal columns. "How does this body part move?" Have them place their hands on their hips and rotate the upper part of their trunks while keeping their hips in place. Have them bend forward, backward, and sideward from the waist. Review the movement of the chest associated with breathing.

d. Hips. Have the children touch and feel their hip bones. Explain that the hips do not move freely because their main function is to support other body parts. Point out how the legs are attached to the hips, and note that the legs can move freely because they are attached to a body part that supports them well. Relate this phenomenon to the arms' attachment to the shoulder girdle. Explain that the entire trunk of the body is designed to support the arms, legs, and head, just as the trunk of a tree supports its branches and the shaft of an umbrella supports the top.

e. Arms. Challenge the children to move their arms as many ways as possible. Discuss the movement of each joint. Have them swing their arms and then let the swing become a full circular motion. Point out that this wide range of motion is made possible by the way the shoulder joint is structured. Compare the movement of the shoulder joint with that of the elbow. Explain that the elbow joint is a hinge joint and compare its range of movement to that of other hinged objects, such as a door or a box lid.

f. Legs. Challenge the children to move their legs in different ways. Compare the movement of the hip joint with that of the shoulder joint. Point out that the shoulder joint has a greater range of motion, which enables one to do a wider variety of things with one's arms. But the hip joint is structured to support movements requiring greater strength. Compare the movement of the knee and elbow joints. Have the children put one arm beside a knee and turn the arm so that it is bending in the same direction as the knee. Doing so will enable them to see that the knee and elbow joints are both hinge joints, though in ordinary use they bend in opposite directions.

g. Wrists and Hands. Have the children bend and rotate their wrist joints and then flex and extend the joints of their hands and fingers.

"How would you have to move if there were no joints in your wrists and hands—if there was one long bone from your elbow to the ends of your fingers? What difference would it make if you didn't have a thumb?" Challenge them to experiment with picking up and holding objects as if they didn't have thumbs.

h. Ankles and Feet. Ask the children to move their feet in different ways. Then have them compare the structure and function of hands and feet. Have them put one hand palm down on the floor beside a foot and look at the similarities and differences between the two body parts. Explain that hands and feet were made to do different things. "What are feet made to do?" (support the body) "What are hands made to do?" (hold and manipulate objects)

Challenge the children to pick up objects, such as a piece of cloth or marbles, with their toes. When they have become fairly adept at picking up and holding marbles with their toes, make the exercise into a relay race. Initially instruct the children to pick up a marble with only one foot; then have them pick up one with each foot and hold both while walking on their heels a certain distance. A further challenge is to see who can pick up the most marbles with his or her toes.

Have the children support their body weight on their hands. Point out that this is much more difficult than supporting their weight on their feet and that picking things up with their toes is much harder than doing so with the hands.

My muscles (1) help hold my body together and give it shape, (2) pad my body parts, and (3) move my body parts.

2. Ask the children to touch the muscles of different body parts, such as the arms, legs, seat, neck, and abdomen. Explain that muscles help to hold bones together and to give the body a rounded shape. Have them again touch arms, legs, neck, and seat and note that all these body parts have rounded shapes.

Explain that muscles also pad body parts. Have the children gently bounce their seats and legs on the floor, noticing how their muscles pad these body parts.

Explain that the most important thing muscles do is to help the body move. Have the children bend and straighten various body parts and execute some of the locomotor movements.

Explore how the muscles work. Explain that muscles are attached to bones, and that the muscles move the bones by pulling them in different directions. This process can be demonstrated by attaching a piece of elastic to the model of the skeleton. Tie one end of the elastic to the shoulder and the other end to the upper part of the forearm to simulate the biceps muscle. Pull the elastic tight enough so it stretches when the arm is fully extended. Grasp the wrist joint of the skeleton and pull it upward a short distance; then let go and allow the elastic to flex the elbow joint. Repeat the experiment, asking the children to note that the elastic gets shorter as it pulls on the forearm. Explain that muscles too get shorter when they pull on bones. Have the chidren place the palm of the left hand on the right biceps and feel the contraction of the muscle when the elbow joint is flexed.

3. At the intermediate level, you can introduce the concept of *antagonistic muscles*. Explain to the children that muscles can only contract, creating a pulling force. Therefore each body part has two sets of muscles, one on the front and one on the back; one set flexes the joint and the other extends it. In most movements one set of muscles relaxes while the antagonistic muscles contract. However, one can contract both sets at the same time so they pull against each other. Have the children experience this phenomenon by contracting both sets of muscles in the arms and legs. Ask them to note that doing this restricts the affected body part's range of motion; the pull of the muscles against each other prevents freedom of movement. The concept of antagonistic muscles can be illustrated by tying an additional piece of elastic on the back of the model skeleton's upper arm to simulate the triceps muscle.

4. Advanced Level. Show the filmstrips *The Skeletal System* and *The Muscular System* from the series "Systems of the Human Body."[1] In these filmstrips, the concepts introduced above are reviewed and pictorially related to a variety of movement activities. You may also use the filmstrip *The Nervous System* to relate the functions of the nervous and muscular systems.

Key Concept
□ *The force created by my muscles controls the way I move.*

> *My muscles control (1) where my body, my body parts, or an object moves; (2) whether a movement is weak or strong; and (3) the speed of a movement.*

5. "Make a small movement with your right hand. Now hold your

---

[1]Available from Educational Activities, P.O. Box 392, Freeport, New York 11520.

right forearm in your left hand like this (demonstrate) and move your right hand around in different directions. Can you feel the muscles of your right forearm? Can you feel them controlling how your right hand moves?"

Have the children hold one lower leg with both hands while moving the foot. Explain how the muscles of the lower leg control the movements of the foot.

Have the children use their hands to pull their bodies along the floor in a front-lying position. Explain how the arm muscles provide the force.

Have them slide on their backs by pushing and pulling with their arms and legs. Discuss how the muscles move the arms and legs, and thus the whole body.

6. Give each child a balloon; challenge the children to keep their balloons up in the air. Afterwards discuss how they moved their body parts in order to control the movement of the balloon.

"Tap your balloon lightly to see how high it goes. What must you do if you want your balloon to go higher?" (hit it harder) Challenge the children to make the balloons go as high as they can.

Discuss the different amounts of force used to tap the balloon lightly and to hit it hard. (This concept will be reviewed and reinforced in the section on basic ballhandling skills.)

Note: Tying one end of a piece of yarn to the child's wrist and the other end to the balloon helps the child visualize the effect of a striking force. It also helps small children control the movements of their balloons.

7. Have the children experiment with weak and strong movements of their body parts. Some movements that may be used are:
    bringing the hands together softly/clapping them together vigorously
    walking with ordinary steps/stamping the feet
    jumping and landing softly/jumping and landing hard
    pretending to throw a ball hard/pretending to toss a feather lightly
    walking like a fairy/walking like a giant
    walking like a cat/walking like an elephant
    walking weightless in outer space/walking with a heavy load on your shoulders
    moving like an angry gorilla/moving like a happy bird
    a crash/a tinkle
"Which movements felt heavy, strong, or hard? Which ones felt light, weak, or soft?"

Ask the children again to bring their hands together softly and to clap vigorously. Note that one of these movements is soft and the other is hard, and ask if there is any other way in which these two movements differ. (one is fast and the other slow)

Challenge the children to move through space slowly; then rapidly.

Challenge them to execute heavy slow movements; then heavy fast movements.

Challenge them to move light and slow; then light and fast.

Ask each child to select an animal and move as it moves. Have some of the children demonstrate their animal movements, and let the other children guess the animal and describe its movements in terms of time and force.

Have each child select a second animal that moves differently from his or her first selection and imitate it.

8. Intermediate Level. Develop problems involving several movement elements, such as the following.

"With a partner, make a series of large, light movements on three different levels."

"With a partner, tell a story in movement using heavy slow movements."

"Develop a short sequence in which you use heavy fast movements. In your sequence move toward and away from your partner and on two different levels."

"Develop a sequence in which one person moves fast while the other moves slow and one uses strong movements while the other uses light movements."

9. Advanced Level. Design more complex movement problems by increasing the size of the group and adding additional elements. Some examples of advanced movement problems follow.

"Develop a sequence that has a beginning, a middle, and an end. Begin on a low level with slow light movements, in the middle use some body parts other than your feet to support your body weight, and have your body form a strong angular shape at the end."

"Develop a sequence with your partner. Include fast and slow movements and strong and weak movements. At some point in your sequence, one of you must support the other's body weight in some way."

"With four other people, develop a moving sculpture using strong slow movements on three different levels."

"With your partner, develop a sequence in which one of you leads and the other follows. Move in a curved pathway using light slow movements."

1. Develop a series of learning activities in which children will experience the difference between feeling tense and feeling relaxed.

2. Develop a lesson in which beginning or intermediate children explore the use of different body parts as bases of support.

3. Develop a lesson in which children explore rocking and then progress to rolling forward and backward. Emphasize the feeling states associated with these movements.

4. Teach the lesson you developed in activity 3 to a group of children. Evaluate the learning outcomes. If any of the children have difficulty executing the rolls correctly, analyze the source of the problem and suggest ways to eliminate it.

5. Work out a solution to one of the movement problems on pages 203–205.

6. Practice developing movement problems involving weight transference and the use of different body parts as bases of support.

7. Develop a sequence of learning activities designed to introduce children to the concept of the center of gravity. Then progress to the study of moving on and off balance.

8. Practice falling and landing in various positions.

9. Develop a group of learning tasks designed to familiarize children with the correct way to land.

10. Explain the concept of the line of gravity. What is the relationship of this line to stable and unstable body positions?

11. Develop a lesson in which children explore the relationship between the body's structure and its functions.

12. Develop a lesson in which children explore creating and controlling force. Emphasize the feeling states associated with these movements.

**SUGGESTIONS
FOR FURTHER
READING**

BARLIN, ANNE, and BARLIN, PAUL. *The Art of Learning Through Movement.* Los Angeles: Ward Ritchie, 1971.

BILBROUGH, A., and JONES, P. *Physical Education in the Primary School,* 3rd ed. London, England: University of London Press, 1968.

BROER, MARION. *Efficiency of Human Movement,* 3rd ed. Philadelphia: W. B. Saunders, 1973.

DIMONDSTEIN, GERALDINE. *Children Dance in the Classroom.* New York: Macmillan, 1971.

GILLIOM, BONNIE. *Basic Movement Education for Children: Rationale and Teaching Units.* Reading, Mass.: Addison-Wesley, 1970.

JOYCE, MARY. *First Steps in Teaching Creative Dance.* Palo Alto, Cal.: National Press Books, 1973.

MAULDON, E., and LAYSON, J. *Teaching Gymnastics.* London, England: MacDonald and Evans, 1965.

MORISON, RUTH. *A Movement Approach to Educational Gymnastics.* London, England: J. M. Dent and Sons, 1969.

MURRAY, RUTH. *Dance in Elementary Education,* 3rd ed. New York: Harper & Row, 1975.

Part Four

Developing the Basic Skills

Once children have developed awareness of their movement potential, they are ready to enhance their understanding and skill levels, this is the primary concern of Part Four.

Part Four presents a systematic sequence of learning activities designed to enhance the children's basic skill development.

Chapter 14 is devoted to an in-depth analysis of the basic movement skills, followed by a series of learning activities that progresses from simple exploratory movements to complex structured sequences. Chapter 15 focuses on the basic skills employed in controlling the movement of an object. These skills are designated *manipulative*, because the child is learning to control his or her own body while maneuvering an external object.

The content of this chapter emphasizes the movement needs of children in the early elementary grades, but some activities requiring more advanced skill development are included.

The subject matter of chapters 16 and 17 is designed for the upper elementary grades. Chapter 16 introduces the physical laws and mechanical principles that regulate movement, and then applies them to the correct execution of the basic sports skills. In Chapter 17 the fundamental physical skills are analyzed and guidelines for teaching them proposed.

The subject matter of Part Four is designed to help the child understand the components of efficient movement.

Because such understanding is an essential aspect of the child's education, this material is presented as a guide to the development of this area of the curriculum. This content is specific and its arrangement in the text is sequential. When utilized as lesson content for a particular group of children, however, it should be arranged and presented in a way that will enhance individualized instruction.

14 The Basic Movement Skills

The basic movement skills are the body actions common to all movement activities. There are two types of such skills, those that move the body *through* space (locomotor skills) and those used to assume various bodily positions *in* space (nonlocomotor skills). The purpose of the basic movement skills component of the physical education curriculum is to enable each child to use his or her own body as a more efficient and expressive movement instrument. This goal is attained by studying the relationships between the basic movements and movement elements (time, space, and force), by practicing correct execution of each basic skill, and by increasing the children's awareness of the feeling states evoked and expressed by executing these movements in certain ways.

THE LOCOMOTOR MOVEMENTS

When studying the locomotor movements, children should learn how the various body parts contribute to their correct execution: how the feet function as the base of support and how other body parts are used to create force and help maintain stability during weight transference. Young children are capable of discovering these principles in broad outline, and older children should be able to analyze each movement verbally.

Walking

In walking, each leg alternates between a supporting phase and a swinging phase. One foot or the other is in contact with the floor at all times, and they are in simultaneous contact with the floor for a brief period. The body's weight is transferred sequentially from the heel to the outside edge of the foot, the ball of the foot, and the toes. The feet should move parallel to each other, the toes pointing straight ahead. The arms should swing freely and rhythmically in opposition to the legs; that is, the right arm and left leg swing forward simultaneously, as do the left arm and right leg. Correct walking is free-flowing and rhythmic. Walking is also a relatively stable movement, since at least one base of support is always in contact with the supporting surface.

You should observe each child's walking pattern, preferably without letting the child know he or she is being scrutinized: self-consciousness can cause children to move tensely and awkwardly, and may prompt some to perform. In observing, you should give attention to the following factors:

1. *Posture.* The body should be in proper alignment, with the head erect. Watch for forward tilt of the head and rounded shoulders.

2. *Foot position.* Feet should be close together, with toes straight ahead. Children who "toe out" slightly may nevertheless be walking correctly, but exaggerated toeing out causes the child to walk on the inside of the foot rather than transferring weight from the heel to the outside edge of the foot. (See Figure 14.1.) "Toeing in" (walking pigeon-toed) results in a flat-footed step. If the feet are too close together or far apart, movement will appear jerky.

3. *Transference of weight.* A smooth, gliding step is a function of transference of weight from the heel to the outside edge of the foot and from there to the ball of the foot, pushed off by the toes. Too much vertical thrust of the leg and/or incorrect weight transference will result in bobbing or bouncing of the body.

4. *Ankle, knee, and hip flexion.* Correct flexion of the knee, ankle, and hip joints gives the movement a flowing quality. Locked knees or tenseness in the joints causes the movement to appear to be "jarring" the child's body.

5. *Arm swing.* The arms should appear to swing freely and smoothly in opposition to the legs. A well-coordinated walking pattern will have a rhythmic, flowing quality that makes the child appear to be moving effortlessly through space. (See Figure 14.2.)

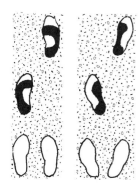

Figure 14.1 Normal Walking Pattern and Toeing Out Compared

Activities for Children

The following learning experiences constitute full exploration of all the dimensions of walking. If the children have already been introduced to them, these activities can serve as a review. In such a case, you may wish to omit some activities and to review the factors they employ

**Figure 14.2 Normal
Walking Pattern**
The arms swing freely in
opposition to the legs.
Mickey Adair

The Basic Movement Skills

later, in conjunction with other locomotor movements. If you are working with older or more experienced children, certain activities should be combined to create more challenging movement problems.

1. a. "Walk freely through general space."

b. "Walk, and stop when you hear the signal" (a drumbeat or some other sound).

c. Have the children walk on different levels (high, medium, low).

d. Have them walk in different directions (forward, backward, sideways).

e. Have them walk along different pathways (straight, angular, curved).

f. "Walk taking small steps, and then large steps. Take a small step with one foot and a large step with the other."

g. "Walk slow and then fast."

h. Have the children make different body shapes (narrow, wide, twisted) while walking.

i. "Take heavy steps and then light steps."

j. "Walk with your body tense and then relaxed."

k. Have the children walk in different directions (*along* the sidewalk, *across* a line, *around* a tree, *through* the door, *out of* the room, *toward* the school building, *away* from the street).

l. Have them walk with their body parts on different levels (arms overhead, knees raised high on each step, head down, arms straight out from your shoulders, elbows overhead, upper body bent forward).

m. "Raise and lower your body while walking."

n. Have the children use the supporting body parts in different ways while walking. "Walk with your feet close together and then far apart. Walk on tiptoe. Walk on your heels. Walk with your toes out, in, and straight ahead. Walk with your legs stiff. Lift your heels backward and spank them on your seat on each step."

o. Have the children use different body parts as bases of support while walking. (See Figure 13.1.)

p. Combine two or more dimensions. For example, "Walk forward on a low level and backward on a high level. Use small steps while walking fast and big steps while walking slow."

q. "Swing the arm and leg on the same side of the body in unison while walking."

r. Have the children express different emotions (happy, angry, frightened, tired) by walking in different ways.

2. Imagery is a very effective means of drawing the children's attention to the potential expressiveness of walking.

a. "Pretend you are holding a beach ball and your knees spank it each time you take a step."

b. "Walk like the tightrope walker in the circus. Walk like an astronaut in outer space. Walk like a giant. Walk like a fairy. Walk like soldiers marching in a parade. Walk as though you were sneaking up on someone. Walk as though your body were very heavy. Walk as if you were walking on ice, in deep snow, in water. Imitate the walks of different animals."

3. Have the children walk to a rhythmic beat. A drumbeat is a sharp, clear sound to which children can readily respond and is therefore very useful for introducing them to rhythmic accompaniment.

a. Instruct the children to take one step to each drumbeat. Beat out a moderate tempo they can follow easily as they walk freely about the room.

b. "Were you walking fast, slow, or in between?" (in between)

c. "This time I'm going to beat the drum a little faster, so you'll have to walk faster—but be sure to walk with the beat."

d. Beat the drum slowly.

e. Begin slowly and gradually increase the tempo.

f. Begin fast and gradually decrease the tempo.

g. Alternately increase and decrease the tempo.

h. Have the children execute fast and slow walking steps in combination with other variations in movement. Some examples follow.

(1) "Walk forward on the fast beat and backward on the slow beat."

(2) "Take small steps on the fast beat and large steps on the slow beat."

(3) "Walk on a high level on the fast beat and a low level on the slow beat."

(4) "Walk along a straight pathway on the fast beat and a curved pathway on the slow beat."

(5) "Take heavy steps on the slow beat and light steps on the fast beat."

(6) Challenge older children by combining several such variations in each problem. For example, "Use small steps while you are walking forward on a fast beat and large steps while you are walking backward on a slow beat."

4. Introduce the concept of an *accented beat*, explaining that it is harder or stronger than other beats. Demonstrate by beating out a phrase in 4/4 time, accenting the first beat of each measure. Explain

that you are grouping the beats. Challenge the children to count the beats in each group. "How could you tell how many beats were in the measure?" (the accented beat marks the beginning of a new group) "How can you accent your walking steps?" (by stamping our feet)

a. Instruct the children to group their walking steps in the same way you group the drumbeats, by accenting the first of the four beats.

b. Challenge them to walk in an angular pathway by turning on each accented beat.

c. Have the children practice walking backward, accenting the first beat in each measure.

d. Have them reverse direction on each accented beat. (forward four steps, backward four steps)

5. Have the children form a circle, and increase the length of the movement phrase by having the children walk forward eight steps and backward eight (moving into and out of the circle, or around the circle counterclockwise while moving forward and clockwise while moving backward).

a. Add variations in tempo, level, size, and force.

b. Challenge the children to develop a sequence of movements to a specified number of beats.

6. Introduce musical accompaniment and have the children walk in time to the beat. Marches are very suitable for beginners, but they should also experience more lyrical music.

7. a. Introduce singing games and folk dances in which walking is the basic step. Some that are suitable for the beginning level are: The Farmer in the Dell, Go Round and Round the Village and Pussy Cat (Bowmar Singing Games, Album 1); Gay Musician (RCA LPM 1625); Jolly is the Miller (Folkraft 1192B or RCA 45 41-6153); Jack and Jill (E-Z 78 903-A); Mulberry Bush (RCA 45 41-6151); Sing a Song of Sixpence (E-Z 78 1003-B); The Snail (Bowmar Singing Games, Album 2); and Did You Ever See A Lassie? (E-Z 78 902-A).

b. At the intermediate and advanced levels, introduce the following concepts central to the rhythmic analysis of walking patterns.

(1) Ordinary walking steps have a moderate tempo approximating that of a quarter note. Thus walking is usually accompanied by either 2/4 or 4/4 time. A very slow walk may be performed in 2/2 time.

(2) Each step takes the same amount of time and therefore the rhythm is even.

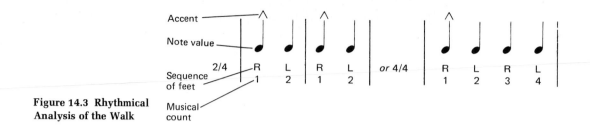

Figure 14.3 Rhythmical Analysis of the Walk

(3) Walking patterns may be rhythmically analyzed as shown in Figure 14.3.

(4) If on the first beat of the above measures you step forward with the right foot, the accented beat will always coincide with a step on the right foot.

c. Teach intermediate and advanced students folk dances with more complex movement patterns, such as: The Thread Follows the Needle (E-Z 78 4225); Shoo Fly (Folkraft 1102 and 1185); and Bingo and Glow Worm (RCA LPM 1623).

8. Introduce activities involving walking on a balance beam. Introduce young children to balance beam activities by having them walk forward and backward along a straight line on the gym floor. Then have them walk on a low balance beam. (The same skills are required whether the beam is high or low, and some children fear walking on a regulation-height beam. Children who are ready to do so should be allowed to, but those who are afraid should not be forced.)

a. Have the children practice walking forward and backward in the following positions:

(1) both arms out to the side, shoulder height

(2) both arms hanging beside the body

(3) hands clasped behind the body

(4) arms folded over the chest

(5) arms straight out in front of the body

(6) arms straight overhead

b. "Walk sideward, right foot leading."

c. "Walk sideward, left foot leading."

d. "Walk forward to the center, turn around, and walk backward to the end of the beam."

e. "Walk sideward to the center, turn, and continue walking sideward to the end of the beam."

f. "Walk to the center, kneel, rise, and walk to end of beam."

g. "Walk with a beanbag balanced on your head."

h. Have the children execute all of the foregoing maneuvers with their eyes closed.

The Basic Movement Skills

i. Have them walk with a weight in each hand, and then with a weight in one hand.

j. "Walk forward and backward while bouncing a ball."

k. "Walk using four body parts as a base of support."

l. "Walk using three body parts as a base of support."

Running

Running differs from walking in the speed of locomotion. It is a less stable movement than walking, because the body has no base of support from the time the back foot pushes off from the supporting surface until the forward foot touches the floor. The position of the running body in space and the movements of the body parts resemble those of walking. However, the increased tempo and momentary period of nonsupport necessitate some bodily adjustments.

The body leans forward slightly while running. This position is attained by increasing the amount of flexion in the ankle joint of the driving leg. The knees are lifted higher in running than in walking. The elbows are bent. The bent arm swings diagonally in front of the body when the opposite leg is exerting the driving force (that is, when the left leg is pushing off from the floor, the right arm swings diagonally forward across the chest).

The more rapid tempo of running results from three factors: the greater propulsive force exerted by the leg muscles; the increased length of the stride; and the increased frequency of weight transference.

In a slow run, the ball of the foot makes the first contact with the floor; as the upper body moves forward over the foot, the heel is lowered. As the body's center of gravity moves farther forward, the heel of the driving foot is lifted, permitting a pushoff from the ball of the foot and the toes. Thus a slow run is characterized by a two-phase movement of the driving foot, consisting of a transfer of weight from the ball of the foot to the heel and back to the ball of the foot. As the tempo of the run increases, the amount of the foot's surface that contacts the floor decreases; in a full-speed run, only the ball of the foot and the toes come in contact with the floor.

The driving force of the leg is exerted in a more horizontal direction in running than in walking, as is shown in Figure 14.4. Thus the propulsive force of running causes the body to move more forward and less upward than when walking. Friction is an important factor in running, due to the small base of support, the increased length of the stride, and the amount of propulsive force exerted in a horizontal direction. If the foot slips when contacting the floor, some of the driving force will be absorbed, the rhythm of the movement will be broken, and it will be more difficult to maintain balance. Thus children should run

Figure 14.4 Direction of the Moving Force in Walking and Running
Mickey Adair

barefoot or in shoes with non-slip soles and should not run on wet or slippery surfaces.

Most children do not need to be taught how to run, since they automatically progress from walking to running when the tempo of the movement increases. Children who run a lot and are allowed to run freely usually teach themselves how to execute running patterns correctly. Nevertheless you should observe the children in order to identify those who do not run correctly. The key factors you should check are:

1. *Foot position.* The toes should point straight ahead. Toeing in or out causes the child to push off with the side of the foot, resulting in a lack of driving force. When the children run fast, check to see that they push off and land on the balls of the feet. Landing on the heels and running flat-footed are common errors. It may be necessary to have some children walk on the toes and the balls of the feet until they "feel" the correct foot position. And having them exaggerate the forward lean of the body enables them more readily to feel their weight coming forward over the ball of the foot, rather than backward over the heel.

2. *Body position.* The entire body should be inclined slightly forward. Some children may bend at the waist, rather than flexing the ankles. If the entire body is not inclined forward, the force of the legs will cause vertical motion and the child's body will appear to move up and down in a "jogging" pattern. Correct body position can be practiced by having the children stand facing a wall. Ask them to stand on

the balls of the feet, support themselves by placing their hands on the wall, and incline their bodies forward.

3. *Leg position.* The knee of the driving leg should be slightly flexed during the pushoff phase of the run; a straight-leg pushoff will jar the body. Knee flexion should be increased as the leg is brought forward, and the leg is then extended as the child strides forward. Insufficient knee flexion and extension cause a shortened stride and decrease speed. It may be necessary to tell children to bend their knees more and extend their legs more fully as they "reach out" with the forward foot.

4. *Arm swing.* The bent arms should appear to swing freely in opposition to the legs. The arms should swing close to the body, the hands moving diagonally forward in front of the chest. The arm swing should originate in the shoulder joint and the shoulders should appear relaxed. Tension may be apparent in elevation or rounding of the shoulders. If so, children should practice freely swinging their arms in different directions while standing and running. You may also ask them to shrug or pull forward their shoulders and to contrast those feeling states with that experienced when the shoulders are relaxed.

In a skilled running pattern, all the body parts appear to be working together to produce a smooth, flowing movement.

Activities for Children

1. a. Have the children run through general space. Caution them to remember to stay in their own personal spaces.

b. Have them run and stop on a signal.

c. Have them walk and stop, then run and stop. Compare the two experiences. (With older children discuss why it is easier to stop suddenly when one is moving slowly, introducing the concept of forward momentum. Also discuss the need when stopping to shift the body's center of gravity from a forward position backward over the center of the base.)

d. Ask the children to run in the following ways, and to compare the feeling states they evoke:

(1) forward and backward
(2) fast and slow
(3) taking small steps and large steps
(4) on different levels
(5) along different pathways
(6) taking heavy steps and light steps
(7) with the body tense and relaxed
(8) at a moderate tempo and in slow motion

e. Combine two or more of the above variations. For example, have the children run forward fast and backward slowly, or run forward in an angular pathway and backward in a circular pathway.

f. Have the children run in place and through space with different body parts assuming different positions. For example, instruct them to run with the arms overhead, straight out in front of the body, clasped over the chest, and hanging down at the sides; run lifting the knees high and then with the knee joints barely flexed; and run with the feet as far forward as possible and then making the heels strike the seat after each step.

g. Have the children play follow-the-leader while running, and while alternately walking and running. Challenge the leader to vary the level, pathway, tempo, and positions of various body parts.

h. Have the children run while keeping in step with a partner. Have older children do the same with three and then four people.

2. a. Designate spaces on the floor by positioning jump ropes in different shapes. Have the children run into, out of, around, and between the spaces.

b. Have the children run and dodge stationary objects and/or people. Then have them gradually increase the tempo as they dodge other children.

c. Have the children play games that involve running and dodging, such as tag games.

3. Organize activities, such as races and relays, in which running speed and agility are factors.

4. Have the children run to a rhythmic beat.

a. Ask the children to run to slow, moderate, and fast drumbeats.

b. Gradually increase and then decrease the tempo of the drumbeat as they run.

c. Have children on the intermediate level respond to the accented beat by taking a heavy step. Progress to a *waltz run,* instructing them to increase the flexion in the knee joint of the leg that takes the weight on the first beat of 3/4 accompaniment. Once they are familiar with the rhythm of the running waltz, have them add a slight body lean to the side of the leg that takes the weight on the accented beat.

d. Play music in various tempos and ask the children to run in time to it.

5. Combine walking and running.

a. Challenge the children to walk on the slower drumbeat and run on the faster beat.

b. Specify the number of walking and running steps they are to take in time with the drumbeat (for example, "walk eight steps, then run sixteen steps"). Ask how much faster the running steps are than the walking steps. (twice as fast)

c. Play musical accompaniment with a distinct change of tempo, and challenge the children to run in time to the fast phrases and walk to the slower phrases.

d. Combine walking and running with other variations. For example, have the children walk backward and run forward; walk in an angular pathway and run in a circular pathway; walk on a low level and run on a high level; walk backward using small steps and run forward using large steps; and walk with heavy steps and run with light steps.

6. Introduce singing games and folk dances in which running is a basic step. Some of those that are appropriate for use on the beginning level are: Pussy Cat (Bowmar Singing Games, Album 1); Chimes of Dunkirk, Seven Steps, and Turn Me Round (Bowmar Singing Games, Album 2); Bluebird Through the Window, Nixie Polka, Swiss May Dance, and Ten Little Indians (Bowmar Singing Games and Folk Dances, Album 3); and Dance of Greeting (RCA LPM 1625).

7. At the intermediate and advanced levels, introduce rhythmic analysis of running, treating the following concepts:

a. Running steps have an even rhythm because each step occupies the same amount of time.

b. Running steps may be executed to a moderate or fast tempo.

c. Running may be performed in various meters, usually 2/4, 3/4, 4/4, or 6/8. If performed in 3/4 time with a lilting quality, it is referred to as a running waltz.

d. Moderate running steps are usually executed in temporal intervals equivalent to quarter notes; fast running steps are equivalent to eighth notes, and very fast running steps equal sixteenth notes.

e. Running patterns may be rhythmically analyzed as shown in Figure 14.5.

8. Introduce some of the more advanced folk dances that include running steps such as: Mayim (Folkraft 1108); Norwegian Mountain March (RCA LPM 1622); and Troika (Hoctor LP 4027).

9. Invent movement problems for intermediate and advanced

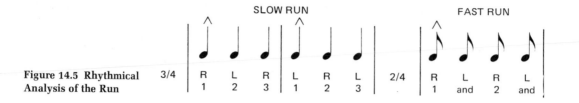

Figure 14.5 Rhythmical Analysis of the Run

children in which they must utilize running. Possible themes for such problems are approaching apparatus; approaching forward and backward rolls, cartwheels, and round-offs; and developing movement sequences that include various dimensions of the movement elements.

Jumping

A jump is executed by taking off from one or both feet and projecting the body upward into space. The body is momentarily suspended at the highest point of the lift; then the force of gravity causes it to drop back to the supporting surface. The landing is always on both feet. (See Figure 14.6.)

The force necessary to project the body is produced by flexing and then quickly extending the legs. When the purpose of the jump is to gain height, the knees are bent and the arms lowered with the elbows slightly flexed. The arms swing upward as the knees are straightened and the body stretched. Children should be encouraged to reach as high as they can on the extension phase. (See Figure 14.6.) The balls of the feet should contact the floor first on landing, and the knees should be flexed to absorb the landing force. When jumping for distance from a standing start, force is increased by assuming a crouching position. The forward lean of the body is counterbalanced by swinging the arms backward and upward. The sudden extension of the flexed ankle, knee, and hip joints and the forward and upward swing of the arm give the jump an explosive quality that propels the body forward and upward. When landing, the heels contact the floor first, and the body's center of gravity must be quickly carried foward in order to maintain a balanced position. (See Figure 14.6.)

In many activities a jump is preceded by a run and a takeoff from one foot. The forward momentum of the preparatory run adds force to the projection of the body. The initial phase of such a jump is identical to that of a leap; the two movements differ only in landing pattern. In a takeoff from a preparatory run, the forward knee is lifted forcefully to produce upward momentum and to shift the body's center of gravity

The Basic Movement Skills

backward over the driving leg. In this position the extension of the supporting leg forces the body upward and forward. During the suspension phase of the movement, the driving leg is thrust forward so as to land on both feet simultaneously. The momentum of the body in such a jump makes for an increased landing force, which must be gradually absorbed by flexing the ankle, knee, and hip joints. Balance is more easily regained if the feet are hip-width apart during the landing.

Children naturally begin jumping as soon as they develop sufficient strength, balance, and coordination. Small children jump vertically because balance is relatively easy to maintain; they usually begin by jumping down from stairsteps, boxes, or other objects. As skill and coordination increase, children should practice jumping over objects, jumping for height and distance, and combining jumping with other basic movements.

Although most children have developed a satisfactory jumping pattern by the time they enter school, some children are "earthbound" and others do not use their body parts efficiently. You should therefore conduct a screening test to detect such problems. This test can also serve as a pretest if you use the data to establish performance objectives and as a basis for the selection of activities.

The type of screening test you administer is determined by the children's developmental level. The jumping patterns of younger children may be evaluated by requiring them to perform the following sequence:

1. From a height of twelve inches, take off from two feet and land on two feet.

2. From the same height, take off from one foot and land on two feet.

3. Jump up from two feet and land on two feet.

4. Jump forward from two feet and land on two feet.

5. Jump up from one foot and land on two feet.

6. Jump forward from one foot and land on two feet.

7. Run and jump from one foot and land on two feet.

8. Jump backward from two feet and land on two feet.

9. Jump backward from one foot and land on two feet.

10. Jump from two feet, turn a quarter-turn, and land on two feet, continuing around to the starting position; then do the same with half-turns.

11. Jump over a stationary object.

Figure 14.6 Correct Jumping Patterns for Covering Maximum Distance
Top across: vertical jump; Bottom across: horizontal jump
Mickey Adair

12. Jump back and forth over a rope that is raised slightly after each jump.

13. Jump over a moving object (such as a rope that is swinging back and forth).

The most common measures of older children's jumping skill are the vertical jump and the standing broad jump. National norms for children ten years of age and older on the standing broad jump are provided in the AAHPER Youth Fitness Test Manual.

The most common errors in jumping are:

1. failure to flex the hip, knee, and ankle joints on takeoff and landing

2. incorrect body position due to the center of gravity being too far forward or backward

3. failure to extend the legs fully on takeoff

4. failure to use the arms to gain upward momentum

5. incorrect timing of arm movements

6. sideward rather than upward swing of the arms

7. landing on the heels or flatfooted

8. unequal distribution of weight on both feet in landing

Activities for Children

1. Challenge the children to jump.
   a. forward, backward, and sideways
   b. in straight, angular, and curved pathways
   c. on a low level and on a high level
   d. while making narrow, wide, and twisted shapes with their bodies
   e. slow and fast
   f. landing hard and landing softly

2. Place bicycle tires or rope circles on the floor and have the children jump into, out of, and around them.
   a. Have the children jump onto and off of old tires, inner tubes, or bedsprings covered with a piece of plywood.
   b. Place an object such as a shoe, rope, or handkerchief on the floor and challenge the children to jump over it forward, backward, and sideways.

3. a. Challenge the children to jump and turn a quarter-turn, a half-turn, and as far as they can turn.

b. Challenge them to jump and initiate turns with the following body parts:
  (1) shoulders
  (2) hips
  (3) ankles and feet
  (4) arms (with elbows bent and then with arms fully extended)
  (5) arms overhead and the body twisting like a corkscrew

4. a. Challenge them to jump as high as they can and land as softly as they can.
b. Place a pole across two milk cartons or wooden blocks cut off at a height of two inches, and have the children jump over it.
c. Arrange a series of several poles, increasing their height at one-inch intervals to the maximum height the children can jump (landing on two feet). With older children, start with the first poles placed at the minimum height they can jump and increase the height at one-inch intervals.

5. a. Suspend balloons from the basketball backstop or another overhead structure. Challenge the children to jump and hit them.
b. Have the children jump and reach for marks at various heights on the wall.

6. a. Jump the Pole. Have the children form a single circle with a radius of approximately eight feet. Stand in the center holding one end of a nine- or ten-foot bamboo pole extended so that its other end rests on the floor slightly beyond the children. (See Figure 14.7.) Tell the children you are going to move the pole around the circle and they are to jump over it when it reaches them. Slowly move the pole around the circle, keeping the far end on the floor.
b. Increase and decrease the speed at which the pole is moving. Change the direction it is moving, and then alternate directions. Do not eliminate the children who miss: they are the ones who need the most practice.
c. Jump the Shot. In the upper grades, substitute a rope with a shoe tied to the far end for the bamboo pole. When the rope is swung around the circle, the weighted end will rise off the floor, forcing the children to jump higher. The height and speed can be gradually increased.

7. Jump the Brook. Position two long jump ropes on the floor so that the distance between them is 18 inches at one end and approximately 48 inches at the other end (See Figure 14.8). Challenge the children to jump across the brook, starting at the narrow end and gradually moving up until they can no longer jump clear across. Challenge them to take

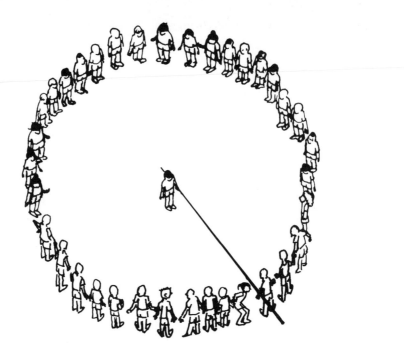

Figure 14.7 Formation for the Game *Jump the Pole*

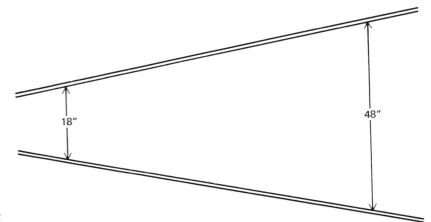

18″

48″

Figure 14.8 Diagram for the Game *Jump the Brook*

The Basic Movement Skills

off from a standing position until they miss; then change to a running approach.

8. Imagery. Challenge the children to jump as would popcorn popping, a jack-in-the-box, a bouncing ball, a frog, a rabbit, and a kangaroo.

9. Jump and Roll. Have the children practice transferring their weight from a forward jump into a forward roll and from a backward jump into a backward roll. Then have them jump over an object and go into a forward roll.

10. Jump and Fly. As soon as the children have developed the skill and confidence necessary to perform a satisfactory jump, introduce the concept of flight. The body is in flight whenever it moves unsupported through the air. (See Figure 14.9.) The three phases of flight are the takeoff, the flight through space, and the landing.

If the landing is on both feet, flight is an extension of a jumping pattern; if the landing is on one foot, flight is an extension of hopping or leaping. In jumping, emphasis is placed on takeoff and landing. The children's attention should now be directed to the flight phase, which begins when the feet leave the supporting surface and continues until a body part again contacts a supporting surface.

a. Explain the concept of flight to the children.

b. Challenge them to take off from the floor, moving forward, then backward, and then sideward.

c. Have the children take off from a bench forwards and backwards.

d. Have them fly onto and then off of the bench.

e. Gradually increase the height of the flight by having the children jump from higher objects.

11. a. Challenge intermediate and advanced children to make different narrow, wide, curled, and stretched shapes with their bodies while in flight.

b. Challenge them to twist and turn their bodies in flight.

c. Challenge them to vary the movements that follow landing. For example, have them land, stop, and hold the landing position; land and roll; land and jump; land, turn, and roll.

d. Have children fly over an object, a partner, or a bench. Then progress to flying over, landing, and rolling.

e. Challenge them to fly with a partner.

f. Introduce the children to the concept of assisted flight and have them practice jumping, grasping, and hanging onto a bar, rope, or piece of apparatus.

g. Discuss the following points:

**Figure 14.9 Take-Off,
Flight Through Space,
and Landing**
Mickey Adair

The Basic Movement Skills

(1) what one must do in order to fly higher (increase the driving force)

(2) why more force is required to propel the body upward than to move it forward (one must push against the force of gravity)

(3) why a greater landing force is created by flight than by transferring one's weight in rolling or stepping (due to the momentum of the falling body)

12. Have the children jump to a rhythmic accompaniment.

a. Ask the children to jump to slow, moderate, and fast drumbeats. Discuss the difference in the feeling states associated with jumping at each tempo.

b. Gradually increase and decrease the tempo as the children are jumping.

c. Have the children jump with a heavy step on the accented beat and light steps on the unaccented beats.

d. Have them jump in place to the beat, then forward, then backward, and then sideward.

e. Specify the number of beats they are to jump in place and in each direction, such as four beats forward, four backward, and so on.

f. Instruct the children to jump and turn quarter-turns to the beat. Increase the beat from slow to fast.

g. Combine walking and jumping, and then running and jumping, to the beat. For example, have the children walk eight steps forward (or backward) and then jump eight steps forward (or backward). Add variations in such dimensions of movement as level, pathway, size, shape, and force.

h. Read a story or poem about an animate or inanimate object that jumps or bounces, and have the children interpret the story in creative movements that include jumping.

13. At the intermediate and advanced levels, introduce rhythmic analysis of jumping, emphasizing the following concepts:

a. Jumping has an even rhythm.

b. Jumping steps may be executed at slow, moderate, or fast tempos.

c. Jumping may be performed in any meter.

d. Slow jumps may be executed at temporal intervals equivalent to whole or half notes; moderate jumping steps equal quarter notes; and fast jumps equal eighth notes.

e. Jumping patterns may be rhythmically analyzed, as shown in Figure 14.10.

14. Introduce intermediate and advanced children to the Bunny Hop. Explain that the movements are actually jumps and that bunnies do in fact jump, not hop.

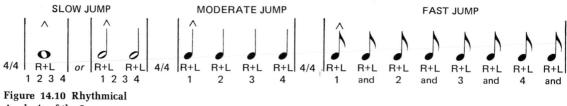

Figure 14.10 Rhythmical Analysis of the Jump

15. Invent movement problems in which intermediate and advanced children must use jumping in various ways. The themes of these problems should include:

a. taking off and landing in various ways

b. jumping as a preparation for and recovery from flight

c. jumping onto and off of objects and apparatus of varying heights and structure

d. developing movement sequences characterized by variations in the movement elements and smooth transitions between phases

e. creative rhythms that utilize jumping and flying patterns in conjunction with other basic movements

16. Help the children develop skill at vertical jumping and improve their ability to broad jump. Use objective measures of these skills in pre- and posttesting.

17. Additional jumping activities are:

a. Jumping stunts

(1) "Jump and slap your heels, both at the same time."

(2) "Jump and click your heels together before landing."

(3) "Jump over the stick. (With the palms of the hands downward, hold a wand horizontally in front of your body. Swing the wand backward as you jump forward over it.)"

b. Jump rope activities. Be sure to distinguish between the different kinds of steps utilized in rope jumping. The children should learn to distinguish between skipping, running, hopping, and jumping over a rope.

c. Jumping races and relays

d. Jumping while keeping in step with a partner, and then with three other people

e. Jumping on the trampoline. Children should be introduced to trampoline activities as early as possible, and children in the upper grades definitely need the movement experiences associated with jumping and rebounding from such a surface.

　　　　The Basic Movement Skills

Hopping

A hop is performed by taking off from one foot and landing on the same foot; otherwise the execution of a hop is the same as that of a jump. A hop is a much more difficult movement than a jump for two reasons: (1) balance must be maintained over a single, small base of support; and (2) the force necessary to project the body into space must be exerted by one leg.

In the preparatory phase of the hop, the body's center of gravity must be shifted sideward over the supporting foot. The hip, knee, and ankle joints of the supporting leg are flexed so that a driving force may be exerted by their sudden extension. The elbows are flexed. Raising the arms during the liftoff phase helps to elevate the body, and the arms also serve as a means of balancing the body.

In hopping, one takes off and lands on the ball of the foot. The hip, knee, and ankle joints should be flexed to absorb the landing force. In a series of hopping steps, the reaction to the landing force helps initiate the next step.

In order for a child to execute a hop, he or she must have developed sufficient strength to lift the entire body weight using the muscular force of only one leg. Hopping also requires the ability to maintain static and dynamic balance on a very small base of support, the ball of the supporting foot. Most children begin hopping at approximately four years of age, and thus have developed a well-controlled hopping pattern by the time they enter school. However, some children have considerable difficulty hopping; thus individual children's skill should be assessed. Gross motor problems may be detected simply by asking each child to hop on the right foot, the left foot, over a line, and over a small object such as a beanbag. Followup tests should be administered to children who have difficulty on this screening procedure, in order to determine the nature of their problems. Some factors that may adversely affect a child's hopping patterns are:

lack of leg strength

inability to maintain static balance

inability to maintain dynamic balance over such a small base

inability to lift the body off the floor (being "earthbound")

lack of practice

As this list suggests, the problem usually involves balance. Thus the remedial program should focus first on helping the child develop the physical ability and confidence necessary to maintain a well-balanced body position while moving. Only then should you progress to the development of a hopping pattern.

1. Challenge the children to hop on one foot and then the other:
a. in different directions
b. in different pathways
c. slow and fast
d. on different levels
e. while making different shapes with their body parts

2. Place bicycle tires, ropes, a ladder, or geometric designs on the floor, and have the children hop into, out of, and around them. (See Figure 14.11.)

3. Play Jump the Pole (see page 243), substituting hops for jumps.

4. Have the children hop over a rope that is being swung back and forth for them. Then have them hop over the rope while turning the rope themselves.

5. Challenge the children to combine a hop and a turn. Then have them combine a hop and a jump, incorporating the variations listed in Activity 1 above.

6. Encourage the children to play hopscotch.

7. Combine a step and a hop, having the children step-hop in different directions and along different pathways. Have them step-hop, pretending to be Indians.

8. Have the children hop to a rhythmic accompaniment.
a. Repeat activities 12a–f on page 247, substituting hopping for jumping.
b. Combine walking and hopping; jumping, hopping, and walking; and jumping and hopping, having the children execute each movement a specified number of beats.
c. Have them step-hop to a drumbeat in 2/4 time, stepping to the accented beat and hopping to the unaccented beat. If necessary, call out "step, hop, step, hop" as they execute the movement.
d. Introduce folk dances in which the step-hop is a basic step. Two such dances that can be used on the beginning level are Crested Hen (RCA LPM 1624 or Hoctor LP 4027) and Ten Little Indians (RCA 45 41-6150 or E-Z 78 1002-A).

9. At the intermediate and advanced levels, introduce the rhythmic analysis of hopping. Explain that the only difference between hopping and jumping is that in hopping the weight is supported and transferred on one foot rather than two feet.

Then explain the rhythmic structure (see Figure 14.12) and execution of a step-hop. Have the children practice the step-hop to a drumbeat as

Figure 14.11 Hopping Through a Ladder
Mickey Adair

Figure 14.12 Rhythmical Analysis of the Step-Hop

| 2/4 | step
R
1 | hop
R
2 | step
L
1 | hop
L
2 | *or* 4/4 | step
R
1 | hop
R
2 | step
L
3 | hop
L
4 |

you count the beats. Begin with a relatively slow beat and then increase the tempo.

10. Introduce intermediate and advanced children to the Indian War Dance (Bowmar Singing Games and Folk Dances, Album 3).

Then teach the folk dances Hora (Hava Nagila) (RCA LPM 1623) and Bleking (RCA LPM 1622).

11. Teach intermediate and advanced children a basic Schottische step.

a. Explain that the basic step consists of three short running steps followed by a hop.

b. Have the children listen to a Schottische with a strong accent, such as the Bummel Schottische (RCA LPM-1622). Have them clap out the rhythm and identify the meter (4/4).

c. Have them practice the basic step alone and then with a partner (couples in skaters' position, facing counterclockwise in a double circle).

d. Introduce the second basic Schottische step, the *step-hop, step-hop*.

e. Combine the first and second basic steps, performing two measures of each.

f. Introduce the rhythmic analysis of the basic Schottische step (see Figure 14.13).

g. Introduce variations on the Schottische step.

(1) Have the children practice the combination of the two basic steps, with the variation of kicking the nonsupporting leg forward and upward on the hop in both of the basic steps. Next have them kick the leg backward on the hop; then sideward. Finally instruct them to kick forward in the first and third measures and backward in the second and fourth measures of each of the basic steps.

(2) Have the children, in couples, perform two basic Schottische steps in a forward direction, drop hands, and do the four step-hops in individual small circles, turning away from each other. (The children on the outside of the circle will turn clockwise and the children on the inside will turn counterclockwise.)

(3) Repeat (2), having the children on the inside of the circle do the four step-hops in place while the children on the outside turn under their right arms. After the next two Schottische steps, the children on the inside turn under the left arms of the children on the outside. Continue alternating.

(4) Have the couples do the four step-hops clockwise in a small circle while holding each other in a shoulder-waist position.

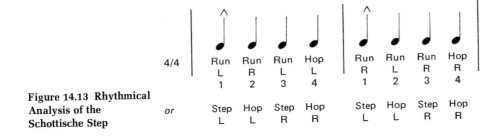

Figure 14.13 Rhythmical Analysis of the Schottische Step

4/4	Run	Run	Run	Hop	Run	Run	Run	Hop
	L	R	L	L	R	L	R	R
	1	2	3	4	1	2	3	4

or	Step	Hop	Step	Hop	Step	Hop	Step	Hop
	L	L	R	R	L	L	R	R

(5) Have the partners move diagonally forward away from each other on the first Schottische step and diagonally forward toward each other on the second step, followed by the pattern described in (3) above on the four step-hops.

(6) After two regular Schottische steps in a forward direction, have the couples turn back-to-back and do four step-hops. (The children on the inside of the circle will be moving toward the center of the circle, while those on the outside will be moving toward the walls.) Then have them turn around and move back to place while executing step-hops to the beat of the next two measures.

h. Review the movement concepts pertinent to the basic Schottische steps and variations. Points that should be noted are:

(1) basic movements (running and hopping)

(2) meter (4/4)

(3) tempo (fast)

(4) spatial dimensions

(a) direction (moving forward; kicking forward, backward, and sideward)

(b) pathway (curved while moving in a circle, angular while moving diagonally)

(c) relationship to partner (side-by-side and back-to-back, moving away from and moving toward)

(5) feeling states (lively, active, fast, exhausting, and the like)

i. In an advanced class, the study of the Schottische may be concluded by teaching the folk dance Weggis (Hoctor LP 4029).

Leaping

A leap is actually an exaggerated running step, in which the stride is elongated and the body lifted higher into the air. The body is suspended in the air for a longer time, and more force must be absorbed when landing.

The elongation of the stride is brought about by more fully extending the legs during the suspension phase of the leap. The higher lift results from a more vertical and more forceful pushoff from the floor and an upward swing of the arms when landing. The ball of the foot contacts the floor first; the force of the landing is absorbed by lowering the heel to the floor and flexing the ankle, knee, and hip.

Successive leaping steps are difficult for children to execute because the body's center of gravity does not move forward over the leading foot during landing. Running steps are therefore often combined with leaping. The running steps make for a forward momentum that helps lift the body into the air on takeoff.

Children will usually leap spontaneously when challenged to step over an object or space on the floor while running. A leap enables them to do so without breaking the pattern of movement.

The teacher should invent movement problems that involve leaping and observe the children as they participate. Due to the difficulty of the movement, the children's leaping patterns may vary considerably. Some may not exert enough pushoff force to elevate the body adequately and some may use their arms incorrectly. Those who find it difficult to maintain balance during the suspension and landing phases of the leap may compensate by landing on two feet. Specifying a reasonable distance to cover and encouraging the children to reach out with the legs and continue running after the leap will help to correct their landing patterns. Music with a distinct lifting quality may help by stimulating greater elevation of the body.

Activities for Children

1. Have the children run several steps and then leap, continuing until they appear to have mastered the rhythm of the movement.
   a. Challenge them to run and leap over:
      (1) a shoe
      (2) a rope on the floor
      (3) two ropes laid parallel on the floor to simulate a stream of water (Gradually increase the width.)
   b. Limit the number of running steps in the approach to three, so that the sequence becomes *run, run, run, leap*.
   c. Lay jump ropes on the floor at evenly spaced intervals and challenge the children to run and leap over them. Have them count the running steps they take prior to each leap and then attempt to standardize the approach so as to take the same number of steps between each rope.
   d. Substitute sticks balanced on milk cartons, blocks, or road cones for ropes. Let the children practice leaping over these objects, and then use them as the ropes are used in (c) above.
   e. Have two children hold the ends of a jump rope parallel to the

The Basic Movement Skills

floor while the other children leap over it. Have them raise the rope about two inches after the others have successfully leapt over it at a given height. (See Figure 14.14.)

2. Have the children perform continuous leaps across the floor in step with a partner. Have them keep in step while executing two running steps and a leap.

3. Play Jump the Brook (pages 243–245), substituting leaps for jumps.

4. Leaping and flying
a. Challenge the children to fly onto and off of objects or apparatus using a leaping pattern.
b. Have them leap onto the box or bench and jump off of it.
c. Have them fly over objects, a partner, or a bench, using a leaping pattern.
d. Have them fly with a partner using a leap.

5. Leaping to a rhythmic accompaniment
a. Have the children leap to a drumbeat.
b. Have them move with the drumbeat while executing a series of *run, run, leap, run, run, leap*.
c. Introduce intermediate and advanced children to the rhythmic analysis of leaping and of leaping combined with running. (See Figures 14.15 and 14.16.) Have them repeat activities (a) and (b) above while attending to the rhythmic analysis.

Skipping

A skip combines two other basic movements, the walk and the hop. It is executed as is the step-hop, except that the timing is different. Both phases of the step-hop occupy the same amount of time, giving the movement an even rhythm. In the skip, the walking step occupies more time than does the hop; thus the rhythm is uneven (see Figure 14.17 on page 259). Skipping consists of stepping forward on one foot (the right), quickly hopping on the same foot, stepping forward on the opposite foot (the left), and quickly hopping on that foot. Swinging the arms forward and upward in opposition to the legs helps to maintain balance and to provide the body upward momentum during the hopping phase. The weight is on the balls of the feet throughout the movement. When skipping forward, the body's center of gravity is shifted forward over the toes. When skipping backward, the center of gravity is shifted backward over the heels.

Skipping is a very rhythmic movement; the unique feeling state that accompanies it is associated with the lifting phase of the step. When correctly executed, the skip expresses joy, happiness, and freedom.

Because it combines two other basic movements and has an uneven

Figure 14.14 Leaping over a Rope
Mickey Adair

Figure 14.15 Rhythmical Analysis of the Leap

4/4 | Leap Leap Leap Leap |
      R   L   R   L
      1   2   3   4

Figure 14.16 Rhythmical Analysis of the Leap Combined with the Run

4/4 | Run Run Leap Run Run Leap |
     R   L   R   R   L   R
     1 and 2 and 3 and 4 and

The Basic Movement Skills

rhythmic pattern, skipping is a complex movement. Some children have difficulty learning to skip, and some can skip on one foot but not the other. You should therefore ask the children to skip around the room in general space and observe their skipping patterns. When you note a child experiencing difficulty, attempt to determine the source of the problem: some children cannot hop, while others are unable to combine the two movements into a coordinated pattern. In both cases, you must work with the child on a one-to-one basis. First check his or her ability to hop (see page 249). If a child can execute a well-coordinated hop, have him or her practice walking and hopping. Then slowly progress to a step-hop. When the child can perform a step-hop satisfactorily and confidently, explain the timing of the skip and demonstrate skipping steps while supplying the verbal cues "s-t-e-p hop, s-t-e-p hop" or " s-l-o-w quick, s-l-o-w quick." Take the child's hand and skip with him or her beginning at a slow tempo. Provide additional practice by having a partner skip with the child and by playing music with a strong lifting quality.

Activities for Children

1. Have the children skip forward through general space.

2. Have them skip in and out of spaces and around objects.

3. Challenge them to skip in circular and angular pathways.

4. Challenge them to skip in step with a partner.

5. Have them skip to music:
a. alone
b. in a single circle, moving counterclockwise
c. taking eight skipping steps counterclockwise and eight clockwise
Repeat.

6. Challenge them to turn as they skip.

7. Challenge them to skip backward.

8. Have them skip rope.

9. Imagery. Have the children skip in such a way as to show they are:
a. happy
b. free
c. on the beach
d. eating something that tastes good
e. feeling very light

10. The many folk dances and singing games in which skipping is a basic step are an ideal medium for practice, since the children can relate the music and the movement. Some folk dances and singing games that can be used with children in the primary grades are: Did

You Ever See a Lassie?, How D'ye Do My Partner,[1] and Mulberry Bush (Bowmar Singing Games, Album 1); Come Skip With Me, A Hunting We Will Go, and I See You[2] (Bowmar Singing Games, Album 2); Hansel and Gretel and Shoemaker's Dance (RCA LPM 1624); Seven Jumps and Pop Goes the Weasel (RCA LPM 1623); and Round and Round the Village (RCA LPM 1625).

11. Introduce intermediate and advanced children to the rhythmic analysis of skipping, emphasizing the following concepts:

a. Skipping has an uneven rhythm.

b. The uneven rhythmic pattern results from the hop phase receiving one-half or one-third the time allotted to the step phase.

c. The skip is usually done in 6/8 time, although it may be executed to 2/4 time. It may be rhythmically analyzed as shown in Figure 14.17.

12. Have the children invent movement sequences that combine skipping with other basic movements. Such sequences may include changes in level, direction, pathway, and range, and combinations of the following relationships between partners: side by side, leading and following, approaching and parting, close together and far apart.

13. Teach folk dances in which skipping is a basic step. The following dances contain movement patterns that challenge children in the upper grades: Oh Susanna and Virginia Reel (RCA LPM 1623); Gustaf's Skoal and Come Let Us Be Joyful (RCA LPM 1622); Jingle Bells (Folkraft 1080); and Skip to My Lou (Bowmar Singing Games and Folk Dances, Album 3 or Folkraft 1192).

Sliding

A sliding step is always executed in a sideward direction: see Figure 14.18. (If the same movement is performed forward or backward, it becomes a gallop). In a slide to the right, the right foot moves sideward and takes the weight. The left foot is then drawn up beside the right and the weight is transferred to the left foot in preparation for the next step. In a sequence of slides in one direction, the same foot continues to lead. Because its first phase is a slow gliding step and the second phase is a quick closing step, the rhythm of the slide is an uneven long-short pattern similar to that of the skip. Although the slide may be executed slowly, it is usually performed at a rapid tempo, the feet staying close to the floor.

[1]Also on RCA LPM 1625.
[2]Also on RCA LPM 1625.

The Basic Movement Skills

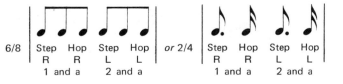

Figure 14.17 Rhythmical Analysis of the Skip

Children usually slide spontaneously if you ask them to move sideward without crossing one foot over the other. A child who has difficulty executing the rapid weight change in the last phase of the slide should practice the step at a slow tempo. When the sequence of the movement has been learned, the tempo can be increased.

Activities for Children

1. Have the children form a single large circle and slide counterclockwise (right foot leading), then clockwise (left foot leading). Have them begin slowly and gradually increase the tempo.

   a. Have them slide eight steps in each direction, then four, then two.

   b. Have them form a single circle, face counterclockwise, and slide four steps to the left (toward the center of the circle) and four steps to the right (back to place). Repeat.

   c. Add music.

2. Challenge the children to slide in straight, angular, and circular pathways.

3. Have them slide around and through objects placed on the floor—road cones, beanbags, ropes, hoops.

4. Challenge the children to keep in step with a partner while sliding side by side; face-to-face (arms sideward, palms touching); and back-to-back (hooked elbows).

5. Play the singing game Oats, Peas, Beans (Bowmar Singing Games, Album 1), using the slide as the basic step.

6. Teach the folk dance Carousel (RCA LPM 1625).

7. Rescue Relay. Divide the class into teams, five or six children to a team. Position one member of each team on one side of the room and have the rest of the team members line up on the opposite side, as shown in Figure 14.19. At a signal, the single player slides across the room and takes the hand of the first teammate in line (circled), and the two slide back across the room together. The first player stays put and the player who has just been rescued returns to rescue the next player. Play continues until all the team members have been rescued.

The Locomotor Movements   259

Figure 14.18 The Slide
Mickey Adair

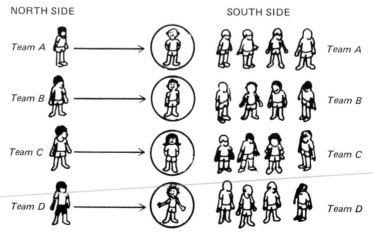

NORTH SIDE

SOUTH SIDE

Team A

Team A

Team B

Team B

Team C

Team C

**Figure 14.19 Diagram for
the Game *Rescue Relay***

Team D

Team D

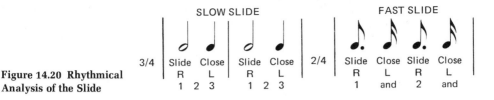

Figure 14.20 Rhythmical Analysis of the Slide

8. On the beginning level, teach some of the following folk dances: Polly Wolly Doodle and Pattycake Polka (RCA LPM 1625); Cshebogar (Hoctor LP 4001); Here We Go Round the Mountain (Rise Up, Sugar, Rise, EZ 78 2004-A); and Paw Paw Patch (EZ 2003-B or Folkraft 1189).

9. Introduce intermediate and advanced children to the rhythmic analysis of the slide. (See Figure 14.20.) Have them execute slow and fast slides to a drumbeat.

10. Challenge intermediate and advanced children to invent movement sequences that combine sliding with other basic movements.

Galloping

A gallop is similar to a slide except that it is always performed in a forward or backward direction. (See Figure 14.21.) In the gallop, the leading foot steps forward and takes the weight; the rear foot then moves forward to a position just behind the leading foot, and in a quick lifting movement the weight is transferred to the rear foot in preparation for the next step. In a sequence of gallops, the same foot continues to lead. When galloping forward, the body's center of gravity is shifted forward. One pushes off from the ball of the rear foot and lands on the ball of the forward foot. The knee and ankle joints remain slightly flexed throughout the movement. The uneven long-short rhythm of the gallop is the same as that of the slide, the first phase of the movement being a slow step and the second a quick catch step. The gallop is always executed at a relatively fast tempo.

A gallop combined with a turn is known as a *buzz step*. The forward foot remains stationary on the floor, acting as a pivot, while the rear foot travels around it in a circular pathway. Because the rear foot travels in a sideward rather than forward direction, the space between the feet remains the same throughout the sequence of the steps. The buzz step is too difficult for children in the lower grades, but should be added to the movement vocabularies of children in the upper grades.

Most children know how to gallop when they enter school and execute the movement readily. They may not, however, know the movement by name. You may therefore demonstrate the gallop and ask the children if they recognize it, or challenge them to move like horses and point out the movement of those who gallop.

The Locomotor Movements

Figure 14.21 The Gallop
Mickey Adair

It is essential to point out the similarity between the slide and the gallop so the children will recognize the relationship. This point may be made by having them slide sideward around a circle and then asking them to execute the same movement in a forward direction.

Activities for Children

1. Have the children gallop freely around the room.

2. Challenge them to gallop in different pathways and on different levels.

3. Place objects on the floor (road cones, beanbags, hoops, ropes) and have them gallop around the objects and in and out of the spaces between lines on the floor and play equipment.

4. Ask the children to form a single large circle. Have them gallop clockwise and counterclockwise.

a. Have them gallop eight steps in each direction, then four, then two.

The Basic Movement Skills

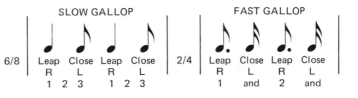

Figure 14.22 Rhythmical
Analysis of the Gallop

b. Have them gallop to music, in the circle and then through general space.

5. Challenge the children to gallop in step with a partner in the following relationships: side by side; leading and following (one may pretend to drive the other); approaching and parting; and close together and far apart.

6. Challenge them to combine galloping with other locomotor movements.

7. Imagery. Ask the children to gallop while pretending to be:

a. a small pony

b. a large horse

c. a racehorse

d. riding a stick horse (perhaps using wands)

e. a horse on a merry-go-round

f. a horse carrying a very heavy rider

8. Have the children interpret in movement the Dance-A-Story "The Magic Mountain" (RCA).

9. Introduce intermediate and advanced children to the rhythmic analysis of the gallop (See Figure 14.22). Point out the similarity between the rhythmic pattern of the gallop and that of the skip and slide. Have the children gallop to rhythmic accompaniment and identify the long and short note values.

10. Challenge intermediate and advanced children to invent a movement sequence pantomiming a story that involves galloping. Require that it have a definite beginning, middle, and end. Ask them to identify the movements they execute and the dimensions of the movement elements involved.

THE NONLOCOMOTOR MOVEMENTS

Children normally perform the nonlocomotor movements as part of their everyday physical activities. And because children are very active, they tend to combine the nonlocomotor movements with forms of locomotion. However, in order to provide for adequate practice of these movements and knowledge of the factors pertinent to their execution, it is necessary to study each movement separately.

**Bending and
Stretching**

A bend is a movement in which body parts are brought closer together. A bend is executed by flexing a joint, causing the angle at the joint to become smaller; bending is also referred to as *flexion*. A small bending movement occurs when a small body part is flexed or when a joint is only slightly flexed. Larger bending movements involve increasing the range of motion in the bent joints or flexing more and larger body parts. For example, bending only the fingers or slightly flexing the forearm are small bending movements; bending the fingers, wrist, and elbow forward until the fingertips touch the chest is in a large bending movement.

The capacity of a body part to bend is determined by the structure of the joint. A joint structured so the body parts it joins can move only forward or backward is called a hinge joint, because it functions like a hinge on a door or box lid. Hinge joints are found in the fingers, toes, elbows, and knees.

Joints in which the rounded end of one bone fits into another bone shaped like a cup or a dish are called *ball-and-socket* joints. A ball-and-socket joint permits the contiguous body part to bend sideward, as well as forward and backward, and to move circularly. Examples of ball-and-socket joints are the hip joint and the joint connecting the upper arm and the shoulder.

The bones of the spinal column (vertebrae) fit together in such a way as to function somewhat like ball-and-socket joints. The vertebrae in the neck permit the range of motion necessary for the head to bend forward, backward, and sideward and to twist (rotate) from side to side. The vertebrae in the back allow the trunk of the body to move in a similar manner.

The wrist and ankle joints are constructed so the feet and hands may bend forward, backward, or sideward and may rotate circularly. The structure of the wrist and elbow joints also permits the hands to be turned 180 degrees.

A stretch is a full extension or hyperextension of the body parts. *Extension* is defined as the return of a body part to an extended position after it has been flexed. *Hyperextension* is extension beyond that point or beyond a straight line (180° angle). For example, if the wrist is flexed so the hand bends forward, it may then be extended so the hand and arm form a straight line or hyperextended so the hand bends backward.

Most movement activities employ several body parts, each of which may be flexed, extended, or hyperextended during various phases of the movement.

Almost every movement activity is characterized by bending and stretching actions, which may be pointed out, emphasized, and/or discussed. Children should become aware of the sensations associated with bending and stretching various body parts, and should develop cognitive awareness of the relationships between bending and stretching and the spatial dimensions of movement (size, level, direction, and shape). Thus the children should be encouraged to attend to the feeling states evoked by each of the following activities, and the dimensions of the movement elements should be reviewed and discussed.

Activities for Children

1. Challenge the children to bend and stretch given body parts as you call out the name of each. Progress from small body parts (fingers, toes, hands, and feet) to large body parts (arms, legs, head, and back) and from single to multiple parts (one arm to both arms; one arm and one leg to both arms and both legs; arms and head to arms, head, and trunk; and so on).

2. Have the children bend one arm while lifting it and extend it while lowering it. Repeat this movement with both arms, one leg, both legs, arms and legs.

3. Have them slowly stretch one arm while extending it sideward and bend it while moving it back toward the body. Repeat with the other arm and with both arms.
   a. Speed up the tempo.
   b. Have them bend quickly and stretch slowly and vice versa.

4. Challenge the children to bend and stretch one (two, three, four, five) body parts.

5. Have them bend and stretch different body parts in different directions while using various other body parts as bases of support (see Figure 13.1).
   a. While lying on their backs, instruct them to:
      (1) "bend (stretch) your head (arms, legs) sideward (upward),"
      (2) "bend your back until it is very rounded."
      (3) "raise your arms straight overhead and stretch."
   b. While standing, instruct them to:
      (1) "stretch and reach to the very tip-top of your personal space, then bend and touch the bottom."
      (2) "stand on one foot while bending your head, arms, and other leg."
   c. While sitting, instruct them to:
      (1) "bend your knees, head, and trunk until your forehead touches your knees."
      (2) "press the soles of your feet together and bend your head and back until your forehead touches your feet."

6. "Bend your body parts and curl up into a very small shape. Then stretch your body parts and make a large shape."

7. "Stretch and move on a high level, and then bend and move on a low level."

8. "Bend one arm (leg) and stretch the other."

9. "Bend the fingers of one hand into a tight fist while stretching the fingers of the other hand." (On the intermediate level, point out that activities 8 and 9 are examples of asymmetrical movements. Discuss the concept of symmetrical and asymmetrical movement with regard to bending and stretching.)

10. Combine bending and stretching with rocking, rolling, walking, and jumping.

11. Use the Dance-A-Story "At the Beach" (RCA), pointing out and discussing the bending and stretching movements.

12. Have intermediate and advanced children bend and stretch to a drumbeat and to musical accompaniment.

13. Challenge intermediate and advanced children to bend and stretch various body parts while hanging by the hands, elbows, and knees.

14. Have them stretch while leaping.

15. Have them stretch their legs high with their bodies in an inverted position.

16. Have intermediate and advanced children develop a movement sequence that includes transitions from bent to stretched positions.

Twisting and Turning

A twist is a rotation of the body or a body part around a long axis. In a twist of the body, the base of support does not move. The structure of the joints determines which body parts may be twisted. The head, shoulders, trunk, and hips may be twisted around the long axis of the spinal column. The ball-and-socket joints of the shoulders and hips permit rotation of the arms and legs. Twisting can only occur in a circular direction.

A turn is a movement in which the body or a body part is rotated. When the entire body is turned, the base of support shifts from one position to another. A body part is turned by twisting the adjacent body parts. For example, the head is turned from side to side by twisting the neck, and the hand is turned by twisting the forearm. A turn can be either clockwise or counterclockwise. Twisting and turning movements are shown in Figure 14.23.

Children commonly perform twisting and turning movements in

The Basic Movement Skills

Figure 14.23 Twisting and Turning
Mickey Adair

their everyday activities. Therefore, the portion of the curriculum devoted to these movements focuses primarily on developing sensory and cognitive awareness. The children should become more keenly aware of the feeling states associated with twisting and turning movements, and should develop an understanding of the relationships between these and other basic movements.

Activities for Children

1. Have the children twist various body parts (neck, shoulders, trunk, arms, and legs).

2. Challenge them to make narrow twisted shapes and wide twisted shapes.

3. Instruct them to make twisted shapes while using a variety of body parts as bases of support (see Figure 13.1).

4. Challenge them to make twisted shapes with one, two, three, four, and five body parts.

5. Ask the children to make twisted shapes while they move through space, using different locomotor skills and varying the level, direction, and pathway.

6. Have them twist their arms around their bodies in various ways holding each position to create a statue with a twisted shape.

7. "Twist different body parts around each other" (arms around legs, arms around head, and so on).

8. "Lie on your back on the floor and twist your hips until you turn over. Now lie on your back again and twist your shoulders until you turn sideward. Now once more, twisting both hips and shoulders."

9. "Turn your head from side to side."

10. "Turn your legs and feet (arms and hands) in and out."

11. "Turn one hand clockwise, then counterclockwise. Turn both hands clockwise and counterclockwise."

12. "Turn your body slowly while moving through space. Turn fast. Turn in small circles and large circles. Now gradually increase the speed (size) of your turns. Now gradually increase the speed while decreasing the size."

13. "Vary your level (direction, pathway) while you turn."

14. "Jump and turn quarter-, half-, and full turns. Do these movements slow then fast."

15. "Turn clockwise and then counterclockwise while using different body parts as bases of support" (for example, back, one foot, both feet, hands and knees, hands and feet, seat and feet).

16. Have the children execute twisting and turning movements to a drumbeat and then to musical accompaniment.

17. Imagery. Have the children pantomime the movements of a:
a. spring
b. screwdriver
c. top
d. machine with turning parts

18. Have intermediate and advanced children twist and turn in pairs.
a. "Stand face-to-face and twist in unison and then in opposition."
b. "Twist in unison while standing back-to-back and side by side."
c. "Stand face-to-face. Then turn away from each other, making a full circle so that you move from face-to-face to back-to-back and to face-to-face again. Continue moving diagonally across the room in this way, in unison with your partner."

The Basic Movement Skills

19. Challenge intermediate and advanced children to invent movement sequences that include twisting and turning.

20. Teach them folk dances characterized by twisting and turning movements.

Pushing and Pulling

To push is to exert one's bodily force against a resistant force. Pushing is used to move an object away from the body or to move the body away from an object or surface. Pushing motions may be made with the hands and arms, feet and legs, shoulders, and hips. The arms and legs are bent preparatory to pushing, and the extension of the joints contributes additional force to the push.

To pull is to move or draw an object toward the body. Pulling motions are usually executed with the hands and arms, though the feet and legs can be used. At the beginning of the movement, the arms are usually extended, the feet and legs in a stride position, and the body and knees bent. Force is exerted by bending the arms and straightening the body.

Children should be introduced to the concepts of pushing and pulling through exploratory activities in which the sensations associated with these movements are emphasized. The curriculum for intermediate and advanced children should include analysis of the movements and practical applications of the mechanical principles.

Activities for Children

1. Challenge the children to push different body parts into space in different directions. For example:
   a. "Push one hand forward (sideward, up, down)."
   b. "Push one foot (shoulder, elbow, knee) upward."
   c. "Push both feet (hands, knees, elbows) sideward."
   d. "Push your hands and feet upward."
"Repeat these movements with your body on a low, medium, and high level. Now repeat them pushing slowly and then quickly. Then make strong hard pushing movements and gentle light movements."

2. "Lie down on your back and use your hands and feet to push your body along the floor. Turn over and use your hands to push your body backward."

3. "While lying face down on the floor, use your hands to push your body away from the floor. Push away slowly and resist the force of gravity by lowering your body slowly."

4. "Stand approximately a foot away from the wall. Place your hands on the wall and bend your arms until your forehead touches the wall. Slowly push away from the wall and return to your starting position."

5. "Assume a crouched position, with your arms beside your legs and the palms of your hands on the floor. Push your body upward into space with your arms and legs."

6. "Sitting on the floor with your legs crossed and your arms folded across your chest, lean forward and push your body up to a standing position. Then let the force of gravity push you back down to a cross-legged sitting position. (This is called a Turk stand.)"

7. Imagery. Have the children pretend to push:
a. someone sitting in a swing
b. a wheelbarrow or lawnmower
c. a piano or automobile
d. the pedals of a bicycle
e. a small snowball and then a large snowball

8. Have them use different body parts to push a beanbag along the floor (see Figure 14.24) and to push a ball across the floor.

9. Use the Dance-A-Story "Little Duck" (RCA), pointing out the pushing movements.

10. Have the children pair off, and challenge one partner to push the other around the room. "Use different body parts (head, shoulder, hip, knee) to push your partner, and push him or her in different directions. Push fast and slow."

11. Have one partner attempt to push the other across a line or out of a circle. Specify the body part to be used for pushing.

12. Partner Stunts
a. Chinese Get-Up (Grades 2–6). The partners who should be approximately the same size, sit on the floor back-to-back with their elbows locked, knees flexed, and feet flat on the floor. They try to rise off the floor by pushing their backs together and taking short steps backward.
b. Crab Fight (Grades 3–6). The partners sit side-by-side in the crab walk position (facing in opposite directions so that one person's knees are next to the other's shoulders). Using their hips, they try to push each other off balance.
c. Shoulder Wrestling (Grades 3–6). The partners kneel facing each other with their hands behind their backs. By moving about on their knees and pushing against each other's shoulders, they attempt to push each other off balance.
d. Foot Push (Grades 3–6). Partners sit on the floor facing each other, using hands, seat, and feet as bases of support. They place their toes and the balls of their feet together. At a signal they push against the

Figure 14.24 Pushing a Beanbag
Mickey Adair

soles of each other's feet, each attempting to force the other out of position.

e. Toe Push (Grades 4–6). The partners sit facing each other in the V-sit position, hands clasped under their knees. At a signal they attempt to force each other off balance by pushing against each other's feet with their toes.

f. Rooster Fight (Grades 4–6). Each partner stands on one leg, arms folded across the chest, inside a circle. At a signal they push against each other's shoulders, each attempting to knock the other off balance. The contest ends when one person touches the floor with the free foot or hops outside the circle.

13. Repeat activity 1 above, substituting pulling for pushing. (With older children, you can combine the study of pushing and pulling.)

14. "Using one hand (foot), pull a beanbag toward you from in front (in back, the side) of your body."

15. Imagery. Have the children pretend to pull:
a. on a rope hanging from the ceiling in front of (behind, above) the head.
b. an empty wagon; a wagon bearing a heavy load
c. as if paddling a canoe

16. "Lying on your back with your knees bent and your arms crossed over your chest, slowly pull yourself up to a sitting position. Slowly lower your body back down to your starting position."

17. "Lying face down on the floor, use your hands to pull your body along the floor and to pull it around in a circle."

18. "Using your seat as a base of support, pull your body across the floor with your feet."

19. "Grasp a horizontal bar or rope and pull yourself up as far as possible."

20. Have the children pair off, and instruct one to sit and one to stand. "Using both hands, pull your partner up from a sitting to a standing position."

21. Have one partner pull the other across a line or out of a circle while the one pulled stands, sits, and lies on the back and the front.

22. Leg wrestling (Grades 4–6). Two children lie on their backs beside each other, heads in opposite directions. At a signal both raise their inside legs and hook them together. By pulling the leg downward, each attempts to roll the other over backward.

23. Have the children execute pushing and pulling movements to a drumbeat and to music with slow and fast tempos. Discuss the different feeling states created by changes in tempo.

Swinging and Swaying

A swing is a circular or arclike movement of a body part around a stationary center point. Swinging results from releasing the muscular force necessary to hold the body part stationary, which allows gravity to pull it downward; the momentum created by the downward swing then carries the body part upward in the opposite direction. The size of the arc will rapidly diminish if gravitational pull is the only force. It is therefore necessary, if the original size of the swing is to be maintained, to exert some muscular force to lift the body part upward to its starting position. Thus the size of the arc is determined by the amount of muscular force exerted. The arc may become a full circle if sufficient force is exerted to carry the swinging part far enough upward to allow the motion to continue in the same direction. The only bodyparts whose structure permits them to swing freely in full circles are the arms. The legs can swing one at a time in an arclike motion. The upper trunk and head can also swing, but their range of motion is limited.

Swaying is a sustained rocking movement of the entire body, controlled by the trunk. It is a relaxed flowing movement executed at a slow or moderate tempo, from side to side or forward and backward.

Swinging and swaying movements are easy to execute, but some children have difficulty achieving the appropriate flowing, rhythmic quality. Thus you should emphasize awareness of the feeling states associated with a rhythmic and well-controlled response.

1. Challenge the children to swing the right arm, the left arm, and then both arms in unison as follows:
   a. sideward diagonally in front of the body
   b. forward and backward (see Figure 14.25)
   c. in a full circle diagonally in front of the body
   d. in a full circle beside the body, first forward and upward (clockwise) and then downward and backward (counterclockwise)
   e. in a figure eight, swinging diagonally forward and backward

2. "Swing your arms forward and backward in opposition."

3. "Swing your arms forward and backward in large forceful movements and then in soft light movements."

4. "Swing your arms fast and then slow. Next swing them in small pendular movements, gradually increasing the size of the arcs until they are full circles."

5. "Stand with the right side of your body near a wall. Place your right hand on the wall at shoulder height. Swing your left leg forward and backward. Vary the size (tempo, force) of the movement."

6. "Standing in a sideward stride position, drop your head forward and swing it from side to side."

7. Have the children swing while hanging from a rope. Then have them swing while hanging from a horizontal bar or overhead ladder.

8. Imagery. Have the children swing as would:
   a. a child in a swing
   b. the pendulum of a small (large) clock
   c. a windshield wiper (using the head and then the whole body as the wiper)
   d. a tree or a flower in a breeze
   e. an elephant's trunk

9. Challenge the children to combine a swing with the following locomotor movements:
   a. Walking. "Swing your arms in opposition to your legs as you usually would, and then exaggerate the arm swing."
   b. Skipping. "Skip forward and backward while swinging your arms."
   c. Jumping. "Swing both arms forward as you jump."
   d. Sliding. "Take one sliding step to the right as both arms swing sideward to the right. Then slide one step to the left as your arms swing back. Repeat.

10. Have the children swing different body parts in combination.

Figure 14.25 Swinging the Arms Forward and Backward
Mickey Adair

a. "Swing your head from side to side, allowing your shoulders and trunk to join in the movement. Keep your arms relaxed so they swing freely from your shoulders."

b. "Slowly bend your upper body forward as you swing so you are gradually swinging closer and closer to the floor."

11. "Raise your right arm sideward to shoulder level and hold it there. Suddenly let it drop and swing across the front of your body. When it reaches its full height on the left side of your body, hold it there. Then let your arm swing back to its starting position. Repeat this movement several times, and then do the same with the left arm."

12. "Swing your right arm back and forth in front of your body, keeping it moving at an even moderate tempo. Let your body sway with the swing of your arm." (The swaying movement should result from the

body's center of gravity being smoothly shifted over the left foot as the arm swings forward across the body and back over the right foot as the arm swings back.) "Repeat with the left arm. Then use both arms and allow your body to sway freely from side to side as your arms swing through."

13. "Standing in a forward stride position with your left foot forward, swing your right arm forward and backward. Let your right shoulder move forward and backward, and let your knees bend so your body sways as your arms swing. Then repeat with the left arm, placing the right foot forward."

14. "Standing in a sideward stride position, swing both arms forward and backward in unison, allowing your knees to bend and your head to move forward and backward. Note how the structure of the shoulder joints permits your arms to swing farther forward than backward."

15. "Standing in a sideward stride position with both arms overhead, let your head and upper body suddenly drop forward while your arms swing freely backward. Then let your arms come forward, carrying your body upward to a standing position. Continue the movement at an even, moderate tempo."

16. "Standing in a sideward stride position with your left foot slightly forward, swing both arms upward until they are fully extended on the left side of your body and the center of gravity is over your left foot. Then swing your arms, head, and upper body diagonally downward to the right while bending your hips, knees, and ankles so your hands swing close to your right foot. Allow your arms to swing beyond the right side of the body. Your weight will shift over your right foot as your body swings to the right. Then reverse the movement, returning to your starting position. Repeat the movement until its execution is rhythmic and well controlled."

17. Have the children pair off.
a. "Stand beside your partner, hold hands, and swing your arms forward and backward. Swing your arms in a small arc, gradually letting the arc get bigger and bigger. Swing your arms slow and then fast."
b. "Stand facing your partner, hold both hands, and swing your arms from side to side. Let your bodies sway as your arms swing."

18. Have the children swing and sway to rhythmical accompaniment.
a. Have them swing different body parts to a 3/4 drumbeat.

b. Have them let their bodies sway as the body parts swing in response to the drumbeat.

c. Have them swing and sway to music that has a lilting quality.

Falling and Rising

There are two types of falls: one type occurs when the body is moving on balance, and the other is the result of moving off balance. (The falling movements associated with off balance positions are discussed on pages 205–208.) In any fall by definition, the body or a body part moves from a higher to a lower level. A fall may be either a sudden movement or a gradual lowering of the body. A sudden fall occurs when the muscular force supporting the body is abruptly and totally released; a gradual fall results when energy is released slowly. A fall may also be partial or complete. In a partial fall, balance is regained or the downward motion of the body is stopped without the base of support changing (as in a drop to a crouch position). In a complete fall, balance is lost and the downward motion continues until a new base of support is established.

Rising is the opposite of falling. In rising, the body or a body part moves from a lower to a higher level. In order to rise, the body must be on balance, it must have a stable base of support, and sufficient muscular force must be exerted to overcome the force of gravity.

When children are being instructed in falling, precautions should be taken to prevent injury. Initially, the children should work on padded surfaces. Emphasis should be placed on the development of well-controlled movements and the correct use of body parts.

Activities for Children

1. Have the children sit on the floor cross-legged.

a. "Let your head fall forward and then raise it slowly. Let it fall forward and jerk it up quickly. Feel the difference between falling and rising and between raising the head slowly and jerking it up."

b. "Let your head fall back and forth from one side to the other."

c. "Let your head fall backward, allowing your mouth to open as your head falls. Close your mouth while your head is tilted backward and feel the stretch of the muscles on the front of your neck."

2. "Raise your right hand up to your chin. Suddenly let go and let your hand drop into your lap. Do the same thing with the left hand, and then with both hands."

3. Have the children lie on their backs with their arms at their sides, palms down.

a. "Keeping your forearm on the floor, raise one hand and let it fall. Repeat with the other hand, then both hands."

b. "Bend your elbow, raising your hand and forearm until your fingers point to the ceiling. Let your hand and arm fall back to the floor. Repeat with the other arm and both arms."

c. "Raise your whole arm a little way off the floor and let it fall back down. Gradually raise it higher and higher so it falls farther and farther. Repeat with the other arm, both arms, each leg, both legs, both arms and both legs together."

4. "Fall forward from a kneeling position, catching your fall with your hands, bending your elbows, and gradually lowering your body to the floor. Reverse the movement and push yourself back up to a kneeling position."

5. "In a sitting position, place one hand on the floor beside your body and lean your weight on it. Let your hand slowly slide out to the side until you fall over sideways. Use your arm to push yourself back up to a sitting position."

6. "Stand up, raise your arms to shoulder height, and let them fall down to your side. Then let your upper body fall forward and bounce as your arms dangle."

7. "Let your body gradually fall from a standing position into a crouch. Then fall backward to a sitting position. Cross your legs and rise, as in a Turk stand."

8. "Fall to a crouch and go into a forward or backward roll."

9. Have the children fall and rise repeatedly to a 3/4 drumbeat.

10. Have them combine falling and rising with walking, jumping, twisting, turning, pushing, and pulling.

TOPICS FOR REVIEW AND FURTHER STUDY

1. What is the difference between locomotor and nonlocomotor movements?

2. How is the goal of enabling each child to use his or her body as a more efficient and expressive movement instrument pursued in the new physical education?

3. Note the factors you should check when observing a child's walking pattern.

4. Develop a lesson on walking. Include the following concepts:
a. moving on different levels
b. moving in different directions
c. moving slow and fast
d. taking light steps and heavy steps

5. Develop a lesson in which children respond to a rhythmic beat by walking.

6. Develop a lesson in which children explore various ways of walking on a balance beam.

7. Describe the errors that commonly occur when children run.

8. Develop a lesson in which children explore several variations in the movement elements while walking and running.

9. Describe correct execution of a jump when the goal is height and when it is distance.

10. Evaluate a kindergarten child's ability to jump. Design a series of activities that will enable the child to jump more skillfully.

11. Develop a lesson in which a group of first- or second-grade children explores the concept of flight.

12. Evaluate a six-year-old child's ability to hop. Design a series of activities that will enable this child to hop more skillfully.

13. Develop a lesson in which a group of children will learn the Schottische.

14. Describe how you would teach a group of children to leap skillfully.

15. Describe how you would teach a child to skip.

16. Develop a sequence of learning activities that will stimulate children to explore skipping to a rhythmic beat. Include variations in the dimensions of the movement elements.

17. Teach a group of children an activity involving a slide and/or gallop.

18. Develop a lesson in which children explore some of the nonlocomotor movements. Include the use of imagery.

19. Develop a series of learning activities for a specific group of children in which they will explore some locomotor and nonlocomotor movements while varying the dimensions of the movement elements.

20. Design a lesson in which children utilize the basic movement skills in expressive, creative activities.

SUGGESTIONS FOR FURTHER READING

AMERICAN ASSOCIATION FOR HEALTH, PHYSICAL EDUCATION, AND RECREATION. *Knowledge and Understanding in Physical Education*. Washington, D.C.: AAHPER, 1973.

BROER, MARION. *Efficiency of Human Movement*, 3rd. ed. Philadelphia: W. B. Saunders, 1973.

SCHURR, EVELYN L. *Movement Experiences for Children* 2nd. ed. Englewood Cliffs, N.J.: Prentice-Hall, 1975.

WICKSTROM, RALPH L. *Fundamental Motor Patterns*. Philadelphia: Lea and Febiger, 1970

15   The Manipulative Skills

Children's inherent need to explore motivates them to handle and experiment with objects. Adults often mistakenly assume that a child manipulating an object is merely "playing." In fact, the child is also learning to sense and control his or her body's relations to movable objects. In the educational setting, the child should also learn how the physical characteristics of the object and the movements of the human body affect the object's movement. Like the basic movement skills, the manipulative skills should be practiced during the primary school years. When the child has mastered these skills, he or she is developmentally ready to learn the more complex basic sports skills.

BALLHANDLING

One of the most important and frequently neglected components of physical education is ballhandling skills. It is often erroneously assumed that because children play with balls, they automatically develop efficient movement patterns. However, the trial-and-error method of learning often leads to habits and attitudes that inhibit, rather than facilitate, skill development. Children should be introduced to ballhandling skills in sequence, beginning with rolling and catching and then progressing to bouncing, tossing, kicking, and striking.

The ballhandling ability levels of the children in a given age group usually vary widely. Some who have had a great deal of experience handling balls will be fairly proficient, while others who have spent very little time practicing these skills may appear awkward and fearful. It may thus be necessary to group the children and individualize instruction in order to challenge the more highly skilled, while motivating and encouraging the less skilled.

The activities presented in this chapter are arranged sequentially so that those appropriate for younger and/or less experienced children appear first. Exploration is stressed to insure that the child initially becomes familiar with the ball and feels comfortable with it. In the activities that follow, control of the ball is emphasized first; gradually, the child is required to increase accuracy, speed, and distance.

Manipulating a yarn ball is an excellent introduction to ballhandling skills. The yarn ball is soft, colorful, safe, and easy to control. Holding, rubbing, and squeezing it stimulates the senses. The yarn ball poses no threat of injury and is easy to retrieve when lost. Also, the yarn ball's tendency to travel slowly enables the child to visually track its pathway through space.

Activities for Children

1. a. "In a sitting position, move the yarn ball around your body on the floor."
b. "Move it around the middle of your body, and then around your chest (shoulders, neck, head)."
c. "Move the ball around your body on the floor using body parts other than your hands."
d. "Using your seat and feet to support your body weight, move the ball under your knees and around your body."
e. "Use your right hand to roll the ball under your knees. Catch it with your left hand. Roll it back through with your left hand and catch it with your right hand. Keep it going back and forth."

2. "Lying on your front with your head and chest raised, roll the ball from hand to hand."

3. "In a squatting position, roll the ball around your feet. Roll it around one foot and then the other in a figure eight pattern."

4. "Standing in a sideward stride position, move the yarn ball in a circle around one knee. Now around the other knee."

5. "Move the ball around one knee and then the other in a figure eight pattern."

6. Have the children kneel or sit, and instruct them to toss and catch the yarn ball as follows:

    a. "Toss upward with both hands and catch with both hands."

    b. "Toss with both hands and catch with your right hand."

    c. "Toss with both hands and catch with your left hand."

    d. "Toss with your right hand and catch with your right hand."

    e. "Toss with your right hand and catch with your left hand."

    f. "Toss with your left hand and catch with your left hand."

    g. "Toss with your left hand and catch with your right hand."

7. "With your hands close together, toss the ball from one hand to the other. Keep the ball moving. Gradually increase the distance between your hands and the height of the toss."

8. "Using your seat and feet to support your body weight, roll the ball under your knees with your left hand, catch it with your right, toss it over your knees, and catch it with your left hand. Repeat and then reverse hands."

9. "Toss the ball with other body parts (wrist, elbow, shoulder, knee) and catch it with your hands."

10. "In a standing position, hold the ball in your left hand with your left arm extended at shoulder height. Drop the ball and catch it with your right hand before it hits the floor. Next drop it with both hands and catch it with both hands. Drop it and catch it with the right hand, and then with the left."

11. "Stand on your left foot with your right knee raised in front of you. Drop the ball with your right hand from shoulder level and let it hit your knee. Repeat, moving your knee upward as the ball strikes it so that the ball is pushed back up into the air. Catch the ball and repeat."

12. "Toss the ball into the air and push it back up with the back of your hand (wrist, elbow, shoulder, head, foot)."

13. "Toss the ball a little way ahead of you and walk forward to catch it. Toss it farther and run to catch it. Remember to stay in your own personal space."

14. Stretch a rope across the room at a height of about five feet. Have the children toss the ball over the rope, run under the rope, and catch it.

15. When the children are familiar with the foregoing movement possibilities and have demonstrated ability to control the yarnball, challenge them to roll and toss the ball while moving in different directions, on different levels, and along different pathways. Challenge them to make different shapes with their bodies or body parts and to move the ball in relation to these shapes.

16. Discuss the physical characteristics of a yarn ball: its color, its shape, why it rolls, the material from which it is made, and how it feels to rub and squeeze it.

Rolling and Catching

Because the motion of a rolling ball is two-dimensional (forward-backward and sideward) while that of a tossed or thrown ball is three-dimensional (also moving up and down), rolling is the best way to begin developing the skill necessary to control a ball's direction and speed.

Rolling is a pushing movement. The hands are placed against the sides and back of the ball, and the elbows are flexed. Both hands move forward simultaneously as the ball is released, and should continue to follow through in the direction the ball is moving. Failure to follow through inhibits full force production and restricts the movement of the ball. Some children impart more force with the dominant hand, causing the ball to roll diagonally.

Children should be instructed in catching and should feel confident of their ability before being expected to catch a ball thrown by another person. It is all too common for an unprepared child to have a ball thrown "at" him or her, thus becoming a "live target" (see Figure 15.1). Children's ability to catch is determined by their hand-eye coordination and other developmental factors discussed in Chapter 3. Thus a child's catching patterns undergo change over time. Younger children catch a thrown ball with the arms and body. As skill and confidence increase, they learn to catch with the hands and body. Finally they become developmentally capable of catching with the hands alone, first both hands and then one hand. (See Figure 15.2.)

A rolling ball provides excellent catching practice, since the child must relate to only two dimensions of movement. Also, the friction between the ball and the floor slows the momentum of the ball so that very little force remains to be absorbed when catching it.

Activities for Children

1. With younger children and those who display fear of the ball, yarn ball activities 1–5 on page 280 may be repeated using an eight-inch playground ball.

2. Have the children pair off, provide one eight-inch playground ball for each pair, and instruct them to stand back-to-back on the center line of the gym floor. "Now take four giant steps forward and turn around to face your partner. Sit down with your legs wide apart." (With the children in this formation, you can stand at either end of the line and readily observe each child's rolling and catching patterns). Start with all the balls on one side of the formation, and instruct the children

Figure 15.1 A Child Who Is Having the Ball Thrown "at" Her
Mickey Adair

Figure 15.2
Developmental Differences in Catching Patterns
Top left: a young child catching with the arms and body; Top right: a child in the early elementary grades catching with the hands and body; Bottom right: a child in the upper elementary grades catching with the hands
Mickey Adair

on that side to push the balls toward their partners. Watch to see if they follow through after release. When every child on the opposite side has caught the ball, have them roll the balls back. Have the children continue to roll the ball back and forth, slowly and smoothly. Help individual children as necessary.

3. Explain how the children should position their hands when catching. Point out that they should place their hands apart with their fingers pointing outward and catch the ball with their palms and the tips of their thumbs and fingers (see Figure 15.3).

4. Challenge the children to roll the ball faster. Discuss what makes the ball go faster. (pushing harder, using more force) Some pairs of children may need to move further apart to increase the challenge.

5. Challenge them to roll a ball along a line on the floor, slowly and then faster.

6. When a child exhibits confidence and accuracy at rolling in a sitting position, have him or her stand and roll the ball by bringing it back between the legs. Emphasize follow-through with the arms.

7. Have the children stand with their backs to their partners and roll the ball backward between their legs toward their partners.

8. When a child can satisfactorily execute a two-hand underhand roll, progress to a one-hand side roll. Explain as you demonstrate (see Figure 15.4):

**Figure 15.3 Correct Hand
Position for Catching a
Rolling Ball**
Mickey Adair

a. The body is in a crouched position.

b. The ball is held at the side of the body, with the right hand behind the ball and the left hand in front of it (if the individual is right handed).

c. The feet are in a forward stride position, with the left foot forward.

d. As the arms move back, the weight shifts backward over the right foot.

e. As the arms swing forward, the left hand is removed from in front of the ball and the weight is shifted to the forward foot.

f. The right hand pushes the ball forward onto the floor.

Have the children practice rolling the ball back and forth, gradually increasing the speed and distance.

9. "In your own personal space, roll a ball and then run and catch it."

10. "Roll the ball with your feet."

11. "Roll the ball against the wall with your hands and catch it after it rebounds." Then challenge them to hit a particular spot on the wall when they roll the ball.

12. Have them roll the ball between the feet of a partner standing in a sideward stride position.

**Figure 15.4 Correct
Hand, Body, and Foot
Position for the One-Hand
Side Roll**
Mickey Adair

13. Challenge the children to roll the ball and knock over an object such as a milk carton or Indian club.

14. Discuss the physical characteristics of a ball, mentioning:
a. how it feels (its texture and softness or hardness)
b. the material of which it is made
c. why it rolls and bounces
d. the fact that it is filled with air
e. the effects of the amount of air in the ball (too much or too little)

15. Rolling games
a. Tunnel Ball. Six or more players stand in sideward stride position in a circle, with one player in the center. The center player rolls the ball toward the circle, attempting to pass it between the legs of a player or between two players. Variations are to make the circle larger or smaller and to have the players in the circle close their eyes.
b. Rolling Relay. Five or six players stand one behind the other, leaving enough space between them so they can bend over. The leader bends over and rolls the ball between his or her own and the others' legs. The players help move the ball to the end of the line. The last player picks up the ball, runs to the front of the line, and rolls the ball backward through the legs. Play continues until the leader is again at the head of the line.

Bouncing

Bouncing is an important skill because it prepares the child to learn to control a rebound from the floor. The child learns to impart varying amounts of force to the ball and to regain control of the ball by absorbing this force after the ball bounces. A well-controlled bounce requires good hand-wrist action and fingertip control of the ball.

Activities for Children

1. "In your own personal space, hold the ball between both hands, drop it, and count how many times it bounces before it stops moving. Drop the ball from different levels (knee, waist, shoulders, head) and count how many times it bounces at each level. Compare the numbers of times it bounces at each level." (Explain to older children that the greater the distance the ball falls, the more momentum it has; hence a greater reaction force is created when it hits the floor.)

2. "Drop the ball and turn your body around as many times as you can before it stops moving. Count how many times you can turn when the ball is dropped from different levels."

3. "Drop the ball, let it bounce once, and catch it before it bounces a second time."

4. "Bounce the ball continously (dribble) using both hands (one hand, the other hand, alternating hands)." (See Figure 15.5 for an illustration of the correct position for a one-hand bounce.)

5. "Turn your body all the way around while dribbling the ball with one hand."

6. "Dribble the ball, swinging one leg over it after each bounce."

7. Have the children bounce the ball:
a. strongly (hard) and lightly (softly)
b. high and low
c. slow and fast
d. while moving forward, backward, and sideward
e. while moving in different pathways
f. using as much space as possible
g. while walking, running, jumping, hopping, skipping, bending, and stretching

8. "Bounce the ball, turn all the way around, and catch it before it bounces again."

9. "Dribble the ball with your eyes closed."

10. "Dribble the ball while walking forward and backward on the balance beam."

11. Have the children dribble the ball around road cones and between the rungs of a ladder lying on the floor.

Tossing

A toss is a movement in which an object is lightly thrown into the air. Because tossing activities are easily executed, they are an excellent introduction to the more advanced skill of throwing. Younger children and children who appear fearful should practice tossing and catching yarn balls and beanbags before working with playground balls. Older and more confident children should practice tossing playground balls and rapidly progress to the basic sports skill of throwing.

Activities for Children

1. Repeat yarn ball activities 6–10 on page 281, substituting a beanbag for a yarn ball.

2. When children demonstrate ability to control the movement of a beanbag, challenge them to toss it accurately. A wide variety of targets may be used:
a. "Try to hit the certain area marked on the wall."
b. "Try to make the beanbags land inside a hoop or bicycle tire lying on the floor. Gradually move back."

**Figure 15.5 Correct
Body and Hand Position
for the One-Hand Bounce**
Mickey Adair

The Manipulative Skills

c. "Toss the beanbag through a hoop your partner is holding." (Specify that the hoop should be held vertically, and then horizontally.)

d. "Practice tossing the beanbag into a box, wastebasket, or can, or through the face of a target."

3. Discuss the physical differences among a beanbag, a yarn ball, and a playground ball, noting:

a. relative size

b. shape and its effect on movement

c. weight and its effect on flight

d. method of grasping

4. Have the children toss a playground ball.

a. "Toss the ball straight up and catch it before it bounces. Gradually increase the height of the toss."

b. "Toss the ball up and see how many times you can clap your hands before catching it."

c. "Toss the ball up, jump up, and catch it while you are in the air."

d. "Toss the ball up, turn around, and catch it before it bounces."

e. Have the children practice tossing the ball accurately by repeating activities 2a–d above.

5. Call Ball. The children form a circle, with one child in the center holding a playground ball. The child in the center tosses the ball into the air and calls out the name (or number) of another child. The child whose name is called must run into the center and try to catch the ball before it bounces (or after only one bounce). If the second child catches the ball, he or she tosses it and calls out a name. If he or she fails to catch the ball, the first child takes another turn.

Using a Scoop[1]   Catching and tossing with a scoop are activities that serve as a natural transition between catching with the hands and striking with an implement. A scoop made from a plastic bottle is easy to grip and manipulate, and may be used to catch or toss a beanbag or small ball such as a tennis ball, fleece ball, yarn ball, or paper ball. Children should experience catching objects of varying weights.

[1]Instructions for making scoops, yarn balls, coat-hanger rackets, and other improvised equipment may be found in Christian (1973), Corbin (1972), and Werner and Simmons (1976).

Figure 15.6 Diagram for the Game *Scoop Ball*

Activities for Children

1. "Toss a yarn ball into the air with one hand and catch it with a scoop held in the other. Try tossing with your dominant hand and catching with the other, and then the reverse."

2. "Toss a tennis ball into the air with the scoop and catch it with the scoop."

3. "Toss a tennis ball against the wall, let it bounce once, and catch it with the scoop. Then catch it on the fly."

4. Have one partner toss a ball and the other catch it in the scoop.

5. Have partners toss the ball back and forth, using scoops to toss and to catch.

6. Scoop games

a. Scoop Ball. Mark two circles on the floor and have one player stand in each circle, as shown in Figure 15.6. The players toss the ball back and forth, using scoops to toss and to catch. A point is awarded for each catch. If a player tosses the ball in a manner that causes it to land outside the opponent's circle, the opponent is awarded a point. (This rule penalizes inaccurate tossing, thus making tossing as important as catching.)

b. Team Scoop Ball. Mark two rectangles on the floor. Each team of two players stands within a rectangle, as shown in Figure 15.7. Play and scoring are the same as in (a) above, either player being allowed to toss or receive the ball.

c. Hoop Scoop Ball. A hoop is suspended from a rope so that its bottom is approximately four feet from the floor. One player stands on each side of the hoop, and a tennis ball is tossed back and forth with scoops, as shown in Figure 15.8. One point is awarded for each toss that passes through the hoop and for each catch made on the fly or after one bounce.

Striking

A strike is an action in which the hand or an implement is used to give impetus to an object. Striking with an implement is a difficult skill because it requires controlling the weight and mass of an extended lever. (An implement held in the hand, such as a paddle or racket, acts

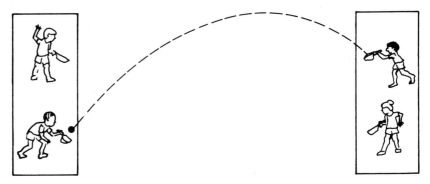

Figure 15.7 Diagram for the Game *Team Scoop Ball*

as an extension of the lever of the forearm; see Figure 16.11.) A child cannot effectively manipulate a striking implement until he or she has developed the muscular strength and hand-eye coordination necessary to control its movement in relation to an object. Most children in the primary grades are not developmentally ready to execute a skilled striking pattern. They can advantageously practice these skills, however, if the size and weight of the equipment are appropriate to their developmental level. Thus the equipment supplied these children should consist of coat-hanger rackets or table tennis paddles and yarn-balls, beanbags, or tennis balls. When they have developed sufficient strength, children should progress to the use of larger, heavier wooden paddles.

Activities for Children

1. "Balance a yarn ball on a coat-hanger racket and walk around the room, keeping the racket and the ball balanced. Then run (jump, hop, skip) without dropping the ball."

2. "Hold the racket in a backhand position (the palm of the hand facing the floor) and repeat activity 1."

3. "Flex the wrist and toss the ball upward with the racket. Catch it on the racket."

4. "Bounce the ball up and down continously."

5. "Toss the ball upward with the racket in a forehand position, quickly turn the racket over, and make the next toss with the racket in a backhand position. Try to keep the ball in the air while switching repeatedly from forehand to backhand."

6. "Toss the ball upward with the free hand and catch it on the racket."

7. "Now toss the ball upward with the racket and catch it with the free hand."

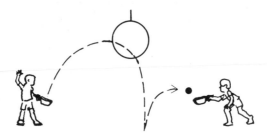

Figure 15.8 Diagram for the Game *Hoop Scoop Ball*

8. "Hold the racket with a forehand grip and in the other hand hold the ball waist-high. Drop the ball and hit it against the wall." (This movement resembles a badminton serve.)

9. "Hit the ball back and forth with a partner. See how many times you can pass it between the two of you before it touches the floor."

10. Have the partners hit the ball back and forth over a rope or bamboo pole three or more feet high.

11. Have four people (two teams of two) hit the ball back and forth over the rope or pole. Challenge them to pass the ball to each player in turn (see Figure 15.9).

12. Have the children repeat activities 1–7, using a table tennis racket and a beanbag. When a child demonstrates ability to control a beanbag (a relatively heavy object), he or she may concentrate on using the paddle to toss the beanbag accurately (see tossing activities 2a–d on pages 289–291).

13. Older children can use larger wooden paddles and five-inch playground balls or tennis balls to repeat activities 8–11 above. You may modify the rules to allow the ball to bounce once before it is returned.

14. Paddles and tennis balls can also be used in the following activities.
   a. "Volley the ball against the wall."
   b. "Move back, and return the ball after one bounce."
   c. "Hit the ball against the wall so that your partner can return it after one bounce. Keep the ball going."

Kicking

A kick is a striking movement executed with the foot. The three kicking patterns that should be practiced by primary children are dribbling the ball with the feet, kicking a stationary ball, and kicking and stopping a moving ball. The children must understand that the purpose of a kick is

The Manipulative Skills

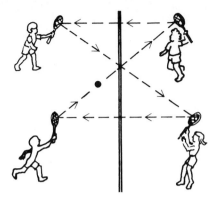

Figure 15.9 Striking a Ball Back and Forth Across a Rope

not merely to propel the ball, but also to control its movement through space.

Activities for Children

1. Place a beanbag on the floor in front of each child. Tell the children to push the beanbag along the floor with the inside of the foot, alternating the right and left feet as shown in Figure 15.10. (Using a beanbag to teach the foot dribble permits the child to learn how the feet are used before having to control a rolling ball.)

2. Have the children dribble beanbags along a straight line, around a circle, and in and out of the spaces between road cones.

3. Instruct the children to kick the beanbag diagonally forward with the inside of the right foot, and then with the inside of the left foot. Point out that the beanbag is moving in a zigzag pathway (see Figure 15.11).

4. Have the children pair off. Have one partner pass the beanbag diagonally forward to the other, using the inside of the right foot to pass. Have the second child stop the beanbag with the inside of the left foot and pass it diagonally forward to the first child, who has run ahead. (See Figure 15.12.) Have the children move down the floor passing and stopping the beanbag, turn around, and move back up the floor. (As they change direction, they will be passing the beanbag with the opposite foot.)

5. Repeat activity 4, having the children dribble the beanbag forward a little way before passing it.

6. Repeat activities 1, 2, 4, and 5, substituting a playground ball for the beanbag. In activities 4 and 5, have the children trap the ball by placing their foot on top of it.

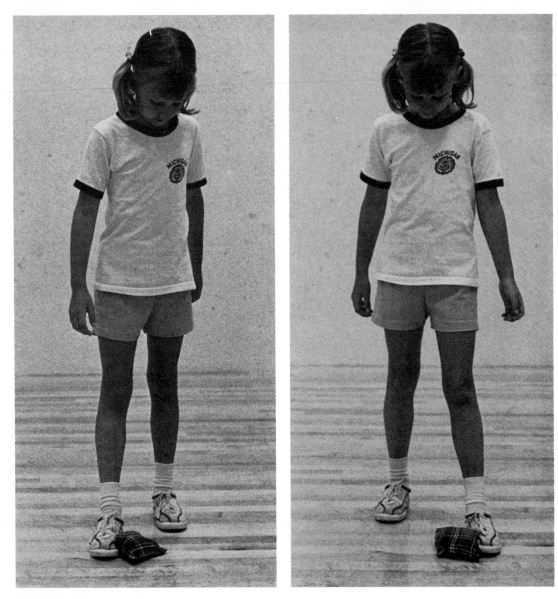

Figure 15.10 Dribbling a Beanbag
Mickey Adair

Figure 15.11 Kicking a Beanbag Diagonally in a Zigzag Pattern

　　　　The Manipulative Skills

Figure 15.12 Passing a Beanbag Diagonally

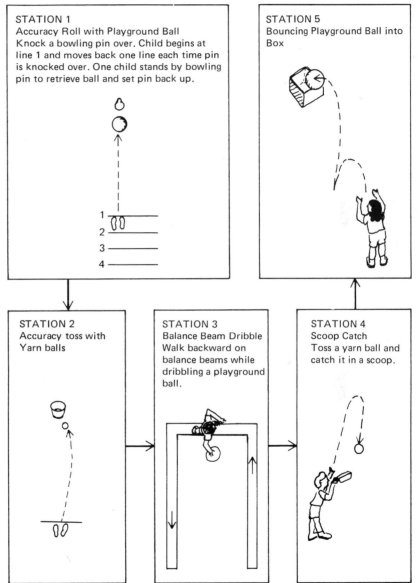

STATION 1
Accuracy Roll with Playground Ball
Knock a bowling pin over. Child begins at line 1 and moves back one line each time pin is knocked over. One child stands by bowling pin to retrieve ball and set pin back up.

1
2
3
4

STATION 5
Bouncing Playground Ball into Box

STATION 2
Accuracy toss with Yarn balls

STATION 3
Balance Beam Dribble
Walk backward on balance beams while dribbling a playground ball.

STATION 4
Scoop Catch
Toss a yarn ball and catch it in a scoop.

Figure 15.13
Ball-Handling Circuit
Have children change stations when the music stops.

Ballhandling

7. Demonstrate the correct execution of a place kick (See Figure 16.31.) Point out that, when kicking with the right foot, the ball should be just inside the left instep. The ball is contacted with the top of the right instep and the right leg swings forward on the follow-through.

8. Have the children stand approximately eight feet from the wall and practice place kicking against the wall.

9. Have the children pair off. Have one partner place kick to the other, who stops the ball by trapping it with the foot and then place kicks it back. Emphasize correct form and accuracy, rather than speed and distance.

A ballhandling circuit such as the one shown in Figure 15.13 allows for ballhandling skills to be reviewed and individual practice supervised. The activities at various stations can be modified or changed to suit the skill levels of different children. For example, if the bounce into a box is too difficult for some children, a toss may be substituted. A foot dribble could replace the hand dribble at station 3 and beanbags could be used instead of yarn balls at station 2.

USING A WAND

A wand is a stick ¾ of an inch in diameter and 36–40 inches long. Broom or mop handles sawed off at the desired length can be used. A wand 36 inches long is easiest for young children to manipulate. Working with a wand helps children develop flexibility and agility, and also enables them to experience balancing an object vertically and horizontally. As with other manipulative activities, control of the object should be emphasized. Children should be cautioned not to use wands as weapons and to restrict the movement of the wand within the boundaries of their own personal spaces.

Activities for Children

1. "Hold your finger on the top of an upright wand whose bottom is resting on the floor. Let go, turn your body around quickly, and try to catch the wand before it falls to the floor. When you can do so turning one way, try turning the other way."

2. "Stand about two feet from your partner. Each of you hold your wand in a vertical position with its bottom resting on the floor. Let go of your wands at the same time and run to catch each other's wands before they hit the floor. Gradually increase the distance between you." (This activity may also be performed by a group of three or more, standing in a circle. All the players move clockwise or counterclockwise to catch the next person's wand.)

3. Balancing the wand

The Manipulative Skills

a. "Balance the wand horizontally on different body parts (the palm of your hand, the back of your hand, one finger, your elbow, the top of your foot, your knee)."

b. "Keep the wand balanced while moving the body part or your whole body."

c. "Balance the wand in a vertical position while your body is on different levels. See how many different body parts you can use to balance it."

d. "Hold onto the wand at both ends and step over it. Then try to jump over it."

4. Thread-the Needle. "Grasp the wand at both ends, bend forward, and step over it one leg at a time. Move the wand up your back, over your head and down in front of your body. Then reverse the movement by moving the wand up over your head and down your back and then stepping backward over it."

5. Twist under. "Rest the bottom of the wand on the floor and grasp the top with your right hand. Bend over and twist under your right arm without letting go of the wand, lifting it off the floor, or touching your knees to the floor. Repeat this maneuver holding the wand in your left hand."

6. Drive the Pig to Market. "Grasp one end of the wand and use the other end to push a beanbag, yarn ball, or tin can along the floor." After the children have practiced, organize this activity as a relay, prescribing the distance they must run while controlling the object with the stick.

USING A HOOP

Activities involving hoops have become very popular in elementary schools. A hoop is a versatile, safe, enjoyable piece of equipment, and such activities contribute to the child's education by promoting general coordination, body awareness, spatial relationships, and eye-hand coordination.

Activities for
Children

1. "Roll the hoop and run along beside it."

2. "Roll the hoop and run ahead of it."

3. "Roll the hoop and run around it as it is rolling."

4. "See how far you can roll your hoop."

5. Instruct the children to roll the hoop:

a. in a circle

b. while weaving around road cones

c. in a figure eight around road cones

Using a Hoop

6. "Crawl through the hoop while your partner holds it stationary, its bottom resting on the floor."

7. "Run through the hoop while your partner rolls it slowly."

8. "Roll your own hoop and run through it."

9. Twirl the hoop on your wrist. Twirl it clockwise and counterclockwise. Twirl it on the other wrist. Now transfer it from wrist to wrist without letting it stop twirling. Try twirling it around your ankles, neck, and waist."

10. "Roll the hoop with a reverse spin so it comes back to you."

11. "Use the hoop as a jump rope. Jump it while turning it forward, turning it backward, walking forward, and running forward.

12. "Use the hoop to play catch with a partner: each of you rolls your hoop to your partner with one hand, and catches his or her hoop with the other hand. Then roll your hoop and catch your partner's hoop with the same hand. Then try throwing the hoops instead of rolling them."

13. Use the hoops for relays.
a. "Roll the hoop to a goal while moving forward, and return to the starting position moving backward."
b. "Roll the hoop around obstacles to a goal and back."

14. Discuss the characteristics of a hoop, noting:
a. its color, shape, and size
b. the ways it can move and how its structure determines its movement possibilities
c. the size the child must be in order to move through the hoop

15. With older children, measure its diameter and calculate its radius and circumference.

USING A ROPE

Jumping rope is a rhythmic skill that requires the child to coordinate several body movements and promotes eye-hand and eye-foot coordination, agility, endurance, rhythmic responses, and an eye for spatial relationships. Working with long ropes and elastic ropes allows children to use their imaginations to create designs and invent activities.

The child learning to jump rope should progress from jumping over stationary objects to a simple jumping step and then to a variety of other steps, including response to a rhythmic beat. Boys often hesitate to participate in rope-jumping activities, but this prejudice can be overcome if appropriate challenges are presented. The learning experiences should be varied and challenging and the element of fun should be retained. Children rapidly lose interest in an activity they consider laborious and repetitive.

The Manipulative Skills

As the children jump, check to see that they are taking off and landing on the balls of their feet. Also be sure that they are flexing the ankle, knee, and hip joints to absorb the force of their landings. Though some children may find it easier initially to jump a single rope, it is usually easier to begin jumping the long rope: the child's full attention can thus be focused on jumping, rather than on turning the rope as well.

Activities for Children

1. Long Rope Activities

a. "Jump back and forth over a rope that is lying on the floor."

b. "Jump back and forth over a long rope that is slowly swinging back and forth."

c. "Stand beside the rope while it is resting on the ground. Jump it as it is turned. See how many times you can jump without missing."

d. "Repeat activity (c), running out of the rope when you are tired."

e. "As the rope is turning toward you (front door), run through it."

f. "Run in the front door, jump several times, and run out the other side."

g. "Run in as the rope is turning away from you (back door), jump, and run out."

h. "Run in the front door; make quarter-, half-, and full turns while jumping; and run out."

i. "Run in and hop the rope, on one foot and then the other."

j. "Run in, jump, and try to touch the floor with your hands on alternate jumps."

k. "Jump with a partner standing side by side holding hands, face-to-face holding hands, face-to-face with your hands on each other's shoulders, and back-to-back holding hands."

l. "Jump while the rope is being turned very fast" (Hot Pepper).

m. Challenge children to jump Double Dutch (two long ropes turning toward each other) or jump an individual rope and a long rope simultaneously.

n. Have the children jump to rope-jumping rhymes (Kirchner, 1974, pages 492–494.)

2. Single Rope Activities

a. "Jump while turning the rope forward and backward. Count how many times you can jump without missing."

b. "Hop over the rope on your right foot, your left foot, and alternate feet."

c. "Do a rocker step: in a forward stride position, the forward foot passes over the rope and takes the weight; the rope then passes under the back foot, and as the rope moves upward behind the body, the weight is transferred to the back foot."

Using a Rope

**Figure 15.14 Jumping
Rope with a Partner**
Mickey Adair

d. "Skip the rope."

e. "Swing one leg forward and the other backward, hopping over the rope and taking a rebound step on the rear foot. Swing one leg and then the other forward alternately."

f. "Jump while doing quarter-turns."

g. "Travel through space while running, jumping, skipping, and leaping the rope."

h. "Cross your arms in front of your body each time you turn the rope."

i. "Jump with a partner, standing face-to-face."

j. "Jump the rope with your partner standing behind you."

k. "Jump with your partner standing beside you, both of you turning the rope with your outside arms." (See Figure 15.14.)

Figure 15.15 Formation for Elastic Rope Activities
Mickey Adair

3. Elastic Rope Activities

a. Have three or more people (depending on the length of the rope) use different body parts to stretch the rope while forming different body shapes, geometric shapes, spatial designs, numerals, or letters. Have them use different body parts as bases of support.

b. Have two people stretch the rope into the shape of a rectangle (see Figure 15.15). Challenge the children to:

    (1) leap over it

    (2) jump into it and hop on each foot five times

    (3) leap into it with the right foot, quickly take the weight on the left foot, and leap out with the right foot leading

    (4) jump to a ¾ beat, jumping astride the elastic on the first beat and into the middle on the second and third beats; repeat, jumping out of the rope

c. Use an elastic rope as a Chinese jump rope (See Anderson, Elliot and LaBerge, 1972, pages 63–64).

Using a Rope

**Figure 15.16 Walking on
Stilts and Tin Cans**
Mickey Adair

The Manipulative Skills

USING STILTS   Children enjoy the challenge of balancing and walking in an elevated position. Young children should first practice maintaining balance and coordinating the movements of their hands and feet while using tin can walkers. Older children may use tin can walkers to walk a balance beam or climb stairs, but should soon progress to regular stilts. (See Figure 15.16.)

Activities for
Children

1. Tin Can Walkers
   a. "Walk in different directions (forward, backward, and sideward)."
   b. "Walk in different pathways (straight, circular, and angular)."
   c. "Walk through an obstacle course."
   d. "Race with a partner or in a relay."
   e. "Walk on a low balance beam in different directions."
   f. "Walk up a short flight of stairs."

2. Wooden Stilts. "It is easiest to mount the stilts if you lean your back against the wall while placing one foot and then the other on the steps of the stilts. Once you have become accustomed to balancing on such a small base of support, you may be able to mount while the stilts are free-standing."
   a. Have the children repeat activities 1a–d above.
   b. Have them walk up and down a small incline.
   c. "Try to walk in unison with a partner."

TOPICS FOR
REVIEW AND
FURTHER STUDY

1. In what sequence should ballhandling skills be taught?

2. When is it necessary to individualize ballhandling instruction?

3. Why are yarn ball activities an excellent introduction to ballhandling skills?

4. Develop a lesson that will challenge the children to control the movements of a yarn ball in a progressively more difficult sequence of activities.

5. Why is rolling taught before tossing or throwing?

6. Demonstrate the correct way to roll a playground ball.

7. Why is it imperative for children to be instructed in catching before being expected to receive a ball from another person?

8. Develop a series of progressively more difficult ball-rolling tasks.

9. What should the children learn about bouncing a ball?

10. Design a lesson in which the children explore various ways to bounce a playground ball.

11. What sequence should be followed in teaching a child who is afraid of the ball?

12. Develop a lesson in which children practice tossing different kinds of objects.

13. Make a set of scoops and design a lesson in which the children use them to practice tossing and catching.

14. Make a set of coat hanger rackets and develop a lesson in which the children use them to practice striking.

15. Develop a series of lessons demonstrating the sequence in which kicking should be taught to children in the early primary grades.

16. Develop a series of verbal cues that will stimulate the children to explore moving in relation to a hoop.

17. Develop a series of lessons designed to enhance children's ability to move in relation to a rope.

18. Make a set of tin can walkers and design a lesson in which children practice walking on them.

SUGGESTIONS FOR FURTHER READING

ANDERSON, MARIAN; ELLIOT, MARGARET; and LABERGE, JEANNE. *Play With a Purpose,* 2nd ed. New York: Harper & Row, 1972.

BUTLER, FRANCELIA, and HALEY, GAIL. *The Skip Rope Book.* New York: Dial Press, 1963.

CHRISTIAN, QUENTIN. *The Beanbag Curriculum: A Homemade Approach to Physical Activity for Children.* Wolfe City, Texas: The University Press, 1973.

CORBIN, CHARLES. *Inexpensive Equipment for Games, Play, and Physical Activity.* Dubuque, Iowa: Wm. C. Brown, 1972.

KIRCHNER, GLENN. *Physical Education for Elementary School Children,* 3rd ed. Dubuque, Iowa: Wm. C. Brown, 1974.

SKOLNIK, PETER L. *Jump Rope!* New York: Workman, 1974.

WERNER, PETER, and SIMMONS, RICHARD. *Inexpensive Physical Education Equipment for Children.* Minneapolis, Minn.: Burgess, 1976.

16   The Basic Sports Skills

Sports skills are goal-directed and performance-oriented; that is, children execute these skills to achieve a definable end. Performance can usually be assessed by objective measures (a performance score) and by the outcome (win or loss).

The nine basic sports skills described on page 87 are movement patterns that can be adapted to serve specialized functions in different sports. In track-and-field events, for example, a jumping pattern is modified in one way if the goal is to jump as high as possible and in another way to jump as far as possible. The overhand throwing pattern used in the one-hand basketball pass differs from the overhand throw in softball. One type of striking pattern is used to hit a tennis ball and another to hit a softball.

All the variations on each basic sports skill are executed with the same instrument (the human body), governed by universal physical laws and principles, and performed in the same general way. Variations in the way a particular skill is performed in different sports are determined by the purpose of the movement, whether or not an object and/or an implement must be moved, and the physical characteristics of the object and/or implement. The component of the curriculum devoted to basic sports skills should provide for the study of all these factors.

The behavioral objectives of this area of study are for the child to:

1. demonstrate correct execution of the basic sports skills

2. demonstrate the ability to adapt these skills in age-appropriate games

3. demonstrate a knowledge of:

a. how the body and body parts function in the correct execution of each skill

b. the physical laws and mechanical principles relevant to performance of these skills

c. similarities and differences in the ways these skills are executed in different movement activities

d. the effect of the movement's purpose on the manner of its execution

e. the objects and implements used in games and sports and the effects of their characteristics on their use

Execution of the four basic sports skills that are also locomotor movements has been analyzed in Chapter 14. Here pertinent movement principles will be discussed and applied to these movements. Throwing, catching, striking, and kicking have been explored as manipulative skills in Chapter 15. In this chapter, the execution of these skills will be analyzed and movement principles will be applied to their execution.[1] While Chapter 15 focuses largely on the primary level, this chapter introduces subject matter appropriate for the upper elementary grades.

SCIENTIFIC CONCEPTS UNDERLYING THE BASIC SPORTS SKILLS

Most of the concepts introduced in this chapter are included in the science curriculum of the upper elementary grades. It is therefore assumed that their application in the physical education curriculum will serve as review and reinforcement. Ideally, the science and physical education curricula are taught through integrated learning experiences, which save valuable teaching time by eliminating unnecessary repetition. Also, the child's learning is more meaningful if he or she can apply it in situations that are personally relevant.

Equilibrium

Key Concept

□ *The stability of my body is affected by the size and shape of my base of support and by the relationship of my center of gravity to my base.*

In order to maintain my balance, my center of gravity must be within and above my base of support.

---

[1]Swimming is not analyzed in this text. To deal adequately with the various strokes and with the unique principles that apply to this movement medium would require a discussion beyond the scope of this text.

I am more stable when my body is supported by a large base and less stable when supported by a small base.
I can increase my stability by lowering my center of gravity.
When I apply or receive force, my stability is increased by enlarging my base in the direction of the moving or opposing force.

Activities for Children

1. Challenge the children to assume body positions that place their centers of gravity as high as possible, as low as possible, and at a medium position. Point out that the lower the center of gravity, the more stable the body; the higher the center of gravity, the less stable the body. Illustrate this principle by inserting a golf ball in one end of a paper-towel roller and a table tennis ball in the other end. Stand it on end, with the golf ball toward the bottom. Point out that the empty roller's center of gravity is at the geometric center, but that its location is altered by placing a heavy object in one end and a light object in the other end (see Figure 16.1). Have the children tip the object over by tapping the top of it. Then have them stand it on the other end and push it over. Ask them which position of the two positions is more stable and why.

2. Challenge the children to show you the least stable body position they can assume, and ask them to explain why it is so unstable. (standing on tiptoe on one foot, because of the small base and high center of gravity)

3. Challenge them to show you the most stable body position and to explain why it is so. (lying on the floor, because of the large base and low center of gravity)

4. Explain to the children that the locations and relationships of the body parts affect the location of the center of gravity. Have them experience the change in arm position resulting from an increase in the forward lean shown in Figure 16.2. Then have them stand on tiptoe, with their arms at their sides and then with their arms fully extended overhead. Discuss how elevating the weight of the arms raises the body's center of gravity. Instruct the children to stand on one foot, in a relatively stable position, and move various body parts, noting how different positions affect stability.

5. Have the children pair off and stand side by side. Have them experiment with pushing each other as in Figure 16.3, the top photos. Point out that when a moving or opposing force is present, simply enlarging the base of support does not necessarily make one more stable. Stability is increased only when the base is enlarged *in the direction of* the moving or opposing force. Review the tilting of the

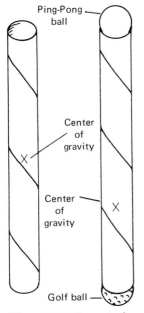

Ping-Pong ball

Center of gravity

Center of gravity

Golf ball

Figure 16.1 Change in the Center of Gravity

Figure 16.2 Effect of a Change in the Center of Gravity on the Body Position
Left: The arms are extended backward and upward to compensate for the forward lean of the body. Right: The forward lean increases and the line of gravity falls outside the base of support, necessitating an adjustment in the body position to prevent a fall.
Mickey Adair

body forward, backward, and sideward in Figure 16.2, pointing out that when one tilts, the body is creating a moving force, and the base must be enlarged in that direction.

6. Have the children experiment with pushing each other as shown in Figure 16.3, bottom. Explain the principle to them: "If you are being pushed from the right side, flexing your left knee serves to absorb part of the force of the push and thus helps keep you from being pushed off balance."

7. Explain that the principle of enlarging the base in the direction of the moving or opposing force is the reason for using a *position of readiness*. The position of readiness in throwing is a forward stride, since the force of the body will move forward during the backswing, release, and follow-through. In batting a sideward stride is the position of readiness because the force will move sideward. (See examples of these positions in Figure 16.4).

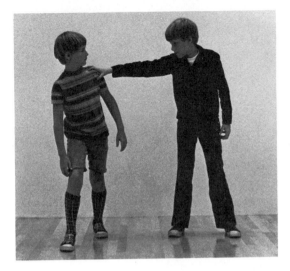

**Figure 16.3 Factors
Affecting Stability When
There Is an Opposing
Force**
Top left: The body
position is unstable
because the base has not
been enlarged in the
direction of the opposing
force. Top right: A wider
base of support provides a
stable body position when
the opposing force is
coming from the side.
Bottom right: Leaning to
the side and flexing the
knee helps to absorb the
opposing force.
Mickey Adair

**Figure 16.4 Positions of
Readiness**
The size of the base of
support is increased in the
direction of the moving
force.
Mickey Adair

The Basic Sports Skills

Motion

Key Concept

☐ *The act of moving involves setting in motion one or more body parts, the body as a whole, and/or an object.*

In running, jumping, hopping, and leaping, the body as a whole is set in motion.
In throwing, the throwing arm, supported by the body as a whole, sets an object in motion.
In striking and kicking, the hand, foot, or an implement sets an object in motion or changes its direction and/or speed.
In catching, the movement of the hands and arms stops the motion of an object.

Activities for Children

1. Write the Key Concept and subconcepts on the board and discuss them with the children. Then have the children complete the circuit illustrated in Figure 16.5. Challenge them to perform each skill with the best possible form, and ask them to notice how they use their bodies and body parts to execute the skills, and control objects. While the children are following the circuit, observe their execution of the various skills. Doing so will give you insight into their skill levels and enable you to identify those who have difficulty controlling their bodies or the ball. You can then work individually with these children in practice situations. When everyone has completed the circuit, move from station to station with the entire class and discuss the subconcept pertinent to each.

Key Concept

☐ *In each of the basic sports skills, something moves; its motion is subject to Newton's three laws of motion, the Law of Inertia, the Law of Acceleration, and the Law of Action and Reaction.*

The *Law of Inertia:* a body at rest will remain at rest, and a body in motion will continue moving at the same speed in a straight line until acted upon by an outside force.
The *Law of Acceleration:* the acceleration of an object is proportional to the force that creates it and inversely proportional to the mass of the object.
The *Law of Action and Reaction:* when force is applied, there is an equal and opposite reaction force.

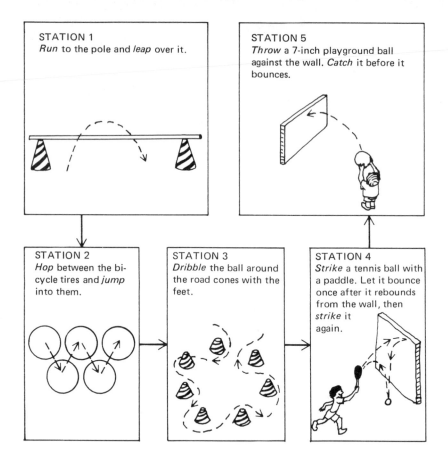

Figure 16.5 Review Circuit: The Act of Moving

STATION 1
Run to the pole and *leap* over it.

STATION 5
Throw a 7-inch playground ball against the wall. *Catch* it before it bounces.

STATION 2
Hop between the bicycle tires and *jump* into them.

STATION 3
Dribble the ball around the road cones with the feet.

STATION 4
Strike a tennis ball with a paddle. Let it bounce once after it rebounds from the wall, then *strike* it again.

2. Have the children stand facing each other in two lines approximately twenty feet apart. Have each child in one line kick a playground ball to the child opposite, who traps it with his or her foot. After the children have kicked the ball back and forth several times, challenge them to kick it harder. Insist that they trap the ball before returning it, so it will not be kicked into the air.

3. Call the class together and discuss the relationship between activity 2 and the first two laws of motion. Note the following points:

a.   The Law of Inertia states that the ball does not move until acted upon by some force.

b.   The ball is set in motion by the force exerted by the kicker's leg.

c.   The fact that the ball continues to move until acted on by the child who stops it is an example of the second part of the Law of Inertia (see Figure 16.6).

Figure 16.6 Applications of the Three Laws of Motion
Top: The Law of Inertia —the ball will remain at rest until acted upon by an outside force; it will continue in motion at the same speed, in a straight line, until acted upon by an outside force. Bottom left: The Law of Acceleration—more muscular force is required to produce the increased acceleration in running than is required to produce the slower movement of walking. Bottom right: The Law of Action and Reaction—the counterpressure from the floor is equal to the downward pressure exerted by the ball. *Mickey Adair*

d. The movement of the ball is also affected by rolling friction, which slows its movement, and the force of gravity, which keeps it on the floor.

e. The acceleration of the ball is directly proportional to the force that causes it to move; that is, the harder the child kicks, the faster the ball rolls.

4. Have the children return to their positions, move the lines closer together, and bounce pass the ball back and forth.

5. Have the pairs scatter about the room. Challenge one child to dribble the ball while the other tries to gain control of it. When the dribbler loses control of the ball, the partners change roles.

6. Call the class together and discuss the relationship between activities 4 and 5 and the Law of Action and Reaction:

a. A reaction force is created when the ball strikes the floor.

b. The reaction force is equal to the downward momentum of the ball. Thus the harder the ball is pushed or thrown against the floor, the higher it will rebound.

7. Explain how the three laws of motion relate to the locomotor movements executed in the circuit illustrated in Figure 16.5:

a. The child's body will not move until the leg muscles exert enough force to set him or her in motion. (the Law of Inertia)

b. The speed of the child's movement is determined by the amount of muscular force exerted. (the Law of Acceleration)

c. When the foot contacts the supporting surface, an opposing reaction force is created and the body is propelled forward. (the Law of Action and Reaction)

8. Extend and reinforce the children's learning by applying the three laws of motion to riding a bicycle:

a. The bicycle will remain motionless until it is pushed or pedaled. Once it is set in motion, it will continue moving in a straight line until some force changes the direction of its front wheel. (the Law of Inertia)

b. The speed of the bicycle's movement is determined by the amount of force the rider's leg muscles exert. This amount may be varied by (1) how hard the rider pushes with the legs and feet and (2) how fast he or she pedals. (the Law of Acceleration)

c. It is easier to ride a bicycle on a sidewalk or paved street than on a lawn or soft dirt. Because pavement is a solid surface, the upward counterpressure of the pavement equals the downward pressure exerted by the bicycle's tires. Grass and soft dirt absorb part of the

The Basic Sports Skills

force, and thus do not exert an equal reaction force. As a result the rider must exert more muscular force to compensate for the lack of reaction force. (the Law of Action and Reaction)

Key Concept
□ *There are three types of motion: angular, linear, and curvilinear.*

Angular motion, also called rotary motion, is movement of a body part around a central axis.
Linear motion, also called translatory motion, is movement of the body as a whole through space.
Curvilinear motion is movement in an arc or circle.

9. Have the children pair off and toss a yarn ball back and forth to each other. Tell them to stand ten to twelve feet apart and use an underhand toss.

10. Write the names and definitions of the three types of motion on the board and identify an example of each in activity number 9 (see Figure 16.7).
   a. The swing of the arm used to toss the ball is an example of angular motion. The shoulder joint is the central axis around which the arm moves.
   b. As the swinging arm moves forward, the hand holding the ball moves in an arc. The ball also travels through space in a curved pathway. Thus the angular motion of the arm results in curvilinear motion of the hand and ball.
   c. As the children walk to and from their positions on the floor, the angular motion of their legs results in linear movement of their bodies. (The hip joint serves as the central axis for the angular motion of the legs, and the child's body as a whole moves from one place to another.)
   d. At least two types of motion occur in each of the basic sports skills. In the four locomotor movements, angular motion of the body parts results in linear motion of the body. In throwing, catching, kicking, and striking, angular motion of the body parts results in linear or curvilinear motion on the part of an object.

11. Review the distinction between the *laws* of motion and the *types* of motion.
   a. The types of motion describe the pathway in which a body, body part, or object moves.
   b. The laws of motion describe why a body or object moves at a certain speed or in a certain direction.

Figure 16.7 The Three Types of Motion
Top left: *Angular* motion of the arms and legs results in *linear* motion of the body as a whole. Top right and bottom: Angular motion of the arm results in *curvilinear* motion of the hand and the ball.
Mickey Adair

The Basic Sports Skills

Leverage

Key Concept

☐ *The human body functions as a system of levers.*

A lever is a rigid bar that moves about a fixed point, or axis.
Movement of the lever results from the application of force.
There are three types of levers, determined by the relationship of the axis (also called the fulcrum), the weight (also called the resistance), and the point of application of the force.
Levers are used to lift weight, to increase the amount of force applied, and to increase the speed of movement.
In the human body the lever is the bone, the fulcrum the joint. The force that moves the lever is supplied by muscular contractions.

Activities for Children

1. Write the Key Concept and first three subconcepts on the board. Review the three parts of a lever. Demonstrate how each type of lever functions (see Figure 16.8).

2. Point out that in each of the examples shown in Figure 16.8, the lever is being used to lift a weight.

3. Demonstrate how the first-class lever is used in conjunction with a prying movement to increase force.

4. Explain that the mechanical advantage of a third-class lever is to increase the speed of movement.

5. Attach one end of a piece of elastic to the shoulder joint of a cardboard skeleton, and the other end to the upper portion of its forearm (see Figure 16.9) to simulate the biceps muscle. Tie the elastic so that it is stretched when the arm is extended and relaxed when the arm is bent at a right angle. Explain to the children that the muscles of the body function by contracting (getting shorter) and pulling on the bone, which causes it to move. Point out that the biceps makes the bone into a third-class lever, since the force is pulling on the bone between the axis (the elbow joint) and the resistance (the weight of the arm and hand).

6. Have the children pair off and face their partners. Ask child A to make a fist with his or her right hand and bend the right elbow at a right angle. Have child B place his or her right hand on top of B's right hand and push down, while A resists. Tell A to place the index finger of the left hand on the inside of the right elbow and feel the biceps tendon. (See Figure 16.10.) Have A and B change places and repeat the activity.

7. Draw a diagram of the forearm on the board (see Figure 16.8). Point out the similarity between the components of the forearm and

Figure 16.8 The Three Types of Levers
Top: First-class lever—the axis is between the force and the point of resistance. To demonstrate push downward on the end of the board (force). Middle: Second-class lever—the resistance is between the axis and the force. To demonstrate lift the end of the board upward. Bottom: Third-class lever—the force is exerted between the axis and the resistance. To demonstrate tie a rope around the board between the axis and the resistance and use it to pull the lever upward.

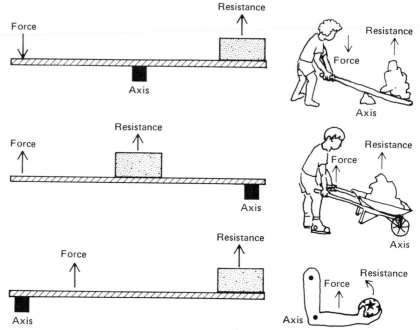

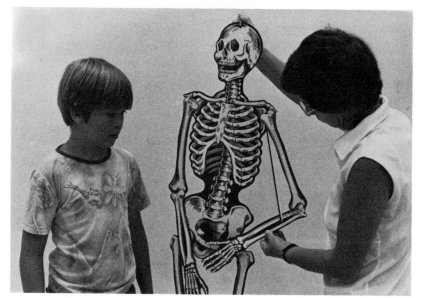

Figure 16.9 The Forearm as a Third-Class Lever: Demonstration with a Cardboard Skeleton
Mickey Adair

Figure 16.10 The Forearm as a Third-Class Lever: Demonstration with Two Children
Mickey Adair

those of the levers used in activities 5 and 6 above: the axis, point of application of the force, and resistance, arranged to function as a third-class lever.

8. Explain to the children that because most of the levers of the human body are third-class levers, we are structurally designed to favor range of motion and speed rather than force production. Point out that human beings do not need to be as strong as some animals because they can use their highly developed brains to invent machines to perform heavy work.

9. Explain that a paddle, bat, or racket extends the length of the arm lever, causing it to make a bigger arc when it moves through space (see Figure 16.11). Increasing the range of motion in this manner enables the person to strike an object with more force.

10. Challenge the children to name as many sports as possible in which an implement is used to impart force to an object. (archery, badminton, baseball, billiards, croquet, golf, hockey, softball, shuffleboard, table tennis, tennis)

11. Explain that a person who uses an implement must be strong enough to exert the force necessary to control its movement, and that for this reason most sports equipment is available in different weights and sizes. The size and weight of such implements as bats, paddles, archery bows, and hockey sticks should be matched to the size, strength, and skill level of the people using them. Equipment that is too

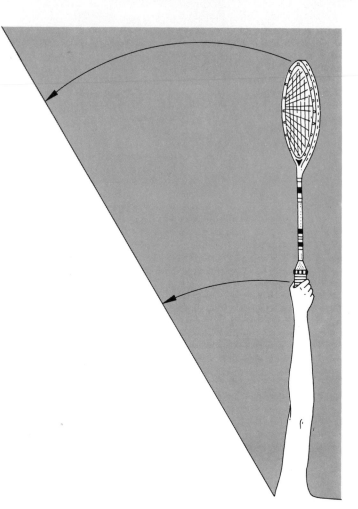

Figure 16.11 Extending the Length of the Arm Lever

large or heavy to be manipulated effectively prevents one from contacting an object accurately.

12. Have the children practice striking a tennis ball with a large wooden paddle. Then have them do the same with a regulation tennis racket. Point out that their superior control over the movement of the paddle enables them to strike the ball more accurately.

13. Have the children practice striking various objects with various implements. For example, have them strike a tennis ball and a five-inch playground ball with a large wooden paddle, a short-handled tennis racket, a wand, a croquet mallet, a gym hockey stick, and a plastic bat. Discuss the size, weight, and shape of the various implements and the effect of these factors on the force imparted to the objects.

Mass

Key Concept

□ *Mass is the quantity of matter making up an object.*

The size and mass of an object affect its movement through space. An object's weight is determined by the amount of force gravity exerts on its mass.

Activities for Children

1. Show the children several pairs of objects that are similar in size but dissimilar in mass (see Figure 16.12). For example:

   a. a table tennis ball and a golf ball
   b. a nerf ball and a softball
   c. a whiffle ball and a softball
   d. a tennis ball and a baseball

2. Have the children practice throwing and striking these pairs of balls, comparing how far and fast they travel, how high they bounce, and how far they rebound from the wall.

3. Relate the children's observations in activity 2 to the Law of Inertia (the ball will not move until some force acts on it) and the Law of Acceleration (the speed of the ball is determined by the amount of force applied to it and by its mass: the more mass the ball has, the more force is required to move it).

4. Show the children pairs of balls of similar mass but dissimilar size. For example:

   a. a cage ball and a basketball
   b. a large playground ball and a croquet ball

5. Have the children roll these pairs of balls. Discuss the differences in the distances they roll.

6. Point out the relationship of the composition, size, and mass of an object. The croquet ball is made of solid wood; because its mass is very concentrated, it is relatively small. The playground ball is made of heavy rubber and is hollow. The cage ball has a thin rubber lining and a canvas cover and is also hollow; its mass is spread over a much larger area.

7. Show the children pairs of objects the larger of which has less mass than the smaller. For example:

   a. a balloon and a five-inch playground ball
   b. a large playground ball and a bowling ball

8. Have the children toss the balloon into the air and let it bounce on the floor. Then have them do the same with the playground ball.

9. Ask the children why the balloon stays in the air longer and

Figure 16.12 Similarities and Differences in the Size and Mass of Objects
Top: balls that are similar in size but different in mass; Bottom: a large ball that has less mass than a smaller ball
Mickey Adair

The Basic Sports Skills

bounces less high than the playground ball. (The balloon has less mass and is therefore subject to less gravitational pull; the ball has more mass and therefore strikes the floor harder, creating a greater reaction force.)

Momentum

Key Concept

☐ *The momentum of an object is the force with which it moves against resistance.*

Momentum is the product of mass times velocity.
The momentum of one object may be transferred to another object.

Activities for Children

1. Simultaneously roll a nerf ball and a softball across the floor. Ask the children why the softball rolls farther. (It has more mass.)

2. Roll the two balls again, this time letting them rebound from the wall. Ask the children why the softball rebounds farther. (Because it has more mass, there is a greater reaction force.)

3. Roll two softballs across the floor, one slowly and one fast. Ask the children why the faster one travels farther. (It has more velocity.)

4. Have the children roll a playground ball at an Indian club. Ask them to describe what happens to the ball after it strikes the club. (It changes direction.)

5. Explain that when a moving implement strikes an object, it transfers its momentum to the object. It is for this reason that a correct backswing is important: as the implement moves forward from the backswing, it builds up a momentum that is transferred to the struck object.

6. Instruct the children to walk through general space, stopping immediately and completely when they hear a drumbeat. After repeating this process three or four times, instruct them to run and stop at a signal. Repeat. Ask the children to compare the amounts of time it takes to stop walking and to stop running. Tell them to run as fast as they can and stop at a signal. Ask if it is easier to stop when walking or when running. Explain that the body has mass, and when it is moving, it has velocity. Since momentum is the product of mass times velocity, the faster one moves the more momentum the body has and the harder it is to stop.

7. Have the children note how far their bodies travel after they hear the signal when walking, running at a moderate speed, and running fast. Point out that they can stop immediately when walking, but may have to take one or more steps before they can stop running. Relate this

phenomenon to the momentum of the moving body. Point out that the risk of injury in case of collision increases as momentum increases.

8. Point out that two objects moving toward each other are both building up momentum, and that if they run into each other the impact will be twice as hard as if one were stationary. Explain that for this reason they should try to avoid running into each other when playing.

9. Explain that a running approach to jumping or leaping builds up momentum by giving additional impetus to the forward motion of the body, and thus enables the person to jump or leap farther.

Friction

Key Concept
□ *Friction is a force that opposes the motion of an object across a surface.*

The amount of friction created between an object and a surface is determined by their physical characteristics and the amount of force pushing them together.
There are three types of friction: starting friction, sliding friction, and rolling friction.

Activities for Children

1. Explain that the size, shape, and weight of an object affects the amount of friction it will create. Demonstrate this concept by rolling a golf ball and a croquet ball across the floor. Point out that the smaller, lighter ball creates less friction.

2. Simultaneously roll the croquet ball and slide a small wooden box in the same direction across the floor. Ask the children why the ball travels a greater distance. (Much more of the box's surface area is in contact with the floor, and sliding creates much more friction than rolling.)

3. Demonstrate that an increase in the weight of an object increases the amount of friction. Have one of the children slide an empty box across the floor. Then put some books in the box and ask the child to slide it again.

4. Demonstrate that rolling decreases friction by placing the box of books in a wagon and asking the child to pull it.

5. Discuss the effects of friction on execution of the locomotor movements.
   a. The leg exerts a downward and backward force (see Figure 16.13).
   b. When the foot is in contact with a solid surface where maximum friction is created, there is an equal and opposite reaction force. (the Law of Action and Reaction).
   c. If the foot slips on the floor, very little friction is created and the

The Basic Sports Skills

Figure 16.13 Friction and Walking
The leg exerts a downward and backward pushing force in walking. With maximum friction, an equal and opposite reaction force is exerted by the floor.
Mickey Adair

reaction force is decreased, causing a loss of force for the movement.
d. One should wear tennis shoes or no shoes in a gymnasium because the adhesive friction of the soles gives one additional traction.

e. Very little friction is created when walking on wet or slick surfaces, and one must compensate by taking smaller steps. Small steps cause more of the force of the legs to be exerted downward than backward.

6. Have the children take small steps and large steps while walking. Have them pair off and observe each other taking steps of various sizes, noting the direction of the pushing force.

7. Have them compare the amount of friction created when they walk barefoot, in stocking feet, and in tennis shoes.

8. Have them try to perform a Chinese-Get-up while wearing socks. Then have them repeat the stunt barefoot or in tennis shoes.

9. Point out that movement activities involving sliding use equipment designed to minimize friction. Examples are roller skates, ice skates, skis, and metal platters or plastic sheets for sliding down snow-covered hills.

Projection

Key Concept

□ *A projectile is an object moving through space without a base of support.*

Any object that is thrown or hit becomes a projectile.
The motion of a projectile is affected by:
    a. *the amount of force imparted to it*
    b. *its physical characteristics*
    c. *the angle of release*
    d. *gravitational pull*
    e. *air resistance*
When an implement is used to strike an object, four additional factors affect the flight of the projectile:
    a. *the physical characteristics of the striking implement (its length, shape, and mass)*
    b. *the physical characteristics of the projectile (its mass, shape, and elasticity)*
    c. *the type of contact made between the implement and the object (the speed of the implement at the moment of contact, the direction it is moving, and the relation of the striking force to the object's center of gravity)*

The Basic Sports Skills

d. *the state of motion of the object at the moment of contact (still or moving; if moving, the speed and direction of its approach to the striking surface)*

Activities for Children

1. Have each child toss a playground ball straight up, gradually tossing it higher and higher.

2. Have the children pair off and throw the ball back and forth, first in a high arc and then gradually decreasing the size of the arc until it is a straight line. Have one partner take a step backward each time he or she catches the ball, so that the distance between the two increases as the angle of the arc decreases.

3. Discuss the following principles:
a. When the gravitational pull equals the upward force of a thrown ball, the ball will begin falling back to the earth.
b. Gravity and air resistance counteract the momentum of the ball. Gravitational pull forces the ball vertically downward and air resistance creates an opposing horizontal force.

4. Copy Figure 16.14 on the board. Have one of the children throw a softball, releasing it at the angles illustrated in the figure. Point out that the greater the angle of projection, the more nearly vertical the pathway of the ball. Thus if the ball is thrown in a high arc, it will stay in the air longer, but more of the distance it travels will be upward than forward. Relate this phenomenon to stepping backward after each catch in activity 2: as the size of the arc decreased, the horizontal distance the ball travelled increased.

5. Point out that the ball travels the greatest horizontal distance when it is released at an approximately 45-degree angle. If the angle of release is greater than 45 degrees, more of its momentum is expended travelling upward; if less than 45 degrees, gravitational pull soon overcomes the ball's upward momentum and it begins travelling downward.

6. Show the children such striking implements as a table tennis paddle, large wooden paddle, tennis racket, badminton racket, croquet mallet, hockey stick, and bat. Compare the length, weight, size, and composition of the striking surfaces of these implements (see Figure 16.15).
a. A non-slip material is affixed to the surface of the table tennis paddle, while the wooden paddle has a slick face.
b. The tennis racket has a larger face and heavier strings than the badminton racket.

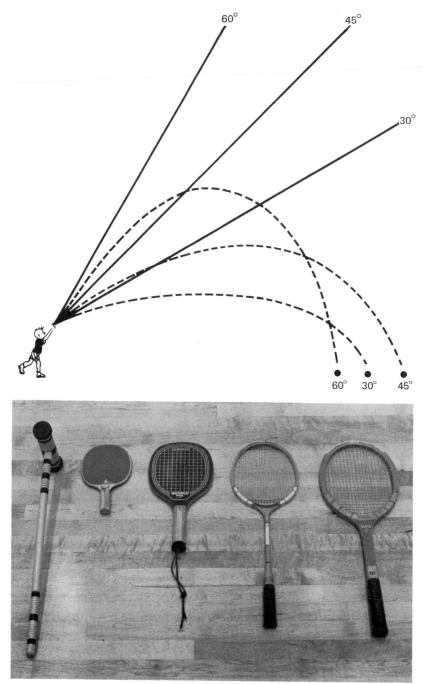

Figure 16.14 The Effects of the Angle of Projection on the Distance an Object Will Travel
A ball will travel farthest if released at a 45-degree angle.

Figure 16.15 Relative Size of the Striking Surface of Various Striking Implements
Mickey Adair

c. The croquet mallet has a small circular striking surface and the hockey stick has an oblong surface.

d. The bat has a long rounded striking surface.

7. Discuss the relationships between implements and objects designed to be used together.

a. A small light ball is used with a small light paddle in table tennis.

b. A larger ball (a tennis ball or five-inch playground ball) is used with a larger wooden paddle.

c. A badminton racket and shuttlecock are both lightweight, whereas a tennis ball and tennis racket are heavier.

8. Discuss the relationship between the design of objects and implements and the size of the playing area in which they are used (see Figure 16.16).

9. Show the children various objects used as projectiles, such as a playground ball, volleyball, tennis ball, shuttlecock, baseball, hockey ball, and table tennis ball. Discuss the relationship between the structure of each object and the way it is used.

a. Playground balls and volleyballs are large and quite elastic because they are struck with a body part. If small, hard objects were used, the body part would be bruised by the impact.

b. A tennis ball is very elastic because it is played on the bounce and must travel a considerable distance when it rebounds from the face of the racket.

c. Because a shuttlecock is always played in the air and travels a relatively short distance, it is constructed to travel slowly and need not bounce accurately.

d. A baseball and a hockey ball are both designed to travel long distances. They are solid, hard objects that are struck by solid wooden implements.

10. Press a playground ball against the floor or wall to demonstrate to the children that an object with an elastic quality is somewhat flattened at the moment of impact. Explain that it resumes its original shape as it moves away from the striking surface, and that the reaction force of this change in shape combines with the striking force to increase the speed and distance it will travel.

11. Simultaneously bounce a partially deflated playground ball and a fully inflated playground ball of the same size. Do the same with a new tennis ball and a "dead" tennis ball. Explain that the partially deflated ball and the "dead" tennis ball have both lost much of their elastic quality and therefore absorb force rather than reacting to it.

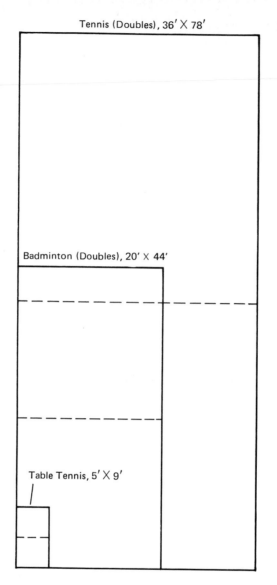

Tennis (Doubles), 36′ X 78′

Badminton (Doubles), 20′ X 44′

Table Tennis, 5′ X 9′

Figure 16.16 Relative Size of Playing Areas in Three Games

The Basic Sports Skills

12. Place a softball on a batting tee and ask one of the children to swing at and strike it in slow motion. Have the child gradually increase the speed of the striking movement. Ask the children to note that the distance the ball travels increases in proportion to the speed of the striking implement.

13. Ask the child to strike the ball through its center of gravity, to "top" the ball, and finally to swing upward and strike the ball from underneath. Compare the effects of these different points of impact. (Striking the ball through its center of gravity will result in a line drive; topping the ball will cause it to be a grounder; and striking it diagonally upward will make it a fly ball.)

14. Have the children strike tennis balls with large wooden paddles. Instruct them to let the ball rebound from the wall and bounce once before striking it again. Have them strike the ball while the face of the paddle is tilted in various upward and sideward directions. Discuss the effect of the angle of the paddle face on the direction the ball moves.

15. Have the children bounce playground balls against the floor, using different amounts of force. Ask them to note the differences in the distance the ball travels after it rebounds. Point out that the distance it rebounds increases as the speed of its movement at the moment of impact increases. Explain that the same thing happens to a pitched ball; that is, the harder it is pitched, the faster it will be travelling and the farther it will travel in the opposite direction after it is hit.

16. Have one of the children kick a stationary ball to a child standing across the room. Have the second child trap the ball and kick it back. Then repeat the movement, having the second child kick the ball without trapping it. The first time the ball will roll along the floor when it is returned, but the second time it may rise into the air. This occurs because the rolling ball has top spin; when it is kicked, the pathway of the ball is only partially, rather than totally, reversed.

17. Have the children dribble balls while standing in place, and then while moving. Ask them to note that the ball rebounds at an angle equal and opposite to that at which it strikes the surface. If it is moving straight down, it will bounce straight up; if it is bounced diagonally forward, it will rebound forward on the same diagonal. Further illustrate this principle by having the children execute bounce passes to partners. Have them pass the ball so it travels at different angles. Explain that this principle applies to a basketball rebounding from a backboard and to any moving object that strikes an implement.

The laws and principles that regulate movement have been discussed separately in order to provide the child a comprehensive knowledge of them. In the following section these factors will be applied to analysis of throwing, catching, striking, and kicking.

THROWING

In throwing, the motion of the body is directly transferred to an object held in the hand. The speed and direction the hand is moving at the moment the object is released determine the velocity, direction, and distance the object will travel. Increased throwing speed is attained by transferring the momentum of the body to the throwing arm. Thus correct and coordinated movement of the entire body is essential to a skilled throwing pattern.

A skilled throwing pattern develops gradually as a child matures and practices its correct execution. Many children's throwing patterns are incorrect and underdeveloped because they have not received proper instruction. Incorrect use of the body parts restricts freedom of movement and hinders control and accuracy. Children should first learn to throw accurately and then work at increasing speed and distance.

There are three basic throwing patterns: underhand, overhand, and sidearm. The underhand pattern, in which the arm is held relatively straight and swings close to the body, is the easiest for children to execute. It is used when a short accurate throw is desired. The overhand pattern is used when the goal is increased speed and distance, and the sidearm pattern is used to impart force to heavy objects.

The Underhand Throw

The position of readiness for the underhand throw is a forward stride position. This position is more stable, because the base of support is enlarged in the direction the force will move during the throw. The foot *opposite* the throwing arm (the left foot[2]) is ahead, permitting proper hip and trunk rotation. The body's center of gravity is over the center of the base of support, the body is relaxed, and the knees are slightly flexed, as shown in Figure 16.17.

As the right arm moves straight back in the backswing, the weight is shifted backward over the ball of the right foot and the body rotates slightly to the right. At the end of the backswing, the right arm should be fully extended in a horizontal position.

To throw, the right arm swings forward close to the body. The trunk rotates back to the left so that the body is squarely facing the target when the ball is released. The body's center of gravity moves forward as

---

[2]For reasons of consistency, all skills will be analyzed for right-handed participants. You will need to reverse all references to right and left when working with left-handed children.

The Basic Sports Skills

**Figure 16.17 The
Underhand Throw**
Mickey Adair

the arm swings. The ball is released at the bottom of the arc (when the arm is perpendicular to the floor).

In the follow-through, the right arm swings forward toward the target as the weight is shifted over the left foot. In an underhand pitch or other throwing motion in which it is desirable to give the ball maximum impetus, a step forward with the right foot should accompany the follow-through.

Activities for Children

1. Have the children stand facing each other in two lines approximately ten feet apart. Ask them to stand in a forward strike position, with the left foot forward if they are right-handed and the right foot forward if they are left-handed. "Rock your body backward and forward, shifting your center of gravity backward over your rear foot and forward over your front foot. Let your arms swing freely with your body." Emphasize the rhythm of the movement, and ask the children to close their eyes and think about how the movement feels.

2. "Imagine you are holding a yarn ball. Let the imaginary ball swing back and forth in your hand. Close your eyes and feel the rhythmic pendular swing of your throwing arm."

3. "Open your hand as if you were releasing the ball just after your hand swings past your right leg. Follow through with your throwing hand so that the ends of your fingers point toward your partner at the end of the swing."

4. Give each child a yarn ball. Have the children practice the arm swing and weight shift without releasing the ball.

5. Have the children stand facing the wall approximately six feet from it. Have them execute the same movements, releasing the ball as the throwing hand swings past the right leg.

6. Mark a spot waist-high on the wall and challenge the children to hit it when they throw.

7. Have the children pair off and throw back and forth.

8. Exchange the yarn ball for a beanbag. Have the children throw the beanbag at the spot on the wall and then to a partner.

9. When the children's form, rhythm, and accuracy are satisfactory, exchange the beanbag for a softball and repeat activity 8.

10. Gradually increase the distance the children are required to throw, but continue to emphasize accuracy.

11. Check each child's throwing pattern, watching for the following common errors:

a. failure to take a full backswing with the throwing arm

b. failure to shift the weight backward during the backswing

c. release of the ball too soon or too late

d. failure to shift the weight forward or to follow through

The Overhand Throw

The position of readiness for the overhand throw is the same as for the underhand throw. During the backswing, the elbow is bent as the throwing arm swings backward and upward. The shoulders and hips are rotated to the right, and the weight is shifted backward over the right foot. The left arm is raised forward and upward. (See Figure 16.18.)

In preparation for releasing the ball, the body's center of gravity begins to move forward and the hips start to rotate to the left. The hip rotation continues as the spine and shoulders begin to turn. The left arm swings downward and backward. The elbow leads the forward motion of the throwing arm, and as it moves forward the forearm begins to extend. When the hand has moved forward in line with the head, the wrist snaps forward and the ball is released.

In the follow-through, the shoulders continue to rotate to the left as the throwing arm continues its forward motion. The throwing motion is completed as the right foot steps forward and takes the weight.

Activities for Children

1. Demonstrate the overarm throwing pattern, pointing out the positions of the arms; the weight transference; and the sequential rotation of the hips, spine, and shoulders.

2. Have the children perform the sequence of movements several times without a ball.

3. Have them face the wall and throw yarn balls. Emphasize correct form. Check each child's throwing pattern for the following common errors:

a. incorrect position of the elbow (The elbow may be held close to the body or elevated above shoulder level.)

b. failure to rotate the hips or shoulders

c. failure to transfer the weight backward on the backswing

d. failure to snap the wrist on the release

e. stopping the forward motion of the body at the moment of release, rather than completing the follow-through

4. Have the children throw to partners. Gradually increase the distance between them. Carefully check each child's form.

5. Replace the yarn balls with tennis balls, and have the partners continue throwing back and forth.

Figure 16.18 The Overhand Throw
Mickey Adair

The Basic Sports Skills

6. Challenge the children to throw accurately by having them throw tennis balls at pieces of construction paper taped to the wall.

7. Transform activity 6 into a contest by allowing each partner to throw five times. The partner who hits the paper most often wins. Have the children move forward or backward according to skill level.

8. Play keep-away, using a tennis ball and specifying that throws must be overhand. Add to the challenge by placing two children in the center of the circle and using two balls.

9. Record the distance each child can throw and challenge the children to increase their distances when they are rechecked at regular intervals.

The Sidearm Throw

The position of readiness for the sidearm throw is the same as for the underhand throw. If a small ball is used, it is held with a tripod grip (see Figure 16.19). If a larger ball is being thrown, the palm of the hand holds it against the lower arm. During the backswing, the throwing arm swings backward in a horizontal arc as the body rotates to the right and the weight is transferred to the right foot.

In preparation for release, the hips, spine, and shoulders rotate as the throwing arm swings forward. The ball is released when the arm is parallel to the target. If a small ball is being thrown, the wrist is snapped when the ball is released.

In the follow-through, the throwing arm continues moving forward toward the target, and the body continues to rotate until it squarely faces the target.

Activities for Children

1. Demonstrate the sidearm throw, pointing out the correct position of the throwing arm; the weight transfer; and the proper rotation of the hips, spine, and shoulders.

2. Have the children perform the sequence of movements several times without a ball.

3. Have them face the wall and throw yarn balls. Check each child's throwing pattern for the following common errors:
   a. failure to rotate the hips
   b. failure to transfer the weight to the right foot
   c. failure to snap the wrist
   d. incorrect timing of the release (Releasing the ball too soon will cause it to veer to the right; releasing it too late will make it swerve to the left.)

4. Have the children throw to partners. Gradually increase the distance between them as their accuracy improves.

Figure 16.19 The Sidearm Throw
Top left: the tripod grip, for small balls; Bottom left: the palm grip, for large balls; Right: correct body position
Mickey Adair

The Basic Sports Skills

Throwing

5. Replace the yarn balls with tennis balls or five-inch playground balls, and have the partners continue throwing back and forth.

6. Challenge the children to test the accuracy of their throws by attempting to hit a target on the wall. Have the partners compete to see who can throw accurately from the greatest distance.

Movement Principles Teaching the laws and principles that pertain to throwing will enable the children to understand the reasons for correct form. The primary factors that apply to throwing are the principles of equilibrium, the laws of motion, and force production.

The principles of equilibrium, which must be observed if a stable body position is to be maintained, are as follows:

1. The body's center of gravity must remain within the base of support.

2. The base of support is enlarged.

3. The base is enlarged in the direction of the *moving* force.

The ball acquires the motion of the throwing hand in accordance with Newton's first two laws of motion:

1. The Law of Inertia: The ball will continue to move at the same speed and in the same direction it is travelling at the moment of release until acted upon by another force (gravity and air resistance).

2. The Law of Acceleration: The acceleration of the ball is proportional to the force projected by the momentum of the body and the throwing arm.

The amount of force imparted to the ball is increased by (1) the full backswing of the arm, (2) the sequential rotation of the body parts, (3) the transfer of body weight, and (4) the release of the ball at the moment the throwing hand is moving forward with the greatest speed. Additional force is attained by means of a wrist snap in overhand and sidearm throws.

CATCHING Catching involves reducing and stopping the momentum of an object and gaining control of it. The catching pattern has four phases:

1. The child must position the body and hands in line with the trajectory of the oncoming ball.

2. He or she must judge the height of the ball at the time it will be received and place the hands in the correct preparatory position.

3. The hands and body must absorb the force created by the ball's momentum.

4. He or she must grasp and hold onto the ball.

The catching pattern employed depends on the size and weight of the ball and its height at the time it is caught. A large ball is easier to catch than a small one, and a two-handed catch is easier than catching with one hand. Thus children should not undertake unilateral catching until they have developed skilled bilateral catching patterns. Most children in the upper elementary grades are capable of highly skilled catching patterns. However, fear of the ball may cause some to dislike catching. These children should work with yarn balls, beanbags, and playground balls until they have become confident and at ease with balls.

Two-Handed Catching

The correct preparatory hand and body positions for bilateral catching are shown in Figure 16.20. The preparatory hand position is determined by the height of the ball; the body position, which is always the same, consists of a forward stride position with the left foot forward. This position enlarges the base in the direction the ball will be traveling, and enables the child to maintain balance while moving the body backward to absorb the force of the ball. Also, the ball is usually thrown immediately after it is caught, and this is the position of readiness for throwing.

In catching, the arms reach out to meet the ball, the fingers are spread and the hands slightly cupped. The ball is received against the palms of the hands and the fingers close around it. The arms "give" with the ball by bending at the elbow and shoulder joints. If the ball has a great deal of momentum, the body also "gives" with the ball and the child may step backward (see Figure 16.20).

Activities for Children

Catching should be introduced and practiced in conjunction with throwing. The children should practice receiving balls of different sizes at different heights and speeds, while standing still and on the move. As the children practice, you should closely observe their form, watching for the following common errors:

1. reaching out to the side for the ball instead of moving the body in line with it

Figure 16.20 Correct Hand and Body Positions for the Two-Hand Catch
Top left: hand position for catching a large ball that is above the shoulders; Bottom left: hand position when the ball is approaching at a level between the waist and the shoulders; Bottom right: hand position when the ball is below waist level; Top middle: correct body position for catching; Top right: correct body position to absorb the force of the ball
Mickey Adair

2. incorrect hand position (fingers not pointed in the right direction; fingers straight and rigid rather than curved and relaxed; heels of the hands too close together or far apart)

3. failure to "give" with the ball

4. failure to close the hands over the ball and maintain control of it

When the children demonstrate ability to control the ball with both hands, they are ready to be introduced to the more advanced skill of catching with one hand.

One-Handed Catching

Catching the ball with one hand is a skill employed in softball and baseball. Because the ball is small and usually travels quite fast, a glove should be worn on the catching hand. The padding of the glove serves as a shock absorber, reducing the amount of force that must be absorbed by the hand and arm.

The correct preparatory positions for catching a fly ball and a ground ball are shown in Figure 16.21. The feet are in a forward stride position and the body and hands are in line with the ball.

As the catch is made, the child reaches out for the ball and stops it with the gloved hand. The bare hand immediately covers and grasps

Figure 16.21 Correct Body Positions for the One-Hand Catch
Left: correct body position for catching a fly ball; Right: correct body position for catching a ground ball.
Mickey Adair

Activities for Children

the ball. The wrist, elbow, and shoulder joints bend to "give" with the force of the ball.

Catching with one hand is usually taught in conjunction with batting and advanced throwing. Thus most of the following activities involve all three skills.

1. Demonstrate the correct form for catching a fly ball. Point out the position of the trunk, arms, and hands. Show the children how the right hand closes over and grasps the ball.

2. Have the children practice throwing and catching fly balls with partners.

3. Have the children take turns batting fly balls from a tee and fungo batting to a small group of fielders who try to catch the batted balls.

4. Demonstrate the correct form for catching a ground ball. Emphasize correct body and hand position.

5. Have the children pair off to practice, one partner rolling the ball and the other catching it and rolling it back.

6. Repeat activity 3, having the batter hit the ball so it will roll.

7. Play games that emphasize catching and throwing.

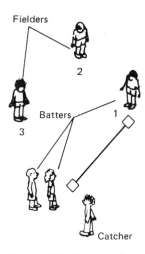

Figure 16.22 Diagram for the Game *Throw Ball*

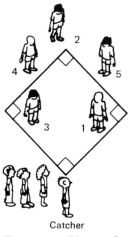

Catcher

Figure 16.23 Diagram for the Game *Beat the Ball*

a. Throw Ball. Six or more players assume the positions shown in Figure 16.22. One of the batters throws the ball into fair territory and attempts to run to the base and back. The fielders try to catch the ball and return it to the catcher before the batter returns. If the batter beats the ball, he or she remains at bat. If put out, the batter takes the place of fielder 3, the catcher becomes a batter, and fielder 2 becomes the first baseman. The following variations of Throw Ball may also be introduced:

(1) The distance to the base may be adjusted to match the skill level of the group.

(2) The batter may stop at first base and run home when the second batter hits. Thus the batter may be put out at either first base or home.

(3) An additional batter may be introduced and the three bases of a softball diamond used. The batter may be put out at any base.

(4) A fielder who catches three fly balls may exchange places with the batter who threw the last ball he or she caught.

b. Beat the Ball. Nine players assume the positions shown in Figure 16.23. One of the batters throws the ball into fair territory and runs around the bases. The fielders throw the ball in turn to first, second, third, and home. A batter who beats the ball home remains at bat. If the ball beats the batter home, he or she is out and takes the place of the number 5 player; the catcher becomes a batter and everyone moves up one position.

c. Teacher Relay. Relay teams line up in file formation, as shown in Figure 16.24. The teacher throws to the first person on the team. If a player catches the ball, he or she throws it back to the teacher and goes to the end of the line. A player who fails to catch the ball on the fly must recover the ball, throw it back to the teacher, and stay in place to receive the ball again. When the first child is again at the head of the line, the team is finished. If the teams are competing, the first team finished wins. Another child takes the place of the teacher and play begins again.

d. Shuttle Relay. The teams line up as shown in Figure 16.25. Player 1 throws to 2 and runs to the end of the opposite line. Player 2 throws to 3 and runs to the end of that line. Player 3 then throws to 4 and so on. The first team to arrive back in starting position wins. This formation may also be used to give children practice in catching ground balls.

Movement Principles   The movement principles that apply to catching are those relating to equilibrium and force absorption.

Catching

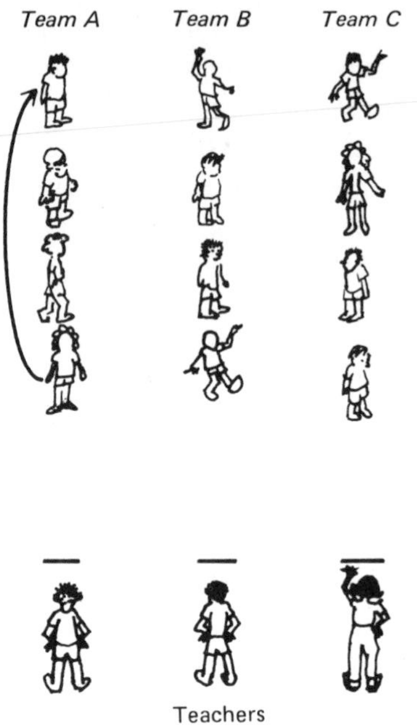

Figure 16.24 Diagram for the Game *Teacher Relay*

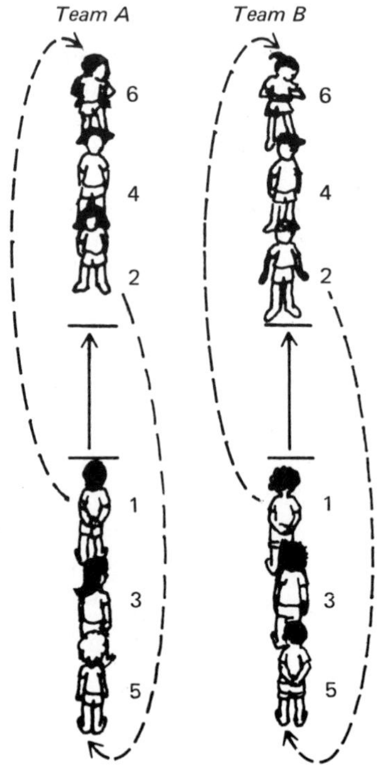

Teachers

Figure 16.25 Diagram for the Game *Shuttle Relay*

The principles of equilibrium that serve to maintain a stable body position during catching are as follows:

1. The body's center of gravity must remain within the base of support.
2. The base of support is enlarged.
3. The base is enlarged in the direction of the *opposing* force.

When a moving ball strikes a surface, its entire momentum must be absorbed or it will rebound (in accordance with the Law of Action and Reaction). In catching, force absorption is affected by three factors:

1. the distance and time over which the force is absorbed
2. the number of body parts receiving the force
3. the nature of the body surface being contacted by the ball

The distance and time over which the force is absorbed are increased by "giving" with the ball. The wrists, elbows, shoulders, hips, knees, and ankles all flex as the body "gives" to absorb the force. Thus a maximum number of body parts are used. A child's bare hands are somewhat padded by muscles, which contributes to force absorption. When more force must be absorbed (as in baseball), a padded glove is used.

STRIKING

Striking is a swinging motion in which force is imparted to an object for the purpose of propelling it through space. In sports activities, a body part or implement is used to strike a stationary or moving object. It is easier to strike a stationary object, since one is not required to judge the speed and direction the object is moving or to relate spatially to these factors. For this reason, it is advisable to use a batting tee during the initial stages of batting instruction.

Striking patterns are influenced by the size, weight, and length of the striking implement; the nature of the object to be struck; and the desired goal. Striking involves the same movement patterns as underhand, overhand, and sidearm throwing, and is characterized by the same sequence of movements: a preparatory phase, the striking movement, and a follow-through.

Basic striking patterns are developed in the process of acquiring the manipulative skills. The sports skills component of the curriculum, then, should introduce children to the specific striking patterns utilized in certain sports. Batting a softball will serve as an example of how such skills can be analyzed and practiced.

Batting

The batter stands with the left side of the body toward the pitcher, legs in a sideward stride position with the weight toward the back foot. The elbows are elevated and the bat is cocked around the right shoulder (see Figure 16.26).

The striking motion is initiated by cocking of the wrists and a weight shift toward the oncoming ball. As the weight is transferred to the left foot, the hips, spine, and shoulders rotate forward and the wrists and arms are uncocked. The ball is contacted in front of the batter.

In the follow-through, the weight is transferred to the left foot, the body completes its rotation, and the bat swings through in the direction of the intended flight of the ball.

Activities for Children

1. Demonstrate correct batting form, pointing out the positions of the body and the bat.

2. Have the children practice swinging imaginary bats. Emphasize the weight shift and the sequential rotation of the hips, spine, and shoulders.

3. Observe each child swinging a bat, and make necessary corrections. Check the following factors:
   a. correct stance
   b. correct position of the arms and the bat
   c. cocking of the wrists
   d. properly timed rotation of the hips, spine, and shoulders
   e. transfer of the weight to the left foot
   f. completed follow-through

4. Have the children practice batting from a tee (see Figure 16.27). A plastic bat and wiffle ball may be used until the children gain sufficient control to progress to a wooden bat and softball.[3] Again check the factors listed in activity 3.

5. Have the children stand at various points in the batter's box while striking: close to the tee, a bat-length away from it, ahead of it, and behind it. Point out the effects of the various positions on the point of contact with the ball.

6. Challenge each child to place the ball in an area of the field you specify by standing at the appropriate point while batting.

7. Play the game described in activity 7 on page 339, substituting batting from a tee for throwing.

8. Play Work-up. Twelve or more players assume the positions shown in Figure 16.28. Regular softball rules are observed, except that

[3]Suggestions for improvising batting tees may be found in "New Ideas for Playgrounds," *Journal of Health, Physical Education and Recreation* 36 (May 1965): 70.

**Figure 16.26 Position of
Readiness and Correct
Sequence of Movements
in Batting**
Mickey Adair

Striking   351

Figure 16.27 Batting from a Tee
Mickey Adair

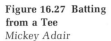
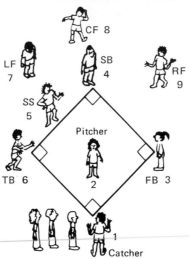

Figure 16.28 Formation for Play Work-Up

　　　The Basic Sports Skills

the ball is hit from the tee rather than pitched. A batter who is put out takes the right fielder's position, and all the players move up one position. You may establish a rule limiting the length of time a batter may stay at bat (for example, to rotate after making three runs). Also, children may be rewarded for catching fly balls by being allowed to exchange places with the batter.

9. Play regulation softball using the tee in place of a pitcher. In place of innings that end after three outs, let every child on a team have an opportunity to bat in each inning.

10. When the children demonstrate consistent ability to execute a satisfactory striking pattern, they should progress to batting a pitched ball. Adequate practice with a consistent pitcher should be provided before the children play regulation softball. All too often children are rushed into games in which most of their time is spent standing or sitting which do not provide the practice or active participation necessary in a learning environment.

Movement Principles Most of the laws and principles that relate to human movement are applicable to batting. The levers of the forearms are extended by using the bat, thereby increasing the amount of force imparted to the ball. The struck ball becomes a projectile and the laws of motion determine its pathway through space.

The principles of equilibrium that serve to maintain the stable body position essential in batting are as follows:

1. The body's center of gravity must remain within the base of support throughout the striking motion.

2. The base of support is enlarged in the direction the force will be moving when the ball is struck.

The laws of motion are pertinent to batting in the following ways:

1. The Law of Inertia. The ball on the tee will remain at rest until the force exerted by the bat overcomes its inertia. A pitched ball will continue moving at the same speed and in the same direction until acted on by another force. (A fast ball will follow a linear pathway through space because gravitational pull will not force it downward in the short distance between the pitching mound and the batter's box; a slowly pitched ball will follow a curvilinear pathway because the force of gravity soon overcomes its forward momentum.) The direction of the ball will be reversed when the force of the bat is sufficient to overcome its forward momentum.

2. The Law of Acceleration. The acceleration of a ball hit from a tee is proportional to the amount of force created by the bat. Because the ball is a stationary object, the total force of the movement is exerted by the bat. A pitched ball, on the other hand, has momentum, and is therefore subject to another law, the *Law of Conservation of Momentum*. This law states that when two objects collide, the total momentum after the impact is equal to the total prior momentum of both objects. Thus the momentum of the struck ball is equal to the momentum of the bat plus that of the ball prior to being struck. (The forward momentum of the bat during follow-through must, strictly speaking, be subtracted from the momentum of the struck ball.) The Law of Conservation of Momentum explains why a struck pitched ball travels farther than a ball hit from a tee (see Figure 16.29).

3. The Law of Action and Reaction. A struck ball reacts to the force of the bat in the same way a bouncing ball rebounds from the floor. If the object and the implement are both moving (that is, if the ball is pitched), two equal and opposite reaction forces occur. One force is exerted by the ball striking the bat; the other by the bat striking the ball. Therefore, the total amount of reaction force is determined by the speed of the pitched ball and the speed of the swinging bat. (Refer to the Law of Conservation of Momentum.)

Batting is characterized by several types of motion. Angular motion of the arms and the bat produces linear motion of the ball, but the action of gravitational pull and air resistance on the ball cause its pathway to become curvilinear.

The lengthening of the arm lever by means of the bat allows for greater range of motion, enabling the individual to impart more force and thus greater speed and distance to the ball.

The momentum of the bat then equals the momentum transferred to it by the arms and body times the mass of the bat. Thus the larger and heavier the bat, the more momentum it will have. If the child cannot control a heavy bat, however, its mechanical advantage is lost. The size and weight of the bat should be matched to the individual's strength and level of skill.

The following principles govern the flight of projectiles.

1. The angle at which the ball is struck determines the angle of its projection. It will rebound from the bat at an angle opposite but equal to the angle at which it contacts the bat.

2. If the ball is struck through its center of gravity, it will travel in a

Figure 16.29 Application of the Law of Conservation of Momentum
A ball will travel farther when it is struck in flight than when it is struck from a stationary position because the momentum of the ball is added to the momentum of the bat.
Mickey Adair

straight line. A ball struck off-center will have spin, and will travel diagonally upward or downward.

3. Accurate batting is relatively difficult because the bat has a small, rounded striking surface.

The first two principles are equally applicable to any ball struck by an implement.

KICKING

Kicking is a relatively difficult sports skill because balance must be maintained on a small base of support while the swinging leg imparts force to the ball. Children should begin learning to manipulate a ball with their feet during the preschool years. In the primary grades they should learn to control the movements of the ball; on the intermediate level they should demonstrate the ability to impart force accurately with the inside, outside, and instep of the foot. The inside of the foot is used for dribbling, passing, and goal kicking. Passing and dribbling may also be performed with the outside of the foot. The instep kick is used to pass the ball long distances and for goal-kicking.

To kick with the inside of the foot, the toe of the kicking foot is extended outward and downward. The knee is bent, and the toe is kept close to the ground so that the ball may be contacted below its center with the inside of the foot. (See Figure 16.30, top left.) As contact is being made, the kicking leg swings diagonally forward. The body's weight is carried forward as a step is taken with the kicking foot.

A kick with the outside of the foot is performed in the same way except that the toe of the kicking foot is pointed inward and downward (see Figure 16.30, top right). The amount of force that can be applied with this kick is limited by the narrow range of outward motion of the ankle joint. This factor also makes control of the ball more difficult.

For an instep kick, or place kick, the toe is pointed downward, the knee is flexed, and the leg swings forward from the hip. The ball is contacted with the top of the instep, and force is imparted by a sudden extension of the knee. (See Figure 16.30, bottom.) The leg continues up on the follow-through (see Figure 16.31). Additional force may be applied by taking one or more running steps prior to the kick. When the children have become able to control the ball in a place kick, they should progress to a punt. (See Figure 16.32.) Though the foot and leg movements are the same as for a place kick, the punt is a more difficult skill because the movement of the legs must be coordinated with those of the arms. The ball is held in front of the right leg and a preliminary forward step is taken with the left foot, leaving the right leg extended backward. The movements after the ball is dropped are the same as those of the instep kick.

Activities for Children

1. Demonstrate the correct method of controlling the ball with the inside and outside of the foot, pointing out the correct body and foot positions.

2. Have partners practice dribbling and passing back and forth with the inside and outside of their feet. Challenge the children to become proficient at passing with either foot. Have them practice maneuvering around such obstacles as road cones, hoops, ropes, and chairs.

3. To improve speed and accuracy, have them practice in the file and shuttle formations shown in Figures 16.21 and 16.22. Insist that they trap the ball before returning it. Do not introduce the competitive element until the children have achieved a satisfactory skill level.

4. Position road cones to simulate soccer goal posts and challenge the children to kick the ball between them from various distances.

5. Kick-Pin Soccer. An Indian club is placed in the center of a circle of children (see Figure 16.33). The children pass the ball back and

The Basic Sports Skills

Figure 16.30 Foot Positions Used to Control the Ball
Top left: kicking with the inside of the foot; Top right: kicking with the outside of the foot; Bottom: kicking with the instep
Mickey Adair

Figure 16.31 Correct Body and Foot Position for the Place Kick (Instep Kick)
Mickey Adair

**Figure 16.32 Correct
Body and Foot Position for
the Punt**
Mickey Adair

**Figure 16.33 Diagram for
the Game** *Kick-Pin
Soccer*

forth across the circle, attempting to knock the club over. The ball may not be touched with the hands; if it goes outside the circle, it must be retrieved with the feet and dribbled back to starting position. One point is awarded for knocking over the club. The child who is ahead at the end of the designated time wins.

6. Lead-up games such as Circle Soccer, Triangle Soccer, Mickey Mouse, Line Soccer, and Line-Base Soccer provide practice in the kicking skills. The directions for these games are provided by Blake and Volp (1964).

Movement Principles

Because equilibrium must be maintained over a small base of support (one foot), the kick is a relatively unstable movement. The force exerted by the foot overcomes the inertia of the ball and sets it in motion at a certain speed. If the ball moves along the ground, its speed is reduced by rolling friction. The foot striking the ball creates an equal and opposite reaction force. The greater the momentum of the leg at the moment of contact, the greater the speed of the ball. A stationary ball will rebound from the foot at an angle equal and opposite to the angle of the foot. The pathway of a ball that is moving at the moment of contact will also be affected by its own momentum.

TOPICS FOR REVIEW AND FURTHER STUDY

1. Explain some of the commonalities and differences in the way the basic sports skills are executed in different sports. For example, what are the similarities in the throwing patterns of a softball pitch and an underhand beanbag throw? How do striking patterns differ in table tennis, badminton, and softball?

2. What determines how a particular skill is performed in different sports?

3. Develop a lesson in which children review and apply to human movement one of the following categories of principles or laws:
   a. the principles of equilibrium
   b. Newton's three laws of motion
   c. the three types of motion
   d. leverage
   e. mass and momentum
   f. friction
   g. the movement of projectiles

4. Describe the execution of one of the following throwing patterns:
   a. underhand
   b. overhand
   c. sidearm

5. Develop a lesson designed to teach children how to execute one of the throwing patterns. Include applications of the movement principles pertinent to this skill.

6. Demonstrate two-handed and one-handed catching patterns. Point out the most common catching errors committed by children.

7. Develop a lesson in which children practice throwing and catching. Include application of the movement principles.

8. Develop a lesson in which children learn a striking pattern. Include application of the relevant movement principles.

9. Develop a lesson in which children practice one of the following kicking patterns:
  a. inside of foot
  b. outside of foot
  c. instep kick

SUGGESTIONS FOR FURTHER READING

BLAKE, WILLIAM D., and VOLP, ANNE M. *Lead-up Games for Team Sports*, Englewood Cliffs, N.J.: Prentice-Hall, 1964.

BROER, MARION R. *Efficiency of Human Movement*, 3rd ed. Philadelphia, W. B. Saunders, 1973.

BUNN, JOHN W. *Scientific Principles of Coaching*. Englewood Cliffs, N.J.: Prentice-Hall, 1955.

COOPER, JOHN M., and GLASSOW, RUTH B. *Kinesiology*, 3rd ed. St. Louis: C. V. Mosby, 1972.

SEIDEL, BEVERLY; BILES, FAY; FIGLEY, GRACE; and NEUMAN, BONNIE. *Sports Skills: A Conceptual Approach to Meaningful Movement*, Dubuque, Iowa: Wm. C. Brown, 1975

WELLS, KATHARINE F., and LUTTGENS, KATHRYN. *Kinesiology: Scientific Basis of Human Motion*, 6th ed. Philadelphia: W. B. Saunders, 1976.

WICKSTROM, RALPH L. *Fundamental Motor Patterns*. Philadelphia: Lea & Febiger, 1970.

17 The Fundamental Physical Skills

The fundamental physical skills are the movement patterns used to perform the tasks of everyday living. Most people undertake them without conscious awareness that their bodies are performing a complex sequence of basic movements. The purpose of including these skills in the elementary-school curriculum is to develop such awareness and to enable the child to execute these movements efficiently throughout his or her lifetime. An aspect of this goal is the development of an affirmative attitude toward the functional use of the body. The lessons in this chapter are designed to (1) provide knowledge that will enable the child to understand why a movement should be executed in a certain way, and (2) enable the child to feel the difference between the correct and incorrect ways of performing these tasks. Children must recognize that the efficient way of standing, sitting, lifting, and so on "feels right" because all the body parts are functioning as they were designed to.

Walking is one of the fundamental physical skills, but it has been extensively analyzed and explored in Chapter 14 and will not be recapitulated here. However, a review of walking activities following the study of standing will enable the children to see the relationship between the two skills.

STANDING

Children spend countless hours standing as they wait, watch, listen, and handle things, and standing is also a preparatory stance for other

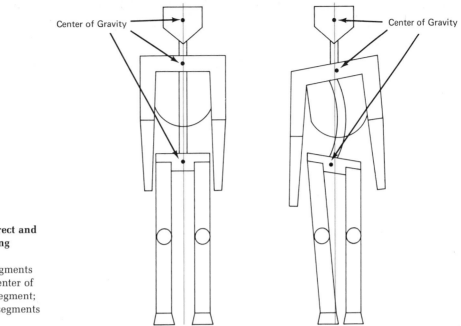

Center of Gravity

Center of Gravity

Figure 17.1 Correct and Incorrect Standing Positions

Left: the body segments aligned on the center of gravity of each segment; Right: the body segments out of line

movement activities. Thus children constantly practice standing. In a standing position the weight is supported by the lower part of the body, leaving the upper part free to execute such nonlocomotor movements as gesturing and manipulating objects.

The human body is composed of moveable segments—the head, trunk, pelvis, legs, and feet—aligned one on top of the other (see Figure 17.1). Each segment has a center of gravity. The body is standing correctly when the center of gravity of each segment is directly above the center of the segment immediately below it. When the body is in this position, the line of gravity extends vertically through the center of gravity of the head, trunk, and pelvis and falls midway between the feet (the center of the base of support). The body parts are thus in a balanced position and their weight has maximum support.

The body segments are held together by ligaments and muscles. The muscles that hold the body in an upright position are called *antigravity muscles,* and contract to resist the force of gravitational pull. The groups of antigravity muscles, shown and identified in Figure 17.2, are identical on the right and left sides of the body, so that when both sets contract equally the body is held in a symmetrical upright position.

In a normal standing position, the feet are a few inches apart with the toes pointing straight ahead. This relatively wide base of support provides for equal distribution of the body weight over the heels, outside edges, and balls of both feet (see Figure 17.3).

Standing

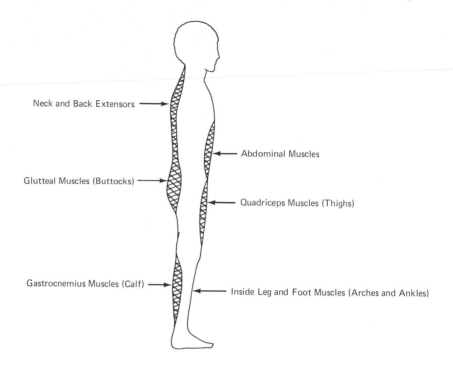

Neck and Back Extensors

Abdominal Muscles

Glutteal Muscles (Buttocks)

Quadriceps Muscles (Thighs)

Gastrocnemius Muscles (Calf)

Inside Leg and Foot Muscles (Arches and Ankles)

Figure 17.2 The Antigravity Muscles

Figure 17.3 Distribution of the Body Weight in a Normal Standing Position

The pelvis is the key to correct standing. All the upper and lower segments must be balanced in relation to the tilt of the pelvis. When the pelvis is tilted forward, its center of gravity moves forward, and the center of gravity of the head, trunk, and feet must be moved backward to compensate. This position causes the back to arch and the knees to hyperextend. When the pelvis is tilted backward, the normal arch of the back must be flattened and the knees slightly flexed (see Figure 17.4). In either of these positions, resisting the force of gravity places a strain on the supporting muscles.

The normal position of the shoulders is parallel to the floor. If the weight is evenly distributed on both feet and the hips are in a normal position, the shoulders will usually automatically assume the correct position. If the hips are tilted, however, the position of the shoulders must be adjusted to compensate for uneven distribution of the body weight. If most of a person's body weight is being supported on one foot, the pelvis and shoulders will be tilted as in Figure 17.1, right, and the sideward curve of the spine will cause the muscles on the outside of the spinal curve to stretch and those on the inside to shorten. For this reason, one should not habitually lean on the same foot; instead, the weight should be periodically shifted from one foot to the other.

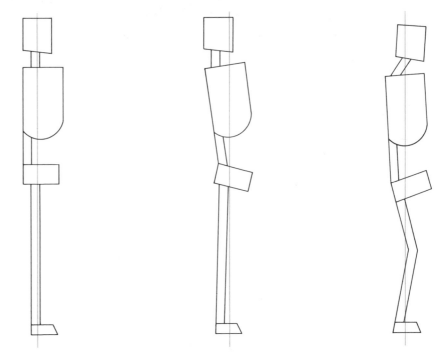

Figure 17.4 Alignment of Body Segments in Various Standing Positions
Left: normal standing position; Middle: pelvis tilted forward; Right: pelvis tilted backward

The head is a very heavy body part, supported only by the muscles and the small bones in the spinal column. It should therefore be held in a well-balanced position. When it is tilted forward or sideward, the muscles on the back or sides of the neck must exert additional force to resist the force of gravity, increasing fatigue and causing muscular tension.

Activities for Children

1. Explain that the body segments must be balanced one on top of the other when in a standing position.

2. Draw a diagram similar to Figure 17.1, left, and point out the approximate location of the centers of gravity of the head, trunk, and pelvis.

3. Review the concept of the line of gravity (see page 363). On the diagram, draw a line of gravity through the center of gravity of the body segments and extend it to a point midway between the feet.

4. Have the children locate the center of gravity of their own body segments and those of a partner.

5. Have each child stand in front of and beside a plumb line. Point out that the plumb line simulates the line of gravity. Check each child's standing position and note instances of incorrect alignment and recommend corrections to the child.

6. Discuss the concept of antigravity muscles. Point out, and have the children touch, the locations of these muscles.

7. Promote kinesthetic awareness of the feeling states associated with correct and incorrect positions of the body segments by having the children assume the following positions:

a. feet

(1) "Standing barefoot, place your feet close together, then far apart, and then a few inches apart. Close your eyes and feel the pressure of the floor on the bottom of your feet. (Tilting your body and wiggling your feet will help increase sensitivity.)"

(2) "Toe out, and notice that this makes it necessary for the weight to be supported on the inside of your feet."

(3) "Look at the bottoms of your feet and observe that the arches are located on the inside. Thus toeing out places a strain on the arches."

(4) "Toe in, and notice which part of your foot must support the weight."

Having the children step in water and then on dry concrete or brown wrapping paper will enable them to visualize the parts of the feet that support the weight in different positions.

b. pelvis

(1) "Stand with your back arched, your knees hyperextended, and your pelvis tilted forward." (The part of the pelvis attached to the legs will move backward and the buttocks will move backward and upward.) "Note that this causes the abdominal wall to distend. Press on your abdomen and feel how this position causes the internal organs to push out against the muscles." Point out that habitually standing in this position causes the muscles to stretch and sag.

(2) "Pull your pelvis back into its normal position. Note that doing so brings the other segments back into alignment and causes the weight of the internal organs to press downward rather than forward."

(3) "Rotate your pelvis upward. Observe that this causes your shoulders and head to slump forward and your knees to flex. Note that this places a strain on the muscles of the upper back and those of the back of the neck. Observe that the muscles on the fronts of your thighs must exert additional force to resist further flexion of the knee joints."

c. shoulders and trunk

(1) "Slouch your shoulders forward. Note that this causes the lower portion of your rib cage to press down into your abdomen.

The Fundamental Physical Skills

Try to take a deep breath. Raise your shoulders upward and backward into their normal position and take a deep breath. Note that your rib cage is free to expand."

(2) "Slouch your shoulders and observe the effect of doing so on the position of your head." (It tends to tilt forward.)

   d. head

(1) "Keep your shoulders in their normal position and drop your head forward. Feel the stretching of the muscles on the back of your neck."

(2) "Tilt your head to one side and then the other. Feel how this stretches the muscles on the side of your neck."

(3) "Rotate your head and then tilt it upward and downward. Notice that these positions move the head's center of gravity off balance and place a strain on certain muscles."

8. Encourage the children to stand in front of a full-length mirror and observe the effects of altering the positions of the body segments.

9. Videotape the children in various standing positions. Review the tapes and discuss the children's observations.

10. Review the concept that a correct standing position is one in which the body segments are balanced one on top of the other so that the line of gravity passes through the center of gravity of the upper body segments and intersects the floor midway between the feet. Emphasize that this position places the least amount of strain on the muscles and joints, and is thus a relaxed rather than a rigid position.

11. Point out that standing is a position of readiness in that it is assumed in preparation for activities involving locomotor and/or nonlocomotor movements.

Because standing is a relatively static position, the only movement principles involved are those that regulate equilibrium. A balanced body position is achieved by keeping the center of gravity of each body segment in line with the center of its base of support. The only force is gravitational pull, and the feet are positioned a few inches apart to enlarge the base in the direction of this opposing force.

SITTING

Children spend a great deal of time sitting—in school, in front of the television, in cars, and while playing. The purpose of teaching children about sitting is to enable them to control efficiently the transfer of weight while sitting down and rising and to help them avoid fatigue and strain while sitting.

The same basic principles apply to sitting and to standing. In sitting,

Sitting

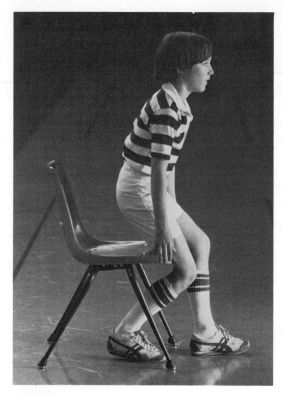 

Figure 17.5 Correct and Incorrect Ways of Sitting Down

Left: the foot supports the pelvis as it moves back and down (correct). Right: the body's center of gravity falls outside the base of support (incorrect).

Mickey Adair

however, the head and trunk are the only body parts that must be balanced. Sitting is a very stable body position because the body has a large base of support and because the center of gravity is close to the base of support.

The correct procedure for transferring one's weight from a standing to a sitting position consists of two phases. In the first phase, one foot is moved backward under the seat as far as possible (see Figure 17.5). In the second phase, the muscles of the thighs and buttocks control the flexing of the hips and knees, permitting the body to be lowered gradually onto the seat.

Placing one foot beneath the seat enlarges the body's base of support in the direction of the moving force. This procedure keeps the center of gravity over the base until the thighs touch the chair, establishing a new base of support. If both feet are in front of the chair and the center of gravity moves backward behind the feet, the child will literally fall into the seat. This can be prevented by counterbalancing the weight shift: leaning the upper body forward while the hips are moving backward. If

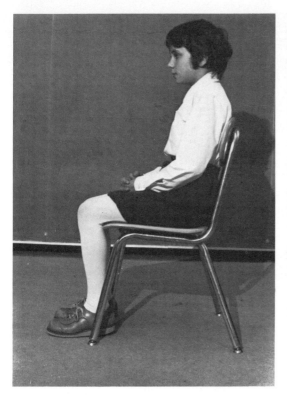
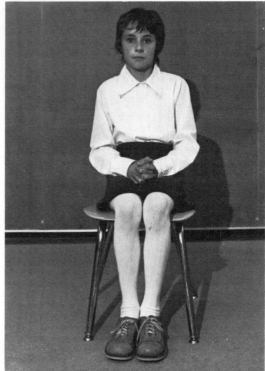

**Figure 17.6 Correct
Sitting Position**
Bonnie Unsworth

a book rack or a rung under the front of the seat prevents a step backward, it may be necessary to lean forward in this manner or to partially support one's weight by placing one hand on the back or arm of the chair.

When rising from a seat, the procedure is reversed. The body's center of gravity is shifted by leaning the upper body forward, one foot is moved backward under the seat, and the thigh muscles contract to pull the body upward into a standing position.

The correct body position for sitting is shown in Figure 17.6. The centers of gravity of the head, trunk, and hips are aligned so that the line of gravity passes through each and intersects the center of the seat. The shoulders and hips are level, and the hips and entire back of the body should rest comfortably against the back of the chair.

The size and design of furniture directly affects how a child sits. The chair should be comfortable and of appropriate size. The child should be able to rest both feet comfortably on the floor, and the shape of the chair back should match the natural contour of the child's back.

Sitting

**Figure 17.7 Correct
Height of a Desk**
Bonnie Unsworth

The Fundamental Physical Skills

The height of a child's desk should be as shown in Figure 17.7. The desk top should be just below the normal position of the forearms when the elbows are bent. A desk that is too high causes the child's shoulders to be elevated while writing, and too low a desk necessitates slouching.

Activities for
Children

1. Have one of the children demonstrate the correct ways to sit and rise. Point out the positions of the feet and upper body and discuss the pertinent movement principles.

2. Have the children practice sitting and rising correctly. Have them experiment with falling into a chair, pointing out that doing so jars the body and damages upholstered furniture.

3. Have the children sit in their classroom seats while you discuss correct sitting. Review the concept of the alignment of body segments. Ask the children to rest their backs against their chairs and to feel the support. Then ask them to sit with their backs about an inch from their chair backs and to feel the difference between a supported and an unsupported back. Ask them to close their eyes and concentrate on the difference.

4. Discuss the correct size for a chair and the correct height for a desk.

5. Have the children sit with their head tilted forward and their shoulders slumped. Ask them to close their eyes and feel the strain on the muscles of their necks and backs.

6. Have the children sit on the floor (preferably in front of a mirror). Point out that the seat is always the base of support in sitting, but that the legs, feet, and hands may be used to provide additional support. Challenge the children to sit in various positions, using various body parts as bases of support (see Figure 13.1). Discuss the effect of these positions on the size of the base of support and the alignment of the body parts.

7. If possible, videotape the children while they are sitting at their desks. Review the tape with the children, pointing out efficient and inefficient movement patterns.

8. Show the children pictures of people sitting and ask them to comment on the positions.

Parents and teachers should remember that children need frequent changes of pace; requiring them to sit for long periods may force them to adopt inefficient sitting positions.

STOOPING AND LIFTING

In everyday life the purpose of stooping is to manipulate or pick up something on or near the floor. Preschool children frequently bend over, rather than stoop, to pick up toys; their bodies are extremely flexible, and bending contributes to their neuromuscular development. Children also spend a great deal of time using their hands to propel objects across the floor, and frequently do so by bending over and walking, which permits greater mobility than do crouching or crawling. Children therefore become very familiar with these movement patterns; faced with tasks involving stooping and lifting, they automatically bend over. This is an efficient method of handling light objects that can be lifted easily from the floor. But as children develop greater strength and stability, they begin lifting heavier objects and manipulating objects located above their heads. Thus elementary-school children should be taught how to do so safely and efficiently as soon as they are ready.

An object remains at rest because the force of gravity holds it in place. When it is lifted, it is being pulled upward against the force of gravity. The heavier the object, the more force is required to lift it. When an object's total weight is supported by the body, its weight is added to that of the body, causing a change in the location of the body's center of gravity toward the added weight. Thus it is easiest to lift an object when it is located in front of the body between the feet (see Figure 17.8). This position places the object's center of gravity immediately in front of the body's center of gravity. It also locates the load between the body parts (the legs) that will exert most of the force to pull the object upward. Another advantage to lifting from the front is that the load is lifted into the correct position for carrying. Lifting from the side provides for a larger base in the direction the body parts are moving during the first phase of the lift but, because it is more difficult to exert force sideward, the load must be swung around to the front of the body in preparation for carrying. The same movement principles apply to both positions.

The correct preparatory position for lifting is to stoop (crouch), rather than bend, the upper body forward. Stooping positions the strong leg muscles under the body's center of gravity, and places the body such that the force of the movement will be exerted directly upward against the force of gravity. If one bends forward to lift, the weaker back muscles must exert the force; as the trunk of the body is lifted, force is exerted diagonally backward and upward in a less efficient movement (see Figure 17.9).

Before lifting an object, one must have a firm hold on it. It is much easier to grasp an object that has a handle. If there is no handle, the

The Fundamental Physical Skills

**Figure 17.8 Correct
Positions for Lifting from
the Front and from the
Side**
Mickey Adair

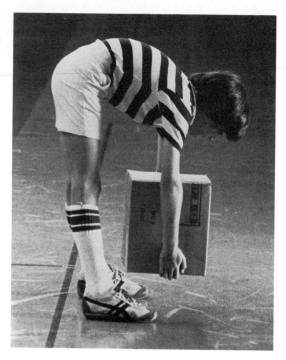

**Figure 17.9 Correct and
Incorrect Positions for
Lifting a Heavy Weight**
Left: correct position, with
knees bent and back
straight; Right: incorrect
position, with legs straight
and back bent
Mickey Adair

hands must be placed securely beneath the object to provide a base of support for it.

When lifting a heavy object, it is necessary to exert a strong initial force to overcome the inertia of the object. Once the object has been set in motion, less force is required to continue moving it in the same direction. The force that lifts the object is exerted by the muscles of the ankles, knees, and hips acting to extend these body levers. Throughout the movement, the object should be kept close to the body; if it is to be carried, it should come to rest tightly against the body.

When an object is lifted down from a shelf, force must be exerted in two directions. The object must be (1) removed from the shelf by moving it forward, and (2) controlled as the force of gravity pushes it downward toward the floor. The correct position in which to execute this movement is a forward stride with the body slightly in front of the shelf and the weight on the forward foot. One slowly slides the object toward the front edge of the shelf, places the fingers under the object, and shifts the weight over the back foot as the object is pulled forward off the shelf. The object must be kept close to the front of the body while it is lowered.

The Fundamental Physical Skills

1. Explain that objects are held in place by the force of gravity and that lifting is an upward pull against gravity.

2. Have one of the children demonstrate a correct lift from the front. (A brown paper package containing some heavy metal tools wrapped in newspaper is heavy enough to be a challenge, but small enough to be easily handled. Be sure the metal is well padded and that the contents of the package are properly balanced. A box containing a few books can also be used, but it is bulkier and less interesting than the package. Interest in the lesson can be enhanced by creating an air of mystery about the package's contents and allowing the children to open it when they have all lifted it correctly.) As the child lifts, point out the following:

a. The weight of the object added to that of the body causes the body's center of gravity to move forward.

b. Lifting from the front places the object's center of gravity immediately in front of the body's center of gravity.

c. The load is between the body parts that exert the major force.

d. The one disadvantage of this position is that it provides a very small base in the direction in which the initial force is exerted (backward).

3. Have the child lift from the side. Point out the following:

a. When lifting from the side, the foot opposite the load is ahead (see Figure 17.8).

b. This position provides a larger base along the forward-backward axis.

c. It is more difficult to lift from the side because the body is not as well balanced (the center of gravity shifting sideward over one foot), the force is not exerted straight upward, and the load must be swung around to the front as it is lifted.

4. Have the children practice lifting from the front and from the side. Check each child's position. Encourage them to notice how their bodies are moving and to contrast the two lifting positions.

5. Ask the children to pretend they are lifting heavy objects by bending forward from the waist. Tell them not to bend their knees. Have them close their eyes and note the muscles of the back contracting.

6. Show the children the cardboard skeleton. Point out that the only bones supporting the lower back are those of the very small spinal column, and that with so little bony structure the muscles must do virtually all the work. Point out that when one lifts from the front or the

side, the strong muscles of the legs and hips contract to move the levers of the legs. Leverage and strong muscles make the movement more efficient.

7. Discuss the difference in the angle of pull between a lift from a crouch position and a forward bend.

8. Point out that a forward bend position may be used to lift small light objects, but that large, heavy objects lifted from this position may strain the back and cause injury.

9. Have a child demonstrate the correct way to lift an object from an overhead shelf (see Figure 17.10). Point out the following:

a. The object must first be moved in a forward direction; then the downward force of gravity must be resisted.

b. A forward stride position is used to give the body a wide base of support.

c. Standing slightly in front of the shelf allows the load to be lowered close to the body.

d. The weight is on the forward foot as the object is being moved toward the front of the shelf, and is shifted backward over the rear foot as the object is lifted from the shelf.

e. The fingers are placed under the object so the hands will form a base of support and so the wrists can bend as the load is lowered. Have the child who is demonstrating place his or her thumbs under the object and lift it down from the shelf. Ask the children to note that this position gives the object a very small base of support (only the thumbs) and prevents it from being moved below shoulder-level unless it is tipped over.

f. Illustrate the amount of force that must be resisted while the object is moving downward by sliding the object to the edge of the shelf and letting it fall to the floor. This enables the children to visualize the effect of gravitational pull.

g. Have each child practice the correct procedure for lifting from a shelf.

h. Have a child stand on a stool and reach for an object on a high shelf. Point out that this position is very unstable because the body's base of support is very small. Furthermore, getting down from the stool while holding the object is a challenge to stability. Then have the child do the same thing using a step ladder. Point out that the ladder has a much wider base of support, that the legs may be braced against the steps of the ladder while reaching, and that the child may hold on with one hand while descending. The hands should be used

The Fundamental Physical Skills

Figure 17.10 Correct and Incorrect Positions for Lifting an Object from Overhead
Top and bottom left: correct position, with fingers under object, feet in forward stride formation, and body placed to allow object to be lowered close to trunk. Weight shifts from forward to backward foot as object is lifted from shelf. Bottom right: incorrect position, with only thumbs under object and feet together.
Bonnie Unsworth

as much as possible when climbing a ladder, since the body must balance on one foot while the other foot is being moved.

HOLDING AND CARRYING

When one holds an object, balance must be maintained and enough force exerted to resist the downward pull of gravity against the object. Both principles also apply to carrying, in which additional force must be exerted to move the weight of the object.

A secure base of support must be provided to prevent the object being held from slipping or rotating. The weight of the object added to that of the body makes it necessary to adjust the body so that the new center of gravity is over the center of the body's base of support. This should be done by shifting the body position from the ankles, rather than by moving individual body segments. If the load is held on the right side of the body, its weight should be counterbalanced by leaning the entire body slightly to the left. If the trunk alone leans to the side, the head, shoulders, and chest are not aligned with the lower body segments and the muscles of the side and back are strained. If the object is not too heavy, its weight may be counterbalanced by lifting the arm on the opposite side (see Figure 17.11).

It is most efficient to hold an object close to the center front of the body. This position places the object's center of gravity close to and directly in front of the body's center of gravity. Thus the object's weight can be counterbalanced by a slight backward lean.

There are four additional ways to carry a load: on top of the head, on the back, from a shoulder strap, or equally divided between the two sides of the body. (See Figure 17.12.) Carrying on top of the head is the most efficient method, since the load's center of gravity is thus directly over the center of gravity of all the body segments; its inherent drawback is that it is difficult to keep the load balanced on such a curved base of support. A backpack is an efficient means of carrying a load, since its weight is supported by the strong muscles of the shoulders and upper back. And if one leans forward, the load is partially supported by gravity pushing the load against the body. The use of a shoulder strap allows the weight to be supported by the muscles and bony structure of the shoulder, which strains the shoulder joint less than when the weight is held in the hand. Dividing the weight of a load equally between the two sides of the body has two advantages: a lighter load is borne by each hand, and the location of the body's center of gravity does not change. Thus the normal alignment of the body parts is maintained.

Figure 17.11
Counterbalancing the Weight of an Object
Left: leaning sideward from the ankles; Right: lifting the opposite arm
Mickey Adair

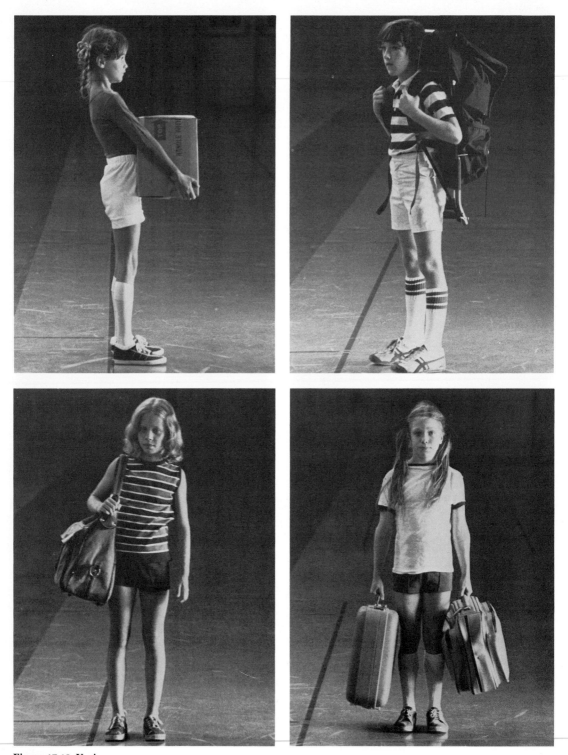

**Figure 17.12 Various
Positions for Supporting
the Weight of a Load**
Mickey Adair

1. Have six children hold and carry loads, using the methods described above and shown in Figures 17.11 and 17.12. Have them stand in front of the class while you compare the various methods and discuss correct body positions. Discuss the principles outlined above, emphasizing the following points:

a. When a load is held or carried, its weight added to that of the body causes a shift in the body's center of gravity.

b. It is highly efficient to carry a load on the head, but maintaining balance is difficult. Some peoples have developed skill at carrying heavy and elaborate loads on their heads. Show the children pictures of people doing so.

c. A backpack is an efficient way to carry a load. The heaviest objects should be placed in the bottom of the pack so that its center of gravity will be as close as possible to the body's center of gravity. The techniques of loading a pack are taught in scouting; having a Boy or Girl Scout demonstrate these techniques adds interest to the lesson. Also ask the child to demonstrate the correct methods of walking on the level and up and down inclines while carrying a pack. Have one of the children demonstrate the use of a backpack while riding a bicycle.

d. A heavy load should be divided in half so that the weight will be borne equally by the two sides of the body. For this reason, it is better to carry two small suitcases than one large one.

e. Supporting a load with a shoulder strap places less strain on the shoulder than does holding it in the hand, which pulls at the point where the shoulder and arm connect. A strap should be placed over the shoulder so that its bony structure and the muscles of the upper back support the weight.

f. When a load is carried on the back, the side, or in front of the body, its weight must be counterbalanced. This should be accomplished by leaning the entire body from the ankle.

2. Explain that a load should be held close to the body. Holding it away from the body shifts the center of gravity further in that direction and lengthens the body lever, requiring additional muscular force to support the weight. Reinforce this concept by having the children compare the amount of muscular force required to hold objects close to their bodies with the force required to hold them with the arms extended forward or sideward.

3. Set up six stations and have the children practice one method of holding and carrying at each station. Supply each station with a poster stating the pertinent movement principles and illustrating the correct positions of the body and the load.

PUSHING AND PULLING

The primary factors in pushing or pulling an object are correct application of force and maintenance of a stable body position. In these movements, force is exerted by the leg muscles and transferred by means of the body levers to the point of contact with the object. The body's base of support is enlarged in the direction of the moving force by the use of a forward stride position.

In preparation for pushing, the hands should be placed on a level with the object's center of gravity. If the hands are placed above this point, the force of the push will cause the object to tilt rather than slide. The hands should be positioned shoulder-width apart or, if the object is not too wide, at the corners. The arms should be straight and the body should be inclined forward. (See Figure 17.13.) The joints of the body should be "locked" so that force will be efficiently transferred through them from the legs to the hands. If the joints are allowed to bend, they will absorb part of the force. A very strong initial push is necessary to overcome the object's inertia. Once the object is set in motion, its speed is determined by the amount of force exerted and the amount of resistance that must be overcome. Sliding friction creates a great deal of resistance if the object is large or heavy; rolling friction offers much less resistance.

A firm grasp is essential in pulling because the resistance pulls against the hands. The appropriate position is a forward stride, facing the direction the load will be moving. The ankle, knee, and hip joints are flexed. Force is exerted by extending these body levers and pushing against the floor with the ball of the foot. (See Figure 17.14.)

Activities for Children

1. A large, square cardboard box filled with evenly balanced objects is an excellent teaching tool for pushing. Ask a child to push the box across the floor. Then challenge the children to answer the following questions by applying the movement principles:

a. "Where on the box should your hands be placed, and why?" (halfway up, if the box's weight is evenly distributed between top and bottom, because this point is level with the center of gravity)

b. "What happens if your hands are placed higher?" (The box tilts forward.)

c. "Should your hands be placed in the center of the box or at the edges?" (At the edges. If the hands are placed in the center, the box may turn instead of sliding forward.)

d. "How should you stand?" (in a forward stride position, which enlarges the base in the direction of the moving force)

e. "Why should your arms be locked in a straight position?" (so the force will be transferred through a straight lever, rather than absorbed by the flexing of the joints)

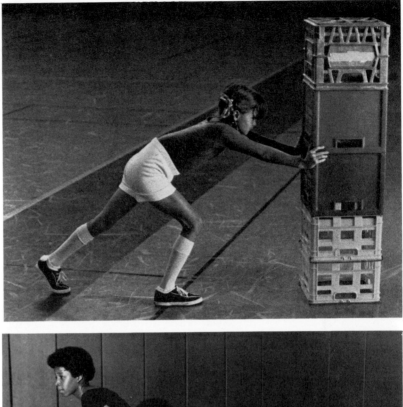

Figure 17.13 Correct Body Position for Pushing a Heavy Object
Feet in forward stride position; hands level with the object's center of gravity, shoulder-width apart; arms straight; body inclined forward; joints locked
Mickey Adair

Figure 17.14 Correct Body Position for Pulling
Bonnie Unsworth

f. "What body parts create the force for the movement?" (the legs)

g. "Why is the body inclined forward?" (so that the force will be transferred diagonally forward rather than upward)

h. "What kind of friction is created between the box and the floor?" (sliding friction)

i. "Why does it require more force to start the object moving than to continue moving it?" (The object's inertia must be overcome.)

2. A wagon filled with bricks is an excellent device for demonstrating pulling; with a rope tied around its center, the box used for pushing serves as a contrasting object. Have one child pull the wagon and another pull the box. Challenge the children to answer the following questions:

a. "Why should you face the direction the load will be moving?" (It is easier to keep your balance and see where you are going when walking forward.)

b. "What body parts create the force for the movement?" (the legs)

c. "Why is friction between the foot and the floor necessary?" (If the feet slide, the force is lost.)

d. "What is the difference between the types of friction created by the wagon and by the box?" (The wagon wheels create rolling friction, and the bottom of the box creates sliding friction.)

e. "Why can you pull a heavier load in the wagon than in the box?" (Rolling friction creates less resistance.)

3. Have each child practice pushing and pulling each of the objects. Then show the children pictures of people pushing and pulling and ask them to comment on the movement patterns.

TOPICS FOR REVIEW AND FURTHER STUDY

1. Describe and execute a correct standing position.

2. Identify the antigravity muscles.

3. Describe the effect of incorrect positioning of the following body parts on one's standing position:

a. pelvis

b. shoulders and trunk

c. head

4. Describe the correct size and design for a child's chair and desk.

5. Describe the correct body position for lifting. Outline the advantages and disadvantages of lifting from the front and from the side.

6. Demonstrate the correct way to lift an object from an overhead shelf.

7. Discuss the advantages of each of the five methods of holding and carrying.

The Fundamental Physical Skills

8. Describe the correct method of pushing and pulling a heavy object.

9. Develop a lesson designed to teach children the correct method of executing one of the fundamental physical skills. Provide for the application of relevant movement principles.

SUGGESTIONS FOR FURTHER READING

BROER, MARION R. *Efficiency of Human Movement,* 3rd ed. Philadelphia: W. B. Saunders, 1973.

COOPER, JOHN M., and GLASSOW, RUTH B. *Kinesiology,* 3rd ed. St. Louis: C. V. Mosby, 1972.

METHENY, ELEANOR. *Body Dynamics.* New York: McGraw-Hill, 1951.

WESSEL, JANET A. *Movement Fundamentals,* 3rd ed. Englewood Cliffs, N.J.: Prentice-Hall, 1970.

Part Five

Studying Movement Forms

Part Five consists of three chapters, each devoted to the study of a specific movement form. A *movement form* may be defined as a group of related activities of a similar nature. The movement forms that comprise the bulk of this area of the new physical education curriculum are dance, games, and educational gymnastics.

Chapter 18 focuses on dance, suggesting ways to stimulate creative dance as well as outlining the study of structured dances. Chapter 19 explores the educational potential of games, discussing the relationship between children's developmental characteristics and games, analyzing the structure of games, and suggesting ways to utilize games as a learning medium. Chapter 20 reviews the contribution of educational gymnastics to the child's development.

Movement themes appropriate for children in different age groups are listed, and these themes are explored in conjunction with various learning activities.

This part of the text outlines some highly structured learning activities. As a teacher of the new physical education, you should constantly consider how each child's participation in such activities will enhance his or her development as an individual. You must ask yourself how you can organize these activities so that instruction will be individualized and each child will be challenged and encouraged to learn at his or her own optimum rate.

18   Dance

Much of what is usually considered the subject matter of educational dance has already been covered in Parts Three and Four of this text. The material has been presented in this order because rhythmic activities are not regarded as a separate component of the new physical education curriculum. Instead, the children's rhythmic responses are viewed as a natural and inseparable aspect of the total physical education program. In the teaching situation, rhythmic experiences should be integrated with the development of movement awareness and basic movement skills so that rhythmic responses to movement stimuli evolve naturally. When a basic vocabulary of rhythmic movements and an understanding of the elements of rhythm and movement have been attained, the study of dance as a specialized movement form can be initiated.

The development of rhythmic responses has been reserved for inclusion in this chapter for two reasons: (1) to present a unified progression that may be adhered to in rhythmic movement instruction, and (2) to facilitate the integration of physical education and music education so that the children's learning in both areas can be supplemented and reinforced and unnecessary duplication of effort eliminated.

MOVING RHYTHMICALLY

The word *rhythm* is a derivative of the Greek *rhythmos*, meaning "measured motion." The motion of the human body can be measured in terms of three factors: the amount of time it consumes, the space it occupies, and the amount of force exerted to bring it about. All skilled movement has the flowing, aesthetically pleasing quality that characterizes a highly developed rhythmic response. This quality may be observed in the movements of highly skilled participants in sports, gymnastics, and dance. In fact, all human movement is rhythmic, but the term is usually associated with dance, in which rhythmic structure is specified and emphasized.

Young children naturally respond to rhythmic impulses and stimuli. However, our culture tends to suppress rather than enhance the development of this ability as children grow older. Boys, particularly in the upper grades, frequently resist participation in rhythmic activities, preferring activities that elicit positive reinforcement from their peers and from adults. The interest of these students can and must be stimulated, since development of their ability to respond rhythmically is a vital aspect of their physical education. When you introduce the children to rhythmic activities, begin with their interests. Then, by means of effective teaching, you can gradually extend and expand their interest to the kinds of movement experiences that are essential to their full development.

THE NATURE OF DANCE

In order to work with children in the medium of dance, it is necessary to be able to distinguish among a movement sequence, a dance, and dancing:

A movement sequence is a *series of consecutive movements.*

A dance is a *rhythmic composition.*

Dancing is a *rhythmic response to a feeling state.*

All of our actions are movement sequences, since the component movements follow one after another. Such sequences may consist of spontaneous or prescribed movements. Most sequences in everyday life are spontaneous, undertaken as the need for them arises. For example, you have probably developed a sequence of movements you routinely perform when you arise in the morning. These movements have no prescribed order, and may be changed or rearranged at will. Games are sequences in which some movements are prescribed and some are spontaneous. A folk dance is an example of an activity all of whose movements are prescribed.

A movement sequence becomes a dance when the rhythmic qualities of the movements are emphasized and the composition has a definable structure. A dance has three distinct phases—beginning, middle, and end—consisting of contrasting but related movements and united by a theme. A dance also has a discernible rhythmic structure and organization.

Figure 18.1 Dancing as an Expression of Feeling
Mickey Adair

A child may *do a dance* without *dancing*. Simply executing the prescribed movements is performing a dance; experiencing the rhythmic response of one's moving body is dancing. *Dancing is a feeling state,* and is therefore always expressive in nature. A dancing child is expressing what he or she feels (see Figure 18.1). In other words, a combination of skipping and turning is a movement sequence. If skipping steps and turning movements are executed to a rhythmic beat, they form a dance. If the child skips and turns *happily,* he or she is dancing.

THE GOALS OF EDUCATIONAL DANCE

The goal of educational dance is to develop the children's sense of rhythm and enhance their awareness in a way that will enable them to respond rhythmically to the world around them. If this goal is to be achieved in an educational setting, the children must be willing, enthusiastic participants. *You can require children to perform a dance, but you cannot force them to feel their rhythmic movement.* Willingness to feel arises within the individual and must be stimulated. The development of a successful dance curriculum depends on your ability to create a learning environment that will stimulate this desire.

The content of the educational dance curriculum includes study of the movement elements, the rhythmic and structural components of dance, and the form and characteristics of dances. The prescribed activities enable the child to explore rhythmic movement, create dances, and develop a repertoire of structured dance activities.

THE DANCE CURRICULUM

Children should begin studying dance in kindergarten or first grade and systematically progress through a curriculum of gradually increasing scope and difficulty. The learning experiences that should be provided for at each learning level are as follows:

1. Beginning Level

a. responding rhythmically with different body parts and with the entire body

b. starting and stopping spontaneously and on a given signal

c. rhythmically executing the locomotor movements walking, running, jumping, hopping, skipping, and galloping

d. developing awareness of simple rhythmic patterns by responding to a drumbeat and to music with a strong beat

e. executing imitative movements portraying how various things *feel*

f. participating in simple action songs and singing games

g. developing a basic understanding of the movement elements by experiencing the following contrasting dimensions:

    (1) high and low

    (2) forward and backward

    (3) small and large

    (4) fast and slow

    (5) heavy and light

    (6) hard and soft

2. Advanced Beginning Level

a. responding to a rhythmic beat with simple combinations of the basic movements

b. responding spontaneously and creatively to different kinds of rhythmic accompaniment

c. recognizing how the basic movements and formations (circle, line, square) are used in singing games and simple folk dances

d. recognizing rhythmic patterns and phrases

e. moving with a partner while responding rhythmically

f. developing a basic understanding of movement and rhythmic elements by:

(1) suddenly and then gradually changing the force; size, direction, levels; and tempo of movements in personal and in general space
(2) varying body shapes
(3) following different pathways
(4) responding to the accented beat

3. Intermediate Level
a. executing all the locomotor and nonlocomotor movements to a rhythmic beat
b. recognizing and reproducing the parts of a dance (beginning, middle, and end)
c. responding to even and uneven rhythmic patterns

4. Advanced Level
a. utilizing the basic skills, movement elements, and rhythmic elements in the solution of movement problems, improvisation, and dance composition
b. creatively interpreting feeling states and the structure of music
c. developing a repertoire of folk dances from around the world and studying them as folk art
d. creating various kinds of rhythmic accompaniment

As the preceding outline makes evident, the children progress from learning experiences that are largely exploratory to those involving a relatively high level of problem solving. This is, of course, an ideal curriculum designed for textbook children who are introduced to rhythmic movement in kindergarten and progress step-by-step through the curriculum. In reality this rarely happens. Most of you will face the challenges of modifying the content so that children in the upper grades can be introduced to the elements of rhythmic movement and then rapidly progress to higher learning levels. The following activities are designed to help you make such adaptations.

RESPONDING TO A RHYTHMIC BEAT

Children may initially have difficulty relating what they hear with how they are to move. Thus their activities must promote the development of such rhythmic responses. You should first introduce a single rhythmic pattern by clapping and by beating a drum; it is much easier for the child to hear and attend to these rhythmic cues than the beat of a musical selection with melodic and harmonic elements.

Key Concept
□ *My body parts can move rhythmically.*

I can clap in rhythm.
I can walk to a rhythmic beat.

Activities for
Children

1. Ask the children to listen while you clap a measure in 4/4 time, as shown in Figure 18.2. Do so one more time while the children listen; then have them clap with you.

2. Echo Clapping. Tell the children you want them to be your echo, clapping what they hear you clap. Begin with one measure; then progress to two, three, and four measures.

3. Beat the same rhythm on a drum, having the children echo it by clapping. Repeat the rhythm, having them clap on the floor with their hands and then their feet.

4. Explain that each clap or stroke of the drum is called a *beat*.

Figure 18.2 One Measure of 4/4 Rhythm

5. Challenge the children to walk to the beat, taking one step on each beat. Instruct them to begin walking when you begin beating and to stop when you stop beating the drum.

6. Challenge them to walk backward to the beat.

I can walk to beats that are fast or slow.
I can accent a beat by taking a heavy step.
An accented beat marks the beginning of a new group of beats.

Activities pertinent to these concepts are listed on page 230, activity 3. As soon as the children demonstrate ability to respond to a rhythmic beat by walking, they should begin executing the other locomotor movements to a beat.

Key Concept
□ *I can move on a high level to high sounds and on a low level to low sounds.*

7. Play extremely high and low tones on the piano; play recorded music characterized by high and low tones; or improvise by striking different kinds of sticks or objects, or by speaking or singing at high and low pitches.

a. Challenge the children to respond to the high tones by standing up and the low tones by sitting down.

b. Increase the challenge by having them respond to very high tones by standing on tiptoe and reaching as high as possible, and to very low tones by lying on the floor.

c. Have the children move about the room, on a high level in response to a high tone and on a low level to a low tone.

d. At the advanced beginner level, explain that the high, medium, and low tones of sounds are called the *pitch*, and that the pitch may gradually become higher or lower. Play piano music or simple

Responding to a Rhythmic Beat

recorded music illustrating this concept, and have the children gradually change the level on which they move in response to the pitch.

Children who are cognitively mature enough to comprehend the concept of numerical fractions should be introduced to the following rhythmic concepts.

Key Concept
□ Rhythm *is the flow of music and movement. Rhythm is determined by the organization of pulsations.*

Rhythmic pulsations are called beats.
Beats are grouped together to form a rhythmic pattern. The units formed by grouping beats are called measures.
A beat that is stronger or heavier than other beats is called an accented beat. *The accent usually falls on the first beat of each measure and serves as a signal that a new measure is beginning.*
Notes are named according to their temporal value.
The number and type of notes in a measure determine the meter.
The meter is written at the beginning of a musical composition as a numerical fraction. The top numeral indicates the number of beats in each measure; the bottom number specifies the kind of musical note that gets the beat.
If all the notes within the measure have the same temporal value, the rhythmic pattern is even. An uneven *rhythmic pattern results from combining notes that are temporally unequal.*
A rhythmic sequence consisting of several measures is called a phrase.

8. Have the children place the fingers of their right hands on the right sides of their necks and locate the pulse. Point out that the pulse results from the rhythmic pulsations of the heartbeat. Relate this phenomenon to the fact that all their movements are rhythmic and that the pulsations are called the *beat*.

9. Beat out a measure of 4/4 meter on the drum. Ask the children how many beats they hear. (four) Explain that a certain number of beats are grouped together to form a unit called a *measure*. Have the children clap their hands to one measure of 4/4 meter; then have them clap their hands on their thighs to a second measure, and on the floor to a third measure.

10. Explain that measures are usually divided by an accented beat on the first note of each measure. Demonstrate by beating several measures of 4/4 meter on the drum, accenting the first beat of each measure. Review the concept of responding to an accented beat.

11. Explain note values.

a. Draw a whole note on the blackboard, and challenge the children to duplicate its shape with their bodies, as shown in Figure 18.3.

b. Explain that all the notes except a whole note are fractions. Draw two half notes on the board under the whole note (see Figure 18.4), and challenge the children to make their bodies into the shape of a half note, as shown in Figure 18.5. Explain that two half notes equal a whole note.

c. Draw four quarter notes under the half notes. Challenge the children to duplicate this shape with their bodies, as shown in Figure 18.6. Explain that four quarter notes equal one whole note or two half notes.

d. Draw eight eighth notes under the quarter notes. Have the children duplicate this shape, as shown in Figure 18.7. Explain that eight eighth notes equal one whole note, two half notes, or four quarter notes.

e. Draw sixteen sixteenth notes under the eighth notes. Have the children duplicate the shape of a sixteenth note, as shown in Figure 18.8. Explain that sixteen sixteenth notes equal one whole note, two half notes, four quarter notes, or eight eighth notes.

f. Explain that because there is only one whole note in each measure, it occupies a lot of time; thus movements in response to whole notes are very slow. Movements to half notes are quite slow. Quarter note movements are of medium speed, like walking. Eighth note movements are fast, like running, and sixteenth note movements are fast running steps.

g. Have the children walk in time to whole notes, half notes, and quarter notes. Signal each step by means of a drumbeat. Challenge the children to run in time with eighth notes and sixteenth notes.

12. Explain how notes are grouped into measures, and how the number and type of notes in the measure determine the meter (see Figure 18.9).

13. Have the children echo-clap 2/2 meter composed entirely of half notes, accenting the first beat of each measure (see the first measure in Figure 18.9, A). Ask them to count the musical count as they clap. Progress to echo-clapping 2/2 meter composed of whole notes. Gradually progress through the rest of the examples in Figure 18.9.

14. Have the children walk in time to different note values in a variety of meters. Challenge them to run in 6/8 time. Accompany their movements with a drumbeat, accenting the first beat of each measure. Review how the note value affects the tempo of the movement.

15. A Movement Orchestra. Divide the class into three groups.

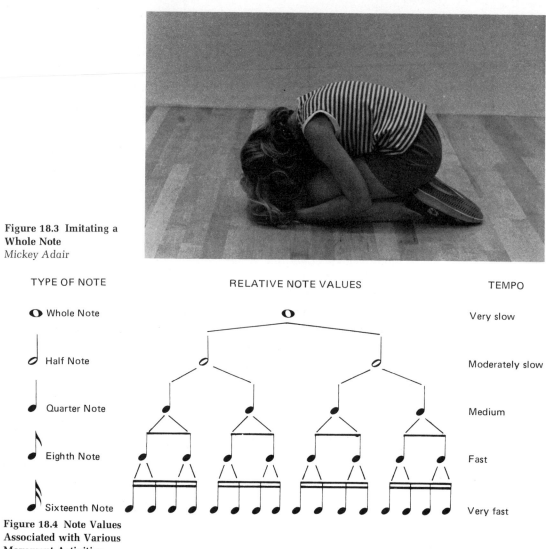

Figure 18.3 Imitating a Whole Note
Mickey Adair

TYPE OF NOTE   RELATIVE NOTE VALUES   TEMPO

Whole Note   Very slow

Half Note   Moderately slow

Quarter Note   Medium

Eighth Note   Fast

Sixteenth Note   Very fast

Figure 18.4 Note Values Associated with Various Movement Activities

Figure 18.5 Imitating a Half Note
Mickey Adair

Assign one group to act as whole notes, the second group as half notes, and the last group as quarter notes. Explain that you are going to beat out several measures of 4/4 meter, and that each group is to respond by taking one step on the appropriate beat. Demonstrate how each group is to move, as follows:

> Whole notes take one step on the accented beat and hold that position on counts 2, 3, and 4.

> Half notes take one step forward on the accented beat, hold on count 2, take a second step on count 3, and hold on four.

> Quarter notes take a step on each beat.

Variations:

> Assign a fourth group to act as eighth notes, taking two running steps to each beat.

Responding to a Rhythmic Beat

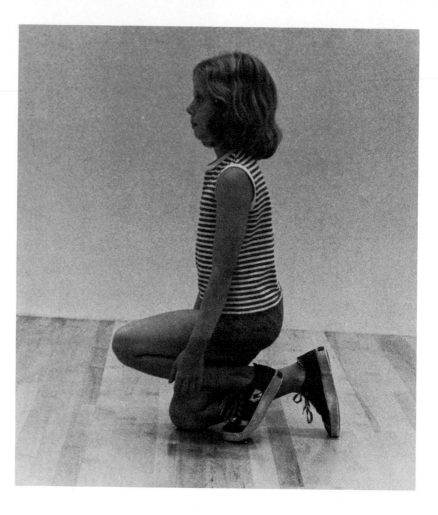

**Figure 18.6 Imitating a
Quarter Note**
Mickey Adair

Use movements other than walking steps, such as the following.

Whole notes jump forward on the first measure, backward on the second measure, and forward and backward again.

Half notes swing diagonally downward on the first count, hold on 2, swing upward on 3, hold on 4.

Quarter notes imitate drum majors, lifting one knee and the opposite arm high on each step.

Eighth notes take very fast choppy steps like robots, bending their arms at right angles and moving their hands up and down on each step.

16. Review and reinforce the concept of note values by having the

Figure 18.7 Imitating an Eighth Note
Mickey Adair

children jump and hop slow and fast. Add the nonlocomotor movements and vary the dimension, direction, level, size, and pathway.

17. Challenge individuals or small groups to develop a sequence of movements to a specified number of beats.

18. Explain the concepts of even and uneven rhythms. Point out that, in all the preceding activities, the rhythm was even because all the notes in a single measure had the same time value; that is, a given measure was composed entirely of quarter notes, half notes, or a single whole note. The locomotor movements walking, running, jumping, hopping, and leaping all have even rhythms, since each step takes the same amount of time. (Demonstrate.) The locomotor movements skipping, galloping, and sliding have uneven rhythms, because the first part of the step is slower than the second part. (Demonstrate this by indicating that when you skip the step phase of the movement is relatively slow, but the hop phase is fast. In the slide the sideward step is slow and the closing step is fast.) Diagram the rhythmic analysis of these

Responding to a Rhythmic Beat

**Figure 18.8 Imitating a
Sixteenth Note**
Mickey Adair

movements on the board (see Figure 18.10), explaining how the steps coincide with the rhythmic pattern. Explain that a dotted note receives one-and-a-half times its ordinary time value. Have the children practice skipping, sliding, and galloping to a rhythmic beat.

19. Explain the concept of a musical or movement *phrase*. Point out that a phrase consists of several measures or movements that express a given theme, and is thus analogous to a sentence composed of words that together express a thought. Have partners compose a movement phrase by joining two locomotor movements and one nonlocomotor movement to express happiness. For example, one child *bends* over to pick up an object lying on the floor. Discovering it has great value, he or she *runs* to show it to a friend and the two of them *skip* away together.

Phrasing is a concept central to dance composition, since movements must be joined to express a theme. The portrayal of the theme is initiated at the beginning of the phrase, expanded in the middle, and brought to a climax at the end. A longer composition may consist of several phrases joined to express a more complex theme.

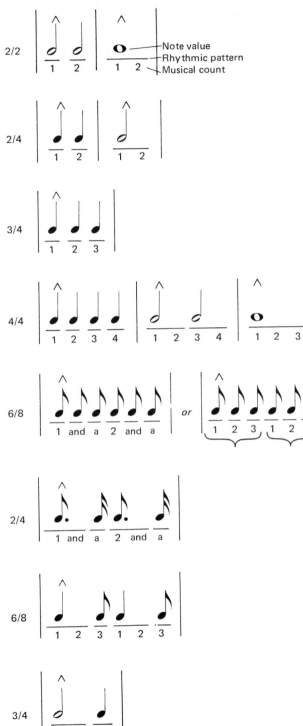

Figure 18.9 Musical Measures in Various Meters

In the meter designation (2/2, 2/4, etc.), the top numeral indicates the number of beats in a measure and the bottom numeral the kind of musical note that gets one beat. Thus in 2/2 meter the half notes each get one count; in 2/4, 3/4, and 4/4 meter the quarter notes each get one count; and in 6/8 meter the eighth notes each get one count. The accent is on the first beat in each measure.

Figure 18.10 Uneven Rhythmic Patterns: Skipping, Galloping, and Sliding

Top: the skip, the fast slide, and the fast gallop; Middle: the slow gallop; Bottom: the slow slide

Responding to a Rhythmic Beat

Figure 18.11 Swinging Movements
Here scarves are used to stimulate movement.
Mickey Adair

DEVELOPING A QUALITATIVE RHYTHMIC RESPONSE

As children experience rhythmic movement, they should become aware that it has a qualitative nature. They should experience the effects of varying force in order to portray different feeling states or lend a movement a certain spirit. Such learning experiences should help them comprehend the following concepts.

Key Concept
□ *The quality of a movement is determined by the amount of force expended and its timing.*

The four principal qualities of movement are:

1. Swinging movements. *Produced by the rhythmic rotation of the arms and legs, these movements may vary from short pendular to-and-fro movements to full arcs. (See Figure 18.11.)*

2. Sustained movements. *Such movements characterized by a smooth, flowing quality and an even rhythm.*

3. Percussive movements. *Strong, sudden, explosive movements resulting from sudden, forceful contraction of the muscles, percussive*

movements may result from body parts contacting each other (clapping), the floor (stomping), or an external object (beating a drum).

4. Vibratory movements. *Vacillating, quivering movements resemble vibrations of the strings on a stringed instrument. Such movement is rhythmic shaking.*

Activities for Children

The exploration of movement qualities is fully discussed in Dimondstein's *Children Dance in the Classroom* (1971, Ch. 10), to which you should refer while developing this component of the dance curriculum.

DEVELOPING CREATIVE DANCES

Structured dances are relatively easy to teach, since the subject matter is prescribed and the learning situation entirely teacher-directed. It is much more difficult to teach creative movement, whose significant content must emerge from within the child. The act of creating is an adventure with the inner self that leads to a personal discovery, *a knowing through feeling.* It is an inner experience that has an outward manifestation. Bringing about creative learning involves developing and using the qualities of openness, alertness, awareness, and sensitivity. Such a learning environment must be carefully planned and maintained, keeping in mind the following factors:

1. The task must be appropriate to the developmental and learning levels of the children. Because the creative act involves manipulation and application of previously acquired knowledge and skill, the child needs confidence in his or her ability to manage the components of the task.

2. The movement theme must interest and challenge the children and must readily evoke appropriate movement responses.

3. Each child experiments, discovers, and relates in a unique way and in accordance with his or her own ability.

4. The creative act must be purposeful. The child must be able to see its meaning, application, and relationships.

5. The process and the outcome must evoke a sense of self-satisfaction.

6. The child's achievement must be recognized and positively reinforced by others.

The study of creative dance is characterized by three phases. In the first stage the children are introduced to the elements of dance through *exploratory movements.* (See Figure 18.12.) They develop awareness of their bodies' actions, the basic elements of rhythm, and the feelings associated with executing the locomotor and nonlocomotor

Figure 18.12 Exploratory Movements
These children are becoming aware of their body actions by using their bodies to create different shapes.
Mickey Adair

movements rhythmically. The teacher leads the children in exploring the lesson's theme by introducing activities that will initiate movement responses. The teacher observes these responses and then extends the children's exploration by means of questions, challenges, or imagery (see pages 114–118).

In movement exploration, children respond to a stimulus with a literal interpretation or imitative movement. As their awareness of their movement potential increases, they should progress from moving *like* something to expressing how it feels to *be* that thing. Thus, in the second stage of the dance curriculum, the children interpret the feeling states evoked by the stimulus and express them through improvisational movement. (See Figure 18.13.) Improvisation is the use of one's imagination and previous experience to invent movements that

Figure 18.13 Interpretive Movements
Here children interpret how it feels to be a crumpled sheet of plastic that is slowly expanding.
Mickey Adair

portray the characteristics of the stimulus. The children use the basic movement skills and the elements of rhythm and movement to symbolize and communicate the expressive qualities of an object or idea.

Let us illustrate the difference between movement exploration and improvisational movement with the following example. You tell children in the exploratory stage to pretend they are waving goodbye to someone. You can then extend their exploration by challenging them to make their movements larger or smaller, or to use more or less space. When the children are ready to improvise, you use the same movement stimulus (waving goodbye) but instruct them to move as though they are sorry or happy to be leaving. The child's perception of the feeling state is them conveyed in the movements he or she selects: small, slow movements to indicate reluctance or large, fast movements to convey enthusiasm and excitement. The child may wave realistically or abstract the gesture by exaggerating or diminishing it in order to draw attention to certain aspects of it.

In the final stage of creative dance instruction, children create their own dances. Creating a dance is a learning task involving all the components of problem solving, which take the form of the following steps:

1. sensing and comprehending the meaning, implications, and expressive qualities of the dance theme (the movement stimulus)

2. exploring the movement dimensions of the theme—that is, considering how the meaning and feelings evoked by the theme can be expressed in movement

3. tentatively selecting movements that express these characteristics

4. placing the movements in a sequence

5. rhythmically phrasing the movements

6. polishing and refining the rhythmic phrasing and execution of the movements

The ability to create dances develops naturally when children's movement experiences follow an educationally sound sequence. If you review the above steps, you will note that steps 1 and 2 are the learning outcomes associated with movement exploration. Step 3 results from learning how to improvise. In all areas of the curriculum, the children should be learning how different movements fit together logically and smoothly to form a sequence. All their rhythmic movement experiences should involve learning about phrasing, and refining the quality of the movement response should be the goal of every movement lesson. Therefore, the only factor in creating a dance that is unfamiliar to the children is the dance's structure. And this is not entirely new to them if they have been learning about structured dances and games.

Children's initial experiences in dance composition should involve simple themes and short phrases. As learning progresses the themes may become more complicated, more movement dimensions may be included, and a higher level of performance may be expected. For example, an appropriate theme for children who are just beginning to create dances is "Walking on the Beach." The children might respond by arising from a prone position (the beginning of the dance); slowly walking along, their attention focused on the floor as if casually looking for something, and bending over to pick up a seashell (the middle of the dance); walking back to their places on the beach and sitting down to examine their discoveries (the end of the dance). A more advanced theme might be "A Day at the Beach." The children's response to this theme would involve a wide variety of locomotor and nonlocomotor movements and variations in the dimensions of the movement elements. For example, they might elect to respond to the ocean breeze, play on the beach and in the water, be sea creatures or birds, or go for a ride in a boat. At first you will be responsible for select workable themes; as the children become familiar with the nature of a satisfactory theme, they will be able to select many of their own.

STIMULATING THE MOVEMENT RESPONSE

A movement stimulus is used to create a mental image that will motivate the children to move in a certain way. The stimulus should suggest the basic movements and dimensions of movement that will be used, as well as the quality of the movement response. For example, the word "popcorn" suggests the basic movements bending, jumping, and falling. (See Figure 18.14.) The suggested spatial dimensions involve moving upward and downward, first with a narrow and then with a wide shape. The tempo is slow, and the force is expended suddenly, resulting in percussive movements. As the children become more familiar with expressive movement, the stimuli should gradually become more complex, requiring multi-dimensional movement responses. Eventually the children must respond with a sequence of related movements that include variations in the dimensions of the movement elements.

The most commonly used movement stimuli are auditory: music or spoken words. These are effective sources of stimulation, but children should also be given opportunities to respond to their visual, tactile, gustatory, olfactory, and kinesthetic senses. The following list suggests the kinds of sensory input that may be used as movement stimuli.

Inanimate Objects

clock: the hands moving, the pendulum swinging, ticking, the alarm going off

big paintbrush: painting the wall, ceiling, floor, or the inside of the child's personal space

lawn sprinkler: going back and forth or round and round

elevator: going up and down, the door opening and closing

balloon: being blown up, floating in various directions, bursting

ball: rolling, bouncing, being thrown, hitting the wall, being caught

clothes: being washed, wrung out, hanging on the line, tumbling inside a dryer, being folded up

Animals

fly: buzzing overhead, stuck on flypaper

bee: gathering honey, stinging someone

bird: jumping, flying, gliding, building a nest, bathing in a birdbath

cat: sleeping, waking, stretching, hunting, being chased by a dog, being petted

Figure 18.14 Responding to a Movement Stimulus: "Popcorn"
Mickey Adair

dog: eating, chasing a thrown stick, barking at a cat in a tree, seeing his master come home

worm: emerging from the ground, crawling

caterpillar: clinging to a leaf, crawling along the ground, spinning its cocoon, resting inside, emerging from the cocoon as a butterfly

bear: walking, climbing a tree, finding honey, waking from hibernation

gorilla: walking, becoming sleepy, becoming angry

giraffe: eating, looking around, running

animals in a circus, in a zoo, on a farm; wild animals

Nature

the ocean: waves, shells, fish, seagulls, sandy beaches

the sun: rising, setting, on a cloudy day, beaming on the earth

a storm: lightning, thunder, wind, rain, snow

a flower: growing, blooming, losing its petals

a snowflake: floating down, landing, resting on the ground, being rolled into a big snowball, melting, soaking into the earth

a drop of water: falling as rain, flowing in a stream, going over a waterfall

Machines

eggbeater	washing machine	tugboat
toaster	percolator	plane
mixer	lawnmower	rocket
gears	jackhammer	train
wheels	car	bulldozer

Objects and Things

paper bags	scarves	bubble gum
matches	jumping beans	elastic
bubbles	popcorn	a magnet

Characters

baby	cowpoke	giant
elderly person	soldier	magician
prince or princess	robot	space traveler

Living Habits

getting up	walking to school	taking a bath
dressing	playing with a friend	brushing one's teeth
eating breakfast	playing with a pet	going to sleep

Situations

being alone	losing something	walking on the moon
being in a crowd	being lost	going fishing
receiving a gift	walking in a forest	going away

Sensory Stimulation

Tactile

flannel (soft)	terry cloth (fuzzy)	cotton (soft)
burlap (rough)	feather (tickly)	rock (hard)
sandpaper (rough)	plastic (slick)	beanbag (lumpy)
fur (fuzzy)	silk (silky)	balsa wood (light)

Visual

Colors	Symbols	Photographs, paintings, drawings
black	numbers	historical events
red	letters	sports
blue	road signs	machines
orange	Indian signs	

yellow
pink
purple

people
places
animals
abstract art
nature

Gustatory

candy	a hamburger	chocolate cream pie
whipped cream	an orange	hot pepper
a lemon	pizza	relish

Olfactory

perfume	a skunk	food cooking
a rose	smoke	wet earth

Auditory
Sounds of things

crashing	screeching	tinkling
rattling	snapping	banging

Sounds of rhythm instruments

clicking instruments: sticks, wood blocks, castanets, coconut shells
ringing and jingling instruments: triangle, bells, tambourine, cymbals
swishing or rattling instruments: sandblocks, maracas

Sounds of nature

birds singing	dog barking	thunder
cat meowing	rain	wind

Music

pitch	rhythm
meter	tempo

Words

the feelings conveyed by the inflection of the voice
the rhythm and tempo of the words
the meaning of the words

Functional or Expressive Body Actions

stretching	stomping	wiggling
drooping	tugging	squirming
crouching	jerking	floating
reaching	shaking	jumping
grabbing	patting	paddling
punching	waving	rowing
pounding	sweeping	hurrying
slashing	swinging	hiding

Figure 18.15 Responding to a Movement Stimulus: "Fear"
Mickey Adair

Feelings, Emotions, and Characteristics

fear (Figure 18.15)	disappointment	confidence
anger	excitement	dignity
happiness	calm	bravery
sorrow	freedom	arrogance
surprise	captivity	shyness

Play Activities

on the playground: play on swings, seesaw, sliding board, climbing pole

on a picnic: spread out the lunch, eat it, clean up; it begins to rain

on a camping trip: pitch the tent, unroll the sleeping bag, gather wood, build a fire, cook over the fire, hike in the woods, wade in the stream

in an Indian village: paddle a canoe, walk quietly through the woods, hunt for game, do a dance

at a carnival: ride the merry-go-round, ferris wheel, roller coaster; drive a bumper car; throw balls at a target

Holidays

Halloween: skeletons, ghosts, witches, cats, scarecrow, jack-o-lantern, haunted house, sound effects

Thanksgiving: pilgrims, Indians, turkeys, hunting, going to church, building homes

Christmas: Santa, reindeer, sleighbells, Christmas tree, toys, snow

Easter: bunnies, chickens, ducks, Easter baskets, Easter eggs

Seasons

autumn: school, birds flying south, harvest, leaves changing colors and falling

winter: wind, snow, ice, skating, skiing, sledding

spring: rain, planting seeds, watching things grow, flying kites

summer: sun, swimming, sailing, taking vacations

Compositions

Poems

"The Night Before Christmas" by Clement Clarke Moore (Random House, 1961)

"The Little Turtle" by Vachel Lindsay (in Arbuthnot and Root, *Time for Poetry* (Scott, Foresman, 1968)

"Fog" by Carl Sandburg (in Johnson, Sickels, and Sayers, *Anthology of Children's Literature,* Houghton, Mifflin, 1970)

"My Shadow" by Robert Louis Stevenson (in Ferris, *Favorite Poems Old and New,* Doubleday, 1957)

"The Mysterious Cat" by Vachel Lindsay (in Johnson, Sickels, and Sayers)

haiku (see page 415)

Stories

Do You Want to Be My Friend? by Eric Carle (Crowell, 1971)

Winnie-the-Pooh by Alan Alexander Milne (Dutton, 1961)

Bambi by Felix Sulten (Grosset & Dunlap, 1929)

A Tree Is Nice by Janice May Udry (Harper & Row, 1956)

I Like to Be Me by Barbara Bel Geddes (Viking, 1963)

Where the Wild Things Are by Maurice Sendak (Harper & Row, 1963)

Themes and Music from Films

Mary Poppins	*The Sound of Music*	*2001: A Space*
Dr. Doolittle	*West Side Story*	*Odyssey*

Recordings by Popular Artists

The Misty Moods	Herb Alpert	Peter, Paul, and Mary
John Denver	Bert Kaempfert	rock groups

Traditional, Ethnic, Classical, and Semiclassical Music

Movement stimuli may be used in a variety of ways, depending on the theme of the lesson. For example, you may select a word that will stress the actions of certain body parts, such as the hands, arms, feet, head, or trunk. You may use stimuli to review the rhythmic execution of certain basic movements or to reinforce certain concepts. You may also use these mechanisms to explore ideas and to enhance the children's awareness of feeling states. The following lesson illustrates the use of movement stimuli in various ways within a single lesson.

SAMPLE LESSON PLAN

Level: Intermediate or Advanced

Unit Title: Creative Rhythmic Movement

Theme: Movement expresses ethnic characteristics.

Performance Objectives

Psychomotor Domain: The children will move in time to music with a very slow tempo. They will correctly execute movements that express the feeling states evoked by the music, the haiku, and the ethnic characteristics of the Japanese people.

Cognitive Domain: The children will demonstrate a knowledge of
1. the relationship between the way people live and feel and the way they move
2. the ethnic characteristics of the Japanese people as expressed in their poetry and the way they move
3. the essential components of haiku
The children will identify the movement concepts contained in the prescribed sequences, as well as in the sequences they create. The specific concepts they will identify are:
1. the spatial dimensions—size, direction, level, and pathway
2. the dimensions of time—tempo and rhythm
3. the locomotor and nonlocomotor movements
4. the qualities of the movements they execute

Affective Domain: The children will experience movements that differ from the characteristic movements of people in the western world. They will demonstrate the ability to work in a small group while developing an expressive movement sequence.

Equipment: A phonograph recording of Japanese instrumental folk music, such as the "Flower Dance," recorded by Katsumasa Takasago from the album *Japanese Folk Melodies* (Explorer Series, H 72020-A); copies of haiku (see page 415)

Teaching Aids: Scale outline maps of Japan and of the children's home state, for a comparison of their sizes; illustrations of traditional Japanese costumes; pictures of Japanese people working and playing

Introductory Activities

1. Have the children form a circle and sit down on the floor with their legs crossed (tailor-fashion).

2. Play a portion of the Japanese folk melody and ask the children if they can identify the country of its origin.

3. Discuss the definition and significance of haiku.

Main Activities

4. Divide the class into seven groups, and give each group a copy of one of the haiku shown below.

5. Tell the groups that you will give them about ten minutes to develop movement sequences that express their haiku. Instruct them to arrange the movements so that they can be executed within the class circle.

6. When the children appear to be prepared, have them return to the circle. Explain that they are going to participate in a movement sequence that expresses a traditional way of life of the Japanese people.[1] Tell them that the movement sequence has three parts; in the first and last parts they are to follow your instructions, and in the middle part each group will perform its haiku.

7. Instruct them that the performance of each group's haiku is to be acknowledged by the rest of the class by bowing and saying, "ah so." (Emphasize that this phrase is the Japanese equivalent of clapping or cheering.)

8. Ask if there are any questions.

9. Turn the music on and tell the children to move to the music whenever they move as a group.

10. Begin the movement sequence by saying, "Here we are in Japan on the shore of a big lake. It is here that the Japanese people come together to plant rice." Have the children kneel. "We must make a mud wall around our field." Everyone moves as if scooping mud from the center and piling it on the wall, in time to the music.

11. "The wall is finished. Now we will make a gate so the water can flow in." The children move as though they are making an opening in the wall.

12. "Now we must step over the mud wall and work the water into

[1]The movements in this sequence were originally developed by Nancy Berling, a student at the University of Kentucky.

414   Dance

the soil with our feet." The children step into the circle and move their feet around as though stamping in mud. They step back to the circumference of the circle and remain standing.

13. "Now we must plant the rice." The children make motions as if scattering seeds.

14. "Now the work is done. We can rest and celebrate." The children sit cross-legged in the circle, and each group performs its haiku sequence. After each performance the class bows. The following are examples of haiku that can be created using movement themes:

Lightning flashes in the
Night sky and the thunder announces
The arrival of rain.

The night wind stirs the
Boughs of the tree and silently
They wave their greeting.

A leaf falls to the
Ground and comes to rest among
The welcoming grass.

The weeping willow
Makes a resting place for the
Happy, singing birds.

The baby sparrows
Hop and fly in the shadow
Of the willow tree.

The sun appears and
The morning mist rises from the
Warm rice paddy waters.

The sleeping cats are
Startled into wakefulness.
They stretch and move about.

15. "After many days and nights the rice grows, stretching toward the sun. The people celebrate by dancing." The children stand in a circle and hold hands. Then they perform the following steps slowly, in time to the music.
  a. "Walk eight steps clockwise."
  b. "Walk four steps forward toward the center of the circle and four steps backward."
  c. "Walk eight steps clockwise."
  d. "Swing both arms downward and backward to the right, and then to the left. Repeat three times."
  e. "Walk eight steps clockwise."

f. "Skip four steps forward toward the center and backward to place."

g. "Walk eight steps clockwise."

h. "Hop four steps to the center and hop four steps backward."

i. "Walk eight steps clockwise."

j. "Walk to the center eight steps."

k. "Walk backward four steps and slowly bow."

Concluding
Activities

16. Have the class sit in a circle. Discuss the feeling state evoked by the movements and the characteristics they portray: calm, quiet, slow, polite, meditative.

17. Show the children the teaching aids and discuss the related information.

18. Review the movement concepts listed in the objectives.

This lesson is highly teacher-directed and could be used to introduce the children to the uses of movement stimuli. In the lessons that follow, the children should become more self-directing. Throughout the creative dance curriculum the children should be encouraged to assume responsibility for their own learning and for the development of self-expressive movements.

STUDYING
STRUCTURED
DANCES

A structured dance has a prescribed sequence of steps. Such dances include singing, games; folk, square, ethnic, and ballroom dances; and dances composed by individuals.

A sequence for introducing structured dances has been outlined in Chapter 14. This program is based on the principle that children first develop the ability to execute the basic skills rhythmically, then combine the movements to create dance steps, and sequentially arrange these steps to reproduce the pattern of the dance.

Folk and square dance should be studied as folk art (see page 90). The children should also learn to recognize the basic movements that comprise the dance and the basic structure of the dance form. A suggested sequence for teaching a structured dance is as follows:

1. Point out the basic movements that compose the dance.

2. Listen to the music and point out the tempo and changes in phrasing.

3. Practice the first set of steps without music.

4. Add the music.

5. Repeat activities 3 and 4 with the second set of steps.

6. Repeat activities 3 and 4 for each figure of the dance, periodically reviewing the parts that have already been introduced.

7. Review the entire dance, with music.

8. Discuss the meaning, significance, and characteristics of the dance.

It is impossible to explore the theoretical and applied aspects of children's dances fully in this text. The subject is so extensive that entire books have been devoted to it. It is thus recommended that you consult the texts listed on page 419. A list of sources for rhythmic accompaniment is also supplied in Appendix C; a review of the companies' catalogues will familiarize you with a wide variety of teaching aids.

TOPICS FOR REVIEW AND FURTHER STUDY

1. Why should the curricula of physical education and music be interrelated?

2. Define the Greek word *rhythmos* and explain its relationship to skilled movement.

3. Define movement sequence, a dance, and dancing.

4. What is the goal of educational dance?

5. Develop a lesson in which a group of children at the beginning level practice responding to a rhythmic beat. Provide for variations in time and space.

6. Feeling your pulse rate
a. Determine the rhythmic structure of your heartbeat. Compare it to your respiratory rate. Which is faster?
b. Diagram the rhythmic structure of your resting heart rate. What kind of musical notes have approximately the same temporal value as your heartbeats?
c. Diagram the rhythmic structure of your heart rate after you have run around the gym. What kind of musical notes must you use?

7. Develop a movement sequence involving walking steps. Use eight measures of 4/4 meter accompaniment. Include very slow steps, moderately slow steps, regular walking steps, and very fast steps. Take one step on each beat. Diagram the rhythmic structure of your sequence.

8. Using 2/4 meter, develop a sequence involving walking, running, bending, and stretching. Indicate the musical count on which each movement is performed.

9. Develop a lesson designed to acquaint children with the relationship between musical notation and movement.

10. Do a series of jumping steps in the meters listed below. Note how the feeling quality of the movement changes as the tempo increases.
   a. 2/2 meter containing whole notes
   b. 2/2 meter containing half notes
   c. 4/4 meter containing quarter notes
   d. 6/8 meter containing eighth notes

11. Express the following emotions and characteristics by using movements of varying tempos and qualities:
   a. happiness
   b. freedom
   c. bravery
   d. frustration
   e. anger
   f. fear

12. Visualize yourself in the following situations, and describe the tempo and feeling quality of your movements:
   a. walking to class on a very hot day
   b. walking home on the first day of spring
   c. being caught in the rain
   d. being chased by a big dog
   e. walking up a steep hill
   f. walking home from class after learning you have flunked a mid-term exam

13. Develop a series of learning activities in which children explore the qualities of movement.

14. Describe the three stages of learning in the creative dance curriculum. Select a theme and develop a series of learning activities in which children at each stage explore its movement possibilities.

15. What kinds of rhythmic movement experiences should precede children's introduction to structured dance?

16. When and why would you have all the children in a class perform a folk dance?

17. Develop a lesson plan in which a group of advanced children study a folk dance as folk art.

18. Review the catalogues of a variety of companies and select the teaching aids you would use to plan and conduct rhythmic learning activities for children at a given learning level.

19. Review three of the references listed on page 419 and specify how you can make use of each as you plan and conduct learning activities.

SUGGESTIONS FOR FURTHER READING

AMERICAN ASSOCIATION FOR HEALTH, PHYSICAL EDUCATION, AND RECREATION. *Children's Dance.* Washington, D.C.: AAHPER, 1973.

BAYLOR, BYRD. *Sometimes I Dance Mountains.* New York: Charles Scribner's Sons, 1973.

BARLIN, ANN, and BARLIN, PAUL. *The Art of Learning Through Movement.* Los Angeles: Ward Ritchie Press, 1971.

BROWN, MARGARET, and SOMMER, BETTY. *Movement Education: Its Evolution and a Modern Approach.* Reading, Mass.: Addison-Wesley, 1969.

CHERRY, CLARE. *Creative Movement for the Developing Child,* rev. ed. Belmont, Cal.: Lear Siegler/Fearon, 1971.

DIMONDSTEIN, GERALDINE. *Children Dance in the Classroom.* New York: Macmillan, 1971.

FLEMING, GLADYS ANDREWS. *Creative Rhythmic Movement: Boys' and Girls' Dancing,* 2nd ed. Englewood Cliffs, N.J.: Prentice-Hall, 1976.

GATES, ALICE A. *A New Look at Movement—A Dancer's View.* Minneapolis: Burgess, 1968.

HARRIS, JANE A.; PITTMAN, ANNE; and WALLER, MARLYS S. *Dance Awhile,* 4th ed. Minneapolis: Burgess, 1968.

HAYES, ELIZABETH R. *An Introduction to the Teaching of Dance.* New York: Ronald Press, 1964.

KRAUS, RICHARD. *Folk Dancing.* New York: Macmillan, 1962.

JOYCE, MARY. *First Steps in Teaching Creative Dance.* Palo Alto, Cal.: National Press Books, 1973.

LABAN, RUDOLF. *Modern Educational Dance,* 2nd ed. London, England: MacDonald & Evans, 1963.

MURRAY, RUTH LOVEL. *Dance in Elementary Education,* 3rd ed. New York: Harper & Row, 1975.

RUSSELL, JOAN. *Creative Movement and Dance for Children,* rev. ed. Boston: Plays Inc., 1975.

SHAW, LLOYD. *Cowboy Dances.* Caldwell, Idaho: Caxton Printers. 1949.

STANLEY, SHEILA. *Physical Education: A Movement Orientation.* Toronto, Canada: McGraw-Hill of Canada, 1969.

STOKES, EDITH M. *Word Pictures as a Stimulus for Creative Dance.* London, England: MacDonald and Evans, 1970.

VICK, MARIE, and COX, ROSANN MCLAUGHLIN. *A Collection of Dances for Children.* Minneapolis: Burgess, 1970.

WIENER, JACK, and LIDSTONE, JOHN. *Creative Movement for Children: A Dance Program for the Classroom.* New York: Van Nostrand Reinhold, 1969.

WOODLAND, E. J. M. *Poems for Movement.* London, England: Evans Brothers, 1966.

WINTERS, SHIRLEY J. *Creative Rhythmic Movement For Children of Elementary School Age,* Dubuque, Iowa: Wm. C. Brown, 1975.

19　　Games

The purpose of playing games in an educational setting is to provide for interaction between the learner and the content of the games. Thus in order to utilize games effectively as a learning medium, you must understand the children, be familiar with the content of the games, and know how to facilitate interaction between the learner and what is to be learned.

READINESS FOR GAMES

Children in the early primary grades are in the final phase of the developmental stage Piaget designates the preoperational stage (see pages 26–27). They are still characteristically egocentric and tend to be parallel players (to play beside others rather than interacting with them cooperatively or competitively). They cannot quite comprehend what it means to participate in a group effort and pursue a common goal. Instead, they function as separate individuals, each pursuing his or her own goal. Nor do they comprehend the concept of striving against others by matching skill and wit, or recognize the abstract principles governing game play. Thus, though they may appear to understand and accept the prescribed conduct of the game, they will tend to interject their own rules and follow their own wishes. These characteristics suggest that children at this level should participate in games whose rules evolve naturally and are adopted by mutual consent (Mauldon and Redfern, 1969).

Because children in this age group learn best through direct experience, their games should encourage the kind of exploration that will maximize direct sensory input and lead to the development of concrete concepts. And because the activities that naturally appeal to these children are those that involve action, fun, and discovery, their games should stimulate them to explore a wide variety of movement possibilities in which they use their bodies, objects, and implements.

The movement responses of children in the early primary grades are general, rather than specific. Children of this age do not possess the control necessary to make abrupt bodily adaptations, such as sudden stops or changes of direction, and their hand-eye and foot-eye coordination is not fully developed. Cognitively, they are still dealing with static images of the dimensions number, length, distance, area, speed, and time. For this reason, they cannot readily estimate and adjust to the height, distance, or speed of moving objects. These children are not cognitively, emotionally, or physically ready to participate in activities that require drill in highly specific skills. They are, however, rapidly developing in each of these areas, and you must be aware of behaviors that signal readiness to develop more difficult skills and participate in more challenging games.

By the time children enter the upper primary grades (approximately ages seven and eight), their gross motor skills are becoming more refined. Coordination, strength, and endurance increase; they exhibit more emotional control; and they are capable of interacting with each other. Such children are entering the stage of cognitive development Piaget calls the stage of concrete operations. Their solutions to problems are no longer totally impulsive generalizations, since they are now becoming capable of relational thought. Thus they can and should begin to associate the parts of a game with the structure and outcome of the whole game. They should study and practice game elements appropriate to their level of cognitive comprehension and psychomotor development, and should be challenged to fit these elements into structured and creative games. As such characteristics emerge, children become capable of participating in more complex games and interested in developing the skills that elicit achievement and recognition.

Children in the intermediate grades are cognitively ready for problem solving. They are thus interested in discovering the underlying principles that govern games and in developing playing strategies that will enable them to outdo opponents. Intrigued by the element of chance in games, they are willing to work and plan to gain an advantage. They are ready to apply the skills learned through exploration and to develop new skills through drill and practice. They are capable of performing the basic sports skills satisfactorily and ready to use them in lead-up games of gradually increasing complexity.

DETERMINING THE LEVEL OF DIFFICULTY

The relative difficulty of a game is determined by the type of body action required and the complexity of its rules and playing strategy. The simplest games are those involving *single-factor movements*, or movements in which only the body is used to perform the movement task. Examples of such movements are:

running	skipping	dodging
jumping	twisting	tagging
hopping	turning	

The principal types of games employing single-factor movements are dramatic games and tag games.

Dramatic games are exciting because of the element of suspense introduced by the necessity of waiting for the signal to move. The locomotor movement is usually running, because it allows for the children to move at full speed. No one wins and no one is eliminated. At the beginning level, all the children run in the same direction from one area to another.

Key Concepts

□ *The game will begin when we are all in line behind the starting line.*
□ *When the signal is given, I will run across the room and stop running when I cross the goal line.*

(Note: The goal line should not be near a wall, since the children may not be able to stop suddenly or relate spatially to the distance involved.)

Activities for Children

1. Have the children stand behind a starting line. Tell them that when you say "Go!" they are to start running toward the goal line (see Figure 19.1). When they cross the goal line, they are to stop.

As soon as the children are familiar with the basic structure of the game, variations may be introduced in the nature of the starting signal (*when* they are to move), the designation of *who* is to move, the basic movement to be executed (*how* they are to move), or the size and shape of the playing area (*where* they are to move).

  a. The starting signal may be any auditory or visual cue. At first you may substitute a drumbeat for your voice; then progress to signals that require the children to make discriminations. For example, you may toss a beanbag into the air and instruct them to run when it hits the floor. Or you may stand behind the children and play different

Figure 19.1 Diagram for a Game Involving a Single-Factor Movement

Starting Line

rhythm instruments, instructing them to run when they hear a certain sound (such as that of a triangle or a drum). When the children have become accustomed to this type of stimulus, you may play music that contains sounds of nature or sounds made by animals, instructing the children to run when they hear a certain sound. You may also use color discrimination by flashing colored cards and instructing the children to run when a certain color appears. (At first you would use only two colors, such as red and green; then you might add yellow, blue, and so on.) Next you might have certain children run on certain signals. For example, you could put red dots on the hands of half the children, and blue dots on the hands of the other half. The children with the red dots run across the playing area when you call "red"; the others run when you call "blue." Or you may tie pieces of yarn on the children's wrists and instruct them to run when you call out the color of their yarn.

b. The game may be varied by instructing the children to jump, hop, or skip, instead of running. For jumping or hopping, the distance between the starting line and the goal line should be decreased. Changing the shape or size of the playing area creates interest and permits additional features to be added to the basic game (see Figure 19.2). The starting area may be a circle, and the goal line a larger circle or square. The use of a square introduces the factor of distance discrimination, since the corners are farther away than the centers of the sides. Discriminating between these distances can become part of the game. When a circle is used, you can add an interesting and challenging element to the game by having half the children stand inside the circle and half outside. At a signal, the children on the inside run between the children on the outside toward the goal line; this requires the children to make bodily adjustments to a specified

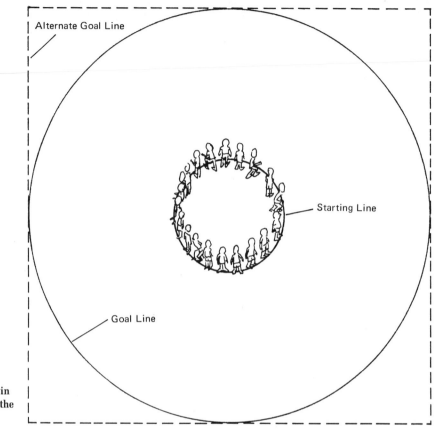

Figure 19.2 Variation in the Shape and Size of the Playing Area

space while moving. You may also have those on the inside and those on the outside change places when the signal is given. The simultaneous movement of both groups of children requires them to relate spatially to moving objects. Because it may necessitate a dodging motion, which is a relatively complex, this variation should not be introduced until the children have demonstrated the necessary bodily control.

c. Interest may be added to any simple game by using imagery. You may suggest that the children move like certain animals or objects, such as cars, horses, or kangaroos. Or you may tell a short story and have the children begin moving at a certain point in the story or when a particular word is used. For example, the children could pretend they are standing on a mountain when they are within the inner circle. Then, when you say "fire on the mountain," they all run to a place of safety beyond the outer circle. You could create a different game by using a starting position outside the large circle;

when you say "fire on the mountain," the children pretend to be fire engines rushing to the mountain to extinguish a fire.

d. In all the above examples, the children respond to a single command. The challenge may be increased by requiring them to respond to more than one signal, such as a command to begin moving and a command to stop. An example is to have them begin moving when you flash a green card, and stop when you flash a red one. Auditory stimuli may be used in the same way by having them move while you shake a tambourine and stop when you strike it. These and other commands can be combined with the elements discussed above to create a wide variety of simple games for children at the beginning level.

On the advanced beginner level, children should progress to games containing additional elements. The next elements to add are roles (different people doing different things) and chance (contest). A game that contains these elements is the running game Squirrels in Trees.

Key Concepts

□ *When I am a squirrel, I must move quickly from one tree to another at the signal and try to avoid being left out of a tree.*

□ *I must take turns being a squirrel and being a tree.*

2. Squirrels in Trees

a. Have the children number off by threes. Numbers 1 and 2 join hands to form a tree; number 3, who is the squirrel, stands inside the tree (see Figure 19.3). There must be one or two squirrels who are not in trees.

b. At a signal (such as saying "change!" or stopping the music), every squirrel must run from his or her tree to another tree. While they are running, the squirrels who were not in trees attempt to find places in trees. Only one squirrel may occupy each tree. Thus, after each change, there will be one or two squirrels who are not in trees.

c. After the squirrels have run a few times, they should exchange places with the 2s; the 1s should have a turn being squirrels before the game is concluded.

d. This game may be made more active by using hoops as trees, which allows all the children to run simultaneously. However, this variation also increases the difficulty of the game, because the children must dodge the other runners.

As soon as the children are familiar with the concept of role-playing in a game, they may progress to games characterized by "runners" and

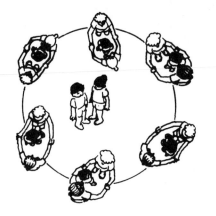

Figure 19.3 Diagram for the Game *Squirrels in Trees*

"chasers." Most such games are tag games. Before introducing tag games, you should anticipate three kinds of problems that may arise. (1) The children may not understand the concept of tagging, and may hit, grab, and hold onto each other's clothes. (2) Some of the children may be unwilling to admit they have been tagged. (3) Some children may consider it a privilege to be tagged so they can be It. You may introduce children to the concept of tagging by having them touch each other on the back while you explain that they should do so just hard enough so the touch will be felt. Point out that hitting hurts and grabbing may tear clothes. The game Brownies and Fairies is an excellent medium in which to practice tagging and being tagged. Children in the early elementary grades do not have team loyalties, and will not mind admitting they have been tagged if they need only change teams, rather than being isolated from the group or eliminated from the game. No advantage is gained by being tagged, so children will not try to be caught.

Key Concepts
□ *When I play a tag game, I should tag the other person by touching, not by hitting or grabbing clothes.*
□ *I should try to keep from being tagged.*

3. Brownies and Fairies[1]
a. Divide the class into two groups and arrange them behind two goal lines (see Figure 19.4). One team is called the Brownies and the other the Fairies.

[1]A version of this game called Cowboys and Indians is modified by having the children clasp their hands in back of their bodies while sneaking and unclasp them as they turn to run.

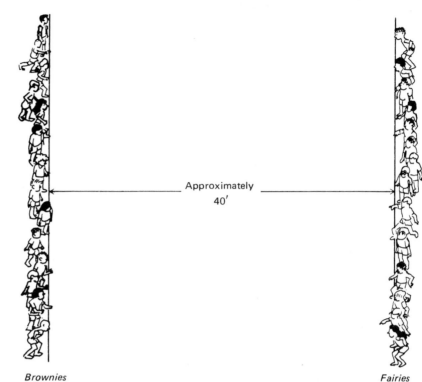

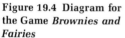

Figure 19.4 Diagram for the Game *Brownies and Fairies*

Brownies   *Fairies*

b. Play begins with the members of one team turning their backs toward the other team (for example, the Brownies turn their backs toward the Fairies).

c. At a signal, the members of the other team (the Fairies) quietly sneak across the space between the two teams. When they are within a few feet of the team whose backs are turned (the Brownies), the teacher calls out, "The Fairies are coming!" This is the signal for the Brownies to turn around and chase the Fairies.

d. Any Fairy who is tagged before reaching the goal line becomes a member of the Brownies.

e. Next the Fairies turn their backs and the Brownies sneak up on them. Play continues by alternating teams.

Brownies and Fairies is a team tag game. It is easy for the children to comprehend the rules because every member of a team does the same thing at the same time. Once the children have mastered these basic concepts, you can progress to games that contain an It. Fox and Squirrel is an example of such a game.

Key Concept

☐ *When the It (the fox) tags the runner (the squirrel), the two players exchange roles.*

4. Fox and Squirrel

a. This game is a more complex version of Squirrels in Trees, employing the same formation, only there is one extra squirrel and a fox. The fox chases and attempts to tag the extra squirrel.

b. The squirrel is safe when he or she enters a tree. The squirrel who was occupying that tree then becomes the runner. The fox can tag a squirrel only when the squirrel is outside a tree.

c. When the squirrel is tagged, the players exchange roles: the fox becomes the squirrel and the squirrel becomes the fox.

The learning sequence next progresses to two team tag games that resemble Brownies and Fairies, Crows and Cranes and Hill Dill. Crows and Cranes is more difficult in that the children must be ready to run in either direction, depending on the signal. Hill Dill is more difficult in that it requires the children to dodge both It and the players on the opposite team. For this reason, it should not be played until the children manifest well-controlled bodily movements.

5. Crows and Cranes

a. Divide the players into two teams and arrange them on the starting lines as shown in Figure 19.5.

b. Call out the name of either team. If you call "Crows!" the Crows run toward their goal line and the Cranes chase and attempt to tag them before they cross it. Any Crow tagged becomes a Crane.

c. Play continues as you randomly call out the name of either team. The team with the most players at the end of the playing period is declared the winner.

d. Suspense may be added to by slowly saying, "Cr———" and then quickly calling out the rest of the team name.

e. This game may be varied by using a visual rather than an auditory signal. A large, square cardboard box may be covered with black paper on three sides and white paper on the other three sides. The teams are designated Black and White. The box is then rolled like dice. The color on the top when the box comes to rest dictates the team that is to run.

6. Hill Dill

a. The same formation is used as for Brownies and Fairies. The child who is It stands in the center of the playing area.

b. It calls out, "Hill Dill, come over the hill!" This is the signal for the

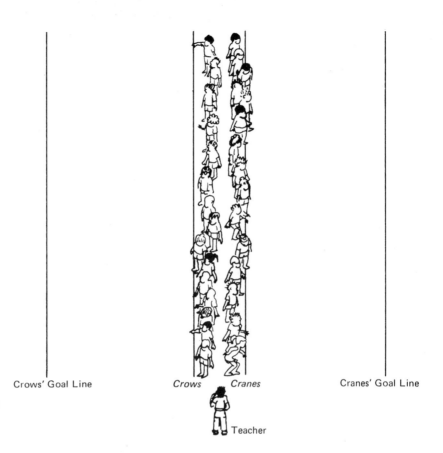

Crows' Goal Line   Crows   Cranes   Cranes' Goal Line

Teacher

Figure 19.5 Diagram for the Game *Crows and Cranes*

players on both teams to run across the center space to a place of safety behind the opposite goal line. Anyone tagged by It must stay in the center and help tag the remaining players.

c. Play resumes when It again calls out the signal. The last player tagged has the privilege of being It when the next game is played.

Intermediate-level children are becoming interested in the concept of a winner and in playing strategy that will enable them to outmaneuver their opponents. Steal the Bacon is a game that contains these elements.

7. Steal the Bacon[2]

a. Divide the players into two teams of from six to eight players apiece. Have the players stand in the formation shown in Figure 19.6 and count off, starting at the right end of each line.

b. Place an Indian club (or other object, such as a beanbag) in the center of the space between the two teams.

[2]If an Indian club is used, this game is also called Club Snatch.

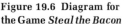

Figure 19.6 Diagram for the Game *Steal the Bacon*

c. When you call out a number, the two players with that number run to the center and try to steal the bacon (grab the object).

d. The player who grabs the bacon then attempts to carry it across his or her own team's line without being tagged.

e. If the player does so, two points are awarded his or her team. If tagged, the opposing team wins one point. The team that has accumulated the most points at the end of a designated playing time is declared the winner.

As soon as children are familiar with the basic structure of games and evidence controlled bodily movements in game situations, they may be introduced to games involving *dual-factor movements*. Such movements require the child to use his or her body to control an object. Children should learn to control their bodies in relation to objects by practicing the manipulative skills. When they can execute a skill satisfactorily, interest may be enhanced and further practice provided by employing it in game situations. Games should provide practice in controlling an object while moving in different pathways and in accurately propelling the object toward a goal. Several such games are described in Chapter 15. Because the rules of these games are simple and the action is emphasized over the outcome, they are appropriate for children on the advanced beginner level.

On the intermediate level children should be practicing the basic sports skills. The games used to practice these skills should be introduced in a sequence of progressive difficulty. If the skills being utilized are unfamiliar or difficult, the rules should be relatively simple; as the children's skill increases, so should the complexity of the rules. At first, the players may simply attempt to reach their own goals. Then the game may be made gradually more complex by introducing more narrowly defined goals, more participants, new rules, and offensive and defensive playing strategy.

The most difficult skills utilized in games are those involving *multiple-factor movements,* or movements in which an implement is used to extend the body lever for the purpose of propelling an object. The most common multiple-factor movements are those involving striking. Others are tossing and catching with a scoop, using a stick to propel an object, and controlling the movement of an object while riding a bicycle. Increasing the number of movement factors adds to the complexity of the movement skill; thus the game itself should be relatively simple. You should not require elementary-school children to execute complex movement patterns while observing complicated rules. These children need to play and have fun while they are learning. When the movement task becomes highly structured, the element of play tends to disappear.

THE STRUCTURE OF GAMES

All games, whether simple or complex, spontaneous or prescribed, have one thing in common: a structure. The structure of a game specifies what is to be done, how it is to be accomplished, and the anticipated outcome. Thus all games specify some combination of the following elements:

1. equipment (the human body, an object, an implement)

2. the way in which the equipment is to be used (the skills that must be mastered in order to perform the movement tasks required in the game)

3. boundaries
a. the size, shape, and dimensions of the playing area
b. subdivisions of the playing area (for example, a center line, goal lines, restraining lines, a safety zone)
c. certain playing areas for participants playing certain roles (for example, It, the runners, the goalie, pitcher, forwards, guards, server)

4. rules
a. the number of players, either limited (for example, five players on a basketball team, six on a volleyball team) or unlimited (for example, a tag game in which any reasonable number of people may play)
b. playing formations (a circle, lines, scattered, shuttle)
c. what players *must* do (for example, move across a certain area at a certain time)

d. what players *may* do (for example, move freely throughout a certain area; choose to move or not to move at a certain time; move when certain events occur)

e. determination of the winner

    (1) scoring

    (2) rewards for performing in a certain way

    (3) penalties for failing to perform in a certain way or for infringing on the rules

5. players' roles

a. every player does the same thing at the same time (for example, everyone runs at a given signal).

b. every player does the same thing, but individuals or teams take turns doing it (for example, an offensive team and a defensive team).

c. Different players do different things (for example, some players stand in place while others run; or each player's role is defined by a playing position).

d. Roles remain unchanged throughout the game.

e. Players change roles when certain events occur (for example, the runner becomes It when tagged or the stationary player becomes a runner if touched by It).

6. the contest (the elements of chance or risk-taking)

a. to keep away or take away

    (1) avoid being caught, left out, or eliminated

    (2) gain or maintain control of an object

b. to move faster than one's opponents (a race)

c. to reach a goal

    (1) with one's own body

    (2) by propelling an object into a certain playing area or into, over, or through a goal

7. playing strategy (ways of gaining an advantage in the contest)

If the outcome of the game includes declaration of a winner, the element of competition is present. The consequences of introducing competition should be carefully considered in light of the type of learning that may occur in the affective domain (see pages 54–55).

A gradual and progressive introduction to the elements of various types of games allows for complex games to evolve naturally from the basic structure of simple games. This process also enables children to see order and relationships and provides for maximum transfer of learning from one game situation to another.

THE CONTENT OF GAMES

When a game is used as a learning medium, the primary consideration is what the children will learn by playing it. The enjoyment and change of pace it provides for are important, but because these outcomes can be attained at recess they are not sufficient reason to teach games in the physical education instructional program. *Games are not the lesson content; they are the learning medium.* Only after the lesson content is clearly specified in the performance and process objective are the games that will help attain these objectives selected. Thus the only educationally sound reason for including games in the school curriculum is to allow for the children to interact functionally with relevant subject matter. The educational value of games may be ascertained by determining how they contribute to the children's development in each of the educational domains. Properly planned and conducted, games can promote attainment of the following general goals of elementary-school physical education:

1. psychomotor domain
to improve the quality of the child's movement responses, manifested as ability to satisfactorily execute and utilize
    (1) the basic movement skills
    (2) the manipulative skills
    (3) the basic sports skills

2. cognitive domain
a. to identify and functionally apply
    (1) a knowledge of the dimensions of movement
    (2) the laws and principles that regulate and control movement
    (3) the elements of games and the principles that govern their conduct
b. to demonstrate the ability to improvise equipment and create games
c. to demonstrate awareness of the kinship of all people by recognizing similarities in the games of different nations

3. affective domain
a. to manifest development of body, spatial, and kinesthetic awareness
b. to be able to follow and obey rules, take turns, care for and share equipment
c. to develop a more positive self-concept
d. to demonstrate willingness to participate in games for their own sake rather than to receive extrinsic rewards

Games' rich learning potential will be fully realized only if you clearly define what you intend to achieve by having the children play and then structure the learning situation so as to do so.

TEACHING GAMES   Children always learn when they play; *what* they learn depends on what they practice and how they are reinforced. For example, a child may learn:

1. to catch the ball confidently or to fear oncoming objects

2. to enjoy playing with others (because it is physically and socially rewarding) or to dread having to play (because he or she is usually unsuccessful and the other children make critical comments)

3. to improvise equipment and create games or to use only standard equipment according to the teacher's instructions

4. to sensorily experience his or her movements or go through the motions only in order to achieve a specified end

5. to play because it is fun or to play only to win

6. to view physical education as a play period or to see it as a situation in which he or she learns by playing

As these paired outcomes imply, *how* you teach games is as important as *what* games are taught. The following pages will help you prepare to teach games in such a way as to enhance the children's enjoyment and maximize the educational outcome.

Games are played in the physical education setting in order to practice skills and to review and reinforce the key concepts and sub-concepts specified in the objectives of the lesson. If the children are to interact beneficially with the content of the lesson, the games must be presented in such a way as to encourage *correct* execution of the skills and the children must be aware of the movement concepts. While you are selecting the games to be played and the teaching methods to be used, these two points should be paramount.

In the game situation, children learn by being physically and cognitively active. That is, *they learn by thinking about what they are doing,* and thus learn more by participating than by watching or waiting. Because children's attention spans are short and they are easily distracted, it is unrealistic to expect them to attend to the elements of the game if they are not actively involved in it. *All* of the children should be actively participating *most* of the time. Quiet games and games in which only a few children move should be played only when the children are physically tired or need a slowdown activity. Elimination

Figure 19.7 The Coconut Shell Relay, an International Game
Mickey Adair

games should not be played; they not only preclude maximum participation, but also eliminate precisely those who need the most practice. When a child is eliminated from a game, furthermore, the attention of the entire class is drawn to his or her lack of success. This experience may reinforce the sense of failure and impair self-esteem.

As we have said, games should be sequentially arranged so that understanding of complex games will naturally evolve from mastery of simpler related games. The children should be able to compare and contrast the elements of various games and should recognize that adding elements to a game increases its difficulty. These concepts can be readily taught by having the children review a simple game and then modify it. For example, if children on the advanced beginner level review Squirrels in Trees and then progress to playing Fox and Squirrels, they will see that the games are basically the same, but that the addition of an It enhances the challenge.

INTERNATIONAL GAMES

The game curriculum should not be limited to the structured games traditionally played in the United States; it should include games the children create and games from other countries. Playing other countries' games (see Figure 19.7) and studying them as folk art (see page 90) make children more keenly aware of the similarities between people in different countries. Harbin's *Games of Many Nations* (1954) and the *ICHPER Book of Worldwide Games and Dances* (1967) are both excellent sources of games for elementary-school children. The latter classifies games by degree of difficulty as well as by country of origin.

CREATIVE GAMES It is important for children to learn that games have prescribed rules and that these rules must be followed. It is equally important for them to learn that rules can be modified and new games created. In the primary grades the latter goal may be achieved by having the children suggest different starting signals, different ways to move, variations in the size and shape of the playing area, and different objects. (See Figure 19.8.) On the intermediate level children's creative games should involve problem solving. You may structure problems by specifying the basic sports skills and dimensions of the movement elements to be included and/or the type of equipment to be used. For example, the problem might be for two children to create a game in which they run, throw, and catch while using a playground ball. To solve the problem the children must determine where they are to run, the type of throw that is to be used, and what is to be done with the ball after it is caught. One solution might be for child A to throw the ball upward and run to a base and back while child B attempts to catch the ball and beat child A back to home base.

If the children find the catcher has an advantage, they can modify the rules by specifying that the ball must bounce once before it is caught. If the thrower seems to have the advantage, they may designate boundaries within which the ball must land. The problem may be made more complex by requiring the children to devise a means of scoring and determining a winner. The children might decide to score the above game by awarding a point on each play: if the thrower beats the catcher back to home base, the thrower receives one point, and vice versa. If boundaries have been established, the catcher receives a point when the ball is thrown out of bounds. There are two alternative ways of determining the winner: they may play a certain length of time and designate as the winner the player who is ahead at the end of that time, or they may designate a certain number of points as the goal and declare as the winner the player who scores that number first. They might also decide that in order to equalize the competitive element, they will change roles at the end of a certain amount of time or when one player has scored a certain number of points.

A similar game might have been created if the teacher had specified the movement elements to be included, rather than the skills. In such a case the original problem might have been to create a game in which (1) the ball moves upward to a high level, and (2) the players move very fast along a straight pathway.

Among of the kinds of equipment that can be used as stimuli for creative games are:

Figure 19.8 A Creative Game
Mickey Adair

beanbags

balls (nerf, whiffle, playground, tennis, cage)

frisbees

striking implements (paddles, bats, sticks)

hoops or bicycle tires

ropes

road cones

If two children are given a bicycle tire and a playground ball, a game like the following might be created. Two players stand behind restraining lines with the bicycle tire on the floor midway between them. Player A bounces the ball into the tire and player B attempts to catch it on the rebound. The players take turns bouncing and catching. The element of competition may be added by awarding one point for bouncing the ball within the tire, and one point for successfully catching the ball after it bounces. The rules may be made more complex by introducing penalties, such as subtracting one point for bouncing the ball on the edge outside the tire or for failing to catch a ball that is bounced within the tire. Again, a winner may be declared at the end of a certain length of time or number of points.

As children gain experience in creating games, the component skills should become more difficult and the number of elements specified should be increased. An effort should be made to recognize the children's achievement by pointing out novel game elements and by having the children demonstrate or teach their games to the rest of the class. Children in the upper elementary grades should also be challenged to write the directions for their games and to specify the component skills, dimensions of the movement elements, and game elements.

Creative games are a vital aspect of the games component of the curriculum because they allow for the children to use their imaginations while working with all the factors characteristic of games. Such experiences enhance their understanding and awareness, as well as encouraging them to create games on their own.

TOPICS FOR REVIEW AND FURTHER STUDY

1. Discuss the relationship between children's developmental characteristics and the types of games that meet their needs and interests at the various stages of development.

2. Review page 27 on children's cognitive development during the stage of concrete operations. Relate this information to the types of educational games that meet the needs of children at this developmental stage.

3. Describe the factors that determine games' difficulty level.

4. Create a dramatic game for children on the beginning level.

5. What are the three principal problems associated with introducing tag games? How can you overcome them?

6. Consult the references on page 439 and select a game from each of the categories below. Analyze each in terms of its specific elements.
   a. a tag game
   b. a game of low organization involving a ballhandling skill
   c. a classroom game
   d. a lead-up game

7. Explain the statement, "Games are not the lesson content; they are the learning medium."

8. Review the list on page 433 of general goals of elementary-school physical education that can be attained through participation in games. Using this list as a guide, specify the learning outcomes that should characterize the games you analyzed in topic 6 above.

9. Why are elimination games educationally unsound?

10. How should games be taught in order to maximize their educational potential?

11. Learn to play a game from another country, and develop a lesson in which this game is the primary learning activity. Include related information that will enhance the children's understanding of the

people of that country. Provide teaching aids that will enrich the children's learning experiences.

12. Design a movement problem that will stimulate children to create a game.

SUGGESTIONS FOR FURTHER READING

ANDERSON, MARIAN; ELLIOT, MARGARET; and LABERGE, JEANNE. *Play With a Purpose,* 2nd ed. New York: Harper & Row, 1972.

BICYCLE INSTITUTE OF AMERICA. *Bike Fun: Games and Competitive Events for Skilled Cyclists.* Bicycle Institute of America, 122 E. 42nd Street, New York, N.Y. 10017.

BLAKE, WILLIAM, and VOLP, ANNE. *Lead-up Games to Team Sports.* Englewood Cliffs, N.J.: Prentice-Hall, 1964.

BOHN, ROBERT. "A Master Game for Teaching Sport Skills in Elementary School." *Journal of Physical Education and Recreation* 47 (April 1976): 23–24.

DOCHERTY, DAVID, and PEAKE, LES. "Creatrad: An Approach to Teaching Games." *Journal of Physical Education and Recreation* 47 (April 1976): 20–22.

HARBIN, E. O. *Games of Many Nations.* New York: Abingdon Press, 1954.

INTERNATIONAL COUNCIL ON HEALTH, PHYSICAL EDUCATION, AND RECREATION. *ICHPER Book of Worldwide Games and Dances,* Washington, D.C.: AAHPER, 1967.

KIRCHNER, GLENN. *Physical Education for Elementary School Children,* 3rd ed. Dubuque, Iowa: Wm. C. Brown, 1974.

KIRK, JAMES. "New Games People Are Playing." *Journal of Physical Education and Recreation* 47 (April 1976): 40.

LATCHAW, MARJORIE, and EGSTROM, GLEN. *Human Movement with Concepts Applied to Children's Movement Activities.* Englewood Cliffs, N.J.: Prentice-Hall, 1969.

MAULDON, E., and REDFERN, H. B. *Games Teaching.* London, England: MacDonald & Evans, 1969.

MORRIS, G. S. DON. *How to Change the Games Children Play.* Minneapolis, Minn.: Burgess, 1976.

NAGEL, CHARLES, and MOORE, FREDRICKA. *Skill Development Through Games and Rhythmic Activities,* Palo Alto, Cal.: National Press, 1966.

RILEY, MARIE. "Games and Humanism." *Journal of Physical Education and Recreation* 46 (Feb. 1975): 46–49.

SCHURR, EVELYN L. *Movement Experiences for Children,* 2nd ed. Englewood Cliffs, N.J.: Prentice-Hall, 1975.

STANLEY, SHEILA. *Physical Education: A Movement Orientation,* New York: McGraw-Hill of Canada, 1969.

VANNIER, MARYHELEN; FOSTER, MILDRED; and GALLAHUE, DAVID. *Teaching Physical Education in Elementary Schools,* 5th ed. Philadelphia: W. B. Saunders, 1973.

20　　Gymnastics

The purposes of educational gymnastics are to increase the children's movement awareness and to promote skillful use of their bodies in relation to both small and large apparatus. Free exploration, guided exploration, and problem solving are all used in educational gymnastics. The children should gradually become more self-directing as they learn to explore movement possibilities and to join movements together to form sequences. Educational gymnastics is an individualized program in which the child progresses at his or her own rate in response to the challenges and encouragement of the teacher.

The cognitive content of the educational gymnastics component of the curriculum was introduced in Part Three, and consists of the concepts children must acquire to orient themselves in space, relate spatially to their environments, and support and transfer their body weight. Educational gymnastics is an excellent medium in which to study these concepts because its central focus is the child's moving body. In addition to teaching concepts and increasing the child's awareness, this area of the curriculum should help develop movement skills and increase the child's fitness.

PLANNING THE CLASSES

An educational gymnastics lesson usually begins with a warm-up period, during which the children explore the lesson theme on their own. The teacher then specifies the subthemes and leads the children's exploration of pertinent skills and concepts. Throughout the lesson, you must keenly observe the children's movement responses and extend their learning experiences by commenting on their actions and asking questions that can be answered in movement. Successful educational gymnastics instruction is dependent on your powers of observation and ability to utilize verbal cues effectively. All the types of verbal cues discussed on pages 114–118 may be employed to guide the children's exploration. Directing the attention of the class to the movement responses of certain children acknowledges each child's achievement and also emphasizes or reinforces certain aspects of the lesson content. Children's demonstrations may be used in the following ways:

1. to recognize children who are executing the skill correctly and effectively

2. to point out the children who are executing a movement in similar way (on the same level, using the same body parts, or making the same shape)

3. to recognize an unusual or novel way of executing a movement

4. to demonstrate similarities and differences in the ways various children interpret the assignment

5. to focus the attention of the class on a particular aspect of the lesson theme

The teacher should move freely among the children, correcting and reinforcing individual actions so that each child is encouraged to perform the assigned task accurately. At the conclusion of the lesson, the children should be responsible for returning the equipment to its proper place.

LEARNING ACTIVITIES

The content of educational gymnastics lessons is developed in relation to movement themes. The theme serves as a central focus for the learning tasks within a given lesson.

Beginner

In the early stages of learning, movement themes should be explored by means of such natural movements as walking, running, jumping, bending, rolling, crawling, and scooting. By exploring these body actions, the children should discover and review cognitive concepts involving contrasting dimensions, such as small-large, forward-backward, high-low, and slow-fast. These activities also enhance the development of laterality and directionality and increase general bodily control.

The educational goals of this learning level may be achieved through the children's natural responses to well-equipped indoor and outdoor environments structured to evoke a variety of such movement responses. These children should be provided stimulating outdoor play equipment that will motivate them to climb, swing, hang, balance, and roll, as well as inviting them to execute freely all of the locomotor and nonlocomotor skills. Examples of such equipment are shown in Figure 20.1. The children should also explore the spatial dimensions and directions by moving over, under, across, around, and through the playground equipment and by moving into and out of spaces of varying size. Indoors, children of this age should use different body parts and explore variations in the dimensions of the movement elements while working with small equipment such as hoops, yarnballs, beanbags, and stepping stones. They should also be encouraged to explore the movement possibilities inherent in mats, small boxes, benches, and balance beams. You can use this equipment to build obstacle courses for the children to move through on their own and while playing follow-the-leader.

SAMPLE LESSON PLAN

Level: Beginner

Theme: Spatial awareness

Subthemes: Movement in different directions; the names of the body surfaces and body parts touching or facing the floor; movement in a circular pathway

Learning Activities

1. Have the children pair off and hold hands. Place a hoop in front of each set of partners. "Everyone place your hands on the floor inside the hoop. Stand inside the hoop. What part of your body is touching the floor? Stand outside the hoop. Jump into the hoop. Jump out of the hoop. Walk around the outside of the hoop."

2. Challenge the children to relate to the hoop in various ways. "Can you walk around the outside of the hoop using big steps? Can you walk around the outside of the hoop using little steps? Can you move around the outside of the hoop with the front of your body close to the floor?"

3. Point out children who are moving on different body parts. (For example, "Jack's hands and knees are touching the floor, Mary is very close to the floor because the front of her body is touching the floor, and Susan has her elbows on the floor." See Figure 20.2.)

4. "Can you move around your hoop with the back of your body close to the floor?" Point out children who have different body parts close to the floor.

5. Have the children respond to your instructions.
a. "Sit down inside the hoop with your partner. Now one partner stand up and the other one stay sitting down. Now the person who is

Figure 20.1 Outdoor Play Equipment for the Beginning Level
Courtesy Playtimber Company

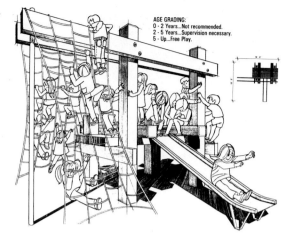

AGE GRADING:
0 - 2 Years...Not recommended.
2 - 5 Years...Supervision necessary.
5 - Up...Free Play.

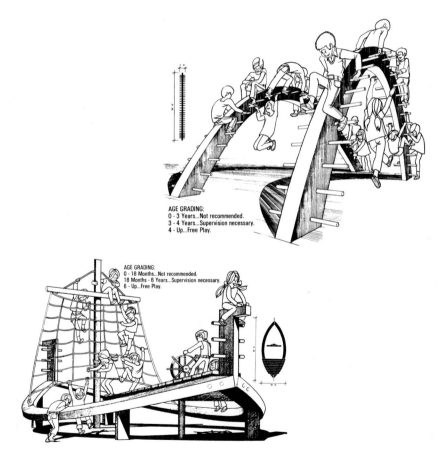

AGE GRADING:
0 - 3 Years...Not recommended.
3 - 4 Years...Supervision necessary.
4 - Up...Free Play.

AGE GRADING:
0 - 18 Months...Not recommended.
18 Months - 6 Years...Supervision necessary.
6 - Up...Free Play.

**Figure 20.2 Moving
on Different Body Parts**
Bonnie Unsworth

standing up, picks up the hoop, brings it to me, and stays here beside me."

b. "All of you who are standing here with me hold hands and help me make a big circle. Let go of hands. Now take one giant step backwards. Stay right where you are until I tell you to move."

c. "Everyone who is sitting on the floor stand up and get in line behind me. We are going to walk in and out of the circle. Follow me."

d. As you walk, challenge the children to vary their movements. "Can you take very small steps as we move in and out? Now can you take big steps?"

e. Have the two groups of children exchange places and repeat (d) above.

**Concluding
Activities**

6. "Everyone standing in the circle stay where you are and everyone who was moving in and out find a space in the circle between two other people and stand in that space." When everyone has found a space in the circle, have the class sit down.

7. Review the lesson. "Today we worked with small circles. What did we use to make a small circle to move around? That's right, we used a hoop. After we moved around the small circle we made a big circle. How did we make a big circle? You held hands and made a big circle using your bodies, didn't you? Can you remember about circles so next time we can make other kinds of circles?" (In the next lesson you could have the children review working with a circle formed by a hoop and then proceed to circles formed by other objects, such as a rope, and circles formed with their bodies and body parts.)

Advanced Beginner

On the advanced beginner level the children should become aware of how their body parts are used to execute different kinds of movements. They should also begin to recognize the terms used to denote the basic movements and movement elements. Advanced beginners should already recognize contrasts in the dimensions of movement, and should progress to the study of gradual changes (for example, gradually moving from a low level to a high level or varying the tempo of movement). They should also work with combinations of two or more dimensions of movement (such as moving forward while taking very small steps or moving forward on a low level while travelling in a curved pathway).

Such children should work with mats, level benches, inclined benches, low boxes, balance beams, ropes, and climbing apparatus (see Figure 20.3). Usually capable of self-direction, they can work with partners and in small groups.

The following movement themes should be explored by children on the advanced beginner level:

1. moving in place—traveling

2. moving and stopping

3. different body parts
a. touching the floor
b. moving in different ways (locomotor, nonlocomotor, unilaterally,[1] bilaterally,[2] cross-laterally,[3] rocking, sliding, rolling)
c. leading the movement
d. creating different shapes

4. spatial dimensions
a. range and size (small–large, little–big)
b. direction (forward, backward, sideward)
c. level (high–low, up–down)
d. pathway (straight–curved)
e. shapes (narrow–wide, small–large, curved–twisted)

5. spatial relationships
a. face-to-face, back-to-back, side by side
b. close together–far apart
c. leading–following

6. environmental directions
a. over, under, around, through
b. into, out of, across

7. force (heavy–light)

8. time (fast–slow)

[1] moving a single body part or only one side of the body
[2] moving both arms or both legs in the same direction simultaneously
[3] moving the body parts on the two sides of the body in different directions, such as the right arm forward and the left arm backward, or the left arm and right leg forward at the same time

Figure 20.3 Equipment
for the Advanced
Beginner Level

SAMPLE LESSON PLAN

Level: Advanced Beginner

Theme: Use of different body parts to support and transfer one's weight

Subthemes: Working in place versus traveling; creating narrow and wide shapes

Learning Activities

1. "Move out onto the floor and find yourself a personal space. What part of your body is touching the floor?"

2. "Stay in your personal space and place some other body parts on the floor. Change to some other body parts."

3. "Look at Bernard, Sally, Alonzo, and Pam. Let's name the body parts they have touching the floor. How many body parts does Bernard (Sally, Alonzo, and Pam) have touching the floor?"

4. Challenge the children to use various body parts to make shapes.

a. "Can you make a narrow shape with two body parts touching the floor?"

b. "Can you make a wide shape with only two body parts on the floor?"

c. "Can you make a wide shape with three body parts touching the floor? Four?"

d. "Can you make a wide shape with your whole body on the floor?"

e. "Can you make a narrow shape with your back on the floor?"

5. "You have used lots of body parts to touch the floor and to make narrow and wide shapes. All this time you have been working in one spot on the floor. Now let's see how you can use these body parts to travel through general space."

6. "Move about through general space using four body parts. Now use three body parts. Make a wide shape while traveling through space on four body parts. Make a narrow shape while traveling using two body parts."

7. Review the lesson. "You have been using different body parts to make wide and narrow shapes on the floor. Now let's see how you can use your body parts to move on the benches." Divide the class into small groups and assign each group a bench. Instruct the members of each group to take turns moving along the bench using two, three, and then four body parts. Challenge them to make wide and narrow shapes while standing on and moving along the bench.

Concluding Activities

8. Ask several children to demonstrate how they moved using different body parts and others to show the shapes they created. Challenge the class to name the body parts supporting the child's weight and the shapes being created. (In future lessons you can add other dimensions,

having the children move across the bench at different speeds, on different levels, in different directions, and leading with different body parts. In related lessons, the children could move on mats, along the balance beam, or on the climbing apparatus.)

Intermediate

On the intermediate level the children should progress from exploring movements to exploring relationships and inventing sequences. The movement themes should challenge them to recall concepts already learned and to apply them in situations requiring relational thought. They should also be challenged to recognize concrete cause-and-effect relationships. Examples of such themes are:

1. using different body parts as bases of support while
   a. working in place and travelling
   b. moving in different directions, on different levels, and along different pathways
   c. assuming different positions and creating various shapes

2. using different body parts to support and transfer the body weight while suspended in the air (climbing, hanging, swinging)

3. transferring the body weight by
   a. rocking
   b. rolling
   c. sliding
   d. step-like movements

4. moving on and off balance

5. using different body parts in different ways in relation to small and large apparatus by
   a. getting on, moving along, getting off
   b. going over, under, around, and through

On the intermediate level the children should work primarily in small groups assigned to particular pieces of equipment. Examples of appropriate themes follow:

1. traveling from the floor onto the apparatus and back to the floor

2. traveling above the floor, using different body parts to support one's weight and varying the dimensions of the movement elements

3. moving on one level while approaching the apparatus and on a different level while on the apparatus (This problem may be varied by substituting other equipment and by specifying different dimensions of the movement elements.)

4. transferring one's weight in one way while approaching a bench

Figure 20.4 Inventing a Movement Sequence
Mickey Adair

(or other equipment) and in another way while on the bench (A third way may eventually be added after landing.)

5. maintaining stillness while supporting one's body weight on three (two, one) body parts on the vaulting box (balance beam, mat, bench, ladder)

6. holding a balanced position on different body parts while creating different shapes (see Figure 20.4)

7. linking together a series of three similar actions (such as a series of continuous rolls, three step-like movements, or swinging while supporting one's body weight in three different ways)

8. composing and repeating a sequence involving a slow movement and a fast movement

9. balancing on two (or three) body parts and then rolling out of the balanced position

Each lesson should be based on a theme, and the body actions and movement elements (subthemes) should be varied to extend and reinforce the main theme.

Advanced

Children on the advanced level should be challenged to explore movement themes that will:

1. develop their awareness of what the body is doing within a sequence of movements (for example, bending; stretching; twisting; moving in different directions, on different levels, and along different pathways; forming different shapes)

2. enhance their understanding of the principles that regulate and control their actions

3. enable them to experiment with different ways of linking movements and of relating their own movements to those of other people

4. improve their movement memories through mastery of longer and more complex sequences

5. increase their body mastery in stillness and in motion

These goals are pursued by having children on the advanced level use various combinations of the dimensions level, direction, pathway, and body shape while:

1. traveling
a. on the floor (weight-bearing)

b. over the floor (weight transference)

c. off the floor (traveling along, taking off from, and landing)

2. using different body parts

a. to support and transfer the weight

b. to initiate and lead the movement

3. varying the tempo of the movement

4. exerting force suddenly and gradually to create strong and weak movements

5. applying the movement principles, that relate to equilibrium, friction, and the creation and absorption of force

Advanced children should explore movement themes through problem solving. The following activities illustrate how the movement themes listed above can be translated into movement problems.

1. "Create a sequence consisting of three balances linked together by travelling movements."

2, "Link three balanced positions that use different body parts as bases of support."

3. "Link a balanced position on a horizontal surface and a balanced position on an inclined surface."

4. "Create a sequence using two pieces of apparatus. Include fast and slow movements."

5. "Approach a piece of apparatus with step-like movements, move along it on a high level, jump off it, and roll when you land."

6. "Using only your hands and legs, support your body in a position of stillness on the climbing apparatus."

7. "Support your weight on the climbing apparatus in three different body positions. Use different body parts to support your weight in each position."

8. "Balance on two body parts; then roll out of this balanced position into another balanced position on different body parts."

9. "Develop a sequence that includes a roll, a balanced position, and a wide shape."

10. "Approach the bench while transferring your weight with a step-like movement, roll along the bench, and land on the mat in a balanced position."

11. "Develop a sequence that includes a wide shape, a narrow shape, and a twisted shape, linked together by step-like movements."

12. "Develop a sequence in which you move on balance, move off balance, and roll."

13. "Develop a sequence in which you move over, under, and around your partner."

14. "Develop a sequence in which you rely on your partner to support your weight while you push together and pull apart."

Lessons involving problem solving should begin with an introduction to the theme and subthemes. The children should then be guided in the exploration of movements like those that will be required by the problem-solving tasks. The class is then divided into sets of partners or small groups assigned to given apparatus stations, movement tasks are assigned, and the children are instructed to begin solving the movement problem. The steps they must follow to do so are the same as those that applied to any other problem-solving task (see page 124). When applied to a problem in educational gymnastics, these steps are as follows:

1. Define the elements of the movement problem.

2. Tentatively select the actions to be performed.

3. Attempt to link the actions together.

4. Make the necessary modifications in content and sequence.

5. Select and practice the final movements and refine the performance of them.

The children should be required to make smooth transitions between their movements, so as to give their sequences a flowing quality. They should also be encouraged to make their actions decisive and to define the different aspects of the sequence clearly. It should have a definite beginning, a well-developed middle in which the theme is expanded, and a well-defined ending. If the sequence involves approaching and taking off from apparatus, they should anticipate the necessary action, executing a smooth take-off and a controlled landing. As children practice solving movement problems, their tasks should become more complex and their movements more refined. They should also invent their own problems by responding to the movement possibilities of the equipment. Advanced children should work with outdoor as well as indoor apparatus. A well-equipped playground is a stimulating environment in which they can further explore the movement skills and concepts introduced in the educational gymnastics curriculum.

1. What is the central focus of educational gymnastics?

2. Explain how an educational gymnastics lesson should be conducted.

3. Develop an educational gymnastics lesson for children on the beginning level. Specify how you will use verbal cues to evoke movement responses.

4. Develop a lesson for children on the advanced beginner or intermediate level, using some of the equipment listed on page 451. Diagram the arrangement of the equipment.

5. Practice solving some of the movement problems listed on page 451.

6. Develop a lesson for children on the advanced level.

**SUGGESTIONS
FOR FURTHER
READING**

ANDERSON, MARGARET E. *Inventive Movement*. London, England: W. and R. Chambers, 1970.

CAMERON, W., and PLEASANCE, P. *Education in Movement*. Oxford, England: Basil Blackwell & Mott, 1963.

GILLIOM, BONNIE. *Basic Movement Education for Children: Rationale and Teaching Units*. Reading, Mass.: Addison-Wesley, 1970.

HOLBROOK, JENNIFER K. *Gymnastics: A Movement Activity for Children Aged Five to Eleven Years*. London: MacDonald & Evans, 1973.

KIRCHNER, GLENN. *Physical Education for Elementary School Children*, 3rd ed. Dubuque, Iowa: Wm. C. Brown, 1974.

LATCHAW, MARJORIE, and EGSTROM, GLEN. *Human Movement with Concepts Applied to Children's Movement Activities*, Englewood Cliffs, N.J.: Prentice-Hall, 1969.

MAULDON, E., and LAYSON, J. *Teaching Gymnastics*. London, England: MacDonald and Evans, 1965.

MORISON, RUTH. *A Movement Approach to Educational Gymnastics*. London, England: J. M. Dent and Sons, 1969.

STANLEY, SHEILA. *Physical Education: A Movement Orientation*, New York: McGraw-Hill of Canada, 1969.

Appendix A

Observation and Evaluation Form

Part I of the following form examines factors that influence the conduct of an elementary-school physical education program. Part II considers the content of these programs. Part III pertains to actual class situations.

This form has been developed to help you become acquainted with the organizational factors, content, and conduct of such a program, and may be utilized in various ways. You may use its questions to guide your review of the information in this text and the suggested readings. You may use some of its topics as subjects for class discussions and/or special reports. Or you may use part or all of the form to appraise a particular physical education program. The first two parts can be modified to serve as the basis for a survey of current conditions and practices in one or more school districts. You may find some of the questions in Part III useful as a guide to preparing an anecdotal report on the behavior of one or more children.

OBSERVATION AND EVALUATION FORM

Name of school _____

Name of physical education teacher_____

Grade levels observed _____

Number of children in each class _____

Time of day each class meets _____

Dates of observation _____

PART I

Organization of the School

1. What grades are included in the school? (check one)

a. _____ K only   d. _____ K–6

b. _____ K–3   e. _____ 1–6

c. _____ 1–3   f. _____ Other (specify)

2. How many students are enrolled?

a. _____ 0–200   d. _____ 600–800

b. _____ 200–400   e. _____ 800–1000

c. _____ 400–600   f. _____ Other (specify)

3. What type of scheduling is used?

a. _____ Traditional

b. _____ Modular (describe)

4. The physical education instructional program

a. Does the school have a regularly scheduled physical education instructional program? _____ Yes _____ No

b. If *yes*, check the appropriate spaces below:

	K	1	2	3	4	5	6
Number of class periods per week							
Average length of class periods (in minutes)							
Average class size (number of children)							

c. Does the classroom teacher have the prerogative to prevent children from attending physical education classes? _____ Yes _____ No

d. How does the size of physical education classes compare to that of classes taught by the classroom teacher?

(1) _____ The same

(2) _____ Larger

5. Recess periods

a. Does the school have regularly scheduled recess periods?

_____ Yes _____ No

b. If *yes*, check the appropriate spaces below:

	K	1	2	3	4	5	6
Number of regularly scheduled recess periods per week							
Average length of recess periods							

c. How are recess periods supervised?

(1) _____ Each classroom teacher is responsible for supervising his or her own class.

(2) _____ Certain teachers are assigned playground duty.

(3) _____ Student leaders and teachers supervise jointly.

(4) _____ Other (specify)

d. Are classroom teachers permitted to schedule recess periods if they so desire? _____ Yes _____ No

6. Does the school have separate physical education classes for children with special needs? _____ Yes _____ No

If *yes*, complete a, b, and c.

a. What kind of classes are provided?

_____ Perceptual-motor programs

_____ Classes for children in the readiness program

_____ Classes for children with physical impairments

_____ Classes for mentally retarded children

_____ Other (specify)

b. Describe the basis for selecting children who would benefit from such special programs.

c. Does the teacher receive assistance from parents or other volunteers?

7. On what basis are children assigned to regular physical education classes?

_____ All the children in a given classroom attend the same physical education class.

_____ Children are classified on the basis of screening tests. (describe the tests used)

8. Does the school have the services of any of the following professions? (Answer *yes* or *no* and indicate whether the person works full- or part-time).

_____ School nurse

_____ Health educator

_____ Counselor

_____ Psychologist

9. Health examinations

Are the children required to have periodic health examinations?

_____ Yes _____ No

If yes, check the appropriate statements below.

_____ The only requirement is evidence that the child has had specified vaccinations.

_____ An annual examination by a physician is required.

_____ An examination by a physician is required every two or three years.

_____ The school administers annual examinations.

_____ The school administers examinations every two or three years.

_____ Periodic screening tests are given by the school nurse or other school personnel.

_____ Other (specify)

10. Does the school maintain accurate growth and weight records?

_____ Yes _____ No

If yes, complete a and b.

a. How often are children checked?

b. Describe the types of records kept.

11. Medical excuse

a. By what procedure is a child temporarily excused from active participation in physical education classes?

_____ A note from a physician is required.

_____ A note from the school nurse is required.

_____ A note from a parent is accepted.

_____ Other (specify)

b. If a child cannot participate actively, what is he or she expected to do during the physical education class period?

_____ Sit quietly and watch

_____ Go to the library

_____ Help by keeping score, retrieving balls, and the like

_____ Other (specify)

Physical Education Personnel

1. Who is responsible for teaching physical education?

_____ Full-time physical education specialist

_____ Part-time physical education teacher

_____ Classroom teacher

_____ Other (specify)

If the school has a physical education specialist, complete 2 and 3.

2. Teaching load

_____ On the average, how many hours a day does the specialist devote to instruction?

_____ How many classes does he or she teach daily?

_____ What is the total number of students he or she teaches?

_____ How much time per week is allocated to program planning?

_____ How much time is available each week for planning with the art and music specialists and/or classroom teachers?

_____ How many hours a week are devoted to other school responsibilities? Check below the duties the physical educator is expected to perform.

_____ Bus duty

_____ Supervision of playground

_____ Supervision of lunchroom

_____ Extra-class physical education activities

_____ Coaching

_____ Perceptual-motor program

_____ Other (specify)

3. Professional preparation

a. What is the extent of the teacher's formal education?

_____ Bachelor's degree in physical education

_____ Bachelor's degree in physical education plus 15 hours

_____ Master's degree or equivalent hours

_____ Some hours above the Master's (specify number)

_____ Degree other than physical education (specify)

b. What grades or subjects is the teacher certified to teach?

_____ Grades K–12 in physical education only

_____ Grades K–6 in physical education only

_____ Physical education plus one other subject (specify)

_____ Physical education plus elementary classroom teaching

_____ Other (specify)

c. If the teacher is certified to teach physical education in grades K-12, what is the extent of his or her preparation in elementary-school physical education?

_____ No courses

_____ Only one required course

_____ Two or more required courses

_____ A program of courses equally applicable to elementary and secondary physical education, but no specifically elementary courses

_____ Other (specify)

d. If the physical education teacher is responsible for the perceptual-motor program, what training has he or she had to plan and conduct such a program?

_____ Familiarity with the literature

_____ Conferences

_____ Workshops

_____ Formal college coursework

e. In-service education

(1) What activities does the state or school system require of the teacher in order to update his or her training?

_____ No requirements once the teacher has a Master's degree or fifth-year certificate

_____ Attendance at workshops sponsored by the school system

_____ Attendance at one or more workshops or conventions sponsored by other professional groups (specify type and frequency)

_____ Attendance encouraged but not required at workshops or professional meetings outside the school

_____ Periodic enrollment in college courses in any field (specify how often)

_____ Additional coursework in physical education (specify how often)

_____ Additional coursework in *elementary* physical education

_____ Other (specify)

(2) What are the school system's regulations on teachers' attendance at workshops or professional meetings?

_____ The teacher may attend only when school is not in session.

_____ The teacher is given release time but required to pay the cost of a substitute teacher if one is necessary.

_____ The teacher is given release time and the school system pays the cost of a substitute teacher.

_____ In addition to paying the substitute, the school system pays part or all of the expenses incurred by the teacher while attending professional meetings.

_____ Other (specify)

(3) What are the system's regulations on teachers' college course work?

_____ The school system does not assist the teacher financially.

_____ The school system pays tuition for any teacher to take one course a year.

_____ The school system pays tuition for any teacher to take one course a semester.

_____ The school system has a reciprocal agreement with a college where it waives tuition for teachers who supervise student teachers.

_____ Other (specify)

Facilities

1. Indoor. Which of the following is available for use in the physical education program? (If an area must be shared with other programs, specify.)

_____ Regulation-size gymnasium

_____ Multipurpose room

_____ Classroom without furniture
_____ Regularly furnished classroom
_____ Swimming pool
_____ Other (specify)

2. Outdoor
_____ No outdoor space available
_____ Grassy area
_____ Hard-surface area with permanent markings (specify type of markings)
_____ Hard-surface area without markings
_____ Apparatus area (specify types of equipment)
_____ Playing field (specify number, type, and type of surface)
_____ Sand or soft dirt area
_____ Natural setting—stream, wooded area, vacant open area (specify)

3. Are community facilities available for use in the physical education program? _____ Yes _____ No
If _yes_, specify below the type of facility and the grades that use it.
_____ Recreation center
_____ YWCA or YMCA
_____ Swimming pool
_____ Camp
_____ Bowling alley
_____ Golf course
_____ Other (specify)

Equipment and Supplies

1. Check below the items that are readily available for use in physical education classes. For items such as balls, hoops, bats, and the like, indicate the approximate number available.

	K	Primary (1–3)	Intermediate (4–6)
Record player			
Tape recorder			
Appropriate records and/or tapes			
Piano			
Videotape equipment			
Drum			
Small percussion and other musical instruments			

	K	Primary (1–3)	Intermediate (4–6)
Beanbags			
Yarnballs			
Nerf balls			
Whiffleballs			
Cageballs			
Playground balls			
Tennis balls			
Soccer balls			
Footballs			
Basketballs			
Volleyballs			
Softballs			
Baseballs			
Jump ropes			
Hoops			
Wands			
Inner tubes			
Tires			
Stilts			
Gym scooters			
Paddles			
Plastic bats			
Wooden bats			
Gym hockey sticks			
Field hockey sticks			
Softball gloves			
Softball bases			
Volleyball net			
Basketball goal			
Tumbling mats			
Mini-tramp			
Trampoline			
Balance beam			
Benches			
Combination apparatus, such as Lind Climber or Gym-thing			

	K	Primary (1–3)	Intermediate (4–6)
Parallel bars			
Horizontal bar			
Climbing ropes			
Vaulting equipment—horse, buck, or box			
Still rings			
Travelling rings			
Stall bars			
Peg board			
Parachute			
Cargo net			
Other (list)			

2. Evaluation of facilities and equipment

	Yes	No	Comments
a. Are the outdoor play areas adequately marked, well drained, clean, and attractive?			
b. Are separate outdoor play areas provided for younger and older children?			
c. Is the outdoor area adequately fenced?			
d. Is the playground equipment adequate, safe, and in good repair?			
e. Are the indoor play areas well lighted, adequately ventilated, well marked, convenient, clean, and attractive?			
f. Is adequate and convenient storage space available for equipment and supplies?			

	Yes	No	Comments
g. Does the physical education teacher have an office or other appropriate facility in which to plan and meet students?			

Program

1. Program planning. How is the content of the physical education program determined?

_____ The content of the entire program is specified by the state and local school system.

_____ The local school system provides a general outline and allows the teacher to select areas he or she prefers to emphasize.

_____ The program is totally determined by the teacher.

_____ The state or local supervisor helps the teacher select content.

_____ Other (specify)

2. Has the school prepared a written statement of the philosophy and purpose of the elementary physical education program? _____ Yes _____ No

3. Evaluation

a. What criteria are used to evaluate the development of the child that results from participation in the physical education instructional program?

_____ Knowledge of program content

_____ Social development

_____ Attitudes

_____ Physical fitness level

_____ Basic skill development

_____ Ability to perform various activities

_____ Other (specify)

b. What tests or techniques are used to evaluate these factors?

_____ Motor development tests	_____ Anecdotal records
_____ Motor skills tests	_____ Subjective rating scales
_____ Written knowledge tests	_____ Observation
_____ Physical fitness tests	_____ Other (specify)

c. Check the appropriate spaces below, depending on whether the child's progress in physical education is reported to the parents.

	K	1	2	3	4	5	6
Reported							
Not reported							

	K	1	2	3	4	5	6
No regular physical education classes, or not applicable to this school							

d. What method is used to report the child's progress?

_____ Grade of *satisfactory* or *unsatisfactory*

_____ Letter grade

_____ Anecdotal report

_____ Combination of grade and anecdotal report

_____ Checklist

_____ Parent-teacher conference

_____ Other (specify)

e. Are students asked to evaluate the physical education program?

_____ Yes _____ No

If *yes*, what is the nature of their evaluation?

_____ Informal comments

_____ Class discussions

_____ Checklist

_____ Written answers to specific questions

_____ Other (specify)

PART II

Content of the Physical Education Program

1. Check the appropriate spaces below, indicating the activities included in the physical education instructional program at different grade levels.

	K	1	2	3	4	5	6
a. No regular physical education classes, or not applicable to this school							
b. Body space and movement awareness activities							
c. Basic skills instruction							
Basic movement skills							
Basic sports skills							
Fundamental physical skills							
d. Warm-up and conditioning activities							
Formal calesthenics							
Creative movement							

		K	1	2	3	4	5	6
	Stunts							
	Exercises with rhythmic accompaniment							
	Circuits							
	Obstacle courses							
e.	Rhythmic activities							
	Singing games							
	Creative rhythms							
	Marching							
	Folk dance							
	Square dance							
f.	Games							
	Classroom and quiet games							
	Games of low organization							
	Games invented by the children							
	Relays							
	Lead-up games							
	Basketball							
	Hockey							
	Soccer							
	Softball							
	Football							
	Volleyball							
g.	Official sports							
	Basketball							
	Hockey							
	Soccer							
	Softball							
	Football							
	Volleyball							
h.	Stunts, tumbling, and gymnastics							
	Individual stunts							
	Partner stunts							
	Combatives							
	Tumbling							

	K	1	2	3	4	5	6
Small apparatus (wands, hoops, scooters, and the like)							
Balance beam							
Benches							
Springboard							
Vaulting box							
Horizontal bar							
Stall bar							
Climbing ropes							
Cargo net							
Horse							
Parallel bars							
Rings							
Peg boards							
Mini-tramp							
Trampoline							
i. Track and Field							
Running and sprinting							
Relays							
Long jump							
High jump							
Hop, step, and jump							
Hurdles							
Softball throw							
j. Acquatics							
Swimming							
Water safety instruction							
k. Parachute activities							
l. Camping							
m. Climbing							
n. Orienteering							
o. Other (specify)							

Appendix A / Observation and Evaluation Form

2. Evaluation of program content

	Yes	No	Comment
a. Does the physical education program provide a variety of appropriate activities for each class?			
b. Is the program content arranged in a logical sequence of progressive difficulty?			
c. Does the program provide for adequate review without being repetitive?			
d. Are program offerings limited by lack of facilities?			
e. Are available facilities well utilized?			
f. Is the development of the child the central focus of program development?			
g. What do you consider the outstanding aspects of the program?			

Extra-Class Activities

1. Does the school provide a program of extra-class activities?

_____ Yes _____ No

If yes, complete 2 through 6.

2. At what time(s) are such activities scheduled?

_____ Before school _____ During the regular school day

_____ During lunch period _____ Evenings

_____ After school _____ Saturdays

3. What types of activities are available to the children? Check the appropriate spaces below, indicating the activities provided at different grade levels.

	Boys			Girls		
	4	5	6	4	5	6
a. Intramural sports competition Soccer						
Touch football						
Basketball						
Volleyball						
Softball						

	Boys			Girls		
	4	5	6	4	5	6
Baseball						
Wrestling						
Track and field						
Swimming						
Gymnastics						
Other (specify)						
b. Activities involving little or no competition Rhythmic activities						
Games						
Stunts, tumbling, gymnastics						
Swimming						
Camping						
Other (specify)						

4. Does the school present programs in which children perform for people other than their classmates? _____ Yes _____ No
If *yes*, check the appropriate spaces below to indicate the nature of the activities performed in such programs.

	K	1	2	3	4	5	6
a. Sports activities (specify)							
b. Rhythmic activities							
c. Stunts, tumbling, gymnastics							
d. Programs that include a variety of activities							
e. Other (specify)							

5. Who is invited to attend such programs? Indicate the number of programs each of the following groups is invited to attend per year.
_____ Teachers and other students at the same grade level
_____ Everyone in the school
_____ Parents

_____ The public
_____ PTA, professional organizations, and the like
_____ Other (Specify type of group)
  6. Approximately how often are such programs presented?
_____ Not at all
_____ Once a month
_____ Once every six weeks
_____ Only when requested by the school administration, other teachers, or groups outside the school
_____ Once every nine weeks
_____ Once a semester
_____ Once a year

PART III

Children

1. Which students attracted your attention first? Why? How did these children interact with the teacher and the other children?
2. What types of interpersonal relations did you see? (pairings, groupings, affection, consideration, antagonism)
3. Do the children appear to be mutually supportive or competitive?
4. Do the children seem to have a sense of belonging—that is, do they appear confident and at ease? Are they comfortable with the teacher?
5. Do *all* the children exhibit enthusiastic attitudes? Do *all* participate willingly? If not, could you determine why not?
6. Are some children extremely quiet? Do some tend to withdraw? Are some hyperactive? Do any appear uninterested?
7. What did you observe about the length of the children's attention spans? Did attention vary from child to child and in different activities?

Class Atmosphere

1. How do the children enter the gym or play area? Where do they go after arriving? How are they organized (squads, teams, one large group, etc.)? How is this organization accomplished?
2. What procedures are followed at the beginning of the class? Are these procedures routine, or do they vary from day to day?
3. What procedures are followed at the end of the class?
4. Does the children's behavior suggest that they realize they are in class to learn?
5. Do the children have some responsibility for obtaining, distributing, and returning equipment?

6. Is the class atmosphere nonthreatening? Do the children feel free to respond openly, both verbally and nonverbally?

7. Do the children become disorderly at any time? If so, under what circumstances? How could this be avoided?

8. Does the responsibility for keeping order rest entirely with the teacher, or do the children assume some responsibility?

9. Does each child appear to experience some success during the class period?

10. What kinds of activities seem to interest the children most? least? Why?

11. Do any of the children appear to be experiencing learning difficulties? If so, could you determine why?

Teaching Procedures

1. Is the teaching time used to the best advantage?

2. Is student leadership utilized? If so, how are leaders selected and what is their role?

3. Are adequate safety measures employed? Do these measures involve self-control on the part of the children as well as adequate supervision?

4. What types of teaching methods are utilized?

5. Does the lesson content encourage individuality, or is every child required to perform in the same manner?

6. Is the lesson content entirely predetermined or modified in response to student response?

7. Does the lesson content have continuity? In other words, is progress from one learning activity to the next logical and smooth?

8. Are individual and group achievements openly recognized and praised?

9. Are auditory or visual aids used?

10. Is discussion and/or review provided for?

11. Is the content of the physical education curriculum related to other subjects or to children's interests outside of school?

Appendix B Annotated Bibliography

Because one text cannot provide adequate coverage of all the specialized areas of the elementary physical education curriculum, the teacher must build a personal library of resource materials. The following references each of which provides the most complete and practical coverage of its subject, can serve as the nucleus of such a library.

BLAKE, WILLIAM, and VOLP, ANNE. *Lead-Up Games to Team Sports*. Englewood Cliffs, N.J.: Prentice-Hall, 1964. Contains a number of lead-up games for each of the official sports, presented in order of difficulty. An essential reference for that part of the curriculum in which the basic sports skills are practiced in game situations appropriate for children in the upper elementary grades. 186 pages.

DESANTIS, GABRIEL, and SMITH, LESTER. *Physical Education Programmed Activities for Grades K–6*. Columbus, Ohio: Charles E. Merrill, 1969. A compilation of numerous physical education activities, organized into subject-matter areas and conveniently printed on reference cards. 1555 cards with 110-page program guide.

GILLIOM, BONNIE. *Basic Movement Education for Children: Rationale and Teaching Units*. Reading, Mass.: Addison-Wesley, 1970. A practical guide to developing lesson plans utilizing guided exploration. Contains exploratory learning activities for children K–6. 224 pages.

INTERNATIONAL COUNCIL ON HEALTH, PHYSICAL EDUCATION AND RECREATION. *ICHPER Book of Worldwide Games and Dances*. Washington, D.C.: AAHPER Press, 1967. Contains descriptions of over one hundred games and dances from fifty-eight countries, classified for grades 1–6 by degree of difficulty and listed under country of origin. 159 pages.

MORRIS, G. S. DON. *How to Change the Games Children Play.* Minneapolis, Minn.: Burgess, 1976. Presents a games analysis model that enables the reader to analyze the components and educational value of games. Emphasizes decision making and problem solving in games. Illustrates how to design and adapt games to meet the educational needs of each child. 127 pages.

MURRAY, RUTH L. *Dance in Elementary Education,* 3rd ed. New York: Harper & Row, 1975. A comprehensive guide to planning and conducting all aspects of a rhythmic movement program. 446 pages.

WERNER, PETER H., and SIMMONS, RICHARD A. *Inexpensive Physical Education Equipment for Children.* Minneapolis, Minn.: Burgess, 1976. Contains ideas for the acquisition and construction of a wide variety of inexpensive or homemade equipment; includes suggestions and instructions for utilizing the equipment in a variety of learning activities. 156 pages.

Appendix C

Sources for Rhythmic Accompaniment

The record companies listed below are sources of excellent rhythmic accompaniment for movement activities.

BOWMAR PUBLISHING CORPORATION, Order Department, P. O. Box 3623, Glendale, California 91201. An excellent source for records with dance themes for creative rhythms, singing games, and folk and ethnic dances.

DROLL YANKEES INC., Box 2447, Providence, Rhode Island 02906. Recordings of genuine sounds of nature.

EDUCATIONAL ACTIVITIES, INC., P. O. Box 392, Freeport, New York 11520. Offers a wide variety of records, including series appropriate for early childhood, perceptual development, primary and intermediate physical education.

EDUCATIONAL RECORDINGS OF AMERICA, INC., P. O. Box 231, Monroe, Connecticut 06468. The series for classroom rhythms and creative dance are recommended for the beginning teacher.

FOLKRAFT RECORDS, 1159 Broad Street, Newark, New Jersey 07114. An excellent source of recordings for the basic movements, dance steps, and folk and square dance.

HOCTOR DANCE RECORDS, INC., Waldwick, New Jersey 07463. Folk dance albums 4001, 4026, 4027, and 4028 include a variety of quality recordings for teaching structured dances.

KIMBO, Box 246, Deal, New Jersey 07723. Offers the widest variety of up-to-date recordings for various aspects of the early childhood and elementary-school physical education program.

MACDONALD AND EVANS LTD. (EDUCATIONAL RECORDINGS), 8 John Street, London WCIN 2HY, England. A series of "Listen and Move" records developed especially for creative activities. Includes percussion, voice, and piano accompaniment.

MERRBACH RECORD SERVICE, P. O. Box 7308, Houston, Texas 77008. Most records from other companies are available through this retailer.

RCA RECORDS, Educational Department, 1133 Avenue of the Americas, New York, New York 10036. An excellent graded series entitled "The World of Folk Dances," a series of square dance records, and the "Dance-A-Story" series.

An additional list of records suitable for dance accompaniment is provided in Geraldine Dimondstein, *Children Dance in the Classroom* (New York: Macmillan, 1971, pages 257–259).

Index

Index